Agribusiness and the Small-Scale Farmer

Also of Interest

Small Farm Development: Understanding and Improving Farming Systems in the Humid Tropics, Richard R. Harwood

Technical Change and Social Conflict in Agriculture: Latin American Perspectives, edited by Martin E. Piñeiro and Eduardo J. Trigo

Environmental Management in Tropical Agriculture, Robert Godland

Farm Management in Peasant Agriculture, Michael Collinson

Agriculture and Employment in Developing Countries: Strategies for Effective Rural Development, Bela Mukhoti

Food Production and Rural Development in the Sahel: Lessons from Mali's Operation Riz-Segou, R. James Bingen

The Transformation of International Agricultural Research and Development, edited by J. Lin Compton

Implementing Rural Development Projects: Nine Critical Problems, Elliott R. Morss and David D. Gow

Livestock Development in Subsaharan Africa: Constraints, Prospects, Policy, edited by James R. Simpson and Phylo Evangelou

Livestock Development in Kenya's Maasailand: Pastoralists' Transition to a Market Economy, Phylo Evangelou

Agricultural Policy and Collective Self-Reliance in the Caribbean, W. Andrew Axline

Food and Development in the Pacific Basin, G. Edward Schuh and Jennifer McCoy

Swamp Rice Farming: The Indigenous Pahang Malay Agricultural System, Donald H. Lambert

Detecting Mineral Nutrient Deficiencies in Tropical and Temperate Crops, edited by Donald L. Plucknett and Howard B. Sprague

Rural Energy to Meet Development Needs: Asian Village Approaches, M. Nurul Islam, Richard Morse, and M. Hadi Soesastro

Westview Special Studies
in Agriculture Science and Policy

Agribusiness and the Small-Scale Farmer:
A Dynamic Partnership for Development
Simon Williams and Ruth Karen

Based on case histories from nine Third World countries, this study examines the successful cooperation between private agribusiness firms and small farmers to increase agricultural production and income in developing countries. In such ventures, small farmers are organized around a core private company that buys their output and provides managerial, marketing, and technical expertise and, at times, credit. The farmers enjoy an assured market and higher income, which in turn stimulates production.

The agribusiness operations described vary from the production of seed corn to the breeding of swine; core companies include multinational corporations, domestic firms, U.S. and other foreign companies, and joint ventures between domestic firms and foreign businesses. The authors conclude with specific policy recommendations for facilitating cooperation between small farmers and agribusiness in the Third World.

Dr. Simon Williams, president of the Center for Rural Development, Inc., has been involved in development research for over twenty years with experience in Israel, Nigeria, Scandinavia, and Latin America. His most recent publications include Credit Systems for Small-Scale Farmers: Case Histories from Mexico (1973, with James Miller). *Ruth Karen* is senior vice-president of Business International Corporation and author of The Farmer and the Money Economy: The Role of the Private Sector in Agricultural Development of LDCs (1982, with Orville L. Freeman) and Toward an Unlimited Future (1983, with Elliott Haynes).

A Study by Business International Corporation
and the Center for Rural Development, Inc.,
for the Bureau for Private Enterprise,
Agency for International Development

Agribusiness and the Small-Scale Farmer

A Dynamic Partnership for Development

Simon Williams and Ruth Karen

Westview Press / Boulder and London

Westview Special Studies in Agriculture Science and Policy

Published in 1985 in the United States of America by Westview Press, Inc.;
Frederick A. Praeger, Publisher; 5500 Central Avenue, Boulder, Colorado 80301

Library of Congress Catalog Card Number: 85-51172
ISBN: 0-8133-0146-7

Composition for this book was provided by the authors
Printed and bound in the United States of America

10 9 8 7 6 5 4 3 2 1

Contents

Tables

Foreword

To elaborate on an ancient Chinese proverb: Give a man a fish and he eats for a day. Teach a man to fish, make it possible for him to have access to credit to buy his pole and a free market in which to sell his production, and he not only feeds himself and his family for a lifetime, he also feeds and builds a nation.

The theme of this volume goes directly to the heart of what the Agency for International Development has been focusing on for the past four years. Difficult--and expensive--lessons of past development efforts have taught us that the transfer of resources alone is futile, even counterproductive. Rather, we must transfer skills, techniques, and know-how, with the proper mix of resources, that motivate farmers to produce more. We must mobilize indigenous private sectors as the principal engines of growth. In agriculture as well as other fields, the private sector is the most dynamic agent for increased productivity that exists. As the book points out, energizing small-scale farmers so they can respond to the incentives of the market is essential to the achievement of positive development results.

The case histories detailed in the book clearly show that the concept of organizing small-scale farmers around a core agribusiness pays dividends. When properly done, the arrangement produces a mutually beneficial association. The farmer benefits from technology, hands-on managerial expertise, assured markets and--best of all--the chance to move from subsistence farming into the market economy. The company benefits from faster-than-usual earnings. An important fringe benefit to company investors and managers is the knowledge that they are actively participating in the substantive and sustainable development of nations and, as a result, a more secure world.

I am especially pleased that the book emphasizes the importance of policies. If the policy environment is right, the dynamic combination of farmer and company will work. During the past four years we at AID have placed policy reform at the highest priority level. We are achieving the beginnings of some significant successes in convincing Third World governments that the practice of paying their farmers a price below the free market in order to provide artificially low food prices to urban people is disastrously counterproductive. Declining food production is evidence that for many farmers, it just isn't worth the cost to continue producing. They join the migration to the urban slums, continuing the cycle of hunger, poverty, and political instability.

As I pointed out, those policies are changing--slowly--but they are changing. Third World officials are coming to the realization that the ability of the individual--the farmer or the businessman, indigenous or foreign--to improvise, compete, and produce self-sustaining prosperity depends on a free market. Things happen when the private sector takes the lead, as shown in the instances cited in this book. The job of government is to produce the proper climate, then stand clear and let the incentives of free market forces work.

The policies of our own country are important, too. As a matter of basic policy, AID is promoting private sector projects--long ignored in AID programming--in cost-effective ways that draw in other resources, such as joint ventures that lend themselves to development and stretch our tax dollars. We are putting together several projects that incorporate the small-scale farmer/corporate arrangements discussed in this book.

This volume, with its case histories and common sense approach to agricultural development through farmer/business relationships, serves as a steady compass to the promise of prosperity and stability in a world that could do with a lot more of both.

M. Peter McPherson
Administrator
U.S. Agency for International Development

Acknowledgments

As may be imagined, literally hundreds of people contributed to the substance of this book: executives at corporate headquarters; management and staff at enterprise sites in the nine countries visited; farmers, farm families, and rural community leaders; government policymakers and technical support staff among many others. Open and thoughtful collaboration was universal. In giving thanks and acknowledging this help, we hope that everyone involved is recognized as a vital and vibrant part of both the intellectual and emotional content of the book.

Above all, we acknowledge the constant support and inspiration provided by four: James O'Connor, Advisor to the Administrator of the U.S. Agency for International Development, in Washington, D.C.; Edgar Harrell, Deputy Assistant Administrator of the Bureau for Private Enterprise, U.S. Agency for International Development; Frances Williams, Vice President of the Center for Rural Development, Inc., Fort Collins, Colorado; and Beth Kilmer, Research Associate at Business International, Inc., in New York City.

It was the commitment, insight, persistence, and skill of James O'Connor that brought the project from an idea to a contracted field investigation, and subsequently to the form of this book. During the entire course of negotiation and follow-up, Edgar Harrell added his constant intellectual and managerial support, without which the actual work might never have been undertaken. Frances Williams made three critical contributions: she participated directly in the field studies in Kenya, Swaziland, and Mexico; she added greatly to the clarity and depth of the entire text as the final report was converted to a book; and she has been the chief editor of the book, giving it a consistent structure throughout. Finally, Beth Kilmer was constant and generous in providing research support, always being there, never failing to be prompt, supportive, and accurate.

Our thanks and appreciation also go to Joyce Oppenheimer, of Fort Collins, Colorado, whose meticulous care, technical capability, and devoted attention helped produce a manuscript of which everyone could be proud, ready for the demanding eye of the camera. She met every deadline and dealt with every contingency. She was invaluable.

S. W.   R. K.

Introduction

Decades of active exposure to farmers and their concerns in the United States, as well as all over the world, have left me with three convictions.

The first is that although there are still millions of farmers around the world who cannot read or write, I have never met a farmer who cannot count. That observation applies to farm families whether the spread they own is large, medium, or small. Experience teaches that farmers don't need an economist to recognize a good deal when they see one.

My second conviction, also based on observation and experience around the globe, is that for-profit companies, again of whatever size or national origin, are the most dynamic mechanism for economic growth and social advancement. As one prescient chief of state in the Third World put it: "I know that companies are not development agencies, but they are agents for development."

My third conviction is somewhat more abstract, but equally universal. I am convinced that the worldwide revolution of expectations, which I consider the prime characteristic of the demanding and inspiring era in which we live, has not run its course and that the great challenge for anyone living today is to participate in that revolution. To do this we must mobilize both private and public agencies. I have been involved in both, locally and globally, in developing countries and in industrial nations. We accomplished this two-track mobilization in the United States with problems and complexities that still stump us, but also with results that still constitute the best hope for the world. Perhaps the U.S. experience cannot be replicated, but it can certainly serve as a model of what can be done and as a demonstration that it can be done.

In sum, I believe that we are our brother's keeper and the question that needs to be addressed here and now is how we can express that commitment in practical terms.

This book addresses the question in terms of the rural population of the world, still by far the largest segment of mankind. The book is based on some specific, concrete assumptions: macroeconomic, structural, and operational.

In macroeconomic terms, it assumes that it is important to the soundness of the global economy, and vital to sociopolitical stability, for the Third World to participate to a maximum degree, and in an optimum fashion, in global productivity. An important ingredient of this participation is that the developing countries make a major effort to feed themselves and to strengthen the agricultural sector of their economies.

The structural assumption is grounded in historical and current evidence that the private sector is the most dynamic agent of development both in industrial and developing countries and is therefore the indicated instrument for a policy that sets productivity as a priority.

Operationally, the book argues--and I believe demonstrates--that in the agricultural sector, the most efficacious way to obtain desirable results, from an economic and from a developmental viewpoint, is to energize small-scale farmers. This is done most effectively by organizing the farmers around a corporate core that offers them the necessary technology and a personal stake in state-of-the-art production.

A concept paper, The Farmer and the Money Economy: The Role of the Private Sector in the Agricultural Development of LDCs, which Ruth Karen and I wrote (Mitchell Prize, 1982), delineated these three components. The concepts developed in that paper were investigated on site in 1983-1984 on three continents (Africa, Asia, and Latin America), in nine countries (Dominican Republic, India, Kenya, Mexico, Philippines, Sudan, Swaziland, Thailand, and Turkey). The case histories cover a range of agricultural production from seed corn to pig raising, and include cash crops and food crops--for family use, for the domestic market, and for the international market.

The companies organizing the investigated enterprises also represent a broad spectrum. They include multinational companies based in the industrial world; host country companies with international dimensions in the form of licensing and/or marketing agreements with multinational firms; joint ventures (including joint ventures with the public sector, domestic or foreign); and purely domestic firms. Companies range in size from very large (Unilever) to very small (Caribbean Basin Investment Agribusiness Group).

In addition, the book addresses what Dr. Simon Williams perceptively describes as "the connective tissue" between these successful private-sector efforts and the public agencies and not-for-profit intermediate organizations actively engaged in pursuing the same goal, that is, the optimum development of farmers and their families around the world.

Finally, the horrors of Ethiopia and its neighbors in the drought- and misery-ridden belt of sub-Saharan Africa make clear beyond argument the urgency of what needs to be done--not in the form of emergency stopgap help, but in the way of fundamental, lasting solutions. What these solutions can and should be is the thrust of this book.

Orville L. Freeman
Chairman
Business International Corporation (1970-1985)
U.S. Secretary of Agriculture (1961-1969)

1
Agribusiness and the Small-Scale Farmer: A Dynamic Partnership for Development

Simon Williams

THEME AND TONE

This book tells a story of a truly remarkable achievement, a global drama about the conception, establishment, and impact of thousands of agribusiness enterprises scattered to the far ends of Africa, Asia, and Latin America and of the changes wrought by these ventures on the lives and hopes of literally millions of people: small-scale farmers, farm families, and the traditional, disadvantaged societies of which they are a part.

People reflecting the myriad cultures of the world have mixed freely to participate in highly productive systems where before both the land and the creative use of human intelligence languished. Quite amazingly, as it grew and proliferated agribusiness found a fit in practically every social structure, every stage of human development, and every political ideology characterizing the Third World, and where the industry has prospered, the people involved have begun to prosper.

These thoughts and feelings are not meant to paint a picture of Utopia, with agribusiness as its capital. No one has yet invented the perfect process of achieving the highest levels of human happiness and serenity. Yet in this troubled world, the challenge is clear and pressing that there can be no let-up in the search for a better place in which all people can live in harmony, in freedom, with hope. This book suggests that the worldwide growth of international and national investment in agribusiness, the impact of these ventures on the supply of food and fiber, and the power generated by individual enterprises to bring traditional but deprived rural people into the process of modernization have to constitute one of the major accomplishments of the twentieth century. This needs to be widely recognized. The strengths and weaknesses of the experience should be carefully evaluated. The instrumentality of agribusiness as a major force for benign agricultural and rural development should be grasped and put into its proper place for the commonweal.

At this point the question arises: What is the fundamental nature of agribusiness that makes it a vitally important tool for development? The answer may be found in three characteristics of

1

the operation and impact of an enterprise in a traditional rural setting.

Agribusiness as a Primary Agent of Change

Whenever and wherever agribusiness becomes a presence in a rural area and manages to prosper, it becomes a compelling force for change. This force is exerted, as a general rule, on relatively large numbers of people simultaneously, at and around the enterprise site; along the food and fiber chain from production to consumption; and at the centers of governmental power. Once public policy has opened the doorways to action, it is at the project site that the most intriguing response to change becomes manifest.

Initially, rural people respond quickly to the economic motivations held out--getting a job and a wage or increasing net cash income on the farm. To participate means accepting a wide variety of changes in behavior and attitude, doing so quickly and in a competitive framework of opportunity. Novel tasks are taken on and new skills acquired, on the job and by means of formal training. New ideas and relationships are introduced. Technical supervision may supersede personal choice on the farm. The importance of quality control; the significance of personal responsibility on the job or on the farm to enterprise success; and recognition of nontraditional lines of authority: these and other abstractions begin to foment in the mind. Upward mobility for men and women becomes a real possibility. New, higher levels of income lift the vision of life from subsistence to more vivacious alternatives for parents and children, visions that may be further brightened by the early impact of corporate public services such as improved housing and schooling, health clinics, and recreational facilities.

Granted, the rapid changes occasioned by agribusiness often generate conflict and some disorder. Rurally sited ventures, especially when they pioneer in a remote area, are prone to breed stresses and strains in family life and in social order when neither time nor talent is allocated to prepare people for abrupt shifts in life-style. New high levels of cash flow in rural communities inevitably attract carpetbaggers and scalawags who prey upon ignorance and awakened expectations. Investment incentives affecting taxes, labor pay scales, land acquisition, management control, repatriation of profit, proprietary rights over technology, and a host of other concerns of investors and governments may one and all, at any moment, be the subject of political, personal, or ideological tension. More than anything else, the radical challenge to investors in the private sector lies in the validity of claims that on-farm increases in net income and increases in family income from wages are truly significant, particularly when compared with corporate profit and management salaries. There may be no argument about the value of doubling, trebling, or quadrupling income, but there is a dispute over the freedoms gained and the equity achieved when in absolute terms income per family remains very low.

But stress, strain, and adjustment are the ineluctable consequences of the process of change. Their existence at an agribusiness site is natural and predictable. This book takes the position that the industry has, in fact, set the stage not only for conflict resolution but also for a further rapid expansion of benefits for rural people and their governments. The signs of this are in evidence throughout the cases described in later chapters. For example, Pinar in Turkey and the Haggar Group in the Sudan (Chapters 5 and 6 respectively) are making company shares available to farmers; Pinar and Hindustan Lever Limited in India (Chapter 2) recognize that the income from small-scale dairy operations cannot adequately support a rural family and are helping to diversify farm output to include other cash crops; in Thailand, the Charoen Pokphand (Chapter 7) operation anticipates that entire villages, complete with houses and all the pig-raising facilities built by the company, will become owned and operated by the people settled originally in experimental villages.

What is of critical importance to intellectual balance in thinking about the potential contribution of agribusiness to rural development is to remember that whatever the shortcomings in the changes the industry brings about in a given period of time, each company galvanizes the rural people at the site into a new state of mind about change. What more needs to be done has an increasingly better chance to be done because both the company and the people have learned something about risking their futures on the dynamics of their interdependence. As anyone with field experience among traditional rural people will testify, receptivity to a break with past constraints on human development is a priceless asset. Achieving this end is usually a costly and time-consuming task. Agribusiness makes this start. Going forward from this point with sensitivity and grace is the true challenge. The limits of past performance only define the opportunity.

Agribusiness Transcends Differences

Agribusiness not only activates the process of change and helps create an environment basic to further development: The experience of the industry also provides conclusive evidence that the response of rural people is remarkably similar worldwide, despite the wide differences of culture, social order, and political form that separate them.

This universality of response is vividly illustrated by competitive companies within segments of agribusiness that span the world. Sugar is a good example.

Sugar is produced on all continents and flows into the marketplace from dozens of countries. Investors may represent public or private interests, separately or in joint venture; variations in the mix of owners and control of cane growing/sugar milling operations are almost endless. Management of the industry, like the capital invested, also derives from many different places. In effect, the personality of the sugar industry cannot be categorized simply by national origin or cultural viewpoint.

What homogenizes the industry is its technology. While there are, of course, differences in the practice of cane cultivation (rain-grown versus irrigated, hand-harvested versus mechanical harvesting, chemical weed control versus hand hoeing, among others), and in refining, the elements of essential similarity dominate. For this reason, it is valid to draw a significant conclusion from the fact that in training farmer-suppliers, plantation labor, or factory workers, wherever the operation is sited in the Third World, the results have been the same. More or less identical training systems are employed and work successfully. The time it takes to reach comparable skill levels is similar. The pride and pleasure taken by management in the performance of their enterprise is manifest wherever production persists. The same pride and pleasure of the local work force, as it moves into this new technical world, are also in evidence at a well-managed plant.

Indeed, if the world were examined only through the lens of sugar enterprises in less-developed countries, people would certainly seem far more the same than different. No matter the language, the clothing, the food eaten, the social order, the traditions of farming and marketing, or the quality of life in general, when the sugar scheme enters the scene, what people do, how they learn, how they change, all fit a common pattern.

What can be said about the sugar industry also applies to the production of grains, vegetables, coffee, tea, tobacco, tree crops, fruits, forest products from tannin to timber, cotton and other natural fibers, and animal products. To some degree, but not as conspicuously, there are similar responses to agribusinesses that interact less directly and continuously with rural people, for instance, manufacturers and marketers of animal feeds, animal health products, fertilizers and other agricultural chemicals, improved seed, and agricultural machinery.

From the viewpoint of this book, the ability of agribusiness investors to transcend differences has three important implications.

1. Most obviously, this ability has led to ventures everywhere; agribusiness dots the earth to its farthest reaches. Thus, a program of agricultural and rural development rooted to agribusiness starts by being truly global.
2. Because both the nature of the changes introduced by agribusiness and the response of rural people tend to be shared throughout agribusiness, the design of a global

policy and its method of implementation is to a considerable extent simplified.

3. The opportunity to promote agricultural and rural development worldwide, put forward by agribusiness, is seemingly independent of the product line and other particu-
larities of each commercial enterprise. Therefore, when
thinking of agribusiness as contributing a force for
rural development, the industry can best be thought of as
a homogeneous entity, rather than as a large, complex
group of discrete, competitive, and very diverse enterprises. Integrating the function of long-range rural
development within each company need not be threatening
to corporate privacy. What is to be capitalized is the
attitude toward change already generated and the assets
flowing outward from the enterprise into the community at
large: money, active intelligence, new and varied
skills, self-respect, and other benefits of equal importance.

Agribusiness Takes the Risk and Intends to Stay

In addition to its power to induce change and to find a fit
throughout a heterogeneous world, agribusiness helps accelerate
rural development in many other ways. Four examples are singularly illustrative.

The company takes the first, large financial risk. In the
start-up phase management must do what any rural developer must
do to induce response from local people whatever their role is to
be, contract farmers or labor. Of a consequence, the industry
has added literally billions of dollars to the global development
budget.

Not only is this investment important because of its sheer
magnitude; from a development perspective it is equally significant for other reasons. Agribusiness often risks capital where
public development funds would not venture (see the Hindustan
Lever case in India, Chapter 2; the Mumias Sugar Company case in
Kenya, Chapter 3; and the Commonwealth Development Corporation
case in Swaziland, Chapter 4), although at times the situation is
reversed (see the Agro Inversiones case in the Dominican Republic, Chapter 10). Agribusiness, when it enters into remote areas
with few social amenities, is able to attract talented professional people to the job as residents with incentives beyond the
capability of most public agencies. Equally important, companies
can and do provide income incentives to farmers and workers that
encourage participation in the enterprise. These early costs can
be very high and may have to be carried for some years; calculat-
ing these costs and their economic justification is a normal part
of corporate feasibility projections. These realities often con-
found the design of publicly financed projects. To this last
point should be added that investors in agribusiness, dealing as
they do with renewable raw material resources, and following

strategies based on an expanding market, actual and potential (as all the cases in the following chapters illustrate), start with a policy that focuses on longevity. This long-range view of growth and profitability allows for flexibility in amortizing start-up costs. As an official from the Commonwealth Development Corporation put it, the company's investments are characterized by "patient money," a resource often denied to public officials.

In sum, once an agribusiness is in full operation, it has financed the toughest, most sensitive, costliest, and riskiest stages of the process of rural development. Although the job is never finished, building upon the early changes to the next broadly conceived, long-range stages of rural development is a creative and prudent utilization of resources.

The company provides an on-site, disciplined management organization. This in itself tends to correct a basic weakness in too many public development programs. Accountability for performance and the use of money is facilitated. The burden of excessive overhead costs attendant to the intervention of bureaucratic personnel located in urban centers far from a project site is sharply reduced. The daily presence of professional staff among their constituency, a critical factor governing success, is ensured. Finally, because the company intends to operate long term, the design of the ongoing rural development program is planned with the necessary continuity in mind. A glaring flaw in development assistance financing has been the short time span of its commitment.

The company can mediate conflictive issues. This is true especially if it is located in a remote area where no other authoritative, competent intermediary exists to mediate between local people and their government, or between divergent groups within the community. As already noted, agribusiness is a primary force for change at an enterprise site, and change is inherently a never-ending process of conflict generation and conflict resolution. Further, the changes set in motion are not, and cannot be, confined to the site. The ripple effect of the entry of agro-industry into a traditional area can circle out for great distances. The universal mosaic of law, agrarian reform, paternalism, finance, investment incentives, internal and external marketing systems, among so many other facets of local, regional, national, and international interaction, is touched at a thousand and one places, each sensitive, each colored by its contact with another.

Generally, the elements of self-interest in this complex structure of interaction are inclined to interfere with one another. Harmonizing these conflicting interests requires both sophisticated understanding and a position of authority as a respected participant in negotiations. Rural people rarely have the knowledge or the power to present their views. Agribusiness management usually has both. This appreciation is particularly relevant as the distance of an enterprise from the centers of public administration grows, and the interdependence of rural people and management becomes closer and more intimate.

The evidence for the growth of management discussions with governments, on behalf of rural people, can be found in some of the cases described in this book. The issues range from gaining access to credit and imported inputs required for new high-yielding farming practices; to prices paid for raw material contracted from farmers; to improvements in local infrastructure; to the establishment of farmer organizations charged to work out solutions to a wide variety of technical and social problems with declining dependency on either company or government.

The company provides a cash flow. This provides a base for a program of economic diversification--often a planned goal of rural development programs that is never reached because of the lack of a first major generator (investor) of cash.

From the moment preoperational construction begins, large cash flows emanate from the enterprise, always with major impact. If there has been no preparation for the use of this money, it may corrupt, disrupt, and otherwise be largely wasted. Preparation or not, prudent personal use or not, the money and the permanence of its source creates a dynamic, immediate opportunity to diversify the area economy in significant ways. More people can share in the benefits of development: more income to diffuse, more variation in job requirements and necessary skills, decreased dependency on the company, increased self-sufficiency and freedom from public support, among many others. The reality of this opportunity is overwhelmingly evident wherever agribusiness has entered the scene and has prospered. The question is: Who, most logically, can and should take responsibility to ensure that the wealth of opportunity created is not lost?

Ongoing agribusiness has built its bridges to the local people. Its interdependence with these people is a matter of self-interest to protect and nurture. It can negotiate with the outside world: the government, banks, markets, and sources of knowledge and expertise, for example. It provides a management system, with a concern for performance. It has the capacity to "see" investment opportunities and to judge their potential viability. Despite disbelief in many quarters, the managers of agribusiness in the Third World, whatever their nationality, are generally professionals with long field experience. They are understanding of the needs of the rural people with whom they live and work. They would want to help if what can be done to broaden and accelerate the development process does not threaten the commercial success of their business.

In effect, all of the foregoing adds up to an extraordinary opportunity to capitalize on the presence of agribusiness at so many places around the world to catalyze rural development far beyond the boundaries of past achievement. The industry cannot, of course, be all things to all people and all nations in need, nor is it likely to be willing or able to take full responsibility even for what is logical and prudent to do. But in partnership with host governments and development assistance agencies, agribusiness could emerge as one of the great forces in the field of rural development by the close of this century.

With this vision in mind, with the vision firmly supported by extensive empirical evidence of reality, and in the certainty of the practicality of its recommendations for policy changes and action programs, this book has been written with the deepest sense of hope and optimism.

ORIGIN

This book results from a study made for the Bureau for Private Enterprise of the United States Agency for International Development (USAID), in support of its policy of working with the private sector to increase the well-being of rural people in less-developed countries. Most specifically, the inquiry was directed toward identifying and evaluating agro-industrial enterprises structured on the principle of "satellite farming," wherein a central processing plant or marketing organization draws all or a significant part of its raw material from a relatively large number of small-scale farmers under contract. The study was not limited to this structure. Any venture that might properly be defined as an agribusiness, or one promoting agribusiness investment, and having the inherent capability of impacting significant numbers of rural people, was given consideration. Evidence of this may, in particular, be noted in Chapter 13.

Prior to the field study, it had been suggested that agro-industrial enterprises with a satellite farming procurement system, sometimes called "nucleus estates," have a unique capability to transfer technology very rapidly and to generate widespread participation by local people. It was opined that this type of company successfully separates investment in processing and marketing from the sensitive issue of land tenure. In many ways, it seemed that agribusiness was an ideal institution through which to implement, in part, public policy directing development assistance toward and through the private sector. However, the literature on the subject is most meager. Hard evidence was lacking. Therefore, the study upon which this book is based was undertaken.

The questions at the outset of the study, therefore, were: Is this suggestion defensible? What would an actual examination of agribusiness experience reveal by way of verification or challenge? Since small-scale farmers are integral members of a larger rural society, what is the impact of agribusiness investment on farm families; on men, women, and children in their different roles; on all the people in the zone of influence of the enterprise? Since rural development is a continuous process, has agribusiness been able or willing to sustain the process it may have put in train? And, finally, if agribusiness can be shown to be a powerful force in generating the first stage of change among traditional rural people, what might USAID (and other development institutions) do to help reinforce the role of the industry as a partner in the general attack on hunger, poverty, and disadvantage among the masses of rural people in the Third World?

The study was conducted under contract to Business International Corporation (BI), which, in turn, shared the investigation with the Center for Rural Development, Inc. (CRD).* Because the role of private enterprise, or even public enterprise that operates for profit, in agricultural and rural development is controversial, it is clear that no study of the subject can be value free. So that readers may have an unambiguous appreciation of the viewpoint of the authors, a brief description of both BI and CRD follows.

Business International is an independent organization providing a comprehensive system of business information to corporations operating internationally and to those who support and govern them, including bankers, attorneys, consultants, universities, and government officials. Established in 1954, its facilities span seventy-five countries, including some 240 full-time researchers, analysts, editors, and executives located in fifteen major markets of the world, plus a network of researchers and editorial representatives spread over sixty other commercial and political centers.

Business International's goal is to advance profitable corporate and economic growth in socially desirable ways. It does so by: providing fast, reliable information needed for corporate decision-making, planning, and management development; alerting corporate management to new opportunities, as well as dangers; discovering, explaining, and interpreting international management techniques that will advance profitable corporate and economic growth; and analyzing government measures that will affect economic growth and international cooperation, and thus pave the way for corporations to make their maximum contribution to human welfare while advancing their own survival and prosperity.

Business International publishes weekly reports that identify and analyze a broad range of business-related information funneled in from all over the world. It also provides to its clients a variety of reference and research services, including economic forecasting, on-line data bases, roundtable conferences, and management education programs. The organization deeply believes in private enterprise and a free, competitive marketplace as powerful forces for economic growth, and it believes that such growth fostered through private sector initiatives has enormous potential for human welfare [1, 2, 3].**

---

*For further details contact Business International Corporation, 1 Dag Hammarskjold Plaza, New York, NY 10017, or Center for Rural Development, Inc., 1432 Meeker Drive, Fort Collins, CO 80524.

**Numbers in brackets refer to the first section of the bibliography, which includes books, reports, and articles used as direct sources. Section 2 of the bibliography refers to other relevant and useful background material.

The Center for Rural Development is also an independent consulting organization, quite different in its experience and
activities, but in its interests and goals, both highly compat-
ible and complementary to BI. On the one hand, CRD works to
apply the principles and practices of well-managed business in
the design and implementation of integrated rural development
projects that start at the village level and build forward to
larger investments. On the other hand, CRD is concerned with
methods that extend the development impact of agribusinesses that
enter the boundaries of a traditional, disadvantaged rural
society. As this book emphasizes again and again, agribusiness,
as it pursues its commercial objectives, hastens technical transfer; generates unprecedented levels of cash flow into and through
its zone of influences; and, in a multitude of ways stimulates
the whole process of irreversible change. CRD sees in this a
vitally important tool for development.

Historically, the roots of CRD are in a two-year, worldwide
study, made between 1963 and 1965, of the role the private sector
might play in alleviating the twin problems of hunger and poverty. This study was sponsored by a major U.S. multinational agribusiness whose objective was to find innovative ways for industry
to contribute solutions to these problems. The results of this
study led to the establishment of an integrated rural development
program in Mexico in 1965. First financed by USAID, since 1968,
the program has been supported entirely by a private sector,
Mexican, multinational corporation. This program, national in
scope, sets the theme, philosophy, and methodology of CRD,
whether action in the field starts in villages untouched by the
creative energy of agribusiness, or starts among people impacted
by prior investment and already launched into the future. CRD
has worldwide experience and at every point tries to encourage
financially self-sustaining systems of agricultural and rural
development, in which improved farming practices, diversified
investment in agribusiness and service industries, and human
development evolve as an integrated, profitable enterprise. A
keystone of the system is that those whose labor and productivity
contribute to success share in ownership of new capital assets
formed at the site, and as rapidly as possible take increasing
management responsibility [4, 5, 6].

CONDUCT OF FIELD INQUIRY

The chapter headings reveal the distribution of work between
Business International and the Center for Rural Development.
Although the nature of the inquiry to be made at an enterprise
site was considered jointly before any studies were conducted, no
rigidly prescribed procedure was followed. It was recognized
that no two corporations would reveal the same kind of information, nor would local conditions allow for identical approaches
to farmers, public officials, local businesses, and corporate

personnel. Each case, therefore, reflects the freedoms and constraints on interviewing. An attempt was always made to discuss the viewpoints of the company, the rural people impacted, host government officials, and donor government representatives. Relevant literature was studied. This book does not pretend to be an in-depth, theoretical, scholarly work. The cases were carefully examined in terms of the purposes of the work, namely, to sketch a picture of the interaction between agribusiness and small-scale farmers, and the eddy effect of this relationship on farm families and their communities. This empirical evidence was then blended with the many years of industrial and rural development experience of the authors to arrive at recommendations for policy and implementation most likely to expand the role of agribusiness in the general attack on hunger, poverty, and disorder in the Third World.

2
Hindustan Lever Limited:
A Milk Processing Operation in India

Ruth Karen

SUMMARY

In the late 1960s, Hindustan Lever (HLL) established a milk products factory in the district of Etah, in the state of Uttar Pradesh. By 1973, it was ready to withdraw; the enterprise simply could not generate sufficient supplies of raw milk. Employees at the factory, supported by the governor of the state, persuaded HLL to reconsider the decision. Between 1973 and 1975, HLL streamlined the plant and changed its manner of working with local farmers. Supplies of milk reached satisfactory levels; the enterprise succeeded; net farm income from dairy herds increased significantly. Encouraged by this success, and because of a deeper sense of appreciation of both the needs and capabilities of the farmers in the area, in 1976 HLL initiated the Integrated Rural Development Program (IRDP), which has since become a model of private-sector intervention in long range, comprehensive economic and social development.

The IRDP covered six villages in 1976. Fifty villages, involving approximately 100,000 people and 50,000 hectares, were impacted by the program in 1983. Net farm income per hectare (1 hectare = 2.5 acres) doubled in this time, and a total additional income of US$10 million flowed into the Etah District. During these years, IRDP concentrated on four programs.

Agriculture. To improve all crop practices; to introduce new cash crops, such as oilseeds, which create a raw material base for a new investment by HLL for oil extraction and animal feed formulation; and to reclaim alkaline/saline land to add to the productive capacity of the area.

Animal husbandry. To raise the quality of dairy herds by cross breeding and providing veterinary and nutritional services.

Community development. With an emphasis on the provision of health delivery services and potable water, renewable energy technology, improved roads and schools, and the creation of cottage industries.

In special projects. For example, the organization of dairy cooperatives and registered village societies.

Future plans for the expansion of IRDP call for the establishment of a research and development center; opening a supply depot to ensure prompt delivery of inputs relevant to improved and diversified crop practices; and readying the farmers for a rapid increase in the production of oilseed crops. IRDP has become so important to HLL top management that selected management trainees, from all areas of the company, spend several months working in the program.

The Etah case clearly illustrates the concept of "satellite farming," with a single-channel marketing system supplying an on-site core processing facility. The case also demonstrates the strength of a truly global, highly diversified private-sector company to take risks, persist in the face of failure, and learn from experience to correct errors in judgment about the range and diversity of economic and social factors governing the success of agribusiness sited among technically backward, traditional people. More than this, the Etah story reveals an extraordinary decision by HLL to invest in the social and economic development of the people affected by the corporate presence, far beyond the limits to which agribusiness normally goes and far beyond the limits that most investors and theorists in the field of rural development would believe allowable by governments in the Third World. The importance of the HLL case, therefore, rests not only on the accomplishments in the Etah District of India, but also on its challenge to all those who tend to restrict too rigidly the leadership role agribusiness might play in accelerating agricultural and rural development everywhere.

COUNTRY BACKGROUND

In India, the lives and fortunes of the rural population are vital to the country's economic, social, and political future. There are 576,000 villages in India, 79 percent with a population of under 1,000. Some 80 percent of India's 700 million people live in rural areas. Despite a quite sophisticated and appreciably growing industrial component, about 35 percent of India's gross national product (GNP) still consists of agricultural output.

Etah District

The state of Uttar Pradesh is one of the least developed states of India. Indicatively, 80 percent of the state lacks all-weather roads. Etah District is one of the least developed areas within the state. It has only two industries: the HLL milk processing plant and a sugar factory. Ninety percent of the population is directly dependent on agriculture. Average literacy is 22 percent; female literacy is 9 percent. The average

land holding is 1.1 hectares. Despite reasonably good soil conditions due to the alluvial deposits of the Ganges River and excellent irrigation potential, major crop yields in Etah District
are considerably below the national average. For Example, measured in quintals per hectare (1 quintal = 100 kilograms), the
present crop yield in rice for all India is 12-plus, for Etah,
4.64; wheat yield for all India is 15-plus, for Etah, 13; sugarcane yield for all India is 500-plus, for Etah, 298; potato yield
for all India is 103, for Etah, 101. The law and order situation
is one of the worst in the country. Dacoits (bandits) still roam
the countryside, and there are areas in the district where trav-
eling at night is considered dangerous.

Economic Conditions

Quoting from the annual report of Etah Gramin Bank, a bank
created in March 1981 that specializes in rural requirements:

Transport, communication and other infrastructural
facilities exist only in skeletal form. The interior
parts of the district are almost inaccessible. Only
about 40 percent of the district's 1500 villages are
electrified.
The district experiences extremes of hot and cold
climate. Rains are irregular and untimely. Dependence
on rainfall for agricultural operations is highly
risky. The district does not have any significant
mineral wealth or forest wealth [7].

Social Conditions

The district is afflicted with many of India's persistent
and pernicious social problems, the most intransigent being the
caste system. The caste structure, still strongly in place in
Etah, has four major segments. The Thakurs, members of the ancient warrior caste, usually constitute a substantial segment of
the villagers. In terms of political power, they are often balanced out by the Yadavs, traditional shepherds and owners of
livestock, who are considered descendants of Krishna. As a result, the Brahmans, who usually constitute only a minority of the
village, often command the swing vote. The remaining castes,
consisting of Harijans (Untouchables) and other "scheduled
castes," are understandably the most enthusiastic about any and
all development efforts, but given their peculiar social status,
they have little political clout. Caste feelings run high, and
demarcations between the various castes and subcastes are still
preserved, restricting the scheduled castes to their own sections
of the village and requiring, for example, separate wells for
these village members.
The stratification of roles and opportunity created by the
caste system is further defined by sexual taboos. For example,
democratically elected (all villagers eighteen years of age can

vote) village councils, which play an important role in village affairs, do not permit women to be elected to their ranks or to attend meetings. In another important area of development, village health workers, the resident paramedics who assist visiting doctors, are women--but selected women. They must be selected from the two top castes in the village, since some villagers will not allow lower castes into their homes and will certainly not permit lower castes to render the kind of intimate service that medical service requires. Yet it is considered unsuitable for women in the upper castes to do any work outside the home!

Nevertheless, despite the limiting aspects of illiteracy, social order, a difficult climate, and severe underdevelopment of the district infrastructure, the Etah Gramin Bank report asserts that "if the farmers are given the necessary guidance and financial assistance, they come forward and can be motivated to make optimum use of the land they hold" [7]. HLL experience bears out this assertion, and the process of trial and error provided a unique demonstration in the area of just what the "necessary guidance and financial assistance" consisted of for the time and place.

ENTERPRISE BACKGROUND

Hindustan Lever Limited (HLL) is part of the Unilever group of companies. Unilever was formed in 1930 through a merger of Lever Brothers of Great Britain and the Margarine Union of Holland. Today, Unilever operates in seventy-five countries, employing about 300,000 people, one-third of these in developing countries. It has a total of 500 subsidiaries or associate companies worldwide and is known for its genuinely international corps of managers. Annual sales are in the vicinity of US$18 billion, with the following product breakdown: edible fats and dairy products, 24 percent; foods, 23 percent; detergents, 18 percent; personal products, 4 percent; chemical products, 6 percent; animal feeds, 6 percent; and others, 19 percent.

Hindustan Lever has a turnover of approximately $460 million, with a breakdown by product category: soaps and personal products, $185 million; detergents, $120 million; vanaspati (hydrogenated vegetable fat) and edible oils, $83 million; milk foods, $5 million; margarine and ghee (clarified butter), $6 million; animal feeds, $15 million; chemicals, $28 million; marine products (exports), $3 million; textile sheeting (exports), $4 million; footwear (exports), $0.36 million; carpets (exports), $1.89 million; others, $3 million. HLL's exports constitute one full percentage point of India's total exports.

Unilever equity in HLL is 51 percent. The remaining equity is in the hands of some 90,000 shareholders, including all of HLL's 10,000 employees. Employee stock purchases were financed by the company and have turned out to be an excellent investment. At a nominal price of 10 rupees (R), the shares were placed on

the market at R19 and in 1983 traded at R70. (The conversion
rate used throughout this case is R10 = US$1.)

Hindustan Lever does extensive research and development,
emphasizing the use of Indian raw materials in the development of
new and improved products. Over 250 scientists are employed at
the HLL Research Center, the largest in the private sector. The
marketing system of HLL is probably unparalleled in India, reaching an estimated 125 million people, many of them in outlying
rural areas.

The mode of the Etah milk products project has its origins
in two conceptual frames of reference: Unilever corporate philosophy and the particular perspective of HLL in terms of rural
India and the future of the company. Both are significant to the
theme of this book.

The corporate philosophy of Unilever. Unilever's philosophy
is clearly defined, sophisticated, and pragmatic and underpins
its global operations.

Unilever believes that social responsibility is at
the heart of any decent business. Unilever is not,
however, a social or charitable institution. It believes that the role of industry is to create wealth.
Certainly it uses its capabilities to produce wealth on
a massive scale. Nearly all the money that comes into
its coffers, some 12,000 million pounds sterling for
the goods it sold in 1981, passes out very quickly
again to people all over the world: its employees,
their dependents and pensioners (who add up to about a
million people altogether), its shareholders (among
them financial institutions, pension and insurance
funds and trade unions), suppliers of raw materials,
governments via taxation, local authorities and communities via rates and other levies. Last, but by no
means least, is the money retained for investment in
future activities, for Unilever aspires to be in business forever.

To achieve its infinity, the company realizes that
next to its financial and commercial obligations it has
an inescapable commitment to society. While its legal
and contractual obligations are clear enough in most
situations, its moral responsibilities are conceived
differently by different people. Unilever knows that
offending people anywhere is bad for business.
Ideally, it would like to be loved by everyone but in
courting the affections of one group (or of one
country) it can easily alienate another. It has to set
its cap at employees, investors, bankers, governments,
suppliers and customers who live and work in 75 countries.

At different times and in different countries,
Unilever has to give priority to the interests of one
group in preference to others. The rapidly changing

social, political and economic scene makes this inevitable. In the long term, a balance must be struck.
Without profits Unilever could not meet any of the
social or other demands made upon it. In its pursuit of
profit, growth and continuity it has, however, committed itself to acting always as a good employer and
citizen in the countries where it operates, respecting
international and local laws, regulations and customs.
It adds the rider that in respecting local customs,
however, it must not be tempted into lowering its standards of behavior [8].

The HLL perspective in India adds the local vision that the
rural people could become the company's major market. In 1983,
HLL's chairman noted that of the total expenditure on manufactured goods in India, 75 percent is spent in rural areas. Significantly, this percentage has remained almost unchanged in the
past two decades. The chairman also added:

> Though consumption and expenditure on manufactured
> items is low in rural areas, the market is approximate-
> ly three times larger. On the assumption that all per-
> sons or families above the poverty line form the market
> for some branded consumer goods, this market has a size
> of 42 million households. If we just take Punjab,
> Haryana, Rajasthan, Gujarat, and Andhra, the target
> market of 72 million people is larger numerically than
> France, the United Kingdom, or West Germany [8].

It is this focus on rural India that prompted the company to
concentrate an important part of its managerial energy in that
direction. The company approach has a sociopolitical ingredient,
a macroeconomic ingredient, and a unique component of managerial
follow-through.

The sociopolitical perspective. As stated by HLL's chairman
in mid-1983,

> The growth of economic activity in rural India is
> attended by per capita numbers and unending debates
> about the poverty line. These are real and cannot be
> wished away. But in a democratic society, uniform
> growth would be an elusive goal. If one set aside for
> a moment the sociopolitical aspects and instead ana-
> lyzed the socioeconomic realities, then the dispersal
> of agricultural and other products into rural India
> represents an important aspect of a possible approach
> for ensuring a measure of uniform economic spread [8].

The macroeconomic perspective. From the same source:

> HLL's experience in marketing and distribution has
> been greatly strengthened by innovations in technology
> and investments in the core sector. Its research

discoveries of chemical compounds which boost agricultural productivity, and its investment for manufacturing inorganic fertilizers, provide added impetus for deeper penetration of the hinterland. National surveys, as well as research undertaken by the company, confirm the view that population growth tends to overshadow progress being made and opportunities which are developing. However, they also clearly bring out the rapid developments taking place in many parts of rural India. We must now get out of the shadow of lopsided growth of the urban centers and carefully plan to service the increasing demands of non-urban India [8].

The company's unique managerial follow-through on its perspective is centered on the Etah project. After an initial false start, which concentrated on economic incentives exclusively, the company realized that only an approach addressed to all the farmer's needs, developmental as well as economic, could work. As this realization grew, HLL made it mandatory for management trainees to work at Etah, in the IRDP program, for at least two months. In this way, as the HLL chairman explains it:

We help urban-bred young men to comprehend the problems of the majority of our countrymen. This, in turn, helps to develop a cadre of people who will be better tuned to the needs, aspirations, and opportunities outside the mainstream of India's urban life. In addition, rural development in India is still a neglected sector and the hands-on involvement of companies like HLL provides on-site transfer of technology, as well as the application of scarce managerial inputs [8].

To ensure that the management trainees appreciate their role and approach village life with utmost sensitivity, the company's approach to all facets of village activities and the needs of the people is spelled out in a succinct set of instructions. The instructions state:

You can contribute in the area of agriculture by studying the economics of various crops which will maximize benefits to the farmer; introducing new varieties of crops, especially cash crops like oil seeds, soybeans, safflower, etc. after studying in detail their economics and chances of success; developing better irrigation aids and reducing cost of existing facilities; helping the farmer to market his produce through cooperatives; identifying farmers suitable for training.
You can contribute significantly in propagating the concept of cross-bred cows and can help in promoting large-scale purchases of such animals through Land Development Bank loans. Generous subsidies from the government are available to farmers for such purposes.

You can check the efficiency of our veterinarians and Animal Health Centers by cross-checking their artificial insemination reports and recording confirmed pregnancies.

You should bring forward your own ideas for devices such as the bio-gas plants and bullock-powered pumps which reduce costs and benefit the villagers.

Your first task on settling in a village is to obtain the cooperation of the villagers. Very often the best way to work on it is through community projects like brick-paved roads; repairs on wells; provision of soak pits; electrification of the village. Subsidies are available for such projects from the government and nominal subsidies are extended by the company to initiate the work.

You can also substantially contribute in areas like adult education and setting up village societies which, in the absence of external leadership, can carry on the developmental work.

Much of the work done involves financial assistance from the government and banks. This is very often a frustrating experience for the newcomer unfamiliar with government procedures. IRDP supervisors, proficient in handling the local government staff, often make this job simpler. However, it is your initiative which could make all the difference between success or failure [8].

Discussions with some of these management trainees reveal that this exposure to the realities of rural life in India does indeed fulfill the expectations of the chairman. All of the trainees confessed to initial culture shock of drastic proportions, and then offered a variety of lessons learned:

I learned two things that will be important to me for the rest of my life. The first is patience; the second is not only intellectual understanding, but actually seeing and feeling other people's viewpoint.

I got a new perspective on rural life in India. The villages are not simple structures in any sense of the word. There are caste relationships; there are power relationships; there are property relationships; and managing all of these requires a sensitivity and adaptability that is a vital management tool everywhere.

I learned to handle myself in an unstructured environment or, more accurately, an environment with structures that I did not know. In that environment I learned what it takes to motivate people, organize them and implement follow-through. In short, I learned that I can create a concept, engineer agreement and make things happen. And that, I was taught at the University, is the essence of management.

ETAH DAIRY PRODUCTS ENTERPRISE BACKGROUND

History

The Etah District was chosen by HLL for two reasons. First, the company had some prior experience in Uttar Pradesh. HLL's first agribusiness venture was a pea dehydration operation in Ghaziabad, also in that state. Second, the district of Etah is situated on the Indo-Gangetic plains and has a rich potential for agriculture and animal husbandry. Indeed, Hindu tradition places Krishna and his famous dalliance with the milkmaids in this region. Thus, both tradition (an important element in all facets of Indian life), and natural resources pointed to Etah as a logical location for a milk-processing facility.

As so often in India, however, the gap between potential and reality turned out to be sizable. The Etah venture ran into a number of problems of which the most important was that the company could not generate a sufficient supply of milk from the farmers, with the result that the factory operated at only 30 percent of capacity to process 30,000 metric tons (mt) of milk per year. In 1973, the company was ready to call it quits and close down the factory. However, both its own employees and the governor of Uttar Pradesh mounted a campaign to have the company change its mind.

During the following two years (1973-1975), HLL streamlined the operations of the factory and concentrated on increasing and improving the supply of milk from the farmers of the Etah region. As the managing director of the HLL dairy operation stated in a conversation: "It was realized at that time that increasing the milk availability of the Etah District was crucial to the enduring existence of the factory and was inextricably linked to the overall socioeconomic development of the region."

In August 1976, the chairman of HLL, T. Thomas, reviewed the situation of the Etah dairy operation in its totality and formulated the concept of an integrated development program. This aimed at improving the prosperity level of the Etah District farmers through their own efforts by providing them with guidance and knowledge in agriculture and animal husbandry. The economic goals of improving the prosperity of the area through this program were integrated with the social goals of helping the villagers to improve local sanitation, health, and education.

By 1982, factory operation had been increased to 66 percent of capacity. Although other operational and managerial elements, such as more aggressive milk collection and new product introduction, were involved in this increase, the company reports that the Integrated Rural Development Program made a major contribution to this important improvement. The company expects its IRDP activities to result in an 80 percent use of factory capacity by 1985.

Integrated Rural Development Program

IRDP was launched with the assignment of five supervisors from the factory to different villages in the district. The five supervisors were assigned six villages: Sirsa Badan, Mamau, Alipur, Patna, Tikathar, and Dharauli. They were asked to collect data on population, landholdings, irrigation, cropping patterns, cattle population, and attitudes of farmers, among other basic data, and to think of ways in which each of them could work with the villagers in improving agricultural output without the company having to subsidize the operations financially. It was always HLL's intention that the farming communities should not become dependent on charitable aid, but that they should have some financial stake in their development and a sense of shared responsibility for the improvement of their production capabilities.

At the end of a six-week stay in these villages, the supervisors met the chairman of HLL in the Etah District for a presentation on the data they had gathered, the impressions they had formed, and the ideas they had formulated for effecting improvements. In their presentation, the supervisors emphasized four obstacles faced by the farmers: lack of financing, forcing villagers to borrow from moneylenders at excessive rates of interest because banks were reluctant to grant loans for fear of defaults in the absence of acceptable collateral; lack of technical assistance, resulting in poor yields; lack of reliable, accessible sources of supply for essential inputs, such as seed, fertilizers, pesticides, and animal health products; and lack of storage and marketing facilities after harvest.

The supervisors also outlined their own ideas on how they could assist and guide the farmers in overcoming these problems, not by financing them but by enabling them to make better use of facilities that were already available, mostly through government schemes. In response, the company structured a four-part program for its integrated rural development activities.

Agriculture. Propagate a scientific system of practices; reclaim alkaline/saline land through a process of chemical treatment with gypsum or pyrites to render it cultivatable; institute seed multiplication, a program that supplies good quality seeds from the National Seed Corporation to selected farmers, arranges for needed inputs, inspection, and certification, and returns harvest seed to the National Seed Corporation. Because certified seeds fetch a substantial premium over the ordinary crop harvest, this adds handsomely to the farmers' income.

Animal husbandry. Encourage crossbreeding, which raises the quality of local cows through artificial insemination using frozen semen of thoroughbred, progeny-tested Holstein or Jersey bulls; improve buffalo breeds; and extend veterinary and nutritional guidance.

Community projects. Establish village health and road programs; repair schools and drinking-water wells; develop renewable energy systems; and develop cottage industries and local handicrafts.

Special programs. Encourage and support village dairy co-operatives (formed in each village or in a cluster of villages by primary milk producers). These cooperatives are supported with free veterinary and nutritional care. Milk generated by the co-operatives is guaranteed for off-take at a remunerative price by HLL. Other programs were to develop bullock-powered pumps for the farmers and promote bio-gas plants that convert animal and plant waste into methane used for cooking and lighting.

In each of the six villages, some of the local farmers were selected on the basis of their willingness to take help and guidance from the supervisors. These selected farmers were given help in deciding on crop rotation, seed selection, fertilizer dosage, irrigation intervals, tilling, weeding, and other essential practices. Their farms also served as demonstration plots, to show others the results of following scientific practices.

In animal husbandry, it was realized that it was essential to upgrade the quality of milch cattle in the Etah District. For this, it was considered advantageous to introduce high-yielding, crossbred cows to replace the hardy but low-yielding buffalo. Assistance was sought from the Bharatiya Agro-Industries Foundation, a voluntary agency near Poona specializing in crossbreeding programs for cows. With their help, a demonstration farm, initially comprised of twenty crossbred cows of the Holstein, Frisian, and Jersey breeds, was established on the Etah factory premises. In addition, a program for the artificial insemination of local cows with the frozen semen of pure Holstein, Frisian, and Jersey bulls was initiated. Veterinary support was also found to be essential to maintain the health and productivity of the relatively more sensitive crossbred cows.

In order to take the program to the community, five registered societies, with many of the participating villagers as members, were formed in the areas where the initial six villages were located. These are presently operated by HLL, but it is the company's intention that such societies should take on the development activities at the village level some time in the future. For the IRDP operation, the overall manager, an HLL employee, directs the work of both the company's own supervisors and the supervisors chosen from existing village societies. The latter are in charge of a single village center, or a cluster of villages located around a center, and oversee the work of village extension workers. Village society supervisors work with company supervisors in directing the efforts of veterinarians and village health workers. Qualified medical doctors and compounders (pharmacists) visit each center on a regular basis.

To facilitate smooth sailing for IRDP, the program must be implemented in the context of the established political structures and the traditional caste system. The functions of the caste are integrated into a hierarchy of civil government, starting in each village with the panchayat (elected community council). In theory, panchayat elections are held every other year, but timing depends on the state government. In some states, intervals between elections have been as long as ten years.

The village councils, in their turn, elect representatives to the pradhan (the block council), which represents a hundred villages and roughly 100,000 persons. The pradhans then elect the pramukh (district council), which consists of fifteen blocks. The district council consists of forty people: one member from each block; ten members at large; the district manager, who is a civil servant; and for the remaining fourteen, members of the state assembly and the federal parliament. In relating to this complex system of government, HLL/IRDP cooperates directly with civil servants, concentrating on the district manager and on officers whose appointments and function parallel the political structure. These civil service functions proliferate into village extension offices, one for each ten villages. At the district officer level, there are also technical specialists, including livestock and agricultural officers and agricultural engineers.

IRDP also maintains close relationships with the Etah Gramin Bank, which in the first two years of its existence managed to set up a network of thirty-two branches covering twelve of the fifteen blocks of Etah District. By 1985, the bank expects to have a hundred branches in fifteen blocks. These branches really do reach the villages. Set up in two rooms of a village hut, they manage to attract village savings as well as make loans in the amounts and for the purposes that the villagers require. In the first two months of its existence, the bank branch in one village had attracted deposits of R5,000, in accounts of R50 to R100, and had made loans for the purchase of fertilizer and seeds. The branch manager reported that he relied heavily on the knowledge of the HLL supervisor servicing the village, for two reasons: the supervisor knows through personal experience who in the village is dependable; and although HLL will not guarantee any loans, it does provide a form of collateral through its regular and dependable purchase of milk from the farmers who have either buffalo or dairy cow livestock.

The progress of the IRDP program was reviewed in February 1977, July 1977, and September 1977, at the end of the winter, summer, and monsoon crops respectively. These reviews indicated that there was a perceptible improvement in the awareness of the farmers as to the need to follow better agricultural practices. Their ability to utilize bank loans and government subsidies had also improved, and an increase in yields and economies in operations was also noted.

Encouraged by the progress made in the first year, IRDP was extended to cover a number of additional activities in 1978. The areas of operation of the supervisors were extended beyond the original six villages and additional supervisory resources were applied. A program was initiated for the reclamation of uncultivatable alkaline and saline land, which then constituted over 5 percent of Etah District. A training program covering mechanical equipment repair was started. Finally, a medical plan was introduced, concentrating primarily on preventive measures such as vaccinations and improving the general cleanliness and hygenic conditions of the homes and village. Training villagers in paramedical techniques was an important part of the plan.

At the time I visited the Etah District in 1983, future projects being planned for IRDP included establishing of a research and development center focused on agriculture and animal husbandry; expanding the organization of dairy cooperatives to 150 villages, with the idea that each one would serve as the nucleus for growth in village self-reliance; rapidly moving toward extensive cultivation of soybeans and other oilseeds, thus laying the groundwork for an investment in processing; and facilitating the supply of basic inputs to farmers applying improved crop and animal husbandry practices by a careful integration of the flow of supplies from different enterprises in the HLL corporate structure.

The initial budget for IRDP was R1 million; this budget had doubled by 1983. HLL hopes that the growing capability of the farmers and their understanding of the need to constantly reinvest part of their newly created cash income to sustain both growth in income and social development will permit the company to hold the budget to R2 million (exclusive of an investment in the research center noted above). The decision to invest in IRDP on a long-term basis clearly fits into the philosophy of Unilever as it applies to its global operations as summarized earlier in this chapter: IRDP is a sound business venture and is a socially responsible activity in an area of great need. Fitted to the objectives of HLL management, IRDP is intended to demonstrate to its own employees at all levels that the company is conscious of its responsibility to the physical and social environment in which it operates; assure the people and government of India that HLL is truly involved and committed to the national effort to accelerate agricultural and rural development; provide an enduring infrastructure to sustain the dairy operations in Etah District; lay down a sound basis for agricultural diversification, of benefit to farmers and to HLL, the latter most particularly in form of opportunities for investment in processing; and build a growing market for HLL products among rural people.

Impact on the Farmer

Starting with six villages in 1976, the company's IRDP program covered fifty villages in 1983, reaching approximately 100,000 people. Agricultural extension work alone has more than doubled income per acre for the farmers involved in the program, covering approximately 50,000 hectares and amounting to an annual total of $10 million of additional income for the district. Targets for the next five years include the following:

- Coverage of at least 10 percent of Etah District. This would mean coverage of 160 villages with a total population of 160,000, occupying a cultivable land area of 100,000 hectares.
- Coverage of at least 5,000 hectares of land for seed multiplication, resulting in an additional income of R8.5 million to Etah farmers.

- Cultivation of 2,000 hectares of reclaimed land under the Usar Reclamation Program, resulting in an additional annual income of R10 million to Etah farmers.
- Improvement of productivity in all covered areas through improved irrigation aids such as animal-powered pumps, and through better farming aids and crop rotation practices, increasing income per hectare by at least 10 percent and making additional income of R27 million available to Etah farmers.
- Generation of additional milk availability of 21,000 tons as a result of propagation of crossbred cattle and distribution of crossbred heifers. The additional milk would be equivalent to new income to farmers totaling R42 million per year.
- Further development of bio-gas plants, animal-powered pump sets, and other energy-saving devices, expected to yield savings equivalent to R6 million per year.

It is thus estimated that by 1990, the activities of HLL's IRDP program will have resulted in net income gains to farmers of R94 million per year. This, when distributed over the 160,000 people covered by the program, represents an increase in per head income of R600 per year. This would, in no small measure, help the government's intention of lifting the rural poor over the poverty line.

Marhera--A Village Experience

Within two years of association with HLL/IRDP, dramatic changes occurred in Marhera. A milk collection system was established that collects milk from the village each morning and transports it to a collection center. The system eliminates the middleman with whom the farmers had to deal previously. This increases the price the farmer is paid by 25 percent.

A seed supply system organized for the farmers, has increased the production both of their food and of their cash crops, and has introduced new crops that span the traditional winter and summer seasons. Farm families in Marhera typically have holdings of one hectare, and the government's National Seed Corporation is organized to supply seed only for farmers owning five hectares or more. To overcome this hurdle, the company has collected ten or twelve of the one-hectare farm families and registered them as one producer. This made them eligible for dealings with the National Seed Corporation.

Before HLL made its organizing and management contributions to the village, Marhera farmers used to sell their crops to traders who took a considerable part of the price for themselves and were not always dependable in how, when, and indeed, whether they paid the producer. After the company's arrival and with its help, the farmers bought a truck and some bullock carts and, using this transportation, began to take their produce to market themselves. The city of Etah, the regional capital, is only eleven kilometers away, but it had never occurred to the farmers that they could do their own marketing.

The company gave the farmers expert advice on fertilizer, crop rotation, and the use of marginal land to grow vegetables. An estimate by the elected head of the village society posits that in two years the company's presence has increased village income by at least 25 percent. In addition, HLL brought regular and dependable veterinary services to Marhera, whereas previously the government had supplied such guidance sporadically and unpredictably.

With HLL help, electricity has been brought to Marhera for the first time by the introduction of bio-gas generators. The village well has been protected from mud by the construction of a simple platform around the well opening. All the pathways of Marhera are now paved with brick. And most importantly, HLL also helped to organize a village health system, mainly by finding and training a paramedic and organizing a ladies' society to instruct women in prenatal and infant care. It has backstopped this service by sending to the village, again on a regular basis, an HLL mobile team of a compounder and a fully qualified medical doctor, who was practicing on the day I visited the village. His consulting room was a gigantic mohar tree at the edge of the village, and his clinic consisted of a bed of plastic webbing. He did not lack patients.

Kisrauli--IRDP and a Village Cooperative

HLL policy is to make village societies entirely self-supporting in about five years, so that the company can move both its services and its finances to new locations. Kisrauli is well along this road.

The village of Kisrauli, with a population of 1,500, has a cooperative of 4,000 shareholders that caters to twenty-six villages in the immediate vicinity. The co-op was organized so that farmers can buy fertilizer and seeds in bulk, and can sell its price-supported products to the Food Corporation of India, a government purchasing agency. Another advantage of such a cooperative is that the government will guarantee credit in a 1 to 10 ratio. This makes it possible for the co-op to purchase in bulk such basic commodities for home use as kerosene, sugar, and cloth.

For the co-op, the arrival of HLL has been an important step up the economic ladder. Not only does the company represent a totally dependable buyer for all of the co-op's milk output, it also has made a major contribution to increasing that output through advice on animal care, the supply of dependable veterinary services, and the operation of an artificial insemination station.

On the marketing end, elimination of the middleman has increased the co-op's income by about 25 percent, with an additional margin added by the quality tests the company conducts in each of its collection stations. One aspect of that test is the fat content of milk. Kisrauli's farmers deliver primarily buffalo milk, which has a fat content of 7.5 compared to the 6.5 that is standard among milch cows. Higher fat content increases the value of the Kisrauli farmers' milk, and HLL pays for the difference.

At the Kisrauli co-op, a point was made regarding the difference between government-supplied services and those supplied by the company. A spokesman for the co-op reported that the government did have a veterinarian visiting the village, but when he was transferred no replacement arrived for several months despite repeated urgent requests. When the villagers approached the company, it responded immediately. As the head of the co-op noted (echoing a statement voiced in Turkey, Chapter 5), "The difference is that the government comes on a bureaucratic schedule, the company comes when people or animals need them."

With their own innate tendency toward organized independent action buttressed by company support, the people of Kisrauli also decided not to wait any longer for the government to start up the school they wanted and had asked for repeatedly. With the mukhaya (head of the village) donating his own house as a school building, Kisrauli has launched its own school. The school consists of grades one through eight, with students sitting in "classrooms" that consist of straw mats laid out in different areas of the house and the yard. The village has hired six teachers for a total student body of 250, 30 of whom are girls. Parents pay R5 per month and there are applications from parents as far away as eight kilometers for their children's admission to the school.

The school day runs from 7:00 a.m. until noon, six days a week, and homework is assigned. The teachers, all of whom are young, lively, and dedicated, report that despite the fact that the children get no help at home with their homework--because most of the parents are illiterate and cannot help--the students do their homework diligently and well. Although there is still some resistance to sending girls to school, the girls who do get to school do as well as the boys. Instruction covers the complete government curriculum (general knowledge, mathematics, general science, social science, geography, and history) and in addition, English is taught.

In Kisrauli, HLL works with the co-op and with individual farmers to facilitate interaction with various government agencies, as well as with the Etah Gramin Bank, which has established a branch in the village. As another sign of the town's new affluence and confidence, Kisrauli has its own doctor, with office hours from 7:00 a.m. to 12:00 noon, and from 3:00 p.m. to 6:00 p.m. every day of the week, in a building he shares with the post office.

HLL's direct involvement in Kisrauli's welfare, aside from its economic, managerial, and intermediary contributions, includes identification of and compensation for a village health worker; introduction of new sanitation habits in village houses; disinfecting of village wells; and support for the local ladies' society that teaches good nutritional and sanitation habits to pregnant women and young mothers.

Village Development--Some Generalizations

The company's approach to village development is to work closely with village societies where they do exist, and otherwise to encourage their formation. Although the company is generous with its organizing, management, and administrative know-how, it attempts to hold its financial inputs to a minimum. For capital expenditures like roads, wells, bio-gas plants, and two new enterprises (animal-powered wells and tree planting ventures), the system the company likes best is for the relevant government agency to provide 50 percent of the required financing in either cash or materials, for the company to contribute 25 percent in either cash or materials, and for villagers to pay a share of 25 percent in either cash or labor.

A symbolic contribution HLL makes to all the villages in which it works is a display board made of steel that defines each village in terms of what it considers to be the main ingredients of its developing identity. The board gives the name of the village; its total population; the number of families; its area; the numbers of buffalo and cows; and, when warranted, the harvest increase of its crops.

One such board illustrates the importance of another contribution the HLL program makes to the development of the area: the Usar Land Reclamation Project, which reclaims unproductive land. Usually, Usar land is assigned to the Harajans, the only caste in the community that will take on the particularly unrewarding task of working this kind of land. The Harajans do this because they have no other choice. What happens when Usar land is reclaimed, a process that consists primarily of covering the area with gypsum and broadening and lining canals with brick to prevent waterlogging, is illustrated by the HLL board at the entrance of Jinaoli Village, which carries the following legend.

	1979/80	1980/81	1982/81
Rice	20	25	32
Wheat	3	6	18
Barley	-	-	18

In all the villages visited, the farmers understood the self-interest of the company. They were also aware of the company's international connection. They had no problem with either. As one headman put it: "They help us and we help them. That's the way it should be. That's how everybody profits and prospers." Within the Indian context, perhaps the most telling indications of how the people of the area feel about the company are that the dacoits who infest the region will not touch anyone who works for the company; and village headmen have offered daughters in marriage to company management trainees.

Government Relations Fostered by IRDP

The company maintains a close and continuous working relationship with the district manager and all relevant district departments. Although it encountered initial resistance and suspicion from the district bureaucracy, that resistance has largely
melted as officials have seen the extent of HLL's effort, commitment, and impact. The district manager, in a discussion with me,
noted that initially the company's concern was simply to obtain
the maximum possible amount of quality milk, which, he added, was
not an objectionable aim in itself. However, he observed accurately: "They've changed their original approach. They realized
that to achieve their own aim, they have to have a comprehensive
outlook on rural development. They have that now, and we consider them good and effective partners in what we ourselves are
attempting to do."

The district manager, who is the senior civil servant in the
region, offered a proposal based on his own experience with HLL.
He suggested it might be an idea for the federal government to
link each district of India with an industrial house that would
give maximum scope to the industry for its own growth and the
development of the district. There are 405 districts in India.
Discussing the political aspects of this notion, the district manager said that "In India, we have four sectors that can
contribute to development: the federal government, the state
government, local government, and the private sector. Each has
its strength and its weakness; that is democracy. But if we put
them all together, I believe we can make sure that the maximum
possible benefits go to the grassroots in the shortest possible
time."

At the national level it may be observed that for all private enterprise, relationships with the government of India are a
full-time occupation and preoccupation. Almost all large companies, domestic or multinational, maintain offices in New Delhi
whose mandate is to deal with the federal bureaucracy and with
the legislature. In India, members of parliament consider it
part of their function to pose questions about individual companies and their activities. The fact that these questions are
often based on gossip and ignorance, and are always politically
inspired, has made no difference to this exercise. Its connection to reality is usually tenuous.

HLL, for example, has major investments in the state of
Kerala and is considering expanding its productive facilities in
that state. The governor of Kerala is a member of the Communist
party who nevertheless maintains excellent relations with HLL
management and, when asked, appears and officiates on such company occasions as plant openings or expansions. His rationale:
"When the revolution comes, I'll nationalize you. Meanwhile I
want the jobs and the economic development that your activities
bring to the state." This pragmatic revolutionary has even been
persuaded on occasion to prevent his comrades in the federal legislature from making unwarranted accusations and from supporting
destructive or obstructive motions that affect the company.

At the international level, HLL does not relate directly to donor countries, in the sense of receiving development assistance. IRDP is a corporate function in its entirety. In a global sense, HLL does receive support, as needed, from its parent, Unilever, who may contribute to the solution of technical and managerial problems, as well as give full moral backing to the social outreach of HLL in India. The Dutch government has actually sent the Queen's consort to visit HLL's facilities, which in the opinion of HLL management, "has added a visceral tool to the home government's own recognition that multinational corporations are not only high technology, high profit, high remittance organizations, which the conventional wisdom holds them to be, but are also concerned with economic, social, and human development in every country, every area, indeed every village in which they operate."

POLICY IMPLICATIONS

For the Company

HLL has been careful to monitor itself and each of its operations and has evolved a variety of policy conclusions concerning rurally-sited, satellite farming procurement systems that involve a core processing facility with large numbers of rural people. These policy guidelines appear to be broadly applicable, in India and elsewhere.

Although it may be attractive to resort to charity to obtain quick benefits, these benefits are of a transient nature. Unless the villagers are also financially involved in the programs, there is little shared responsibility for their ultimate success.

A continuous feedback as to the relevance of the programs to the actual needs of the villagers is essential. In fact, as far as is practical, solutions to the problems of the villagers and the plans of action to apply such solutions need to be developed in active consultation with the villagers themselves. In HLL's program this is made possible by the physical presence of IRDP staff in the villages.

However efficient, no one group can hope to tackle all basic problems of rural development single-handedly. The involvement of government agencies, other voluntary agencies, financial institutions, specialist institutions, as well as local communities, is essential to obtain maximum benefits from the development programs.

When appropriate infrastructural support has been provided, the villagers are quite capable of taking advantage of the available facilities to improve their own lot. This has been clearly demonstrated in the villages covered by the HLL program in the increased ability of the farmers to make use of bank loans and government subsidies and to adopt scientific methods in agriculture and animal husbandry.

Qualitative determination of progress in such a program is only possible over a long-term span of ten years or more. It is nonetheless necessary to monitor the performance of program activities at regular intervals to ensure adherence to objectives and direction. It is also necessary to set quantitative parameters to measure the impact of the program in the shorter term.

In addition, the general manager of HLL's Etah operations has formulated his own unpublished "Ten Commandments for Rural Development."

1. Establish credibility through honesty and integrity. These qualities have to be expressed both internally and externally. They are best conveyed by committed supervisors who are honest, apolitical and corruption-proof, and who can earn the respect of elected officials from the village level up, and of appointed civil servants from the district manager down.

2. Assure that plans are generated at the grass roots by the farmers themselves. There is an initial hesitation by the farmers to make such plans, but the resistance can be broken down by supervisors who know their business and their communities, and by management trainees who actually live in the villages. Both the supervisors and the management trainees have to establish the kind of relationship with the farmer in which they can say "no" as well as "yes" and still retain the respect and trust of the villagers.

3. Set up an effective organizational structure for follow-through. Frequently, government and voluntary agencies have marvelous ideas and brilliant concepts, but no one who is competent or interested enough to follow through. One of the fringe benefits of the management trainees who work in the villages is that they are instructed to provide and are capable of providing feedback on the organizational followthrough that is required.

4. Provide or organize financial support. The need is for onsite banking institutions that operate effectively at the village level.

5. Build a viable communications system, both physical and people-to-people. This includes roads that are accessible throughout the year (at present, 70 percent of India's villages are inaccessible during the rainy season), and every form of transportation including buses, bullock carts, and bicycles. In our system we use them all.

6. Upgrade agricultural practices. This involves everything from water management to crop rotation; from seed improvement to livestock care.

7. Introduce animal husbandry, not as a replacement for existing cultivation of food or cash crops, but as a viable secondary occupation for the farm family.

8. Promote appropriate alternative energy sources, such as bio-gas fueled by cow dung.

9. Aid village industries, particularly those relevant to women.
10. Help to build health and educational infrastructure.

For the Host Country

The key factor at the community level is to build an effective bridge between theory and practice. HLL, acting through IRDP, has done this. Extrapolating the HLL experience to all of India and beyond, the indicated policy would be that if an agribusiness enterprise exists in a rural area and accepts the responsibility as prudent business practice, it should be encouraged to replicate and adapt the HLL methodology, minimizing public-sector cost and intervention. However, because agribusiness cannot be everywhere, policy might well direct civil servants to study the HLL/IRDP program and apply its operating principles as the circumstances will allow.

Logically, then, civil servants should be given the opportunity to observe the IRDP on-site and, perhaps, serve a period of apprenticeship even as HLL demands of its management trainees. Another opportunity for India is to take advantage of the large body of village-level experience embodied in the intermediate development organization (intermediaries between donor countries and host governments) headquartered all over the world. The criteria of selection among these organizations include a rigorous evaluation of performance under diverse cultural, social, and economic conditions.

If civil servants are, as a matter of national policy, supported in their work at the village level by advisors from outside of India, there will be a substantial cost assumed by the rural development program, which, for maximum return on investment, should be obligated for periods of at least three to five years. As the HLL case illustrates, even a global corporation with the resources of Unilever must invest for many years before widespread, in-depth results are evident. As a matter of policy, rural development costs not borne by private enterprise such as HLL in its Integrated Rural Development Program, should be returned over time by an allocation from the new wealth generated. In other words, just as HLL expects that the IRDP program will return a profit in the long run, so should public investment in similar programs. Village-level rural development can be economically viable and self-sustaining, and policy should support this objective.

The paramount need, as easy to advocate as it is difficult to implement, is to debureaucratize the very comprehensive network of services that the Indian government offers its rural population. It is also vital that a way be found to eliminate corruption from the system and to design the paperwork in a way that villagers can understand and deal with. At present, the paperwork required for villagers to obtain any government service is daunting to a point where the overwhelming majority of the rural population simply has no way of obtaining the services to which, in theory, it is entitled.   There may indeed be a place here for intermediate institutions specifically trained to help villagers deal with the administrative tasks that give them access to the considerable array of government services that do exist.

The suggestion that a specific industry house be linked with each of the country's 405 districts to promote growth and development might well work in the Indian context.   As the district manager in Etah pointed out: "Companies are change agents, and we do need change."

Finally, a tax provision that has allowed companies to deduct rural development expenses from their tax as a business expense is now being questioned, alleging occasional abuses by some companies. This questioning seems counterproductive.

For the Donor Country

Rural development clearly appears to be a winning proposition both for the host country, where it raises the GNP and contributes to the overall welfare of the population, and for the donor country, where it creates the possibility of new markets, as well as generating political goodwill.   For these reasons, as well as the medium and long-range self-interest of the companies involved, donor countries should encourage their multinational corporations to pay attention to the developmental as well as the economic aspects of their undertaking. This includes reinvesting in the host country when appropriate commercial possibilities and economic justification exist.   It also includes relevant attention to external constraints such as pollution and environmental safeguards and, where possible, the establishment of appropriate industries in outlying districts so that the wealth-creating process--the basic economic and social justification for multinational corporation (MNC) activity--is distributed as widely and as fairly as possible. The donor country should, to whatever extent possible, encourage its multinational corporations not to be islands in the host countries, but to see themselves as agents for change, innovation, and overall development.

3
The Mumias Sugar Company: A Nuclear Estate in Kenya

Simon Williams

SUMMARY

The Mumias Sugar Company (MSC) is a joint venture of the Government of Kenya (GOK), the Commonwealth Development Corporation (CDC, Chapter 13, Section 1), Booker Agriculture International (BA, Chapter 13, Section 11), and the East African Development Bank. In addition to its investment, BA manages the enterprise under contract. MSC is a model of what is called a "nucleus estate," a system that integrates a core processing plant, a corporate plantation that ensures a supply of high-quality raw material, and an outgrower or "satellite farming procurement program" into which large numbers of small-scale farmers are drawn.

The achievements of the company, which began production in 1974, have been remarkable. In one decade, a poverty-stricken sub-subsistence area with no background of sugarcane production has been converted into a cash economy. The sugar mill now produces roughly half the sugar consumed in Kenya. Twenty-three thousand outgrowers are under contract, supplying 88 percent of the cane requirement. Exclusive of its impact on the farmers, the enterprise employs 5,000 people full time and upwards of 9,000 part time. In ten years, as the sole commercial force in the area, the company has dramatically altered the economic and social characteristics of an area embracing several hundred thousand people.

There are two distinctly different systems of interaction with the local people in operation. With employees of the sugar mill and the plantation, MSC is almost totally involved. Villages have been created to provide housing for the majority of workers and the company provides all of the supporting services, including medical. Technical training facilities are extensive and upward mobility is a common thread of opportunity throughout the enterprise. The enterprise site is a bustling center of energy, almost startling in its impact on an observer first visiting this remote part of Kenya. Relationships with contract farmers are close and continuous insofar as they relate to technical supervision of sugarcane cultivation, but are deliberately

somewhat withdrawn in terms of community and human development.
Unlike the decision of Hindustan Lever Limited (HLL) in the
Etah District of India (Chapter 2), for example, MSC tends to
hold back in taking responsibility for how the people in the area
capitalize on their new opportunities and build for their future
outside of the environment of the company. This responsibility,
it is strongly felt, belongs to the Government of Kenya. To
facilitate bringing the people and their government together, the
farmers have been brought into their own organization, the Mumias
Outgrowers Company, intended ultimately to be the local agency
for development and the interface between the local people and
the company, and between the local people and government officials. As the case reveals, this methodology raises basic questions: Can one organization effectively relate to 23,000 farm
families? With what resources of money and talent is the organization to be endowed? Where are these resources to come from,
with what strings attached?

The questions raised by this important case are not meant to
imply criticism. Rather, they reveal unusual opportunities to
build the Mumias area into a second generation of development
success on the foundations of constructive change that has been
introduced.

COUNTRY BACKGROUND

Agriculture is the backbone of the economy and lies at the
heart of social and political life in Kenya. Currently, even in
the face of a recent decline explosive in relative importance,
the agricultural sector provides nearly 40 percent of the gross
domestic product (GDP), 34 percent of manufacturing inputs,
65 percent of nonpetroleum exports, and 65 percent of total
employment. In a country having no natural resources aside from
land, people, and wildlife, and almost no mineral deposits other
than soda ash, gemstones, limestone, and fluorspar, the vital
importance of vigorous growth in agriculture and agribusiness to
the future prosperity and stability of the nation is clear and
pressing.

The agricultural sector is dominated by four characteristics
of particular importance to investors.

Private land tenure. Ninety-nine percent of the farms and
ranches are privately owned, even though tribal culture is strong
in rural Kenya. Approximately half this land is in about 3,000
so-called "large farms," ranging upward from 20 hectares to well
over 40,000 hectares (1 hectare = 2.5 acres). These farms yield
45 percent of marketed production. The other half is the property of approximately 800,000 smallholders, 70 to 75 percent of
whom farm less than 3 hectares. These farms have become increasingly important to the agricultural economy since independence

and now account for 55 percent of marketed production and 80 percent of all production.

An intriguing development has been the transfer of ownership of some purchased large expatriate farms to groups of smallholders organized into either companies or cooperatives. In either case, part of the land is divided into individually owned small farms and part is farmed as an estate, with paid management.

Increasing productivity on smallholder land is of the highest priority in Kenyan planning. Land tenure realities and the pressing need for more food production exercise a pervasive influence on public policy, popular attitudes, and the design of public and private investments in agro-industry.

Explosive population growth. Kenya has one of the highest rates of population increase in the world. Officially designated at 3.8 percent a year, the figures of 4.0 to 4.2 percent are more widely held to be true. This steadily increases pressure on the land, as indicated by a World Bank estimate of a 0.88 hectare decline in the amount of good farmland per capita from 1970 to the year 2000. The decline in good farmland per capita has also forced agriculture and animal husbandry into marginal areas, with serious negative impact on soil erosion and water conservation in the same vicious cycle that plagues nations throughout the world. Although it is not the sole factor at work, population pressure on the land has surely contributed to the slowdown in farm production growth from an annual rate of 6 percent in the 1970s to a 1983 rate of 2.4 percent [9].

Improved agricultural practice constrained. Improved agricultural practice on smallholder farms is inhibited by the very high cost of all chemical and machinery inputs, weakly structured credit systems, traditional practices, and inadequate pricing and marketing policies. Further, despite high levels of unemployment and underemployment in rural areas, there are acute shortages of labor throughout the country at critical times in a crop rotation. Among the myriad reasons for labor shortages are more children spending more time in school, very low wage for hard work, traditional patterns of the distribution of labor, and migration to urban centers.

Powerful and pervasive force of GOK. Finally, and very importantly, GOK is a powerful and pervasive force affecting practically every aspect of commercial agriculture and agribusiness. It fixes prices and the cost of labor. Public corporations may compete with private enterprise. Marketing boards control much of the domestic and export market. GOK dictates the movement of foreign exchange, the Africanization of management, and the requirements of training, to name but a few of the interventions of the public sector. Yet despite first appearances, GOK exhibits considerable flexibility and pragmatism. Granted that negotiation is never easy and is always slow, it is, nevertheless, always possible. The structure of a few existing agro-industries best illustrates the point.

Some ventures are parastatal and managed by public corporations, for example, the Kenya Tea Development Authority (Chapter 13, Section 3); other parastatals are managed by foreign

38

partners, such as the Mumias Sugar Company. CPC International (Chapter 13, Section 7) has been granted the first commercial exception to the rule that all grain must be purchased from GOK and can now negotiate for maize at the farm gate. East Africa Tannin Extract Company (Lonrho-UK, Chapter 13, Section 6) wholly owns and operates a 46,000-acre diversified farm-ranch, which helps support a central manufacturing complex. East Africa Industries (Unilever, Chapter 13, Section 4) is developing a source of vegetable oil-seed using land leased from absentee owners and managed under contract to private, profit-making companies. Kenya Canners, Ltd. (Del Monte, Chapter 12) leases long-term its entire 22,000-acre estate (10,000 in pineapple) from GOK, but owns and operates a cannery and controls all export marketing of its canned product.

Two of these enterprises have been isolated for more detailed analysis, namely, the Mumias Sugar Company and Kenya Canners, Ltd. This report highlights the former.

ENTERPRISE BACKGROUND

From independence, GOK has given high priority to the attainment of self-sufficiency in sugar. Sugar is basic in the Kenyan diet; it has been established that as much as 10 percent of the food budget per family is allocated to sugar. Kenya needed to save foreign exchange, and it was reckoned that cane cultivation and sugar manufacture could employ large numbers of people and could introduce a cash crop into areas of high population density where subsistence agriculture was the tradition.

A weak start in the early years of independence convinced GOK that expert technical and managerial assistance and external sources of capital were needed. In 1966, GOK approached Booker-McConnell, Ltd., of the United Kingdom, now Booker Agriculture International (BA), a division of IBEC, Inc. (formerly the International Basic Economy Corporation) of the United States, to take on a new development in the Nzoia Valley of the Western Province, centered around the township of Mumias. BA, which had singularly relevant experience in the development of a sugar industry in Guyana, agreed, but with a proviso that GOK accept a three-year preoperational field-testing program to provide a reliable base of information upon which to build future commercial practices on both the nucleus estate and the lands of the outgrowers. Financial projections could be made firm for the investors, public and private. This program was financed by the government, with BA advancing 10 percent of the cost, to be reimbursed when the project went commercial.

This three-year period of study, fact-finding, and demonstration was, in the eyes of BA management, vital to later success. Not only were farm practices verified, but the time was long enough and the contact with farmers and public officials intimate enough to bring about mutual understanding, confidence,

and trust, conditions absolutely basic to the rapid and effective
evolution of outgrower production, as well as to harmony between
the government and BA.

Based upon the results of the BA prefeasibility work, the
Mumias Sugar Company was formed in June 1971. Cane was to be
supplied by a corporate nucleus estate of 8,500 acres, part of
10,000 acres leased from GOK; and by numbers of freehold, small-
scale farmers, the "outgrowers," under contract to MSC. The
shareholders as of 1983 are shown in Table 3.1.

Table 3.1
Shareholders in the Mumias Sugar Company--1983 (in percentages)

Shareholders	Percentage
Government of Kenya	70.76*
Commonwealth Development Corporation (UK)	17.18
Kenya Commercial Finance Corporation	5.00
Booker Agriculture International (IBEC-US)	4.42
East African Development Bank	2.64

*Note: GOK purchased its shares by means of an original loan
        from the British government.

Source: Mumias Sugar Company Limited. Report and Accounts 1982.

The management of Mumias Sugar Company was, and remains,
contracted to Booker. Under the original managing agency and
factory supply agreements, Booker was to

● Provide a factory of 45,000 metric tons (mt) annual capacity, with start-up by mid-1973, expanding by 1979 to
  70,000 mt.*
● Develop the nucleus estate to provide a stable supply of
  cane, leveling off relative to outgrower production at
  roughly 20 to 25 percent of mill requirements.
● Organize outgrower production and provide training at all
  stages from field cultivation to general management.
● Manage the company until Kenyans could take over (estimated to take ten years).
● Take a minor equity position in the Mumias enterprise.

*The conspicuous success of initial production led to the
achievement of 70,000 mt sugar output by 1976. Progressive expansion plans brought mill capacity up to about 90,000 mt in 1978
and 180,000 mt by 1980. Throughout the 1970s, the next stage of
expansion was being planned before the current stage had been
completed.

● Take responsibility for the management of an existing but faltering sugar scheme (Chemelil) in an adjacent province (Nyanza)

Booker brought a high level of professionalism to its task. Very likely, this integrity of purpose would have been sufficient to ensure success. However, at GOK insistence, Booker took a small equity position. The original terms of the Booker management contract are instructive. Though adjusted from time to time, the contract had four components: a relatively small fixed fee, to cover the general manager's salary and certain specified BA overheads, linked to the UK retail price index; other BA staff to be seconded at cost; a percentage commission on net MSC revenues (value of sales less excise tax) on a sliding scale tied to annual output, zero if under 45,720 mt, rising to 5 percent if over 66,040 mt; and 2.5 percent of the net profit of MSC. Since 1978, payments to Booker have been adjusted to take into account the much larger turnout of sugar than had been expected.

It is to be remembered that MSC was created as an import substitution industry. One hundred percent of output is consumed in the domestic market and marketing is the responsibility of the Kenya National Trading Corporation. The prices for sugar and cane are fixed by GOK and promulgated by ministerial order. All sugar is purchased by the Ministry of Commerce; the Ministry of Agriculture handles cane price; the Ministry of Finance sets the sugar price. Profit, therefore, is far less influenced by fluctuations in the world sugar price, international market quotas, or ocean transport costs than by a variety of national and local factors, such as

● Differential between cane and sugar prices
● Magnitude of excise taxes
● Level of subsidy of sugar prices to consumers plus the method of paying for this subsidy
● Climate (all cane at Mumias is rain grown)
● Care with which outgrowers follow recommended cultivation practices
● Cost of transportation of cane to mill
● Default by GOK in repaying MSC for contracted work, for example, maintaining roads
● Cost and efficiency of mill operations, including extensive and intensive training and capital improvements
● Social costs, for example, for housing, schools, and medical services

The play of these variables presents an endless, changing management challenge. It is a tribute to the shareholders and staff of MSC that the system works so well. As will be suggested later in the text, there are indications of problems arising out of the very size of the enterprise and the sheer numbers of people interacting between farm and mill loading dock.

History

During the decade since manufacturing start-up, MSC growth has been truly impressive. The mill supplies roughly half of the sugar consumed in Kenya. For at least another decade, it would seem that Kenya is free of the threat of having to import sugar. A large area in Western Province has been converted from a poverty-stricken and bare subsistence state to a lively cash crop economy touching the lives of hundreds of thousands of people. The nucleus estate, originally planned to supply at least half the cane needed, with a gradual decrease to 20 to 25 percent, now produces but 12 percent, more or less. Outgrowers, numbering almost 23,000 by the end of 1983, deliver roughly 88 percent of requirements. Farmers who fifteen years ago had never grown sugarcane or worked in a factory now manage their cane fields, man the estate, and staff the mill. Proof of the accomplishments of both management and rural people lies in results: cane yields per acre are competitive with any rain-grown crop anywhere in the Third World; mill efficiency is comparable to the best factories in Africa. To date, GOK has been a reasonable partner. Booker has had a relatively free hand in management and has put highly qualified, committed people in the key roles. Kenyanization of management is proceeding more or less on schedule, with thirteen expatriates still on board at the end of 1983 and a plan to reduce this to about five by the end of 1985.

Table 3.2 summarizes the key results achieved over the past five years, and adds data from 1974 for comparison. It should be noted that the losses shown for 1981 and 1982 and the failure to pay dividends for three years do not signal a breakdown of MSC. Rather, the result reflects the risk attendant to operations rooted in temporal farming systems. In this case, a period of excessive rain, followed by two years of drought, has required adjustments in harvesting rates and mill operation to bring back full production by 1985. In addition, GOK pricing policies in the 1979-1982 period kept the price of sugar and cane virtually unchanged, while input costs rose dramatically. A sharp adjustment upwards at the end of 1983 is expected to help the situation greatly. This emphasizes a point often made by the Commonwealth Development Corporation, namely,that investors in agro-industrial ventures like MSC require enough "patient money" to ride through the inevitable short-term downturns.

Organization

MSC operates under a five-member board of directors: three represent the public sector, and both Booker and the Commonwealth Development Corporation have one seat. The general manager is a Booker employee. Finance, manufacturing, and maintenance are tightly organized and classically structured. However, the handling of cane procurement and training, both of fundamental importance and budget significance, is of unique interest to any agribusiness centered within an outgrowers program.

Table 3.2
Five-Year Summary of Performance, Mumias Sugar Company (with reference to 1974)

K£ (Kenyan Pound) in thousands*	1974	1978	1979	1980	1981	1982
Gross turnover	4,635	16,954	21,499	29,564	34,891	33,879
Excise on sugar	1,241	4,396	5,521	7,780	8,451	7,349
Net turnover	3,394	12,558	15,978	21,784	26,440	26,530
Payments to cane farmers**	710	4,131	5,285	8,487	10,141	9,409
Profit/(Loss) before taxation	751	2,278	145	843	(184)	(251)
Taxation	-	707	(246)	(160)	-	-
Profit/(Loss) after taxation	751	1,571	391	1,003	(184)	(251)
Equity on 31 December	3,317	9,582	9,123	10,126	9,865	9,614
Profit after tax as a percentage of equity	22.6%	16.4%	4.2%	9.9%	-	-
Dividends	348	1,274	850	-	-	-
Dividends as a percentage of equity	10.5%	13.3%	9.3%	-	-	-
Direct revenue to government from excise on sugar and income tax	1,241	5,103	5,521	7,780	8,451	7,349
Area under cane (ha)						
Nucleus estate	3,300	3,300	3,300	3,300	3,300	3,300
Outgrowers		12,400	15,400	19,500	24,300	27,400
Cane crushed (thousand metric tons)	-	810	975	1,497	1,566	1,294
Sugar produced (metric tons)	55,700	92,500	109,831	163,510	167,402	140,179
Annual increase/(decrease) in production	-	13.8%	18.5%	49.1%	2.4%	(16.3%)
Number of registered farmers on 31 December	2,271	11,346	13,113	15,142	17,474	20,761
Number of employees on 31 December						
Permanent	-	3,469	4,108	4,716	4,930	4,626
Seasonal	-	141	5,282	4,050	9,218	8,072

* In 1975, K£ = US$2,80; in 1982, K£ = US$1.89; in late 1983, K£ = US$1.48

** These payments are gross before deductions for the services provided under the MSC/MOCO agreement. In 1980/1982, the net payments were of the order of 40 percent of the figures shown. With normal yields and better prices expected in 1983/1984, the net figure is expected to be nearer 50 percent.

Source: Mumias Sugar Company Limited. Report and Accounts 1982 (1974 data supplied separately by Mumias Sugar Company for inclusion in Table 3.2).

Cane Procurement

As already noted, MSC manages a nucleus estate of 8,500 acres that supplies roughly 12 percent of cane requirements, an amount that could decrease proportionately should the mill be further enlarged. Internally, the estate is the joint responsibility of an Agricultural Department and an Agricultural Service Department. The former relates to production, the latter to mechanical inputs affecting land preparation, harvesting, transport, and associated functions.

Both departments are also responsible for the outgrower program. Each of the roughly 23,000 farmers, all voluntarily in the scheme, enters into a contract that covers a minimum five-year period (the time necessary to complete one seed cane crop and two ratoon crops), with specific provisions for termination by either party. The Agricultural Department establishes the practice and is charged with the extension and supervisory functions. It supplies technical inputs, such as disease-free seedlings, fertilizer, and any agricultural chemicals needed; and organizes the cane harvest. Land surveys, land preparation, and cane transport to the mill are all the responsibility of the Agricultural Services Department.

The contract between the company and the farmer allows MSC to enter any farm that in its judgment is not meeting cultivation timing or quality standards, perform the necessary tasks, and charge the farmer's cane account accordingly. When cane is delivered to the mill, the farmer whose crop is involved (or his representative) comes to the mill weighing station, observes the weighing-in, and is given a copy of the machine printout. This record is also sent to the outgrowers organization, the Mumias Outgrowers Company (MOCO).

MOCO is an exceptional experiment in intermediation between farmer and MSC and between farmer and government. When MSC started operations, contract farmers were dealt with individually, the Ministry of Agriculture being responsible for representing farmer concerns and for supplying certain educational and training services. In time, the complexity of relating to very large numbers of outgrowers, the attendant growing cost to MSC, and the ineffectiveness of GOK services led to the need for a grower organization that might eventually take over all the costs of, and control over, the outgrowers program. So, in July 1975, MOCO was legally created.

MOCO has a board of nine directors: three represent GOK, one each from the Ministry of Agriculture and the Ministry of Cooperative Development, and the district commissioner representing the Office of the President; one each from MSC and the Commonwealth Development Corporation; and four elected by the outgrowers, who may be reelected after serving a term of three years. This slight weighting of the board against the farmer representatives reveals a judgment that the transfer of authority to MOCO needs to proceed with great care. Board members are not paid for their services.

The organization and staff of MOCO operate independently of MSC, but there is, as would be expected, close interaction between the Agricultural Department of MSC and the efforts of MOCO. This is clearly reflected in the patterns and functions of staff, as shown in Table 3.3.

Table 3.3
Comparative Structure of MOCO and the MSC Agricultural Department

Staff	MOCO*	MSC Agricultural Department
General Manager	1	1
Zonal Managers**	0 (as yet)	2
Superintendents	3***	6
Supervisors	4	28
Village Headmen	15	96

*   The 1983 Agricultural Department budget was K£310,000 ($459,000); the equivalent MOCO budget was K£63,000 ($93,000). Since MOCO reimburses MSC for part of the cost of services rendered, the net MSC cost was K£117,000 ($173,000). This subsidy added about $0.13 to the cost of production of a metric ton (mt) of sugar. (The conversion rate of K£1 = US$1.48 is used throughout this chapter.)

**   The outgrower area is divided into four zones for administrative purposes. There is one board member representing the farmers in each zone. Because MOCO has no zone managers, the farmer board members try as best they can, utilizing a travel allowance, to fill this function. Within their zones, committees of farmers have been organized into "units," with an elected leader. In addition, taking advantage of the fact that MSC practice requires farmers to form blocks of no less than 15 acres to minimize the costs of production and harvesting (average size of cane field, per farmer, is 3.5 acres), block leaders are elected to reflect farmer concerns more truly and to pass on information more intimately.

***   One of these is being trained to administer a test area with the same level of responsibility as a peer from MSC. It is too early to evaluate this first attempt to transfer more responsibility (and cost) to MOCO.

Source: Date provided during interview with the manager of the Agricultural Department of Mumias Sugar Company.

Financially, the interlocking system of MOCO/MSC is also instructive and has broad implications for project design elsewhere. MOCO is a legally constituted company with no paid-in capital but with what is called "a guaranteed equity." This means that every farmer member guarantees to pay in fifty pence on call by the board of directors. Membership in this sense also includes the organizations represented on the MOCO Board of Directors--for example, MSC.

The financial base of MOCO was secured by loans from the Commonwealth Development Corporation at 5 percent interest; from the GOK at no interest and no definite rate of repayment; from the British Government at 7 percent interest; and, from the Kenya Commercial Bank at 10 percent interest. All interest charges are on the outstanding balance. At the end of 1982, the total loan balance was K£2,700,000.

In addition to loan capital, MOCO receives income from interest charges on credit extended to members. In 1982, interest received was K£68,000. MOCO also receives a levy of 6 Kenyan shillings ($0.45) per mt of cane delivered to the mill. As of December 1982, the balance in the levy account was K£1,728,000. These funds are used first to repay loans.

MSC provides services to each farm, in accordance with its outgrower contract. This service work is, in effect, contracted to MSC by MOCO. MSC bills MOCO in accordance with a fixed schedule of charges and, theoretically, payment is made in full. In actual fact, MOCO cannot sustain 100 percent of the payments and the difference is subsidized by MSC. As noted previously, in 1983 MSC subsidized 38 percent of these costs.

It is premature to judge the potential ability of MOCO as an instrument to optimize the benefits of MSC that flow to the farmers and to establish a relationship of trust, mutual responsibility, and deep understanding between MSC and the rural people. The concept of MOCO is creative and worth the investment. But its task is enormous. What is most likely to threaten its usefulness would be to assign a bold approach and not allocate the resources needed to do the job. At present, what MSC would like for MOCO to do ideally, and what the director and MOCO board agree ought to be done, is far from what MOCO is equipped to do.

Training

To quote from a memorandum prepared by R.M.D. Glasford, general manager of MSC:

From the outset it has been the objective of MSC to train Kenyans for all technical, supervisory and managerial positions. Training has, as a result, received prime emphasis, and the record of the last ten years indicates the success of this policy. The Company carries out training at all levels in agriculture, personnel management, engineering, sugar technology and accountancy. A Training Centre, the first of its kind in the sugar industry in Kenya, was opened in 1977. An apprenticeship scheme is operated for artisans and for several years now, the Company has recruited more apprentices than the rest of the sugar industry put together.

In effect, there are two distinct categories of training provided.

Craft apprenticeship program. This is a national scheme under the jurisdiction of the Directorate of Industrial Training in the Ministry of Labour, financed by a levy against all industry. In the case of sugar, companies such as MSC pay four Kenyan shillings (US$0.30) per mt of production into an industry pool, against which MSC can claim certain costs. Apprentices are recruited by MSC from among the graduates of eight technical schools in Kenya. These graduates would have received the Kenya Certificate of Education. When apprenticed to MSC, the students are then sent for further preparation to one of three training centers run by the Directorate of Industrial Training (Mombasa, Nairobi, and Kisumu). The fact that there are only three such training centers is a constraint on the growth of the program. Any new agribusiness venture in Kenya would be faced with the necessity of integrating this program, physically and in terms of human development, into the enterprise on a long-term basis.

The course goes for three years. Students are given housing and are paid a salary that increases over time, based on a sliding scale of percentages of income set by GOK. Graduates are under no obligation to work at MSC upon completion of the course; MSC is under no obligation to hire graduates. As Glasford notes, however, many want to stay and are hired. This is a natural consequence of mutuality of understanding and a familiarity with MSC conditions of work, gained by on-the-job experience during the three year program. Since the program began, there have been 120 graduates. At the time I visited the mill in late 1983, there were 20 students registered in each of the levels (a total of 57 actually).

Internal development program. This program, fully supported and controlled by MSC, is flexible, adaptive, and aimed at providing upward mobility to every class of employee. New graduates from university are recruited for a two-year management training course. Most of the experience is on the job in different departments of MSC, with occasional opportunity to spend time with other companies, not necessarily with sugar mills. The company suggests that within six months, it is possible to identify those most likely to succeed in management roles. For those judged to have unusual promise, the inclusion of overseas training is considered a must. This program has undoubtedly contributed significantly to the ability of MSC to Kenyanize carefully, systematically, and satisfactorily.

Any employee with a minimum of two years of employment and meeting the requirements of a testing program and certification by his or her superiors may volunteer for one or another of several opportunities. Some may be sponsored by MSC and released to study at either of the two polytechnic institutes in Kenya (Mombasa and Nairobi) while remaining on salary. Others may take courses of varying length, some offered on released time, others at night, aimed at upgrading skills, responsibility, and pay.

Given the remote location of MSC, the traditional culture of the people of the area, and the speed with which MSC introduced cane cultivation and factory operations, investment in human development is both a necessity and an obligation. For the more capable workers, the MSC training program is key to upward mobility, a track not readily followed in rural Kenya. In its totality, purpose, and performance, the MSC training effort is impressive and judged by management to have a high rate of return.

Outreach

What MSC does is extensive. Over the past ten years, MSC has built and maintained over 3,100 housing units on five separate sites centered in local communities reasonably close to the mill. Major roads have been improved in these areas and maintenance is carried out by the company on behalf of GOK.

Under the Mumias Sugar roads scheme, which was financed by a grant from the British Government to GOK, a 316-kilometer (km) network of feeder roads and over 2,000 km of access roads and tracks within a 24 km radius of Mumias Township have been constructed and improved to facilitate cane, personnel, and product transport. These roads have had the additional benefit of allowing access by vehicles to areas that formerly were only accessible by footpath.

When an outgrower enters the scheme, MSC inspects and surveys land intended for cane cultivation. It has been considered important to ensure that no farmer contracts all his farmland for cane. Generally, two-thirds of his acreage is retained for food and other cash crops or animal husbandry.

Medical facilities from a fully equipped MSC health center are available free to all employees. The center is staffed with a full-time doctor, two medical assistants, and three nurses. A laboratory and minor operating theater have recently been added. As well, MSC built and maintains an elementary school that has reached its limit of 1,600 children. GOK pays the teachers.

The company training center has just begun (1984) an outgrower development program, with an initial emphasis on "training the trainers" so that impact can multiply rapidly. This program will focus first on the MSC Agricultural Department extension workers and on village headmen who function as key communicators among the farmers and farm families.

What MSC does not do. Directly, formally, and operationally, MSC does not take responsibility for the further development of the worker communities, the outgrowers and their families, and the people in the extended area so heavily impacted by the establishment of MSC. It was hoped, for example, that outgrowers

would grow the food needed by their families, and possibly produce some other cash crops for the local market. Yet there is no
organized program to encourage this development. The farmer directors of MOCO would like to do more about this, as would the
management of MSC. In the case of the latter, a statement made
by an executive of BA during an interview in London, is revealing
of both need and opportunity:

> Now that the development of MSC is nearly complete,
> a proportion of our energies might well be directed to
> some other activities. On the agricultural side, we
> are particularly interested in three areas: food crop
> development; afforestation; and machinery reclamation.
> On the organization of credit, we would like to find
> means of advancing further credit to farmers for weed-
> ing. We would like to tie it to performance, as weed
> control continues to be a significant constraint on
> yield levels.

Another BA manager commented during an interview:

> My own great disappointment with the scheme (MSC) to
> date is that we have not been able to persuade male
> farm owners to devote their own labour to the cane
> operations. Many farmers depend on their wives and
> children to do the manual farm labour. This is, of
> course, fairly traditional. In effect, the farmer is
> entirely unrealistic, expecting to live like a landlord
> off his small cane area instead of being a working
> farmer.

And, as of early 1984, Glasford reported that on the question of
other cash crops they are still, along with MOCO, trying to get a
credit source to get this program off the ground. As neither MSC
nor MOCO has the resources to do the job, GOK might well be
thought to have the responsibility. However, the truth is that
public extension services in the area are all but nonfunctional.
The challenging question persists: How is this outreach to be
accomplished?
    The MSC development has pumped large amounts of cash into
the area, more every year as the company has grown and the outgrower area enlarged. There was no precedent among the people
guiding the responsible and creative use of this money; no agency
took responsibility; and no program exists today. Though there
are few facts to go by, it is clear that the cash economy created
so quickly has had a widespread and disruptive impact on family
life, on relations between husband and wife (or wives), and on
the food economy, among other aspects of life-style.
    The money flowing from MSC activity into the area, it is
estimated, touches the lives of several hundred thousand people,
as millworker families, farm families, merchant families, and
the families of suppliers of services. In all, MSC has released
a powerful force for diversified economic and social development.

There is little visible evidence and no data to suggest that the opportunity provided is being grasped.

MSC investors and management are aware of, concerned about, and frankly puzzled by these challenges to their outreach program and to the value of their entire enterprise. Discussion is constant. Uncertainty over appropriate action remains. Four broad, difficult, basic questions remain to be answered, not only by Kenya and MSC, but by agribusiness anywhere in the world which is sited in a rural area and which becomes the dominant, if not single new force, for change. As they emerged from interviews in London, Nairobi, and Mumias, these questions may be paraphrased as follows:

- Is not the government the logical and proper agency to take responsibility for capitalizing in diverse ways on the development opportunities created by agribusiness?
- If, however, government cannot and does not take responsibility, for reasons of real economic duress, lack of staff, organizational capability, or for other reasons, as is the current situation in Kenya, then should it be expected that the enterprise involved take responsibility?
- If the profit-making enterprise, whoever owns it, does take responsibility, how can the time and cost necessary to train people and apply them to the job be allocated without jeopardizing the viability of the business, without which everything would collapse?
- If neither the government nor the business can afford the responsibility and yet it is agreed that broad, integrated rural development is both desirable and necessary, will inaction beyond present limits threaten the movement of cane to the mill in the future? Will outgrowers continue to be motivated by the desire to earn money? Will time resolve development problems as people adapt through their own intelligence to changed circumstances?

After a review of the benefits resulting from the Mumias Sugar Company, these questions will be addressed further in terms of their policy implications.

PAYOFF

For the Host Country

Benefits to the people of Kenya have been impressive. MSC supplies approximately half the domestic consumption of sugar. MSC is clearly responsible for attainment to self-sufficiency in this commodity, with resultant savings in foreign exchange estimated to exceed K£100 million ($148 million). In addition, MSC has paid K£45 million ($67 million) in excise and income taxes.

The sugar scheme represents a large government investment in land, equipment, and people, with total current assets valued in excess of K 60 million ($89 million). A poverty-stricken, static, subsistence area of high population density has become the center of a vigorous cash economy. Glasford suggests that "upwards of 350,000 persons are dependent in some way for their livelihood on the Mumias sugar scheme."
For GOK, MSC most certainly is a success.

For Booker Agriculture International

The success of MSC can only be a source of satisfaction and pride for Booker. The achievement has surely been to the advantage of the company's professional image internationally. Also, although exact figures are not available, return on equity and income generated under the terms of its management contract have been satisfactory.

For Other Investors

Returns to the Kenya Commercial Finance Corporation, the East Africa Development Bank, and the Commonwealth Development Corporation, all financed by the public sector, have also been adequate, both in terms of return on equity and in development terms. The latter point is well illustrated by the following excerpts from a publication issued by the Commonwealth Development Corporation* (emphasis added).

CDC is a statutory corporation whose capital derives from the British Government, by means of an authorization to borrow long, medium, and short term funds from the UK Exchequer.
CDC is charged with assisting overseas countries in which it is empowered to operate in the development of their economies. CDC does so by investing its funds in development projects which not only help to increase the wealth of these countries but also yield a reasonable return on the money invested. Its area of operations covers Commonwealth countries which have achieved independence since 1948, the remaining territories dependent upon Britain, and, with Ministerial approval, any other developing country.

---

* CDC itself is a model catalyst for the stimulation of free enterprise, investment in agribusiness and rural development. It has pioneered in adapting the nucleus estate concept to a wide variety of circumstances throughout the world. CDC is an important institution to understand, and as a matter of global policy, perhaps emulate in other developed countries. For more detail on CDC, see Chapter 13, Section 1.

CDC does not offer aid as such; it offers investment in the development of resources. Although the Corporation has no equity capital, it must pay its way like other commercial concerns. CDC aims to revolve its funds and when a project is successfully established, it is prepared to consider offering participations on suitable terms, particularly to buyers resident in the country where the project is situated [10].

The success of MSC, therefore, and even the unresolved problems that have emerged, constitute a major payoff for CDC (and the other public sector investors). There has been a reasonable return on money invested and the decade ahead looks bright. National wealth has increased. People and land, the most basic natural resources in Kenya, have been developed, and much has been learned to apply elsewhere in Kenya, East Africa, and even further afield.

For the Rural People

Returns to the rural people are more ambiguous than those to investors, and depend for their assessment on the definition used for "satisfactory payoff" and whether the focus on the people pinpoints employees, contracted outgrowers and their families, or the hundreds of thousands in the total area impacted.

For the Employees

For the 5,000 employees with steady jobs and regular income, benefits are unequivocal. Along with wages, MSC provides housing, medical care for the whole family, a good elementary school, and the hope that these children might go on to further education. Basic training, upgraded skills, upward mobility, enhanced status, and personal dignity are all practical objectives in the total context of opportunity MSC has created. There is a union through which to speak; management has certainly established an ambiance of openness to discussion. Whatever else might be wished for the workers during the next decade of MSC operations, much that is positive and progressive has entered the lives of these people. To a lesser degree, many of these same benefits accrue to the 9,000 part-time workers. However, their lot may be better considered along with the people in the larger area influenced by MSC.

For the Outgrowers

If money alone is the measure of payoff, then the return to farmers from their participation in contracted cane cultivation has been great. In 1982, Table 3.2 notes that payments to outgrowers reached K£9.4 million. MSC management predicts that in

1983, due to a 33 percent increase in cane price and an expected increase in yield, this payment will almost double. Not only are the sums large but it is to be remembered that only ten years ago, practically all of these farmers lived by subsistence farming, existed in poverty, and few had any hope that the situation would ever change.

Some believe, however, that a money measure is not adequate and that a better indicator of payoff is the response of outgrowers to the income. Though there has been no careful study of the behavior patterns of the outgrowers and their families resulting from the MSC experience, there are indications of a negative nature suggesting that there are serious social and economic distortions taking place.

After a harvest, when MOCO and MSC settle the accounts of the outgrowers, the system calls for the net payment to be deposited in the local bank at Mumias Township. According to the bank manager, little of this money is left in the bank very long. Where it is spent is impossible to determine with any accuracy. What is known, however, is that in all too many instances, the money is dissipated rapidly, leaving families without funds for many months at a time. There may be as few as three harvests in five years for the majority with minimum-sized cane plots. Neither the credit nor contract system, nor MOCO and MSC extension efforts, nor any form of intervention by GOK, seems geared to deal with this problem.

Interviews with women confirm the widespread nature of the problem. Their complaint is that a majority of men (the figure of 75 percent was often used) do not inform their families about the amount of money paid by MSC. Frequently the men go away from home for weeks and months at a time without leaving money for food or other basic necessities, such as school fees, clothing, paraffin, or soap, among other items. Again, the system does not take this possibility into account. There is a procedure whereby a family, with a support letter from the subchief involved, can petition MOCO to apply corrective action, but the effectiveness is questionable.

Historically, subsistence farming involved the labor of the entire family. The advent of schooling decreased the input of children and with introduction of sugarcane, which requires intensive labor for cultivation practices, the absence of children contributed to a labor shortage. This is exaggerated by the fact that weeding is hard labor and the rate of pay is very low. One result has been the influx of needy laborers from Rwanda and Burundi and other distant places; another result has been an added burden on the women. Because the outgrower men have so often been secretive and self-serving in the use of harvest money, women, to get any cash, have been demanding a wage from their husbands for cultivation chores. Many men have refused to pay family labor. In turn, this has led some wives to work for other outgrowers to earn cash, leaving husbands to hire other women or migrant labor.

A complex series of interactions affecting family relations, cost of cultivation, food prices, housing for migrants, personal relations with outsiders, schooling, health, and other basic and intimate aspects of life inevitably and predictably arise out of such conditions. The outgrower community gets little or no help in resolving these issues. Illiterate in the majority, thrust rapidly into a major change process with no ongoing preparation, who benefits, who suffers?

This report is not the place to labor the point further. There are other examples at Mumias of the stresses and strains that develop when rapid change is introduced to large numbers of traditional rural people. Whether or not, if adjustment is left to the people, the potential for societal rupture is a threat to the prosperity of MSC is a difficult question to answer. It is a serious question for investors who are responsible for generating change; for GOK, which has far more at stake than income and foreign exchange savings; and for other governments, that would like to encourage both economic and social development simultaneously, through the instrumentality of private, profit-making enterprise.

For All the Rural People Impacted

There is no doubt that cash flowing from MSC has introduced an unprecedented vigor into the area economy. There is a hustle and bustle in the environment. But the actual payoff to hundreds of thousands of people is almost beyond measure. No one has tried to quantify the impact on their lives. Still, to the experienced eye, an impression of the area comes clearly into view, best characterized by a sense of "futures foregone." The economic energy released by MSC into the area has not motivated area development. True, there are stores; there is a bank in Mumias Township; there are services such as garages; there are busy trucks. However, considering that a decade has gone by since MSC began to produce sugar, it all seems incoherent. There is no guiding force. The place is redolent of lost opportunity.

To speak to area development, what is, what might have been, what could be, is not to imply criticism of MSC. There must be an end to corporate responsibility. The fact is that if the success of MSC had been played out in an early scenario, the opportunity for a much more diversified area development might have been foreseen. It might well be argued that the partners in the Mumias sugar scheme had the knowledge, experience, and creative talent to predict what might take place, as well as how advantage could be taken of the result. In narrowing down on the task of MSC itself, there were indeed "futures foregone." MSC classically illustrates the fact that if development and corporate objectives are to be blended in enterprise creation, then both perspectives are best introduced at the beginning of project planning.

POLICY IMPLICATIONS

For the Company

The dominant policy considerations of the next decade relate
to ensuring an adequate supply of quality sugarcane. The mill
itself is complete. Planned capacity has been reached. It seems
reasonable to suppose that Booker management will go on, despite
the Kenyanization of increasing numbers of key posts. However,
with outgrowers supplying 88 percent of the cane needed, responsible and continuous cane production is vital to future success.
Two main factors will govern what outgrowers are liable to
do: the price of cane relative to the costs of production, harvest, and delivery; and the attitudes held by the farmers toward
MSC. In the first instance, as is thoroughly appreciated by MSC
management, policy calls for continuous negotiations with GOK, to
the end of working out an improved system of price adjustments.
In terms of outgrower attitudes, there is perhaps a need to
broaden and deepen the relationship between farmer, farm family,
and MSC. MOCO represents a policy thrust in this direction.
Realistically, however, MOCO will require many years of nurturing
before it can secure for MSC the loyalty, constancy, and sense of
responsibility needed. MSC may find it necessary to give more
attention to the outgrowers as volatile human beings caught up in
a change process dimly understood, who are not always likely to
act in predictable ways. Economic incentives may not be adequate
to ensure performance. At the least, it is suggested, policy
might provide the means to assess the human development issues
that have emerged out of the dynamic growth of MSC and to set a
course toward a sensitive, skillful program of conflict identification and resolution.

For the Host Country

GOK is not likely to change its role in fixing cane and
sugar prices. Its policy, therefore, should emphasize the need
to change the method of calculation. Price determination should
be based on the necessity of protecting farmer income, motivating
cane cultivation, and ensuring the profitability of the mill.
Present methods of analysis and reporting by the National Sugar
Authority are slow, not fully rational, and create unnecessary
uncertainties. Actually, the situation in the sugar industry
raises questions about the efficacy of all public marketing
boards in Kenya, and the entire system should be carefully examined to determine the cost/benefit relationships to national accounts and consumer income.
In terms of rural development, GOK needs to exercise dynamic
leadership if the benefits of agro-industrial investment are ever
to be fully realized. No investor or prudent manager is likely
to risk scarce resources on an extended socioeconomic development
program unless encouraged by the force of public policy that

makes the will of government unequivocal. But the will of government will be ineffective unless backed by collaboration in financing, labor, and the allocation of other resources necessary to facilitate the task and make it feasible.

Finally, the MSC success story suggests that GOK policy regarding Kenyanization of management should avoid being dogmatic. Agro-industrial ventures are exquisitely complex and sensitive, even when their responsibility for human and area development is narrowly defined. They will become more so, by far, if GOK encourages the enterprise to embrace development responsibility more broadly. To manage and express the necessary qualities of leadership calls for a rare combination of training, experience, and personality. GOK policy should make it possible to tap the talent pool worldwide if it is clearly determined that the need is greater than the urge to national self-sufficiency.

For the Donor Country

If the policy implications for MSC and GOK are defensible and acceptable, then logic suggests certain policies vis-a-vis agro-industrial development in Kenya that might well be emphasized. With reference to agro-industries already in existence in Kenya, U.S. aid might be extended programmatically to ensure that any opportunity created for vigorous integrated rural development is not lost. This policy would not be dependent upon the source of capital in the venture. Rather, it would emphasize the importance of well-managed, profitable, rurally sited enterprise in catalyzing socioeconomic progress. For example, in the MSC case, U.S. aid might focus on the needs and potential of MOCO, in realization of the great potential for area development and the scarcity of resources to capitalize on the opportunity.

In point of fact, every one of the more than ten agro-industrial enterprises studied or contacted briefly in Kenya evidences exciting opportunities to build on commercial success to new heights of extended benefits. Yet, not one company was prepared to take financial and operational responsibility without the full policy support of GOK and without financial support arising outside of their business cash flows. On the other hand, no one with whom the idea was discussed was disinterested in the possibility of a joint venture with aid agencies that would not detract from the profit-making function, even if it risked beyond traditional corporate limits on activities in development.

Beyond capitalizing on development opportunities generated by existing agribusiness, it would seem desirable for the aid agency to relate as closely as possible to potential investors considering new investments in agriculturally related, rurally located enterprises. This would help ensure that feasibility analyses included the costs of integrating the production function with the function of development. In this way, the implications of success in economic terms could be examined for their impact on people and the opportunities to be anticipated relative

to area socioeconomic dynamics. Further, such early collabora-
tion between public and private investors could help in the
invention of the means to blend corporate and developmental ob-
jectives into harmonious, financially viable management systems.
All this would require strong policy backing on the part of the
U.S. government, both to influence acceptance of the approach by
GOK and to ensure adequate financial resources for the country
AID Mission.

U.S. policy might urge GOK to reconsider its role in price
control and marketing, as well as in the ownership and management
of unprofitable agro-industrial enterprise. Such intervention
need not be based on ideological arguments. Rather, AID might
undertake more studies of the type done on the Kenya Seed Company
(Chapter 13, Section 1) [11], which present the case in factual,
analytical terms. It is significant, in this regard, to note
that immediately after the coup d'état of August 1, 1982,
President Moi took steps to reassure investors and, among other
things, promised to remove the government from inefficient
business enterprises and said the government would avoid direct
participation in business, henceforth.

A policy that supports the training of Kenyan professionals
in a wide spectrum of fields has long been basic to U.S. aid.
This policy might well be extended to include an emphasis on
training managers of rural development when this function is integrated into an agro-industrial enterprise. It may be timely to
give recognition to worldwide experience that suggests that
agronomists or other technologists, economists or other social
scientists, or politicians, however skilled, do not necessarily
make good managers of rural development. This is even more likely to be true when development goals are integrated with those of
a profit-making agribusiness.

4
Commonwealth Development Corporation: A Sugar Production and Settlement Scheme in Swaziland

Simon Williams

SUMMARY

The Commonwealth Development Corporation (CDC) of the United Kingdom is very active in Swaziland. The background of CDC and the range of its global investments are reviewed in Chapter 13, Section 1; a tabulation of its activities in Swaziland is included at the end of Chapter 4 to emphasize the pervasive importance of CDC to the economy of Swaziland.

The specific project covered by Chapter 4 is actually a complex of enterprises, namely: the Inyoni Yami Swaziland Irrigation Scheme (SIS), the Mhlume Sugar Company (MSC), and the Vuvulane Irrigated Farms (VIF). The latter is a resettlement satellite farming venture. This case illustrates another "nucleus estate" corporate structure. However, it provides a striking contrast to the Mumias Sugar Company in Kenya (Chapter 3). In Kenya, the contract farmers are landowners and were resident long before the company arrived; in Swaziland, the farmers are not landowners and were settled at the enterprise site with no tradition of landownership. In Kenya, both the nucleus estate and an outgrowers program were integral parts of the enterprise from the outset; in Swaziland, the satellite farming scheme was implemented over a decade after the first investment was made. In Kenya, 23,000 farmers supply 88 percent of the cane for the core sugar mill; in Swaziland, 263 farmers supply 12 to 15 percent. In Swaziland, the farmers have larger land areas, are supplied with irrigation water, and produce other cash crops than sugarcane that they can market freely. Perhaps most significantly from a rural development perspective, in Kenya the farmers have their own organization to act in the interest of the participants, however weak it may be; in Swaziland, the Vuvulane Irrigated Farms, home and mentor of the satellite farm families and a creation of the Commonwealth Development Corporation, is being transferred in ownership and control to the Swazi Nation, raising serious and troubling questions about the future.

The SIS enterprise is a combination of cattle, citrus, and sugar, covering an area in excess of 100,000 acres of land that beforehand was largely a wasteland where game and hunters were

the main inhabitants. The area was brought to its productive
potential by an irrigation system introduced in 1957. This established the feasibility of large-scale sugar production, and
the subsequent spin-off in 1958 of the Mhlume Sugar Company, now
a major producer for the export market. The sugar company now
operates a plantation of 12,000 acres, purchased from SIS. The
estate produces 35 percent of cane requirements; SIS provides an
equal quantity; the outgrowers supply 12 to 15 percent; and the
remainder comes from nearby large commercial farms. All growers
get irrigation water from the SIS system.

It was in 1962 that the outgrower scheme was implemented and
4,000 acres were allocated by SIS as the land base for the
Vuvulane Irrigated Farms. This land was in an area of good soil,
suitable for sugarcane, vegetables, cotton, peanuts, potatoes,
and other cash crops. Settler farms range from 8 to 16 acres,
with 75 percent to 80 percent of the farm devoted to sugarcane
cultivation. By 1983, 263 families were resident. The particularly intriguing element of this scheme is that for the settlers
and for the Swazi Nation, it represented the first and only break
with the tradition of tribal chief control over land use, except
for large commercial farms, mostly owned and operated by non-
Swazis.

COUNTRY BACKGROUND

Despite the country's small size and the common tribal heritage of its people, Swaziland is a country of many striking con-
trasts, important to remember, not easy to understand. These
points of opposition touch every aspect of social, economic, and
political life.

First and foremost, Swaziland has a dual system of government, consisting of modern ministries and an influential traditional system. The supreme head of the Swazi Nation is the king,
who exercises authority in the modern government through a council of ministers and in the traditional government through the
Swazi National Council (SNC). In addition to the SNC, the king
has a senior group of councilors advising him directly. In theory, all adult Swazis are members of the SNC, but in fact its in-
ner decision-making body is composed primarily of chiefs and traditional leaders appointed by the king. SNC authority over tradition and custom is absolute. The council of ministers constitutes the primary interface between the modern and traditional
forms of governance.

A second contrast of great importance is defined by the pattern of land tenure. Fifty-seven percent of the total land area
is classified as Swazi National Land (SNL). SNL falls under the
control of the Swazi National Council and is allocated by some
200 chiefs governing a communal land tenure system. About
13 percent of SNL is divided into approximately 42,000 dispersed
homesteads with a resident population of 350,000 (total Swazi
population estimated at 500,000). The remaining 87 percent of

SNL is used for communal cattle grazing, reflecting the tenaciously held tradition that cattle are the most important store
of wealth a rural household can possess. The high stocking rates
applied have had serious soil erosion implications. All development proposals affecting SNL must be submitted first to the Central Rural Development Board and then to the king for approval to
ensure that developments are consistent with Swazi tradition and
reflect the wishes of the people.

In striking variance with SNL, 43 percent of the land is
held in private farms that fall under the Individual Tenure Farm
Lands (ITFL). There are 850 such farms, ranging from family units
of 50 to 100 acres to large agro-industrial estates of many thousands of acres. The Swaziland Irrigation Scheme, for instance,
started with 105,000 acres. ITFL is the dominant source of commercial agricultural production. Ownership of the ITFL is roughly evenly divided between Swazi families; non-Swazi families; and
large industrialized enterprises that often involve foreign investors. The influence of the Swazi National Council on the style
of operations of ITFLs is more the result of collaboration in
deference to national traditions and the will of the king than it
is to any formal structure of law and authority.

Other significant contradistinctions characterize and color
the Swaziland environment. For example, the Republic of South
Africa is the single largest employer of Swazi labor. South Africa is also virtually Swaziland's only supplier, providing over
90 percent of its total imports; and South Africa is vital to the
maintenance of a balance-of-payments surplus, despite a sizable
balance-of-trade deficit, through Swazi participation in the
South Africa Customs Union. The influence of South Africa is
pervasive, mostly constructive, often limiting, sometimes confusing.

On the wage side, the openness of economic relations between
the two countries tends to raise Swaziland's wage rates. This
trend is encouraged by equating the value of the Swazi emalangeni
(E) and the South African rand (R). (The conversion rate used
throughout this case is E or R = US$1.) Yet, though wages are
high, labor productivity remains notoriously low, especially in
subsistence farming. That this need not be so is shown by the
plantation sugar industry, where the productivity of hand labor
is excellent. In turn, this means that Swazi companies, rural or
urban, must adopt capital-intensive means of production to stay
competitive, with a resultant negative impact on employment.

On the food side, the openness of the border makes the import of low-cost foods from South Africa easy, depressing the
prices that might be paid to farmers on SNL and discouraging efforts to increase productivity and farm income. These influences
combine with others such as lack of credit, lack of effective
extension, inefficient marketing arrangements, fragmentation of
the land, and a decrease in farm labor due to out-migration, to
depress the SNL sector of the agricultural economy.

The picture of Swaziland that emerges illustrates a series
of dichotomies: between tradition and modernization; between the
heavy hand of traditional control on SNL and relative freedom of
control on the ITFL; between a capital-intensive commercial and

industrial sector (including all agro-industrial ventures) and a capital-poor rural sector, depressed by low productivity and rapid population growth; between firm ties to the Republic of South Africa and the goals of self-reliance to which the nation is committed. Within this context, public policy seems to entrust development to a free enterprise economic system. The government interferes minimally with market forces. The challenge to this thrust of public policy is to bring the benefits of free enterprise to the traditional sector, at a speed that allows change to occur with grace and in harmony with old values. The challenge also marks an opportunity for private enterprise.

The case of Vuvulane Irrigated Farms, arising out of the development of the Swaziland Irrigation Scheme and the Mhlume Sugar Company, reveals how one international investor, the Commonwealth Development Corporation, has dealt with the many changes that have characterized Swaziland over the past thirty-five years.

ENTERPRISE BACKGROUND

The three enterprises, SIS, MSC, and VIF, form an interrelated agro-industrial complex created by the Commonwealth Development Corporation with an equity investment over the years of approximately US$40 million.

In a sense, SIS is the "father" enterprise, having originally owned all the land involved. It still owns the irrigation system that supplies all three enterprises in the complex, as well as supplying eleven nearby estates and private farms. Technically, SIS does not sell irrigation water. Rather, users have agreements whereby they pay SIS a portion of the costs of running the system based on their water allocations. In addition, SIS is a profitable, diversified farm and ranch, producing cane for processing at the MSC mill, citrus, and beef cattle (the latter for both domestic and export markets), utilizing approximately 76,000 acres [12].

After long negotiations, arrangements were completed to transfer 50 percent of the ownership of SIS to the Swazi Nation. In 1982, to quote from the CDC annual report: "Heads of Agreement have been signed for this direct project to be transferred with retrospective effect from 1.1.82 to a partnership owned equally by CDC and the Swazi Nation. CDC will continue to manage," [13]. As in other instances of such transfers, a CDC loan to the Swazi Nation, to be repaid long term out of dividends earned, makes this transfer possible. SIS employs up to 2,300 people, roughly 2,000 of whom are permanent.

MSC, wholly-owned by CDC since 1955, is now also a fifty-fifty joint venture with the Swazi Nation, with CDC the managing partner. Unlike SIS or VIF, which are direct operating units of CDC, MSC is a separate corporation. As a result of a major plant expansion program from 1977 to 1979, plant capacity is currently 150,000 metric tons (mt) over an eight-month season. At the end of the 1982/1983 cycle, the mill produced roughly 138,188 mt of sugar for export. MSC owns and manages a sugar estate of over 12,000 acres, purchased from SIS. The estate yields about 35 percent of needed cane. SIS, under contract, supplies about the same quantity, and VIF produces between 12 and 15 percent. The remainder is purchased under contract to neighboring private ITFL farms. MSC employs some 2,300; about 2,000 are on permanent jobs [14].

VIF is an estate of roughly 7,000 acres of CDC land, originally allocated to SIS, on which at present 263 smallholders and their families have been resettled from other areas of Swaziland. In addition to their farms, which they operate under long-term lease (twenty years, renewable) with VIF, roughly 70 acres are managed by the Farmer's Cooperative, primarily for use as a cane nursery. A so-called "Commercial Farm" of 312 acres is managed by VIF staff on land not yet settled. The income from the Commercial Farm is used to subsidize the interest charged by VIF in the extension of credit. Settler farms range from 8 to 16 acres; the average acreage devoted to cane cultivation is 75 to 80 percent of the farm area. The remainder of the land is used for a combination of subsistence agriculture and cash crops (potatoes, cotton, vegetables) to be sold as the farmer wishes. Direct CDC investment in VIF, to date, is roughly US$2.8 million [12].

History

The SIS complex dates back to 1889, when King Mbamdzeni conceded 110,000 acres to John Thorburn in northeast Swaziland, bordering on Mozambique. This remote area, a wasteland really, was a place of unreliable rainfall where game and hunters were the main inhabitants. When CDC acquired the land in 1950, the previous owners had developed 800 acres irrigated from both the Black Umbuluzi and Komati rivers, and 2,500 acres of dryland cultivation on the better soils at Vuvulane, on the eastern side of the property. A survey done by CDC indicated that at least 30,000 acres of soil suitable for irrigation could be developed with the building of a canal drawing water from the Komati River. Water rights were obtained. Dryland and irrigation crop trials were initiated, and over a period of five years, it was decided that sugarcane, rice, and citrus were best for large-scale development; potatoes and a wide variety of vegetables could be grown but were best suited to smallholder subsistence and cash cropping. From the beginning, CDC had included an outgrower scheme in its development plan.

In 1957, a 42-mile canal was completed and named by King Sobhuza II "Mhlume Water," meaning "good growth," and the years of conception, planning, and basic infrastructure shifted into an era of commercial production. In 1958, SIS sold 13,000 acres of uncleared land to MSC, a company formed in the same year as a joint venture between CDC (40 percent) and Sir John Hulett and Sons (60 percent). By 1961, SIS had 4,000 acres under irrigation, mainly for rice production, but including 700 acres of sugarcane, for sale to MSC, and 300 acres of citrus. By this time, MSC had a sugar estate of 7,500 acres and manufactured almost 40,000 mt of sugar,mainly marketed through the South African Sugar Industry. Development of the SIS/MSC complex moved rapidly thereafter. The capacity of the irrigation system was enlarged, enabling it to provide water to other private farms that in some cases became large-scale cane suppliers to MSC. MSC capacity was increased. More irrigated land was brought into production at SIS. CDC bought out Sir John Hulett and Sons, and MSC became a whollyowned CDC subsidiary. In all, more than US$40 million was invested. SIS and MSC have transformed the area into a truly magnificent production system, which has been profitable to all concerned and is a fine example of the productive power of entrepreneurial vision, of risk capital that is ventured with a long-range view and a policy of patience, and of committed, competent management that is willing to pioneer in order to build.

As this scheme proved its viability, two elements of CDC policy were implemented. One related to extending benefits to outgrowers by means of a resettlement scheme; the other related to diffusing ownership of the venture within Swaziland as a whole.

Benefits to outgrowers. In 1961, the first formal studies of a pilot settler project were initiated, and a year later the Vuvulane Irrigated Farms were inaugurated under the control of SIS. Land (eventually 4,000 acres) was allocated in an area of good soils, suitable for multicropping. By 1963, the first 30 settlers were in place; by 1983, 263 families were resident. In 1972, SIS transferred the land and assets to VIF, a direct CDC subsidiary investment that has reached the equivalent of roughly E4 million. Further detail on the structure, results, and implications of VIF, an experiment unique in Swaziland history, will be given later in this chapter.

Diffusion of ownership. In terms of diffusing ownership and benefits widely among the people of Swaziland, CDC has taken three steps in recent years.

First, in 1977, by means of a loan from CDC to be repaid out of dividends, the Ngwenyama of Swaziland (basically a trust that holds the patrimony of the Swazi Nation) acquired 50 percent of the shares of MSC. As described in an interview with W.H. Rodgers, general manager of MSC, "At the time of the stock transfer, CDC also put in hand arrangements whereby the land MSC had bought was to be handed back to the Ngwenyama and a back-to-back leasehold agreement entered into to enable the company to continue its operations." In a letter dated February 10, 1984, Rodgers notes that "Due to technical considerations, the actual leasehold arrangements have taken some time and are only now being finalized. However, the emotive issue of landownership had been accepted and dealt with at the time of the agreement."

Second, in 1982, as noted previously, SIS itself became subject to an agreement similar to that affecting MSC. Finalization of this agreement appears to be temporarily held in abeyance until the transition of power, made necessary by the death of King Sobhuza II in 1982, is completed.

Third, after many years of negotiation, "Heads of Agreement" were signed under which the Swazi Nation was to form a wholly owned, nonprofit, limited company to take over VIF from SIS, effective retroactively to January 1, 1982. As part of these arrangements, CDC agreed to make available the sterling equivalent of up to E1 million for a program of drainage. According to the CDC 1982 Annual Report, CDC will continue to manage VIF [13]. The actual transfer and the formation of new relationships between the Swazi Nation and CDC were completed in December 1983.

Organization

The transition to greater participation by the Swazi Nation in the three enterprises will undoubtedly bring changes in control. The exact nature and impact of these changes was not wholly clear at the time I visited Swaziland in November 1983.

Heretofore, SIS had operated as an unincorporated direct project of CDC, and hence subject to control from London. Under the terms of the proposed new partnership with the Swazi Nation, the locus, and perhaps the focus, of policy-making is liable to shift. The general manager of SIS, a CDC employee, is likely to remain the key operating person on site. This retention of professional management supplied by CDC is in keeping with the policy adopted at the Mhlume Sugar Company when 50 percent of the ownership transferred to the Swazi Nation.

In the case of the new organization created for the total transfer of VIF to Swazi ownership, the situation is less clear and remains to be tested. The new company, Swazi Nation Agricultural Development Corporation (SNADC), will no longer have a direct organizational linkage with SIS. Rather, the general manager (Donald Nxumalo, a Swazi), is directly responsible to the CDC regional controller for Southern Africa in Mbabane, capital of Swaziland. The board of directors is comprised of four senior Swazis appointed by the Nation, two CDC representatives, and two elected representatives of the farmers.

Obviously, there is an important difference in the implications for development between shared ownership of the productive systems of SIS and MSC and the shift of control of VIF to the public sector. Except for an internal reorganization of shareholder interests and the distribution of profit, SIS and MSC are likely to continue operations in much the same pattern as before. VIF, on the other hand, touches very intimately the daily lives and sense of security (or insecurity) of several hundred outgrower families who have become deeply involved in a socioeconomic experiment without precedent in Swaziland. Many of the settlers have now been essentially free of the constraints imposed on rural people by the traditions and culture of their tribal heritage. Their mode of thinking, their method of decision-making, their aspirations, the dynamics of change in every aspect of thought and process, and the nature of their relationship with MSC are all inextricably entwined with feelings and questions about the future. Some questions being asked are revealing:

Will land tenure rights revert back to traditional control by a chief? Will the incentives to build homes, care for the property, exercise good cultivation practices disappear with a reversion to past conditions? In all, since there is little evidence in the traditional agricultural sector that governmental intervention has been able to stimulate economic and social progress, why not leave a good thing alone?

Organizationally, MSC operates independently of SIS and VIF, except as a buyer of cane. The board of MSC already includes representation from the Swazi Nation. Its future is less related to ownership and policy control than to top-quality management (which it has) and the marketing arrangements that govern the entire sugar industry.

In the early years, all sugar was marketed by arrangement with the South African Sugar Association. In 1964, the Swaziland Sugar Association was formed as the statutory agency controlling all sugar sales within Swaziland and on world markets. In 1965, the association joined the Commonwealth Sugar Agreement. The quota and favorable prices assigned to Swaziland became the basis of the industry's growing success, even at a time when prices on the free world markets were very low. With Britain's entry into the European Economic Community, the Commonwealth Sugar Agreement terminated at the end of 1974. Immediately thereafter, the competitive position of the Swaziland sugar industry changed. The country signed the Convention of Lomé, but this provided a quota for export to the European Economic Community of only 120,000 mt. Meanwhile, a third sugar mill was at an incipient stage of discussion. When it came on stream in 1980, Swazi capacity increased to 380,000-400,000 mt annually.* Thus, Swaziland is now cushioned to only a limited extent against prevailing low prices on the world market.

Outreach

Vuvulane Irrigated Farms. VIF is the only outreach program in the system, in the sense of extension of benefits beyond those employed by SIS or MSC. VIF was a bold experiment in 1962 when

---

*The second mill, Ubombo Ranches Ltd., is a joint venture of the Lonrho Sugar Corporation, Ltd.-UK (60 percent) and the Swazi Nation (40 percent), with Lonrho the managing partner. The third mill, the Royal Swaziland Sugar Corporation, is a joint venture of the Swazi Nation and the Swaziland government (65 percent) with the Nigerian government, Tate and Lyle, Ltd., Coca-Cola Export Corporation, Mitsui and Company Ltd., CDC, German Development Company, and International Finance Corporation (IFC). Tate and Lyle Technical Services, Ltd., are the management contractors. Neither of these mills has an outgrower program, in action or planned, that in any way resembles VIF's outgrower venture.

the project was formally inaugurated. To quote from J.R. Tuck-ett, the first general manager of VIF, manager of VIF,

> When the scheme started, it represented to the vast majority of Swazis an entirely new concept in their ap-proach to farming and land use. Payment for the use of land and for the availability of water, complete depen-dence upon arable crops rather than on livestock, the techniques involved in irrigation and modern farming methods, the idea of leasing land rather than receiving rights from the Chief, the new disciplines involved, and the unfamiliarity of sugar production; all these factors and more were foreign to those for whom small-holdings were intended. Also they were foreign and somewhat suspect to many Swazi chiefs and leaders from whose areas the settlers were to come. It was scarcely surprising that at first there was no rush to apply for holdings.
> From the outset, settlers were drawn from all parts of Swaziland, and although applicants were few (84) in the first year, the people applying for farms by 1970 exceeded 1,000 each year. . . . It has, in fact, been obvious enough that whatever problems and imperfections may have been encountered in establishing VIF, these have not been great enough to deter good Swazi farmers from wishing to join the scheme in great numbers [15].

VIF management, either directly or through district adminis-trations, sought applicants for farms throughout Swaziland and gave details of those who fulfilled the selection criteria to a selection committee. This was originally chaired by the district commissioner and included the district agricultural officer and an expert in Swazi genealogy. Later, the committee consisted of representatives of the Ministries of Agriculture and Home Af-fairs, the Swaziland National Council, and VIF management. In general, farmers selected from various occupations have proven satisfactory and 263 farms from ten to sixteen acres were settled by 1974. At that time, further expansion to 400 settlers was halted pending agreement with the government on the future organ-ization to manage VIF.

Four main criteria for selection are used: A farmer must be a Swazi; healthy; of good general character; and prepared to make his home at Vuvulane. All other things being equal, a married applicant whose family can help with the farm work, and who has proved to be a good farmer at home, would be given preference.

Once selected, a farmer is allocated a farm by lot. On ar-rival, the farm will have been cleared, leveled, ploughed, disced once, and will be supported by an infrastructure of roads and ir-rigation canals. All costs to this point are borne by VIF. The farmer is shown where he should build his house, but the style and building of it is left to the family. The 75 percent of land to be devoted to sugarcane is planted by the farmer using seed cane and inputs made available on credit from VIF.

During the first year, building materials are available on credit, as is a subsistence allowance provided from a revolving fund made available by Oxfam (UK) [16]. A monthly statement is issued to each farmer showing amounts due VIF. In all cases of credit, repayment is deducted from the farmer's annual harvest check for sugarcane. If accuracy is agreed to, the farmer signs his confirmation.

The conceptual framework for VIF included the goal of making the project economically profitable so that all costs including administration could be recovered and the high capital cost of developing the land and the infrastructure amortized over a reasonable length of time. To move in this direction, the farmer, based on a leasehold of twenty years originally, pays rent, a standing charge for water, the cost of cane cutting and transport to MSC, and any use made of equipment drawn from a tractor pool operated by VIF. It has become clear that VIF is unlikely ever to recover for CDC the original development costs and still become profitable for the farmers. Figures that do reveal profitability, therefore, really do not include a financial burden relating to land preparation and infrastructure, as these were costs CDC was prepared to bear within the context of the whole agro-industrial complex. Keeping these facts and assumptions in mind, the financial data in Table 4.1, as made available by CDC at mid-year 1981, are indicative of the financial performance of VIF as a CDC investment.

Table 4.1
Financial Status, Vuvulane Irrigated Farms

Total Investment Through 1982	Profit After Taxes	Profit as a Percent of Average Capital Employed
E3,190,000	1978...E 19,000	5.11
	1979... 72,000	6.93
	1980... 177,000	9.92
	1981... 160,000	9.54
	1982... 106,000	3.79

Source: Project Data summary sheets and up-dated information provided by CDC project director during interview in London, December 1983.

Finally, it may be noted that VIF relates to the farmers and their families largely in the technical area involving crop cultivation. A Swazi general manager has under him a total of nine qualified staff, including three expatriates: the senior agronomist, field services manager, and project accountant. Day-today advice to farmers is carried out by four field advisors, each responsible for roughly sixty-five farmers. The advisors offer help on all crops, as well as channeling requisitions for tractors and other required farm inputs. Regular group meetings are held for airing grievances, as well as for teaching new techniques of production, marketing, or whatever.

Every effort is made to build a community spirit, but results to this end have been baffled somewhat by the close relationships maintained by the settlers, even after many years, with the homes they left. A significant part of such investment capital as families save at Vuvulane is actually invested, often in cattle, in their home village. As a general observation, it may be said that while VIF has been very successful on the production side of its goals, it has been less so in bringing the settlers into a coherent social structure capable of taking full advantage of the economic opportunities the VIF experience has created. In this regard, it is questionable that bringing VIF into the structure of a public corporation, with Swaziland carrying the cost of further development, is an ideal approach. This point is discussed further later in this chapter.

Training and Welfare

CDC has a long-standing commitment to the training of nationals, the provision of good housing, medical care, and as wide a range of social and recreational amenities as are feasible. The workers at SIS and MSC clearly benefit from these policies. MSC, for example, has an impressive array of activity. The company maintains a separate training center for on-site skill development and upgrading job opportunity. Included in this program is an extensive scholarship project that sponsors employees to attend either the University College for courses in agriculture and industrial management, or the Swaziland College of Technology for courses in crafts and technical skills. All workers are given free housing and utilities; modern medical services are provided free. In all, MSC management estimates that 25 to 30 percent of all cash paid out in the course of an operating year supports the social outreach of the company.

Mananga Agricultural Management Centre

No discussion of the CDC outreach program in Swaziland would be complete without mention of the Mananga Agricultural Management Centre (MAMC). In 1970, CDC recognized a basic and pressing need in all the developing countries in which it operates for junior and middle-level managers and extension workers, and no existing institution seemed adequate for the purpose. It was agreed that MAMC would be built and staffed on such a scale that it would be able to offer training facilities to satisfy the requirements of CDC projects worldwide, and to help improve project management in developing countries in general. It was then decided to base the program in Swaziland to take advantage of the variety of project, development, and management problems that the irrigation complex provided. Since then, over 1,000 management trainees from over forty countries have taken specialist courses while in residence at MAMC. Programs in the planning and control of agricultural management, senior management in agricultural development, and other shorter, specialized courses are offered.

As of the end of 1982, CDC investment in MAMC stood at E1,240,000. During 1982, 113 students from all over the world were in residence for periods up to three months. In addition, 206 students attended in-company courses at various CDC sites in Swaziland. The revenue deficiencies met by CDC in 1982 amounted to E391,000. The center has been strongly supported by the Commonwealth Fund for Technical Cooperation, and increasingly, scholarships and program support are being provided by a wide variety of international aid agencies.

PAYOFF

For the Host Country

The payoff has been large by any Swazi standard. At very low cost to the nation, a large wasteland has been converted into one of the most productive and profitable agricultural-industrial areas of the country. In the process, the Nation has been able to purchase millions of dollars of assets in improved land, irrigation facilities, infrastructure, and manufacturing plants out of deferred earnings rather than with up-front cash. National revenues have been contributed to very substantially, year after year. For example, in 1982, the foreign exchange earned by the SIS/MSC/VIF complex was E51.39 million. Approximately 5,000 people have gainful employment. VIF has demonstrated the capability of Swazi farmers to reach impressive levels of productivity given the right incentives, thereby providing potentially valuable insights to those concerned with the poverty and low productivity that characterize the Swazi National Lands.

For the Company

The results have been impressive in many ways. All three ventures have been profitable. SIS and MSC pretax profit in 1982 was stated as E4.2 million. The progress of MSC has been excellent, as the results shown in Table 4.2 illustrate. CDC loans have given the Swazi Nation an opportunity to enlarge the national patrimony in a creative way, supportive of the harmony sought in public and private sector collaboration. VIF has expressed CDC development objectives. In all, the sheer accomplishment of the scheme in converting a wasteland into an efficient, profitable, productive area has to be a matter of pride to CDC and the British government.

Table 4.2
Five Year Profit and Loss Summary, Mhlume Sugar Company
(E1.14 = US$1, November 1983)

	1977 E.000	1978 E.000	1979 E.000	1980-81* E.000	1981-82 E.000
Proceeds-Sale of sugar and molasses	20,620	27,457	31,795	41,090	45,022
Less-Cost of sucrose	14,228	18,814	23,028	28,999	30,860
Mill production costs	3,768	4,197	5,675	10,780	9,447
Mill profit	2,624	4,446	3,092	1,311	4,715
Estates profit (loss)	100	2,007	1,805	(793)	1,894
Misc. receipts (payments) net	1,182	1,350	1,079	(62)	133
Profit before interest and tax	3,906	7,803	5,976	2,042	6,742
Less-Interest on debentures	97	94	88	98	60
Interest on temporary borrowings	-	55	287	2,622	2,471
Profit (loss) before tax	3,809	7,654	5,601	(678)	4,211
Less-Income tax	1,524	2,885	-**	-**	-**
Transfer to (from) tax equaliza-tion account	(13)	(45)	-	(758)	
NET PROFIT	2,298	4,814	5,601	80	1,500
Dividend	500	2,000	2,000	4,000	2,701
Retained profit including appropria-tion to reserves	1,798	2,814	3,601	(3,920)	1,500
					1,201

*   16-month financial period, includes two non-income-earning off-crop periods.

** Tax allowance on mill expansion expenditures.

Source: Mhlume Sugar Company, Ltd., project data summary sheet.

For the People

The economic payoff is unequivocal for the farm families at VIF. For the 5,000 employees (more or less) of SIS and MSC, a weekly paycheck, free housing and services, free medical care, opportunity for schooling and upgrading skills, and free recreational facilities clearly add up to an impressive change for the better for all these people and their families. In 1982, sugarcane deliveries from VIF to MSC yielded a gross revenue to the farmers of E2.5 million. After deducting all costs and adding in the cash value of potatoes, cotton, and vegetables estimated to have been sold, VIF management judged that the net return, per average farm in 1982, was between E6,000 and E10,000.

In more personal and social terms, the payoff to the farm families at VIF might be questioned. Some farmers still do not trust VIF to be acting in the best interests of the settlers. Why do rents and water charges keep going up? Why is bad drainage not avoided so that land might produce more? Why was there a water shortage? Why isn't there good potable water? Clearly, the extension services have not made the entire system and its problems understandable to all the farmers. In this broad sense, farmers are not sufficiently participatory.

Further, there is no feeling of community, at least not enough to give everyone a sense of permanence. Where people came from, even twenty years ago, is still home. It has often been said that this is changing slowly, helping to bring about an attitude of allegiance to Vuvulane. However, lack of participation in decisions affecting the future combine with uncertainties over the terms of the leasehold itself to maintain a sense of insecurity. This is now exaggerated by the knowledge that CDC has negotiated a transfer of VIF to the Swazi Nation, without it being clear to the settlers what this transfer implies regarding land tenure, lease renewal, and other factors of constraint typical of the interplay between farmers and the traditional sector of government.

There is also some indication that malnutrition is more widespread among children than might be expected in such a bounteous place. No study exists to quantify the situation. However during interviews at VIF headquarters, with the VIF manager, the head agronomist, several farmers, and the home economist then on the staff (late 1983), all agreed that there was a nutritional problem due to an unbalanced diet. The home economist, who was then scheduled to leave VIF by the end of the year, had recently initiated a program encouraging women to cultivate "kitchen gardens," but support for this program did not seem to be adequate or long range in design.

Finally, one of the concerns of the VIF professional staff has been the frustrating experience of trying to organize the farmers into a marketing system to ensure a better return on their garden crops. Farmers still try to market individually. Vuvulane has attracted buyers to the area, but this method of marketing is disadvantageous to the farmers. In all fairness to the VIF staff, organizing efforts to establish a farmers' cooperative failed even though the cooperative was given four leases in which to grow seed and sugarcane as an underpinning. It is well recognized that only a continuous, sensitive educational effort would have a chance of success. One gets an image of a vigorous, economically self-sufficient venture waiting to be developed, but without the necessary leadership to convert the concept to a practice. A commercial enterprise built around other crops than sugarcane is important to establishing stability in the VIF system, so that any decline in the demand for cane due to excess productive capacity in Swaziland can be quickly balanced by a shift in crop emphasis.

Bringing to light these manifestations of disquiet and unattended economic opportunities to diversify the base of VIF operations is not meant to demean the accomplishments of the past two decades. What is intended, rather, is to emphasize the point that the human and economic dynamics that inevitably characterize a successful outgrower program breed conflicts that threaten success and create opportunities to resolve conflict. Neither of these basic elements of the change process ought to be denied, if the remarkable advantages a scheme like VIF offers are to mature and endure.

In the case of VIF, CDC has built in an unusual capability of the venture to help support the cost of a more comprehensive and integrated program of development. A single market channel for sugarcane simplifies and stabilizes the economy of VIF farm families. By allocating good land to VIF and providing an infrastructure, including irrigation facilities that could be expanded, at a cost not paid for by VIF alone, farmers do have the opportunity to take full advantage of a diversified agricultural potential. Finally, the broad spectrum of foodstuffs that can be grown and that are already partially commercialized provide a base for profitable investments in production, grading and packaging, and marketing. Integrating all elements of the economic potential of VIF, would generate a cash flow that might pay for the costs of management needed by the farmers to convert the opportunity to a profitable operating system. In turn, the system could well support staff to harmonize the needs of people with the demands of sound business practices as well as to anticipate tensions, resolve conflict, and optimize benefits.

This point was frequently discussed during visits in both London and Swaziland, and always a dilemma remained: Could the future of rural development at VIF ever be put into the hands of the people there, or must further development be linked to a role played by external managers? A point of view held within CDC, tempered by long experience, was expressed this way: "It is human, not technical, problems that have to be overcome. Although VIF has been running profitable for the farmers for 20 years, there has been no breakthrough in achieving the growth of a satisfactory system operated by the farmers themselves. This is hardly a cause for optimism." The question raised, in the end, is whether or not the failure to develop a self-sufficient system is inherent in the people or inherent in the methods employed to bring it about. However CDC may answer the question, it is one that challenges the planners of all agro-industrial ventures who give consideration to rural development as an integral responsibility.

POLICY IMPLICATIONS

For the Host Country

There are two significant areas of policy affected by the SIS/MSC/VIF enterprise: one involving little change, the other suggesting a fundamental change. In the first instance, the Swazi policy of encouraging free-enterprise agro-industrial ventures, even while finding means to take an equity position, seems to require little change. This is especially true so long as equal emphasis is placed on competent professional management. This policy has been of great benefit to Swaziland in bringing large underdeveloped areas into production with consequent employment, tax generation, and foreign exchange earnings.

In the second instance, the VIF experiment raises a fundamental issue affecting the possibility of bringing Swazi National Lands to a higher level of productivity and offering the thousands of smallholders farming this land a more satisfactory level of income and quality of life. There is no argument over the validity of Swazi policy that attaches basic and dearly held values to the traditions and customs of the nation. Yet, as the VIF project clearly demonstrates, Swazi farmers are capable, when motivated by modifications in traditional control over land use, of attaining very high levels of productivity and net earnings. The challenge to the Swazi Nation, therefore, is to avoid dogmatism in the perpetuation of custom, even while finding acceptable changes in land tenure and freehold rights to the fruits of investment. Policy might well encourage careful experimentation.

For the Company

The policies of CDC, (as detailed in Chapter 13, Section 1) are already enlightened and comprehensive in their approach to the use of capital invested for profit, competent professional management, and patience as catalysts to development. However, the SIS/MSC/VIF experience in Swaziland (and the Mumias Sugar Company case in Kenya), at least raises the question as to whether or not CDC policy adequately covers either the potential for conflict or the potential for broad economic and social development that arises when rapid change is introduced to large numbers of people with a traditional culture.

Introducing policies that extend the responsibilities of a profit-making enterprise beyond the boundaries of normal, prudent business practice does bring CDC into very delicate areas of action. A real strength of CDC as a development institution is its ability to venture into arenas of higher risk than a privately held international organization might consider. At the same time, this strength, which arises out of the public character of CDC, is tied to political sensitivities that constrain decisions to enter into the lives of rural people impacted by CDC investments.

The dilemma faced by CDC, then, is this: On the one hand, the charter of CDC brings the corporation into situations where it is the primary force for change in the lives of many people and where there is likely to be no other competent leadership to help these folk extract what benefits there may be and to minimize disorder. On the other hand, if CDC accepts too much responsibility for the people and their future, will that be offensive and too costly? By what right, moral or logical, should CDC become the guiding light, illuminating the "best" way for a people to develop? If CDC must choose between a policy that gives first priority to the economic success of an enterprise and a policy that may jeopardize a level of profit judged necessary to attract investment, is there a choice?

In the eyes of some CDC executives, the problem is not, in its most fundamental nature, one of cost versus profitability. To quote from an exchange of correspondence with one CDC executive:

> It is much more a question of where the responsibility of the foreign organization should stop and that of the local government begin. I would see it as the role of government to pick up the essentially social development of the people. It should not be the function of foreign agencies to set up a mini-welfare state. On the other hand, I agree that the opportunities for government action might well be a matter for joint coordination.

Equating action to ensure social development to a welfare state is a seriously flawed proposition. The thrust of socioeconomic change is not toward dependency on government or the private sector. To the contrary, it is toward self-sufficiency, greater knowledge, good management of human and physical resources, expanding opportunities, participation in decision-making, and whatever else helps eliminate charity and paternalism. Obviously, there are no easy answers to these questions. One may argue that just as the Swazi Nation may need to reexamine the play of custom and constraint, so CDC may need to reexamine its policies defining the limits of change to which it can and should direct its resources.

For the Donor Country

U.S. development policy, in Swaziland as elsewhere, is directed to encouraging the maintenance of a free enterprise stance in the country. USAID is certainly also focused on the problem of low productivity and poverty among the rural people on Swazi National Lands. However, it may be important to the total thrust of development in Swaziland to direct both policy and resources toward capitalizing on development opportunities created by the larger farms, ranches, and agro-industrial complexes. It cannot be assumed that the economic resources generated by such capital-intensive enterprises will be sufficient or, even if sufficient, will be allocated to development activity to ensure for the people impacted the "good" inherent in the opportunity. It would seem desirable to examine the possibilities of collaboration with the commercial sector of Swazi agriculture to extend the limits of success, not only economically but developmentally.

The powerful moving force of CDC, in Swaziland and in fifty countries of the Third World, suggests that U.S. policy deliberations at least give consideration to the use of a similar organization to catalyze integrated rural development in the mode of free enterprise. As an example of the impact CDC can generate, the following list of CDC investments in Swaziland is very impressive.

CDC involvement in Swaziland.

1. The SIS/MSC/VIF/Mananga Agricultural Management Centre has already been described.
2. Ezulwini Properties (Pty.) Ltd.--A loan to the Swazispa Holdings, Ltd., to build and operate a 200-bedroom Holiday Inn near Mbabane.
3. Neopac (Swaziland) Ltd.--A joint venture with the government of Swaziland (10 percent), National Containers (Pty.) Ltd. (79.38 percent), and NedBank Nominees, Ltd. (0.5 percent) to produce corrugated cardboard containers, principally for citrus fruit and pineapple.
4. The Royal Swaziland Sugar Corporation, Ltd.--Joint venture with the government of Swaziland (32.4 percent), Tibiyo Taka Ngwane Fund (Swazi Nation, 32.4 percent), federal government of Nigeria (10 percent), Tate and Lyle plc (8.7 percent), DEG-German Finance Company for Investments in Developing Countries (5 percent), Coca-Cola Export Corporation (4.2 percent), Mitsui and Company, Ltd. (3.8 percent), and International Finance Corporation (1 percent). Loans included funds from CDC, the Swaziland government, the Swazi Nation, German Development Company, European Investment Bank, Barclays Bank, and IDC/CGIC (machinery suppliers from the Republic of South Africa). This combination of financial and technical resources was a unique creation of CDC and is a compliment to its reputation and capability.
5. Shiselweni Forestry Company, Ltd.--A wholly owned CDC investment in a 22,732-acre forest of pine and eucalyptus, and in an extraction plant for eucalyptus oil for export.
6. Usutu Pulp Company,Ltd.--A joint venture with Courtaulds, plc (UK), and some participation by the Swazi Nation, to develop and manage a pine plantation of 150,000 acres and to build and operate a pulp mill with a capacity of 175,000 mt/year.

7. Swaziland Electricity Board--A loan, along with other loans from the government of Swaziland, World Bank, African Development Bank, Swaziland National Provident Fund, and German sources, to construct a 20-megawatt hydropower station and a 24 million cubic meter storage reservoir on the Lususwana River.

8. Swaziland Fruit Canners (Pty.) Ltd.--CDC has twice helped to rescue this cannery, which also operates a 3,325-acre pineapple plantation of considerable importance to surrounding farmers.

The range and complexity of CDC activities is almost beyond description. I believe that no new venture in agro-industry, especially programs with a nucleus-estate/outgrower structure, should proceed without reference to the CDC experience. The significance of the model CDC presents for adaptation and replication should be carefully analyzed and possibly adapted as an element of U.S. aid.

5
Pinar: A Milk Processing Operation in Turkey

Ruth Karen

SUMMARY

The case of Pinar, in Turkey, provides an intriguing and instructive contrast to that of the milk processing enterprise of Hindustan Lever Limited (HLL--Chapter 2) in India. HLL is part of a global corporation; Pinar is a wholly Turkish enterprise. HLL does not compete with public corporations; Pinar is the only private company in an industry that had been a government monopoly, a monopoly characterized by constant losses and public subsidy. Pinar, like HLL, realizes that the agricultural economy in its zones of influence cannot prosper without diversification from a base of small-scale dairying, and both companies have instituted long-range development plans to produce and process other raw materials. Both companies have found it wise and profitable to maintain a carefully crafted system of extension and close personal interaction with their suppliers and the life of their communities, and each has been careful in extending its inter-relationships into the problems of human development that grow out of the economic impact of jobs and increased on-farm income. Although Pinar and HLL arise out of strikingly different corporate environments, the manner in which each has developed a profitable industry based on the responses of very traditional rural people is a classic example of the extraordinary power of agribusiness to accelerate change in similar ways, in totally different cultural contexts.

Pinar was launched by its parent company, Yasar Holding, in 1974. By 1983, the company was working with 21,000 farmers in 296 villages. Pinar has 900 Turkish shareholders; forty percent of equity is held by farmers, large- and small-scale, who took up the standing option held out to all suppliers to buy stock.

Pinar is a profitable, growing business. It has brought singular economic benefits to a large number of rural people and holds out the realistic promise of more to come. Problems remain. The cost of credit for farmers remains a constraint. Except for the relatively small number of marketing cooperatives, farmers remain unorganized and thus weakened in their thrust to self-sufficiency, not only economically but also in a social

77

development sense. While the economic base underpinning the farmers who supply Pinar is stronger than ever, their dependency on the policies, actions, and capability of Pinar is, perhaps, a weakness to be addressed by corrective action now. If corrective action is agreed to be necessary, how do the farmers, Pinar, and the government of Turkey join together with mutual responsibility for planning and implementation? This is a question of deep concern to Pinar management.

COUNTRY BACKGROUND

Socioeconomic Overview

After a period of economic, political, and social turmoil that culminated in a disastrous bout of stagflation in the late 1970s, a comprehensive set of stabilization and economic recovery measures launched in 1980 succeeded both in sobering the economy and turning it around. An inflation rate that exceeded 100 percent in 1980 was brought down to 20 percent by mid-1983. Real per capita income, after falling in 1979 and 1980, rose in 1981, 1982, and 1983. GDP growth exceeded 4 percent in 1982 and was heading up in 1983. The balance of trade also improved; from mid-1981 to mid-1983 Turkey's exports doubled while imports remained level.

By 1983 the country was also moving back toward a civilian government and gradually evolving a democratic political structure. Terrorism and banditry, which had been rampant in the late 1970s, particularly in the rural areas of the country, had largely been brought under control. The social tensions this violence had created had been alleviated and the results were evident in the small villages and outlying farms I visited while conducting field research for this case history.

Relationship with the United States

Turkey's relationship with the United States appears to be on a sound footing politically and economically. Evidence that this relationship is becoming closer in productive ways came in June 1983, when the U.S. National Science Foundation signed a memorandum of understanding with the Technical Research Council of the Republic of Turkey. The five-year agreement established an organization of Turko-American scientists with a mandate to transfer technology in order to increase agricultural and industrial productivity, to help remove bottlenecks in the Turkish economy, and to establish effective cooperation between the central government of Turkey, Turkish universities, and the Turkish industrial sector.

The Role of Agriculture

The role of agriculture in the Turkish economy is paramount. Of Turkey's 45 million people, 60 percent are engaged in agriculture. Agriculture develops 21 percent of the gross national income and makes a major contribution to Turkish exports. Turkey is one of the few developing countries that feeds itself, and that has no shortage of arable land.

As a matter of policy, the Turkish government is closely involved in agriculture. There are price supports for all of the country's major crops (tobacco, cotton, grapes, meat, sunflowers, soya, tea, and olives) although support prices tend to be substantially below market prices. Other fruits and vegetables, which do not have support prices and are allowed to respond to internal and external markets, make an important contribution to farmer income.

Turkey has an effective agrarian bank, which has a far-flung network of supervised credit and, in 1983, disseminated US$2.2 billion in rural lending operations; $523 million of that for agro-industry. The bank pays special attention to family farms.

The government also now encourages its network of national and regional universities, particularly those with agricultural faculties, to work with farmers and with agro-industry. Finally, the government is engaged directly in some sectors of agriculture, including stock breeding (sheep, cattle, water buffalo, and goats). It also has extensive operations in milk processing.

ENTERPRISE BACKGROUND

Pinar is a member company of a conglomerate, Yasar Holding, that has a total annual turnover of about US$400 million. The conglomerate began as an industrial enterprise, mainly in the chemical industry, but moved into agro-industries in the early 1970s. The corporate philosophy prompting this diversification was the recognition by the chairman, Seljuk Yasar, that making use of Turkey's existing agro-economy as a basis for industrialization made sense both for the country and for the company. The strategy was endorsed by Deputy Chairman Ali Nail Kubali (who has a Ph.D. in economic development from Washington University), who believes that the most effective way, and the least expensive in terms of hard currency, for Turkey to exploit its comparative advantage is to introduce the technology of production and processing into its existing agricultural base.

Corporate Strategy

The corporate strategy demonstrated its soundness in the chaotic late 1970s, when most industrial firms in Turkey worked at 30 percent capacity, with the industrial enterprises of Yasar

Holding no exception. Yasar Holding's agribusiness, however, continued to operate at full capacity, with the result that Yasar Holding, as an entity, emerged from the economic wringer stronger than before.

Corporate History

Yasar Holding began its diversification process into agro-industry with an undertaking to produce Tuborg Beer, using Turkish barley and importing the most advanced technical know-how from United Breweries of Denmark. The milk processing facility, Pinar, was launched in 1974. At that time, milk processing was a virgin area for the private sector. There were numbers of government-owned and -operated milk processing facilities, but, as the managing director of Pinar notes in an interview, "They didn't work very well. We thought we could do better."

The reason Pinar thought it could do better was that its market surveys showed that the market for high-quality milk products throughout Turkey was not being supplied adequately, and certainly not imaginatively. An illustration of Pinar's innovative approach to the market is its design of special products: prepared salad dressings and packaged cream cheese, designed for Turkish workers and their families who have returned from industrialized countries such as Germany, where they got used to convenience foods.

On the production side, a Pinar survey demonstrated that the Aegean region, traditional heartland of agricultural production in Turkey, had a good number of farmers either already engaged or interested in livestock breeding. The task would be to work with these farmers to upgrade their cattle and to improve the quality and quantity of their milk. This became the company's main objective, along with the construction of a modern, technologically advanced plant, with relevant expertise imported from abroad. Pinar has a licensing agreement with Dart and Kraft (U.S.) for products and with Tetra Pak (Sweden) for packaging.

Equity Arrangements and Growth

Pinar has 900 shareholders. Forty percent of the equity is in the hands of Yasar Holding; 20 percent in the hands of another holding company and a bank; the remaining 40 percent is spread among both large- and small-scale farmers. The financial package to launch Pinar was put together in 1973 and construction of the plant started in 1974. The plant began operations in June of 1975, processing 12 million tons of milk that year. By 1983, the plant was processing 70 million tons.

Pinar operated at a loss only during its start-up year, 1975. It has been profitable every year since then and its return on investment (ROI) has been impressive. With an investment capital of 300 million Turkish pounds (T£), profit in 1982 was T£500 million. (The conversion rate used throughout this chapter is T£4.14 = US$1.)

At start-up in 1975, Pinar operations involved 9,000 farmers in 150 villages, 7 cooperatives, and 50 big farms. In 1983, the company was working with 21,000 farmers in 296 villages. Milk intake in 1983 was derived 68 percent from small farmers, 18 percent from 38 cooperatives, and 14 percent from 155 large farms. Pinar also provides 750 off-farm jobs in its factory, plus another 500 for an array of supporting services.

Future Plans

Pinar's plans for the future are to expand its successful operation based from the Aegean region of Turkey to the Mediterranean region of the country; to expand its own sales organization from the Aegean to other regions of Turkey (where presently it operates through distributors); and to step up its exports, primarily to the Middle East. Pinar now exports, via refrigerated trucks, to Kuwait and Saudi Arabia.

More fundamentally, Pinar's future plans are designed to solve the problems of its supplier farmers for whom dairy cattle alone is not a viable economic proposition. The company is already in the process of establishing a feed plant to supply farmers with quality feed at a reasonable price and plans to construct a meat processing plant so that farmers can raise beef cattle alongside their dairy cattle to produce a higher combined income.

RELATIONSHIP WITH FARMERS

Company Philosophy

The management principle that governs the operations of Pinar was articulated by its chief executive officer.

> The farmer is the base of our enterprise. Our welfare depends on his welfare. The two are inseparable. We know that helping the farmer upgrade the quality and quantity of his milk, and offering him a dependable market for it, is not enough for his human welfare and for the development of the villages and of the region. We have to help solve the farmer's overall problems which are both economic and social.

Company Practice

Pinar expressed its concerns from the beginning. While it was still constructing the plant, it announced the price it would pay for milk. Rather than take advantage of a fluctuating market that brought prices down severely during the summer, Pinar proclaimed that its price would be steady throughout the year.

Moreover, the price that was offered was somewhat higher than the existing market price. In addition, Pinar shared with the farmers its own forecast for milk prices for both the short and the medium term.

Pinar also announced that it would collect milk every day of the year and established a collection system to do that. This contrasted from the outset with the system of government-owned and -operated milk processing facilities, where milk is not collected on weekends or holidays. As one farmer put it: "The government plants run on bureaucratic time, not on cow time."

Also from the beginning, Pinar supplied veterinary services-- "on cow time," not "bureaucratic time"; checked out cattle feed for farmers for both quality and price; procured government certified seeds for forage, which an individual small-scale farmer could not obtain on his own; instituted quality-control procedures for milk; and produced a monthly newspaper designed for the farmer and his family. That newspaper, laid out mainly in comic-strip style with text, deals graphically with any and every problem a small farm family faces in Turkey. It addresses both the men of the family who, in Turkey, do most of the outside field work, and the women to whom, in most cases, the care of animals on the farm is entrusted. There is even a funny page with cartoons and puzzles.

The problem of illiteracy, which still exists among some adults on the farm, has not proven an obstacle. "There's always someone in the family who can read." Quite often that someone is one of the children, for whom reading the newspaper to parents is both a practical education and an important enhancement of value in the family. It is also a demonstration of the practical advantages of going to school.

In an even wider circle developing from the same center, the company sponsors an annual contest for schoolchildren throughout Turkey, who draw or paint scenes of the pleasures and joys of country life. The winning entry gets wide distribution in the form of a note card that the company distributes all over the country.

Pinar has structured its relationship with the producing farmers into a three-layer system. The first layer consists of "collectors," who are assigned a territory that covers anywhere from a half-dozen to twenty villages and who, using their own cars or trucks, make the rounds of their villages each day to pick up milk from the farmers and deliver it to the company's network of refrigerated collection stations. The company trains collectors in milk quality, ledger keeping, and accounting.

The second layer consists of "field representatives," who are assigned a region in which they supervise the collectors, as well as maintaining their own direct relationship with the farmers.

The third layer consists of "inspectors," who fan out from headquarters and act as a triple check on the relationship between the company and the farmers. They look for any problems that may have developed between collectors and farmers, or among collectors, that have not come to the attention of the field representative, or that the field representative has not been able

to solve. They also back up the field representative when economic or sociopolitical problems arise that the field representative cannot handle at his level of operation.

The Field Representative

The most important human link between the company and the
farmer is the field representative, usually an attractive and en-
ergetic young man with at least a high school background and some
agricultural education, who has to combine dynamism with diplo-
macy, a visible concern for the farmer and his problems with a
controlled temper and a capacity for cool judgment. A successful
field representative is regarded by the farmer as an improbable
amalgam of son and consultant, expert and problem-solver. Obviously, such men are hard to find.
The Field representatives are selected primarily from responses
to advertisements the company places in both regional newspapers
and the daily newspapers of Izmir.   The ads are fairly explicit.
They ask for men under thirty-five years of age, who have no restrictions on travel and have a driver's license. The preferred
background calls for agricultural engineering, veterinarians,
agricultural technicians, or health officers for cattle. A minimum requirement is graduation from high school.   The company reports that it has had satisfactory results from high school graduates who have gone on to do their military service, especially
if that military service resulted in some technical or vocational
training.   What is not in the ad but becomes, in fact, a primary
criterion for hiring a field representative, is that he must be a
practical man with a feeling for people, and must be both socia-
ble and trustworthy. The company goes to considerable trouble to
recruit and train candidates and to check on their background,
personal as well as professional.
Field representatives are trained for three months, in the
factory, in the company's laboratory, at milk collection stations, and by visiting farmers in the company of an experienced
field representative. Their training is backed up by a fifty-page
technical manual and a twenty-five-page administrative manual.
After the three-month training period, during which they receive
a basic salary, field representatives are remunerated with a salary plus commissions that relate to the quantity and quality of
milk their region produces.
From the outset, a field representative's job has a sociopolitical dimension. He lays the base of his relationship with
the farmers of a village by calling on the three leading person-
alities of the Turkish rural community: the mukhtar (an elected
mayor); the imam (a religious leader sent by a central religious
authority); and the teacher, who is appointed by the government.
This triad identifies the other influential people in the village, who introduce the field representative to the farmer.
Occasionally, a cultural barrier has to be hurdled, and political resistance overcome.   An imam can be concerned with what
the relationship with the company will do to the role of women,
especially since animal care falls mainly into women's domain.

A mukhtar, or more often the teacher, can turn out to be a political firebrand with anti-capitalist notions, who sees private-
sector companies as class enemies, and is particularly suspicious
of companies that are large and have international connections.
   One field representative illustrated how he had solved such
a political problem. He overcame ideological resistance by point-
ing out how an involvement with Pinar was important to the farmer
and valuable for the village. He did this in a series of discussions to which he brought the opponent's peer, with whom the
company had already established good relations, from another village. He had clinched his arguments with the direct testimony of
farmers with whom the company had worked over a couple of years.
This field representative noted that establishing relationships
with the villagers is very much a two-way street, and stretches
considerably beyond company services that are directly connected
with milk production.
   On the day I accompanied this field representative, two
problems that had nothing to do with milk production cropped up
in one village. One farmer had a problem with his olive crop,
that he discussed at length with the Pinar representative, who
promised he would think about it and come up with a solution by
the next visit. Another farmer needed a particular cotton insecticide that he had been unable to procure on his own. The Pinar
representative undertook to obtain it for him.
   There are problems that cut even closer to the bone. At the
economic level at which small-scale farmers exist in Turkey,
there is a temptation to save money by not feeding the cattle
enough. The result is a loss of either quantity or quality in the
output of milk, which in turn has an economic cost to the farmer.
Explaining this cause and effect takes doing. Sometimes the representative can convey the message himself. On other occasions
he works through the teacher or the mukhtar.

The Milk Collector

   An important ingredient in the field representative's array
of duties is to choose, train, and supervise the collectors for
their areas. Collectors are independent contractors who work on
a draw-plus-commission basis geared to the quantity and quality
of milk they deliver to Pinar's network of collection centers. It
is the collector who picks up milk from the farmers every day,
and it is the collector who pays the farmers in cash every week.
Because the collectors provide their own transport from the villages to the collection center, and the company pays them by
check, they need to have some economic standing of their own.
They have to be entrepreneurs. Above all, they must be dependable and trustworthy in their dealings with both the company and
the farmers. Indeed, the financial and personal integrity of the
collectors can go a long way toward making or breaking the company's relationship with the farmers.
   Inevitably, problems do arise with some of the collectors.
It is the job of the regional field representative to catch these
problems and repair whatever ruptures have been created as

quickly as possible. The most desirable collectors, it turns
out, tend to be young men from the villages whose family--father
or brothers--are local farmers, with a stake of their own in milk
production. This gives the collector a direct knowledge and involvement with both the farmer and the company, and adds to his
own standing in the community as an entrepreneur who contributes
economically to his own family and to the other families of the
village.

Types of Suppliers

Pinar contracts its raw milk supplies from three distinct
sources: individual small-scale producers; cooperatives whose
members are small-scale dairy farmers; and large-scale farmers.
In Turkey, small farms are those with 1 to 10 hectares of land
under cultivation, with the majority working 1 to 5 hectares
(1 hectare = 2.5 acres). Large farms generally are about 200
hectares and may have up to 300 head of cattle in their dairy operations. Big farms usually produce their own forage, an opportunity denied to most small units because of the need to devote
their limited land to food crops or higher-paying cash crops. Cooperatives, whose memberships range from 200 to 500, are primarily marketing organizations with some pooling of purchasing
power. Cooperatives supplying milk to Pinar do not relate to
production directly.

A Typical Small-Scale Farmer

A representative example of a small-scale farmer is Mustafa
Inang, of the village of Dagkizilca, who farms 4.2 hectares. He
lives in a typical family compound sharing one of four houses
grouped around a central courtyard with his wife, his mother, and
two children (a twelve-year-old girl and a ten-year-old boy).
Also typically, the wife takes care of the farm's animals (this
includes milking the cows) while Mustafa works in the fields.
The children attend the public school, which provides the mandatory five years of education, and help on the farm after school
throughout the year and more intensively during harvest time.
Mustafa grows tobacco, grapes, olives, wheat, and corn;
raises lambs and, at present, has three milch cows. He would like
to have between fifteen and twenty cows, primarily because he
trusts the steady and dependable market that is provided. Mustafa
says bluntly that raising milch cows was a doubtful enterprise in
the past, not only because the market was uncertain and chaotic,
but because sometimes the small purchasers who bought his milk
paid either late or not at all. His problem now is to obtain the
necessary credit to purchase the extra cows; he believes that,
with Pinar backing and the economic base of his current livestock, cash, and food crop mix, he can probably work himself up
to his target. With fifteen to twenty cows, he says, both his
children could be sent to high school.

A Typical Cooperative

An illustrative cooperative is one composed of 270 small farmers from the villages of Bagarasi and Yeni Bagarasi, total population 1,300 families, who formed their cooperative twenty years ago. The cooperative has five directors and a general director, who are elected each year and can serve a maximum of five years. The mukhtar of the village is an ex-officio director who can, and does, attend directors' meetings.

The average farm size of cooperative members ranges from 1 to 2 hectares. The farmers grow tobacco, olives, wheat, and cotton, and have from one to fifteen cows. Both the members and the cooperative itself have prospered since the arrival of Pinar. Productivity has zoomed. With the help of Pinar's extension services, the co-op, which produced 60 kilograms (kg) of milk a day in the pre-Pinar period, now produces 2,000 kg a day. In part, this is a result of additional cows purchased by member farmers and in part it is due to the fact that cows that gave 5 kg of milk per day before company extension services existed now produce between 18 and 20 kg per day. Pinar's extension services included introducing Holstein cattle that Pinar brought from Germany, which the farmers bought, via an installment plan, over two years. The financing was extended by agricultural banks that considered the existence of Pinar as a dependable purchaser with sufficient collateral.

The cooperative itself has benefited from its association with Pinar. It now has its own building, a whitewashed square hall that contains five desks, two adding machines, a filing cabinet, bookshelves, and an overhead fluorescent light. The building is situated on the central square of the village facing the coffeehouse where village elections, including the election for the cooperative's directors, are held. The co-op has bought a machine for mixing feed and has acquired a truck. Most important, since the arrival of Pinar, it has been able to distribute dividends to its members, who have used the funds for four major purposes: to buy more cows and build stables; to modernize their homes with important additions like refrigerators; to build or buy houses and furnishings for newly married children; and to provide more education for their children.

The village now has thirty of its children in high school, compared to thirteen before Pinar arrived, and is already sending about a dozen of its boys and girls to technical school, college, nursing school, and military school. "Another ten years of Pinar and we can send all our children to high school and some to universities," says the director of the cooperative.

Problems of Small-Scale Dairy Farmers

There are problems. The basic economic problem is that the cost of feed is still too high, measured against the price of milk. The farmers argue that two kilos of feed should cost no more than the price they receive for one kilo of milk. This ratio does not obtain now but may when Pinar completes construction of its own feed plant.

Another economic problem is that interest rates are too high, although they are coming down. In June 1983, interest rates for agricultural loans to small-scale farmers stood at 20 percent for one-year loans, 22 percent for loans of three to seven years. The manager of the Agricultural Development Bank for the Aegean region said that the bank's target interest rate for small farmers is 10 percent and that he thought this was achievable within a couple of years.

The main social problem seems to be that as the milch cow population rises, most of the new workload falls on the shoulders of the women. The men concede that this does lead to complaints from their wives, but argue that as the economic base expands for the family, they too have more tasks to fulfill. "The quarrel goes on," says one of the cooperative directors, with a satisfied grin.

After one conversation with co-op directors, a Pinar field representative noted a cultural change that is likely to have major implications for the long term.

> Before we started working here, these farmers didn't talk to strangers. They distrusted anybody they didn't know, often for good reason. They got cheated many times by outsiders who came to deal with them on their milk. Now, the Pinar collector who deals with them is practically an adopted son. Quite often, he stays in the village for the night, and any member of the co-op is happy to have him stay at his home. They are not afraid of strangers anymore. As you see, they are quite open now in talking about themselves, their problems, and their accomplishments. They really like visitors now, and I think that makes a big difference in the horizons of their lives.

A Typical Large-Scale Farmer

An illustration of Pinar's effect on a large-scale farmer is Ayhan Gulcuoglis of the village of Ilkkursun. His farm covers 100 hectares, on which he grows cotton, barley, and hay and alfalfa for his 150 cows. He raises lambs as well. His cows, milked by machine, produce 830 kg of milk per day. He sells all his milk to Pinar, and reports that since the arrival of Pinar he finds his cows more profitable than the lambs. Pinar has been helpful in building up his dairy stock both in quality and in quantity. It has extended, in some cases, direct credit for new high-quality cattle, interest-free for three months, and payable in milk. The Pinar field representative visits the farm once a week. Ayhan Gulcuoglis has become a stockholder in Pinar.

CORPORATE RELATIONS WITH THE GOVERNMENT

Pinar relates to the government at three levels: village, regional, and national. In addition, the company has relations with the international private sector through its licensing agreements and its export activities, and relations with the international public sector through its connections with some of the activities of USAID.

At the Village Level

Relationships at the village level have already been described in detail. In this context, the company would like to see more organizations of farmers, especially small-scale farmers. The government's Regional Development Organization feels the same way, and has tried to encourage an association of small-scale farmers, if only because it would make government distribution of feed, seed, and tools easier to accomplish.

A National Chamber of Agriculture does exist, dating back to 1881 and the Ottoman Empire. The chamber was restructured as a modern organization in 1957, and had an important role in providing farmers with information on agricultural implements and techniques before development agencies, universities, and companies took over that task. At present, the Chamber of Agriculture is mainly a political organization in the Turkish context: It negotiates with the government on matters of farmer interest and meets with the leaders of both the political parties and the military services to brief them on agricultural problems and possible solutions to these problems. Its concerns tend to be macroeconomic, dealing with such topics as irrigation systems, the cost of fertilizer, price supports, and the level and cost of agricultural credit. Under the law, all farmers are members of the chamber, with small-scale farmers contributing 3 percent of their gross income, and large-scale farmers 5 percent, as a mandatory membership fee.

Although the problems the chamber addresses do, of course, affect the small-scale farmer in a macroeconomic way, there is little direct contact between the chamber and these farmers, and it is difficult for the farmers to comprehend in concrete terms just what it is they get for the money they pay to the chamber. This militates against attempts to organize small-scale farmers in a way that would have a more direct impact on their lives. Attempts to organize these farmers on a functional basis (such as an organization of livestock producers) or on a socioeconomic basis (such as an association for the protection of private farm property) have failed. The only exception are the marketing cooperatives described earlier, and though a few of these organizations exist, they represent a limited segment of the small-scale farmers in Turkey. In discussing the situation with cooperative members, they seemed more interested in the possibility of becoming shareholders in Pinar than in the broad concept of a national cooperative movement.

When pressed on the subject of organization at the village level, the answer from small-scale farmers tends to be, "We don't have a leader." The Regional Development Organization maintains that it cannot provide leaders for such purposes; and the company feels, probably wisely in the Turkish context, that taking a leadership role in such organizations would be socially and politically suspect.

Perhaps this is an area for international intermediate organizations or institutions. To function effectively in the sociopolitical and cultural milieu of Turkey is likely to be fraught with difficulties, and clearly calls for skilled, sensitive leadership, patiently at work over long periods of time.

At the Regional Level

The company maintains three sets of regional relationships: with the Regional Development Organization; with the Agricultural Development Bank; and with the agricultural faculty of the University of the Aegean, whose campus is on the outskirts of Izmir not far from the Pinar plant.

The Regional Development Organization. This organization has a mandate to build up the livestock population of the region, and particularly to help increase milk production. It does this mainly by working with the larger small-scale farmers, that is, farmers who have five cows now and want to work themselves up to sixty cows. The Regional Development Organization fulfills its task by providing veterinary services; furnishing seeds for farmers to grow their own feed when they have enough land to do so; and assisting farmers in the construction of stables with a capacity of up to sixty animals.

The Regional Development Organization for the Aegean has reached 300 farmers in the ten years of its existence, and reports that the biggest spur for its activity has been the existence of Pinar and the dependable market it provides. Relations between Pinar and the Development Organization are cooperative, cordial, and close.

The Agricultural Development Bank. In existence since the 1960s, the bank had no involvement with agro-industry until 1978, when it studied a dairy operation in Italy and decided that there was a place for a similar undertaking in the Aegean region of Turkey. In 1979, the bank broadened its policy to provide loans not only to small- and large-scale farmers for production purposes, but also to agro-industrial undertakings and to farmers or cooperatives for the export of agricultural products. Previously, the bank's main problem with its loans had been the volatile and undeveloped marketing conditions for the farmer's output. That problem is now being solved, in part by Pinar and in part by the central government's concerted export drive, which is channeling surplus agricultural output to markets in both Europe and the Middle East. The bank is aware that for market purposes, and particularly for the export market, the main problems for the output of small-scale farmers are quality control and packaging, and it appreciates the role Pinar plays in the solution of both.

The University of the Aegean. Historically, the university had little relationship with industry, a characteristic of all Turkish universities. This is changing. As the head of the agrarian faculty at the Aegean University put it in an interview:

> Universities were closed to industry. The universities were afraid of industry, and industry, for its part, did not think of the universities as a practical resource they could use. Over the past five years this has changed, and I find the change a healthy one. At this university we now have good relations with several industrial sectors and we have considerable working contact with Pinar. To illustrate, we are now constructing a laboratory for pilot projects and Pinar engineers and electricians helped us in the construction.
>
> On the other hand, Pinar needed a particular filter for its factory that had to be imported. The government at first said no, then asked us for an expert opinion. We checked it out and agreed with the company. Pinar got its import license.
>
> For the medium term, we are now working with the company on a research project to produce an infant formula for calves based on Turkish raw materials.
>
> For the long term, we could work with the company on new products. For example, on new cheese varieties, where we could do the laboratory research, then set up a joint venture with the company for pilot projects to produce the new product in quantity, and finally hand over the commercialization of the product to the company.
>
> Also, under the general direction of the university, we could address some of the personnel problems that now exist. We could develop training systems for such technicians as master cheesemakers, master butter makers, master yogurt makers, who are needed in the industry. At present, no training institutions exist for personnel categories between the factory worker and the engineer. We could establish a vocational school for milk industry technicians.

Problems in Company/Government Relations

Despite these generally cooperative relations between the company and the government and its institutions, problems do exist. They revolve primarily around two issues.

The first is unfair competition from government-operated milk processing plants. There are now thirty-six government-owned and -operated milk processing plants in Turkey with a total installed capacity of 270 million liters a year (3.785 liters =

1 gallon). Inefficiency in government plants, however, is such that less than 30 percent of the installed capacity is being used. (Pinar, with an installed capacity of 70 million liters per annum, uses close to 100 percent of its capacity.) This inefficiency by the government-operated dairies is compensated in three ways, each one representing patently unfair competition for the private sector.

1. The government dairies pay lower interest rates to government credit institutions.
2. They make no profit, and their losses are made up by the taxpayer.
3. They have a monopoly on institutional sales to such organizations as the army, the police, and the national hospital network.

If the private sector did not have to deal with such unfair competition, it could expand, making possible economies of scale that would lower the price of its products. At present, Pinar products are largely confined to the upper end of the market. With economies of scale, the quality products put out by Pinar could reach a broader range of the population.

The second major issue between Pinar and the government is the government's monopoly on artificial insemination. Were it not for that monopoly, Pinar would be able to import frozen semen from the United States and introduce artificial insemination to all the farmers it deals with.

As the managing director of Pinar points out:

> We do have a representative in each village who collects milk every day. We could send with him a person qualified to administer artificial insemination. In Germany, the Maegli Company, which also collects milk from the farmers, supplies its representative with a doctor's bag that contains gloves and the appropriate injections and he administers the artificial insemination. Israel has a similar project using imported semen. There is no reason why we cannot do the same. It would speed the upgrading of our cattle and the yield of the cows, benefiting both the farmer and the company. The same principle applies to beef cattle. At present, however, the entire artificial insemination program is restricted to government officials who proceed in their own way, at their own pace. It is a slow and cumbersome pace. It also makes the farmer dependent on the government instead of encouraging his own entrepreneurial instincts.

Relations with the United States

Pinar's relationship with the United States has a personal basis: Both the deputy chairman of Yasar Holding and the general manager of Pinar received their graduate education in the United

States. Indeed, the two first met in the United States at a special training program for foreign students at the University of Colorado. The fellowship under which Pinar's general manager got his U.S. training was provided by USAID. At that time, he was an official in the public sector. He is convinced that fellowships of this nature provide valuable seed capital for human resources and strongly advocates that they be furnished for junior and middle executives in the private sector as well as in the public sector. The general manager's experience in both sectors also leads him to advocate that the United States use its aid resources and its political influence, where feasible, to encourage the private sector whenever and wherever possible, and to persuade the Turkish government to withdraw from productive undertakings that the private sector can do as well or better.

Specifically, he would like to see some USAID funds made available for the import of high-yield cattle, the import of frozen semen for artificial insemination administered by the private sector, and the loan of technicians with expertise in veal production. He would also like to see more USAID scholarships for technical training in the milk industry or, for that matter, in other industries in the private sector. And he would like all of this to happen quickly. "In Turkey today," he says, "we are ready to move, and we want to run, not walk."

POLICY IMPLICATIONS

For the Company

The company is aware that its own success depends not only on the increased population of milch cows it can foster and the higher yield and quality of milk it can help farmers produce; in Turkey, an economically viable and progressive small-scale farm requires an appropriate mix of livestock and crops, with a balance of food and cash crops. It knows that achieving this mix and this balance calls for sociopolitical and cultural skills as well as economic organization and technical expertise. Its current plans call for a broad and diversified production base that would provide an expanding, comprehensive market and also act as a technology transfer agent for such integrated development.

What should probably be added to the company's plans is a systematic effort to broaden its existing equity base to include among its shareholders as many farmer cooperatives and individual small-scale farmers as is feasible given economic realities.

For the Community

A prime prerequisite would appear to be streamlining operations of the Regional Development Organization so that its activities relate to the realities of farm life rather than to the organizational convenience of the bureaucracy. In addition,

there seems to be a consensus that it would be desirable for
small-scale farmers to form an organization or association that
could deal effectively with both public and private sector institutions. The driving force of such an organization should clearly be a community leader independent of the traditional triad of
mukhtar/imam/teacher. Who would provide the inspiration and who
would devise the organization is an open question. Apparently,
there are no national institutions skilled in the arts of intermediation among traditional rural people that are working closely
with enterprises such as Pinar. Therefore, an appropriate international intermediate organization might serve to start the process and help create the necessary Turkish organizations.

For the Host Country

Though the pioneer work that the government has done in developing the dairy industry in Turkey is both appreciable and
appreciated, perhaps the time has come for the public sector to
divest itself of its milk-producing plants. Divestiture would
save taxpayer money, lead to substantially increased use of plant
capacity, and make possible economies of scale in the private
sector that could lead to lower prices and wider distribution of
quality products. The government also would probably be well
advised to relinquish its current monopoly on artificial insemination, to make possible a more rapid dissemination of this important technology.

Government resources, both financial and technical, could be
concentrated instead on intensified irrigation projects, for
which there is still a great need in all regions of Turkey. The
country does not lack water resources, but at present only
25 percent of the land that could be supplied with adequate water
for optimum agricultural output by appropriate use of rivers and
dams is, in fact, irrigated. Providing an expanded irrigation
system would quickly increase agricultural output for domestic
consumption and better nourishment, and for export, with a con-
comitant contribution to the country's balance of payments.

Finally, price supports for basic agricultural products
should closely approximate market realities. In 1983, for example, the support price for cotton was T£70, as against the market price of T£150.

For the Donor Country

For the United States, the recommendation to provide scholarships for junior and middle management in the private sector
seems an excellent idea. Related to this educational support,
USAID might facilitate the intervention of experienced, skilled
intermediary organizations to help in the creation of small-scale
farmer organizations that could lead broadly-based programs of
rural development. Earmarking USAID funds for the importation of
high-yield cattle and frozen semen from the United States also
appears reasonable. Another suggestion made by Pinar managers,

that scientists be given an economic education, is an idea that seems to make sense for both donor and host country.

Finally, the United States can exercise what persuasive powers it has to encourage the Turkish government to let the private sector do what it does efficiently and effectively, while concentrating public sector attention on infrastructure undertakings, both economic and social, that are beyond the private sector's resources or competence.

6

The Haggar Group: Cultivation of Tea, Coffee, and Tobacco in Southern Sudan

Ruth Karen

SUMMARY

The case of the Haggar Group of agribusiness companies in the Republic of the Sudan covers the development of a system of supply of tobacco, coffee, and tea in the southern region of the country, currently involving some 2,600 small-scale contract farmers, with plans to reach 7,000 by the end of the decade. These farmers have been brought from their traditional, isolated existence in the bush to become active participants in the cash economy of the nation.

To appreciate the vision, courage, and persistence that underlie this successful private sector venture requires a careful reading of the social and political history of the Sudan and an appreciation of conditions in southern Sudan. In the words of company president Anis Haggar, son of George Haggar, who founded the enterprise fifty years ago:

> Southern Sudan, fifty years ago, was, and to a great extent still is, a remote, primitive, and severely underdeveloped area, with a harsh tropical climate, naturally protected against the rest of the world by the mosquito and the tsetse fly. It is a landlocked area, with negligible communications, and with severe logistical problems for business. It is a region embedded in major differences of ethnic groupings, race, and religion.

Despite the formidable obstacles to the commercialization of agriculture in the region, George Haggar started production and crop development studies relating first to tobacco and tea, and later to coffee, on an estate in the south, over forty years ago. Tobacco production could most readily be extended to outgrowers; a system of extension, credit, favorable pricing, and simple processing methods was introduced. By 1983, the system involved just under 2,500 farmers. While this was happening, over 100 farmers joined another network that added coffee growing to their traditional concentration on subsistence food crops. Currently, an expansion in both coffee cultivation and tea production is under way, each emphasizing a separate body of farmers.

The future of this collaboration between the Haggar Group and the small-scale farmers of the south seems bright. Sudan imports large quantities of all three crops and Haggar production supplies a very small fraction of the domestic market now. The limits to expansion of the program depend more on corporate finances than on farmer interest; far more farmers are expressing a wish to join the system than can be absorbed. Haggar is concentrating its efforts at present on obtaining financial backing from international sources for the outgrowers program.

COUNTRY BACKGROUND

The Extraordinary Potential

From the perspective of agribusiness, the Sudan is unique in a number of ways. Its area is enormous (1 million square miles); its population is relatively small (23 million at latest count, 1982). Of that population, 90 percent is rural, one of the highest percentages anywhere in the world. Most important, more than 200 million acres are suitable for cultivation with a wide variety of crops.

The agricultural potential of the Sudan has long been recognized. As far back as 1839, the possibility of large-scale cotton production was recognized [21], and shortly after World War I, the British government, the British fine cotton spinners, and the government of the Sudan organized the so-called "Gezira Scheme," which is now one of the oldest (the first irrigation dam was completed in 1925) and largest agricultural development enterprises in the world. Originally operated as a private, foreign corporation, control was handed over in 1950 to the Sudan Gezira Board, a public body, which now employs over 60,000 people and organizes small-farm production on roughly 1.2 million acres of irrigated farmland. Cotton was and remains the primary crop, but dura (a type of sorghum), wheat, groundnuts (peanuts), some vegetables, and a variety of fodder crops are also grown. Most recently, there have been some investments in processing facilities, an interesting but as yet not a sweeping innovation.*

With the Gezira Scheme as a central demonstration of opportunity, the Sudan has in recent years been extolled as a potential breadbasket for the Middle East, and there has been much talk, and some limited action, about triangular ventures in

---

*The Sudanese Gezira Board is so important historically and currently to agricultural and rural development in the Sudan that several references to the background and significance of the venture are included in the bibliography. See notations under the names of A. Gaitskell and T. Barrett. Also see Chapter 13, Section 8.

agriculture combining Western technology, Arab money, and Sudanese production potential.

Problems

Also within the past decade, a number of government projects were initiated with technical and financial support from Europe. None of them has been a startling success. The main reason for this appears to be that they are based on a plantation concept, relying for their output on agricultural workers rather than small-scale farmers. In addition to having no long-term personal stake in the success of the enterprise, workers have to leave their own villages and bush farms to work on these plantations. The core problem, however, is that these agricultural project workers are dependent on the government for their pay. In the Sudan, especially in recent years, this means that wages are late in arriving, sometimes as late as six months, with the result that agricultural workers tend to melt back into the bush.

One example of this type of venture is a tea project in Upper Talanga in Eastern Equatoria financed by the European Economic Community (EEC). By 1983, although seven years old, the Upper Talanga Tea Project still had no processing plant, in spite of an investment in the project of US$20 million. Its tea crop at that stage was less than the tea produced by the nuclear estate of the Haggar Group, at nearby Iwatoka, on one-quarter of the acreage.

Policies

A concise summary of government policy vis-à-vis agriculture, and the implications of that policy, was drawn up a couple of years ago in a prefeasibility study prepared by the UK-based agribusiness firm, Booker-McConnell (now Booker Agriculture International, Ltd.). The original document was not available. Anis Haggar provided the following extract during an interview in Khartoum:

> With its economy predominantly agricultural, and with great resources of land which are not fully used, Sudan gives priority to the development of agriculture as the sector with the greatest potential contribution to national economic development. Official policy is for continued self-sufficiency in basic foodstuffs (e.g., grain and livestock) and cotton, and for the increased export of surpluses; for achievement of self-sufficiency in other products with the aim of subsequently exporting surpluses (e.g., sugar); and for a degree of import substitution in other crops (e.g., tea and coffee) for which domestic production is unlikely, in the medium-term, to achieve national self-sufficiency. Production increases are to be achieved

by a combination of large-scale enterprises and small-holder development. In Southern Sudan the emphasis is primarily, though not exclusively, on small farm development.

In view of the limited domestic resources of capital, the Government encourages investment of foreign capital. The Encouragement of Investment Act of 1980 provides guarantees against nationalization and sequestration, and provides for exemption from business profits tax for five years and from payment of customs duties [17].

Land Ownership

Finally, Sudan is extraordinary in its patterns of landownership. For a farmer interested in producing a crop--any crop--getting land to do so is a simple process. A tribal chief in the south explains how it works:

The farmer comes to me and tells me what land he wants and what he plans to grow there. I go with him to see whether his choice of land and product are reasonable. If they are, and if the farmer is a reliable man who knows what he's doing, I will draw up a document that allocates the land to him. A copy of this document goes to the government where it is registered officially.

The farmer does not pay for the land. The land belongs to the tribe, and the farmer receives it on a long-term renewable lease that stays in his family for as long as the land is used for productive purposes. We have enough land to do this for a very long time.

The land allocation process is not quite as arbitrary as it sounds. Although tribal chieftaincies are hereditary, public choices are made among members of the chief's family. In addition, a tribal council advises the chief and has a deciding voice in the allocation of tribal lands.

There is, however, a problematic aspect to the system. Though producing farmers can get long-term renewable leases to the land they work, they do not get legal ownership. As a result, financial institutions do not accept land as collateral. Haggar Ltd., which extends financing at subsidized interest rates to some 110 small coffee farmers and 2,400 tobacco farmers, sums up the reality from a financial point of view: "The only collateral we have is the farmer and his performance."

The South and North/South Confrontation

There is a marked difference in the Sudan between the North and the South, ranging from the cultural to the structural, the religious to the economic. The differences exploded into seventeen years of civil war immediately following independence. A political accommodation was hammered out in 1972, yet few of the differences have been resolved, and tensions continue.

In brief, the North is Moslem and Arab, "Arab" defined in the Sudan as anyone, regardless of ethnic background, who speaks Arabic, identifies with Arab culture, and adheres to the Moslem faith. Under this definition, between two-thirds and three-quarters of the Sudanese are Arabs. Economically, the North is more highly developed, and has nearly all of the country's industry and a considerably better infrastructure, both physical and social. It is also the core of political power. The nation's capital, Khartoum, where the president lives, parliament meets, and the country's major educational and technical institutions are located, is in the North.

The South is African. The population is black and organized along tribal lines. The people are either Christian or animist, and their cultural identification is tribal, southern, and African. Economically, the South is underdeveloped within the Sudanese context, and the central government's policy vis-a-vis the South has historically been one of neglect. Whether or not this neglect is benign is a matter of considerable debate, with sharp and potentially explosive overtones. There are grounds for argument that any project that brings economic development to the South and improves the living standards of people in the southern region makes an urgently needed contribution to the sociopolitical stability of the Sudan.

COMPANY BACKGROUND

History

The Haggar Group consists of eleven companies with a combined annual turnover of approximately 100 million Sudanese pounds (S£). (The conversion rate used throughout this chapter is S£1.23 = US$1.) Corporate headquarters had to be transferred from Juba to Khartoum in 1963 as civil war raged in southern Sudan. Regional headquarters have since been reestablished in Juba. The Haggar Group maintains offices in Port Sudan, Kosti, and El Obeid within the Sudan, and has representative arrangements in Nairobi, Mombasa, and London.

The corporate members of the conglomerate are

Sudan Tea & Coffee Plantation Co. Ltd. (STCP)
Haggar Cigarette & Tobacco Factory Ltd. (HCTF)
Blue Nile Plastics Co. Ltd.
D.K. Aviation International Ltd.
National Air Express (Sudan) Ltd.
Haggar Trading Co. Ltd.
Haggar Engineering & Transport Co. Ltd.

Haggar River Transport Co. Ltd.
Afrograph Company Ltd.
Afrograph Trading Co. Ltd.
Khartoum Aviation Services Co. Ltd.

Although some of these companies were created as recently as the 1980s (for example, Khartoum Aviation Services and Afrograph, an advertising company), the core enterprise of Haggar Ltd. dates back to the first decade of the twentieth century. The two companies directly involved in agribusiness are the Sudan Tea and Coffee Plantation Co. Ltd. and the Haggar Cigarette & Tobacco Factory Ltd., which is engaged in the production, processing, and marketing of tobacco, and in the manufacture of cigarettes for the domestic market.

George Haggar introduced Virginia tobacco to the Sudan in 1948, and manufactured Sudan's first cigarette in 1949 under Haggar Cigarette & Tobacco Factory Limited. The international companies that at that time only imported cigarettes to Sudan did not take an interest until later. The British American Tobacco Company (BAT) established a factory in northern Sudan (Wad Medani) in 1957; Rothmans of Pall Mall established a tobacco growing company, the National Tobacco Company, in 1965. The latter, in turn, established the National Cigarette Company, in which Rothmans held 40 percent of the equity, with the balance offered to the public.

The next few years saw a consolidation of the tobacco industry. Today, Haggar and the National Cigarette Company jointly own the National Tobacco Company (NTC), which grows and sells its leaf to the three cigarette manufacturing enterprises in the Sudan. Two of these three are owned by the Haggar Group; one is owned by the National Cigarette Company, which bought out British American Tobacco Company's Sudan subsidiary in 1967.

In terms of corporate structure, STCP started as a proprietorship in the 1930s and was converted into a limited private company in the late 1970s, capitalized at S£1 million. The intention was to make shares available to any finance company through an equity/loan arrangement, to an international tea/coffee corporation, to local farmers' associations or cooperatives, and to individual local farmers. For the long term, given appropriate growth, STCP is considering going public.

The cigarette company, which was originally owned 100 percent by the Haggar family, has already spun off 16 percent of its equity to its employees, and one member of the staff union and one member of the labor union sit on the company's board of directors. Employees of the cigarette company are encouraged to invest their dividends in other enterprises of the Haggar Group.

The constructive relationship of the employees to the company is illustrated by the fact that there have been no strikes in the company's history. In a recent demonstration of community spirit and company loyalty, employees volunteered to work two shifts without pay on a Friday, the legal weekly holiday, during which workers are paid double time. Employee turnout for this voluntary effort was 100 percent, comprising a total of 700 people. The company, in turn, contributed the wages it would have paid to a national charity. Also, in September of the same year (1983), the company paid each employee a bonus of five months' salary, consisting of one month as a contribution to the celebration of the religious festival of Ramadan, one month as a personal gift, two months as a bonus, and one extra month for productivity. Employees own a substantial equity share in all companies associated with the Haggar Group.

The Haggar Group Agribusiness Enterprises

The Haggar Group's agribusiness enterprises, which employed a total of 5,000 people in the 1950s, fell victim to the Civil War and subsequent political action. In 1970, the Sudanese Government expropriated STCP, and the army occupied the nuclear estate at Iwatoka. A year after the Addis Ababa agreement ended the Civil War in 1972, STCP was denationalized and returned to private ownership. Since then, the Haggar Group has concentrated on expanding production of tobacco, coffee, and tea in southern Sudan by means of a wide-ranging outgrower (contract farmer) program. By mid-1984, some 2,600 small-scale farmers were involved. Subsistence food production has been maintained at self-sufficient levels, even as these people were brought for the first time into the cash economy of their country.
There is an interesting and revealing story behind the expansion of the outgrower program. When the Iwatoka nuclear estate was returned to the Haggars, George Haggar wanted to divide the land that had been devoted to the development of coffee and tea production for many years among the people of the area. However, the ravages of the Civil War had taken such a toll that the people were more concerned about who would pay them their next month's wages and bring foodstuffs to the canteens than they were with owning land and cultivating new cash crops for themselves. In response to this clear message, the Haggar Group immediately embarked on an outgrower scheme to satisfy both farm family and corporate needs.
A belief in the future for both company and their farmer suppliers is based on market realities. Tobacco consumption, in cigarettes, is currently the equivalent of 3,000 metric tons (mt) per annum. Domestic tea production in the Sudan ranges between 70 and 100 mt, while consumption totals 19,000 mt. Sudan produces about 1,000 mt of coffee, of which STCP supplies only 100 mt, while consumption is roughly 16,000 mt. In the words of management, offered during an interview with the company president: "We have a long way to go before we achieve self-sufficiency, but when we finally do, we shall be able to look towards markets with neighboring Egypt, with whom we have a Political and Economic Integration Pact. Egypt produces none of the three crops and totally imports its requirement."
In addition, the company's expansion plans include processing and packaging tea and coffee and marketing both products directly to supermarkets and other retailers. This plan is facilitated by the fact that Haggar Ltd. already has a nationwide distribution network that sells the cigarettes produced by the

conglomerate's cigarette company. Provided adequate and appropriate financing can be secured, expansion could proceed at the
rate of 300 to 400 acres a year for the first three years, with a
possibility of adding 1,000 acres per year thereafter. With the
average family farmer planting one to two acres, this would constitute a profitable undertaking for STCP, and an appreciable
import-substitution project for the Sudan. It would bring some
3,000 additional family farmers into the market economy within
five years.

Corporate Motivation

The outreach program of the agribusiness activities of the
Haggar Group is traditional in most ways. It includes a carefully supervised transfer of appropriate technology employing experts and trained extension agents; the supply at cost of relevant inputs; the financing of these inputs and, in the case of
tobacco, the financing of such special farmer requirements as
tools and barn construction for flue-curing of tobacco. In addition, it comprises some social outreach activities, such as contributions to dispensaries and the operation of nonprofit stores
and canteens, the construction of village schools, and the extension of special loans for personal requirements. These activities are circumscribed by government policies and attitudes and
also by the company's resources.

There is one unique ingredient to the outreach program of
STCP. The company not only finances coffee growers, and intends
to finance tea growers, for a comprehensive package of production
inputs but also advances cash to the farmers for their own labor
and the labor of their families. The motivation for this has a
practical as well as a social aspect.

In the Sudan, and particularly in the southern region, the
constraint on agricultural productivity is not land but labor.
Typically, small-scale farmers who cultivate one to five acres of
"bush plantation" grow a variety of food crops, in the main for
their own use, but with just a little left over for trading
against such basic necessities as salt, oil, fish, and minimal
clothing. The only augmentation to this rock-bottom subsistence
farming is the illegal but widespread distillation of alcohol
brewed from corn and bananas, which is made and marketed by the
women of the family.

All in all, these activities employ members of the extended
family at a level that clearly constitutes underemployment by any
economic yardstick, but is both traditional and acceptable to
subsistence farmers in the bush. Offering these farmers an opportunity to cultivate a cash crop, in addition to their basic
food crops, means that extra labor is required from all members
of the family. Coffee cultivation requires three to four years
of extra effort before the farmer gets any cash return for his
labor. For bush farmers, four years is a long economic horizon,
to which they are not attuned mentally or emotionally and which
they are in no position to finance on their own. The extra labor
is, therefore, financed by the company on a "piecework" basis,

geared to the number of coffee trees planted and the amount of land allocated to the production of either coffee or tea. The company encourages farmers to add the cash crop to their food crops, with the average ratio of one acre of cash crop to four acres of food crops, but not to replace the food crops with cash crops.

The social aspect of this ingredient of the outreach program focuses on a situation in which traditional subsistence practices have created an apathy that is intensified by the widespread availability of rotgut booze, and in which local markets offer very little to buy. A cash income stimulates both the desire and the possibility for these bush farmers to spend their money on consumer items other than alcohol, beginning with the opportunity to afford transportation to market centers that offer such items as clothing, bicycles, transistor radios, torches, salt, dried fish, and canned goods; entertainment in the form of movies and sports events; and perhaps most significant from a developmental viewpoint, higher and better education.

This financing of the farm family's labor does not apply to tobacco planters, who can produce a cash crop in the first season they plant tobacco. Tobacco takes five to six months from land preparation to sale of leaf. NTC therefore does not finance growers' labor, but does provide hand tools, implements, chemicals, fertilizers, and funds for the construction of tobacco-curing barns. Also, most small farmers who grow tobacco do so on a three-year rotation basis. They grow tobacco one year, using between half an acre to two acres of their land, then alternate other crops for the two subsequent years to return to the soil the nutrients that tobacco depletes. Crops for this rotation procedure include groundnuts, millet, maize, sesame, cassava, sorghum, and sweet potatoes--all food crops, and all marketable.

Corporate Strategy

Technical as well as managerial strategy differs for tobacco and for coffee and tea.

Tobacco. The growing of tobacco requires substantially more financing over a very short growing season. Total financing for the company's tobacco farmers in the South amounted to roughly S£100,000 in the 1983/1984 season. The average advance to a farmer planting tobacco in his first season amounts to approximately S£260. This breaks down into S£200 for the construction of curing barns and tools, with repayment expected in two to three years; and S£60 for crop materials, with repayment expected at the end of the season. In tobacco, the company extends all its financing to the farmers interest-free.

The major NTC corporate expenses in tobacco are: management and field extension officers; tobacco storage facilities; the holding of tobacco after purchase from farmers for a minimum twelve-month period, while the leaf matures; and transport from southern Sudan to the factories in the North. Total expenses amount to approximately S£1.2 million per year.

Payroll cost for the extension staff in the 1983/1984 season amounted to S 250,000. The Haggar Group tobacco-growing activities in the South, for the 1983/1984 season, encompassed 1,793 feddans (1 feddan = 1.038 acres), cultivated by 2,434 farmers. This called for a staff of sixty extension agents and experts at various levels. Moving up the managerial ladder, this staff included forty crop supervisors, with a primary or a secondary education; eight area supervisors, with a secondary education and specialized company-supplied training; four tobacco officers, of whom one is a university graduate; six senior tobacco officers, all with agricultural college backgrounds; an assistant leaf manager with a Bachelor of Science degree from the University of Khartoum and a Masters degree from the University of California; and--the sole expatriate in the managerial roster--a leaf manager from the United Kingdom. The company used to operate a training center in the North, but after building a nucleus of supervisors, now does most of its training on the job.

Crop supervisors are recruited locally. They are often the sons of farmers who grow tobacco and live in one of the villages they supervise. Both the crop supervisors and the area supervisors are usually from the same tribe as the farmers with whom they work, and speak the language of the tribe idiomatically.

The managerial ladder is characterized by the type of transportation the extension agents command as well as by their salary and authority. Crop supervisors move around on bicycles; area supervisors have motorbikes; tobacco officers and senior tobacco officers have pickup trucks; and leaf managers have Suzuki or Land Rover four-wheel-drive vehicles.

Crop supervisors are hired on a three-month probation basis, and there is considerable shakeout during these three months. Thereafter, turnover is minimal. The crop inspectors who turn out to be right for the job think of the position as a career path, as does the company. Except for the top job, which is held by an expatriate with decades of experience in tobacco growing, all promotion is from the ranks.

Coffee and Tea. For coffee and tea, direct financing costs are considerably higher than for tobacco, but the expenditure for extension agents is lower. Coffee and tea farmers sign individual ten-year contracts with the company. These farmers undertake

- To furnish evidence of clear and unencumbered ownership or right of use (tribal allocation) of the land or evidence of legal authorization to act fully on behalf of the landlord.
- To provide evidence of the exact location of the land and its quantity, in feddans.
- To show evidence of sufficient work force to farm the land.
- To keep whatever books and accounts may be required of them and to make these records available for inspection by officers of the company.
- To deal with the company on an exclusive basis.

The company undertakes

- To finance the farmer specifically for the payment of salaries and wages of the work force.
- To supply the farmers with suitable seedlings at cost, plus cost for transportation of these seedlings.
- To supply the farmers with tools and implements needed to cultivate the crop.
- To supply the farmer with fertilizers and insecticides, and the transportation of these materials to the farm, all at cost.
- To clean, process, pack, and transport the crop at cost.
- To market the crop.
- To maintain correct books and records of its transactions with the farmers.
- To provide the farmers with a fair financial return.

Unlike tobacco, which is used entirely by the cigarette factories of the Haggar Group of companies, coffee and tea are sold by the company on the open market. The farmers get their proportionate share of the market price, minus a 20 percent charge the company levels for transportation, marketing, and other overhead costs.

In the case of coffee and tea, the company supplies all inputs at cost and, as noted above, finances the farmer's labor. It does charge interest at a subsidized rate. Commercial borrowing rates in Sudan in 1983 were 21 percent; the company charged its farmers 10.75 to 12 percent interest, a subsidy of almost 50 percent.

At the end of 1983, 102 family farms were associated with the company, mainly growing coffee, and advances to these farmers ranged from S£2,000 to S£10,000. As a rule of thumb, financing has to be extended to coffee farmers for between five and ten years. Of thirty-four farmers whose balance sheets I examined in detail, three had paid off all their debts and were in a credit position with the company after five years.

STCP has successfully grown tea on a commercial scale since the mid-1940s. ("Haggar" tea has always commanded a premium price on the market over low-quality imported teas.) Tea growing is now ready for expansion onto family farms, following the coffee-growing model. Expansion into tea growing will be limited by a specific radius from the tea-processing plant. Initially, areas of two to three acres will be recommended per family, and the expansion rate will be determined after early progress is assessed. Unlike the once-a-year picking season for coffee, tea is plucked throughout the year, except for a two- to three-week period at the height of the dry season. Thus, from its third year, when a limited amount of plucking can be done, a tea bush is able to provide continual revenue. The intention is to process the tea in company facilities, and package and retail it for the domestic market. This will require a price-setting system that the company believes should be a tripartite mechanism involving the farmers, the company, and the government. This mechanism will set a price each year, on a cost-plus basis.

Expansion at this rate would require the addition of extension agents with tea expertise. Although a senior tea expert is already in place, additional staff would be required, consisting of graduates from agricultural schools who would need specialized company training for an additional six months. Also, the company's tea-processing facilities would have to be substantially enlarged, and packaging and distributing facilities would have to be organized.

Farmers in the area are inclined toward diversification into tea cultivation because they have suffered losses in coffee from theft and drought. One farmer I visited, who had started with six feddans of land in 1974, had expanded his holdings to twenty-nine feddans in 1983, on which he grew a sizable cash crop of coffee, in addition to such food crops as corn, cassava, groundnuts, millet, and vegetables, including tomatoes, cabbage, and carrots, largely for family consumption. The farmer explained that since his daughter had recently married the local chief, the chief's father had given him five additional feddans of land on which he was prepared to grow tea. His reasoning: In his association with the company since 1974, he had done well by branching out into the cash crop of coffee, as had his two sons, and he felt that tea would prove to be a similarly profitable enterprise. As an additional incentive for moving into tea, he cited the fact that green coffee can be stolen, and indeed is stolen, in this region of the Sudan, because many people roast their own coffee, blending it with spices of their choice. Tea, on the other hand, cannot be stolen because green tea leaves are worth nothing. They have to be processed professionally before they can be sold.

Since tea leaves remain fresh only about eight hours, expansion of tea cultivation outward from the tea-processing plant would be limited in distance. Given the inadequate infrastructure and transportation facilities in the vicinity, the effective range of recruiting farmers for tea growing would be a radius of ten miles, with an outer limit of twenty miles in some areas.

PAYOFF

For the Farmer

Payoff for the farmers associated with the Haggar Group, when they add tobacco or coffee (or tea in the future) as cash crops to their traditional subsistence production of corn or groundnuts, is very clear. For example: Net return per feddan in southern Sudan averages S£250 per year from groundnuts and S£100 (two crops) from corn. A feddan of coffee adds approximately S£1,050 to net income; a feddan of tobacco adds S£500 to S£750 per year and has the advantage of requiring only about four months of attention. An interesting sidelight on coffee prices reveals that in the major market, Khartoum, some 1,500 miles away from the Haggar contract farmers, the wholesale price of bulk coffee beans varies from S£5,000 to S£6,500 per mt; the farmer is paid S£3,500 per mt, on the average.

Viewed from a development perspective, the material effect of increased net income from adding tobacco or coffee cultivation was clearly visible. Where tobacco was being grown, radios, hand calculators, bicycles, and new roofs on the homes were everywhere in evidence. Parents also reported extended schooling opportunities available for the first time to many children, and in some cases this included going on to university. In the coffee-growing zone, one farmer showed off a new house with a zinc roof and hardboard sheets for ceilings; a storage facility for his food crops; four sons and a daughter who had between six and eight years of schooling each; and a radio/cassette player on which he could tune in to not only the regional capital of Juba and the neighboring national capitals of Kampala in Uganda and Kinshasa in Zaire, but also to the BBC and the Voice of America. He also owned a stack of cassettes.

For the Company

For the company, the payback for tobacco is immediate because all the tobacco grown is used in the blended cigarettes the company manufactures and sells itself. The payoff picture is different for coffee and tea. The payback period for these crops is between four and five years, and to make money, the company requires high sales volume and/or its own processing facilities for added value. The highest payoff is obtained when the operation is extended to packaging and retailing, which the company is planning to do for both coffee and tea.

The existence within the Haggar Group of land, sea, and air transportation companies provides an element of self-sufficiency in the Sudan, where public transport is drastically insufficient. Farmers are able to avail themselves of these transport facilities, avoiding the need to purchase or hire unreliable transportation from outside.

Payoff to the company must be evaluated in the context of bringing contract farmers into the system and maintaining extension services. Currently, the annual budget for the management and supervision of the outreach program is S£1.2 million. To defray these costs in part, Haggar borrows approximately S£1.0 million, at an interest cost of S£200,000 annually. To this must be added the following recurrent costs:

● S£260 per feddan to bring each new tobacco farmer into the system
● S£100 to maintain each tobacco farmer already in the system
● S£139 to provide extension services to all tobacco farmers supplying leaf to Haggar (2,343 in 1983, cultivating 1,793 feddans, at a total cost of S£250,000)
● S£900 to S£1,000 per feddan per year, for the full package of services brought to coffee growers

● S£1,200 per feddan, over the first three years leading to the initial harvest, for the full package of services brought to tea growers

Though no exact figures were made available, it was made perfectly clear that Haggar regards these costs as representing a good investment in current operations and in future growth.

Also relevant to payoff is the value of lessons learned and changes introduced or being considered in production, processing, and marketing. A simple example of such change is the plan to introduce mobile teams of knapsack sprayers to administer herbicides at the appropriate time. As has been learned all over the world, under tropical conditions of cultivation family labor rarely is able to control the growth of weeds in a timely and adequate way. The corporate marketing plan to package tea and coffee under its own label has already been launched. The Haggar top management is convinced that agribusiness tied to satellite farming has an enviable opportunity for growth and a broad diffusion of benefits in the Sudan, and the Haggar Group of agribusiness enterprise is leading the way.

For Suppliers and Consumers

For suppliers of inputs, the agribusiness activities of the company obviously offer new markets in a part of the world that in the past has not been a user of sophisticated agribusiness materials. Once Haggar matures its complete program of integration, linking tobacco, coffee, and tea production in southern Sudan with processing, packaging, and marketing of finished products, consumers in Sudan will have the benefit of locally produced goods, at a quality matching international standards, and not subject to price fluctuations resulting from the volatility and availability of foreign exchange. Beyond the benefit of such goods being in the marketplace, the Sudan will save considerable amounts of foreign exchange. Because the Sudan is a semisocialist state, essentially, and because so much of the economy is affected by the financial strength of the central government, foreign exchange savings are particularly important to the Sudanese people as consumers.

POLICY IMPLICATIONS

For the Company

For the company, the policy implications are expansion into tea production as quickly as is feasible as well as expansion into processing, packaging, and marketing of tea and coffee at the retail level. Achieving volume production and integrating that production into a full chain of processing and marketing would make it possible for the company to increase profit margins, to increase payment to the farmers, and to expand its outreach program.

For the Host Country

The major policy implication for the host country is clearly the upgrading, as soon as feasible, of the desperately inadequate physical infrastructure of the southern region. In addition, government encouragement of smallholder production in the private sector is desirable not only as policy, but with administrative follow-through, as a way to convert policy pronouncements into active and concrete measures.

For the Donor Country

Three positive action points seem plausible.

1. To find, or create, mechanisms that will channel funds as expeditiously and inexpensively as possible to "bush planters" for the production of cash crops to supplement their food crops and raise their living standard.
2. To devise ways in which a portion of counterpart funds (which amounted to the equivalent of US$100 million in 1984) can be channeled to the private sector.
3. To use whatever policy-making leverage the U.S. government has to persuade the government of Sudan that encouraging private investment in agribusiness would be an effective method to make use of the Sudan's comparative advantage of arable land to raise the living standards of its people and to contribute meaningfully to adjusting the present negative balance of payments between the Sudan and other countries.

7
Charoen Pokphand: Pig Raising in Four Experimental Villages in Thailand

Ruth Karen

SUMMARY

Charoen Pokphand (CP) is a Thai corporation that started in 1921 as a marketer of vegetables and is now a diversified multinational, the largest agribusiness company in Southeast Asia. In 1977, CP launched an experimental program of rural development, built around the creation of four demonstration villages, each with an economic core of pig production to be purchased by CP, and each with a design aimed at crop diversification, sometimes but not always related to the long-range plans of CP for product diversification. (Chapter 2 gives a description of an analogous corporate approach to agricultural development on the part of Hindustan Lever Limited in India.) Like the Haggar family in the Sudan (Chapter 6), the Thai family that started and still controls CP reflects a special feeling for the interdependence of the company and its economic future and the well-being of rural people as raw material suppliers, buyers of corporate products, and human beings whose needs are more than economic in nature.

Perhaps more than any other case in this book, the CP experience illustrates the extent to which agribusiness management can, at a profit to all concerned and with government approval, entwine itself with the totality of rural development during the early years of transition of rural families from subsistence to a cash economy. Four small villages have been created from nothing. Participating farm families (roughly 225) have been settled in homes provided by CP. Farmers have been given all the necessities to start pig production, and though they participate freely, they have had nothing to do with or to say about the four project designs, each different in structure and operation, into which their lives have been folded. Although philosophically heartwarming, economically successful, and intriguing in the changes the program has initiated, it is still true that the very success of each village has generated an elite that is resented by others. This is a worldwide problem that CP recognizes but has not yet dealt with.

CP has done more than establish four models of agricultural and rural development, each serving the company as a source of supply. It has also demonstrated a unique model that satisfies the demand for immediate profitability for the corporation and the farmer. Each village is designed as a profit center. All development costs have been financed by bank loans, based on feasibility studies. Production levels in each village were predetermined to yield the necessary cash flows at company processing facilities to justify the investment, and these village production goals were predetermined to yield a striking increase in net farm income compared to return from the land used for traditional crops grown in traditional ways. There is a warmth of spirit, ingenuity in planning, skill in management, level of farmer response, and degree of learning by government officials that warrants worldwide respect and study.

COUNTRY BACKGROUND

Thailand has a long tradition of agricultural production as a mainstay of the economy. (The country's classic name, Siam, means "golden" and refers to the golden rice harvest for which the country is noted.) At present, out of a total population of around 50 million, approximately 70 percent are engaged in agricultural pursuits. Nevertheless, agricultural output constitutes less than 25 percent of the gross national product (GNP), indicating an agricultural sector still largely underdeveloped, with minimal use of modern inputs and technology.

The case of Charoen Pokphand and that of Adams International, Inc. (Chapter 11) illustrate successful attempts to introduce modern agricultural practices to traditional small-scale farmers, who are provided with the necessary technical and financial assistance and who are guaranteed a market by agribusiness for the mutual benefit of both farmer and company.

Three Major Problems

The major overall problems in Thai agriculture at present are three.

1. New land for farming, in the past frequently created by clearing woodlands, with the ecological consequences this entails, is becoming scarce. On World Food Day, 1983, Minister of Agriculture Narong Wongman, publicly declared that "New land for farming in Thailand is getting scarce, and yields per hectare must be increased if the country is to remain an exporter."
2. Thailand's exports, overwhelmingly agricultural, constitute a very substantial sector of the gross domestic product (GDP). Thailand's foreign trade, imports and exports, totaled 48 percent of GDP in 1983. This makes the

country vulnerable to world economic conditions, particu- larly to the roller-coaster conditions of international agricultural trade.

3. Thailand, despite appreciable government efforts to limit it, continues to have high population growth, now largely concentrated in the underdeveloped rural areas of the North and Northeast, where children are still regarded as an investment in social security and an insurance for old age.

COMPANY BACKGROUND

History and Structure

Charoen Pokphand is a Thai enterprise that was started in 1921 as an organization selling vegetables. Today, the CP group of companies has proliferated into a range of agribusiness activities that involve fertilizers, agrochemicals, pesticides and herbicides, tractors, animal feed, livestock operations in poultry and swine, crop farming, and processing of farm produce; and in allied manufacturing, jute-backed carpets, polypropylene, and packaging. In addition, the company maintains trading offices in New York and Brussels. It is the biggest agro-industry firm in Southeast Asia.

In Asia, CP has operations in Indonesia, Malaysia, Singapore, Taiwan, Hong Kong, and the People's Republic of China. Indicatively, its joint venture in Singapore with the Singapore government is a swine-raising operation of gigantic proportions, now producing 75,000 head per year and scheduled to produce 250,000 head in the medium term.

From its operations in Thailand, the company exports frozen chickens to Japan, Singapore, the Middle East, Rumania, and Germany; live pigs to Hong Kong and Singapore; cassava and tapioca to the European Economic Community (EEC); corn to Taiwan, Singapore, Hong Kong, Japan, Malaysia, and Indonesia; fish meal to a number of Asian countries; and carpets to the EEC and the United States. Joint-venture partners in the United States are Arbor Acres (poultry); DeKalb (corn, seed, and swine production); PIC (pig stock); and Continental Grain (feed mills).

The company has 10,000 employees worldwide; 6,000 in Thailand. In terms of financial structure, the company is still privately held, with majority equity in the hands of the founding family and key executives. However, equity is being gradually spun off to all employees, and the company expects to go public within the decade.

Corporate Motivation

The company's motivation is grounded in a historical perspective, coupled with sixty years involvement in Thai farming.

Until World War II, Thai farmers were overwhelmingly subsistence farmers, who because of their limited requirements, were largely self-sufficient. They had minimal connection with the money economy. Thailand's development activities after World War II introduced roads, communications, and electricity to these farmers, integrating them into the money economy and increasing their knowledge of and demand for consumer goods. The Thai government succeeded in raising the farmers' standard of living, but that standard of living could not be sustained by traditional production methods. New ways of earning money had to be found: by increasing yields, introducing new crops, and moving into new product lines in the livestock area.

CP, which considers itself primarily an agribusiness company, and therefore closely and inescapably connected with the fortunes of the country's farmers, monitored and moved with this evolution. The company recognized, as it moved along this path, that the material development of the farmers and their symbiotic relationship with the development of the company, had social as well as economic aspects.

The group vice-president responsible for the company's livestock operations, in addition to a number of other product lines, is a former deputy minister of industry. During an interview he delineated the company philosophy:

> For a private company, profit criteria are, of course, fundamental. But profit criteria can be paired with a concern for society and the recognition that the company is an integral part of the society in which it functions. Imaginative management sees the connection between the development of the country and the development of the company. For me, the classic example of imaginative management is Henry Ford's concept of producing a car cheap enough for his employees to buy. Within its own context, each company must come up with a comparable vision. Ours is that the development of the company and of the farmers with whom we work, both as producers and consumers of our products, are intertwined.

> I would add to this that both the production and the social measurements that define this relationship can--indeed must--meet investment criteria, by which I mean a respectable return on investment [ROI].

Corporate Strategy

As a result of this corporate philosophy, CP's outreach program is an integral part of corporate strategy. That strategy is conceived in three developmental, sequential stages.

The first stage is for the company to organize small-scale farmers around the corporate core to transfer modern technology through hands-on operations, with the company providing all the required inputs and the processing and marketing of the product.

The second stage is for the farmers to become sufficiently knowledgeable and independent to employ the company as managers, marketers, or both. The third stage evolves when the children of the farmers who have participated in the first phase go to schools and colleges and acquire enough education to manage the family farm as well as the company could. This is the stage at which the farmers become a major market for the company's products.

At present, CP is engaged in Stage 1, which it launched on a systematic basis in 1977. The company is experimenting with a number of socioeconomic models, and by 1983 it had created four model villages in four different locations. The four villages are primarily concentrated on pig raising, but vary in terms of the cultivation of other farm products, ranging from growing corn and sorghum for feed to cultivating vegetable gardens. There is also a newly introduced experiment in the growing of mangoes for export.

FOUR MODEL VILLAGES

The First Village Project

The first village project was launched in 1977, in the province of Chachoengsao, on the east coast about 120 kilometers from Bangkok. The traditional crop in the area is cassava, a crop that depletes the soil of nutrients and, after several years, produces arid land on which almost nothing else can be grown. The economic implication is that this land can be bought at a relatively low price.

The company bought 1,200 rai (2.4 rai = 1 acre) of this depleted cassava land, partly from resident farmers and partly from absentee landlords. It then created an infrastructure for pig raising by leveling the land, cutting down trees, building a road, bringing in electricity, digging a well, and constructing houses for farmers and sties for pigs. For all of this infrastructure work it hired local farmers who, with cassava as their only crop, were underemployed eight months of the year.

With the infrastructure in place, the company recruited fifty farm families to participate in the pig raising scheme. Thirty-eight of the families were given breeding stock to produce piglets, and twelve families were assigned the task of fattening the piglets until ready for market. The company pays a guaranteed price for each piglet of 70 baht (the conversion rate used throughout is B23 = US$1) and a guaranteed price of B22.5 per kilogram for each fully fattened pig. Each of the fifty families was given 24 rai of land, a house, a pigsty, and full supporting services—breeding sows, appropriate feed, veterinary services, and technical training.

Land set aside for each farmer's house, pigsty, and family vegetable garden totaled 4.8 rai, leaving each farmer 19.2 rai of land to grow crops of his choice. Some farmers continued to plant cassava or rice, but most increasingly switched to the cultivation of feed crops for their pigs--that is, corn and sorghum. By 1983, this first model village had its own small mixing plant to produce the feed for all of its pig raising operations, and depended on company supplies only for the concentrate needed for optimal animal nourishment.

The latest development in this first village is that the farmers have decided to switch part of their acreage into the production of mangoes for export, growing feed grains on the remainder, and also intercropping grains with the mango trees. The company is now considering setting up a processing plant in the village for the fumigation and packing of mangoes for export.

The recruiting process. The company recruited the fifty farm families for the village in careful cooperation with the government's district officers. First priority went to farmers in the vicinity, particularly working farmers who had sold their land, or part of their land, to the company. Second priority went to landless farmers in the area who had good personal records as tenant farmers. Third priority went to casual workers with good records of industry and dependability. Candidates were identified initially by the heads of villages in the vicinity, who sent lists of candidates to the district officers. The district officers culled the list, then sent it on to the company for final selection.

The company/farmer contract. The company makes a contract, which runs for seven years, with each of the selected farm families. In the first year, in addition to providing the house, the pigsty, the land, and all the supporting services, the company furnishes the farmer with a basic stipend that will see him through the eight months it takes to raise a litter of pigs for sale. The farmer, in turn, commits himself to raising a minimum number of piglets, although he is free, and the company encourages him, to produce as many piglets above the minimum as he can. After seven years, if he fulfills his contractual obligations, the farmer gets title to the land, to his house, to the pigsty, and to all other fixed assets.

For the families who engage in pig fattening rather than pig breeding, the same two-way commitment applies, except that the hog shelter that is used for fattening becomes the common property of the twelve families engaged in that enterprise.

The Second Village Project

The second village project, launched in 1979, followed many of the same concepts as the first, but differed in some technical ways. In the first village, families and their land were grouped in four-family units to make possible optimal application of inputs such as insecticides. The insecticide spraying, however, turned out to be uncomfortable for the families during the spraying period, and in the second village, the company put family housing, gardens, and sties on one side of the village and the crop acreage on the other. It also tested new irrigation methods by building a canal from the river and a pumping station, to set up a linear sprinkling system that makes crop rotation possible.

The second village was established in the underdeveloped North, some 400 kilometers from Bangkok, where farmers traditionally grow rice. With the new irrigation system, the farmers can grow seed corn in rotation with their rice crop, which triples their income. The company provides the seed.

The Third Village Project

The third village project was started in 1980, at a location 200 kilometers north of Bangkok. In terms of product, it combines the growing of seed corn on company-irrigated land with the breeding of pigs. It has, however, a different social organization. In the first two projects, farmers are allocated their 24 rai of land on an individual basis, and assume title on an individual basis when their seven-year contract is up. The third village is organized as a common project, similar to the "moshav system" in Israel, where each of the participating families owns an equal share of the common project. Although it is too early to draw definite conclusions, there are indications that this system does not work as well as the organization of villages one and two. Common ownership appears to generate less motivation than the family-owned farms.

The Fourth Village Project

The fourth project, launched in 1981, is located across the river from the third. This last project is designed for company employees who want to retire to the country with their families. The product lines are the same--pigs and corn seed, but the village is designed for seventy-five rather than fifty families. The farmers are former clerks, drivers, and blue-collar workers whose contract with the company runs for eight years (the extra year at the beginning is for training) before they become owners of the property.

CORPORATE ECONOMIC CONSIDERATIONS

Because of its extraordinary flexibility and its broad range of activities, the company reports that its ROI has been satisfactory on each project from the very first year, and that it intends to continue its experimentations with different concepts, different models, and different ways of using the company's wide-ranging resources.

In another area of outreach activity, the company cooperates with government enterprises such as the Electricity Authority of Thailand, for whom it provides expertise on animal husbandry for people displaced by the public flood control system; and with the Ministry of the Interior, which is trying to improve production and income of farmers in the backward regions through chicken-raising projects.

Given the socioeconomic realities in which the four projects are established, and the company's own philosophy and approach, there has never been any separation between the production and outreach aspects of the enterprise. They are inescapably intertwined, and the company's financial and production calculations are based on this cohesion.

Product Strategy

From a production point of view, the company's strategy is simple: to increase productivity through the introduction of modern technology for traditional crops and to introduce new agricultural products, using all available and appropriate inputs and technology.

In an interview a senior executive illustrated the principle:

> A corn farmer in the United States gets a yield of 1.5 metric tons per rai. The traditional Thai farmer gets 350 kilograms per rai. The difference is due to the seed, fertilizer, farming methods, water, insecticides and herbicides, and mechanization. There is no reason for this discrepancy to continue. Thai soil is just about the best there is, and there is plenty of rainfall. The challenge is to approach the farmer with a packet of incentives that he can buy. This includes, in addition to the necessary inputs, appropriate financing, plus hands-on supervision and training. But even that package won't necessarily produce results. Farmers have deeply ingrained attitudes that require change. Economic motivation, while very important, is not enough in itself. The reason for that is that farming--anywhere in the world--is not only a way of earning a living, but is also a way of life.

Sociotechnical Calculations

The company's technical calculations are rooted in this recognition. In determining the optimum acreage per family and the optimum number of families per village, the company proceeded from an estimate of a desirable standard of living for the farmer. It began with a calculation of the farmer's basic spending needs on food, clothing, leisure activities and education, based on the average family size in the area. To this was added a percentage for savings, and some percentage for consumer extras to provide the necessary margin of motivation. Starting with this figure, the company then determined which agricultural products would achieve this standard of living. In the experimental villages, this proved to be a mixture of pigs and crops. Again using the basic yardstick of a desirable living standard, the number of pigs required to achieve this was determined. The company then looked at its calculations from the consumer side and determined what quantity of feed grains the farmers would have to grow for their pigs to produce animals that would meet market needs at a price consumers would find acceptable.

A company executive pointed out that this kind of figuring differs from the approach the government takes toward increasing farmer income and providing development for rural regions.

The government approach is that if they have raised a farmer's income from 50 to 100 percent, that is a great achievement and they are content with it.

The facts of life, however, are that if you increase a poor farmer's income from B500 to B1000, that is still not enough to provide a decent living standard or an effective long-range motivation for the farmer and, above all, for his children. Our calculations are based on providing an incentive not only for the farmer to cultivate his land, but for him to be able to educate his children and have them want to stay on the land.

In that way, you create a sound modern agricultural base for the country, which makes Thai products competitive on both the domestic and world markets, and turns farmers into the kind of consumers that industry needs to grow and prosper.

From a corporate point of view, we are involved in every stage of the process. That is, we provide inputs and technology at the initial stage; management and processing at the second stage; marketing new product lines, and relevant research at the third stage.

Our experience so far is that we can meet our profit criteria at every stage of the process.

Management Strategy

The company's management strategy is based on a comparable calculation. Experience showed that a village of fifty to eighty families is the optimum size for the type of hands-on management the company considers essential. CP management eschews a tall hierarchy, and embraces instead a flat, decentralized structure. For example, each village project operates as a separate profit center. It is staffed by young company managers, most of them college graduates, who put in two to four years living in the village as an ingredient of both their training and the company's career plans for them. Since the company plans to expand its activities along these project lines, it needs to build a cadre of managers who can execute the expansion, and is convinced that the best training is on-site, hands-on experience.

At the same time, the company makes every effort to insure that the village assignment is not a hardship post. It provides the best possible basic facilities for its corporate employees. There is a well-built, well-furnished house for managers, with modern plumbing, television, and pleasant eating facilities including, not unimportantly, a good cook. The company is aware that these young managers live away from their family and friends and, in compensation, tries to make their living facilities more pleasant and their living standard higher than those of their counterparts in the city.

In addition, company compensation is between 200 and 300 percent higher than the salaries these young university graduates would earn in the public sector. It should be pointed out in this context, however, that public sector salaries in Thailand are very low, comparable to the scale of compensation in Indonesia, rather than to the more adequate pay scales of countries like Singapore, Taiwan, and Korea.

To find these young managers, the company has a comprehensive recruiting system that covers all relevant institutions of higher learning in Thailand. A network of scouts, supported by well-cemented relationships with professors and school administrators, identifies candidates during their second year at university. "White elephants," which is the Thai metaphor for the best and the brightest, are offered summer jobs during their sophomore year, which gives them an opportunity to find out what the company is like, and gives the company an opportunity to train the potential employees and to observe how they handle themselves and their jobs. The "white elephants" who find a congenial place in the CP stables are then offered a career path, which can include special training while they are still at school as well as special courses and research projects that are connected with the company and its activities. After graduation, these young men are given formal training on company-owned farms: in general management as well as in specialties like pig raising, poultry cultivation, animal husbandry, veterinary science, and nutrition. In terms of assignment after training, the company has found that the best policy is to assign the trainees to the regions from which they hail, where they relate most easily to the people and their customs.

CP's relationship with the universities is cemented by company funding for eighty scholarships a year, not only in agriculture but also in the social sciences, economics, and administration. In another facet of the company's educational outreach program, CP offers one scholarship a year in each of Thailand's seventy-one provinces for the education of a poor farmer's child either in primary or in secondary school. Finally, the company is in the process of organizing a training center for farmers that offers formal courses in general management, including advance planning.

PAYOFF

For the Farmer

For the farmers, the short-range economics of this arrangement are as clearly beneficial as the long-range returns. On the
average, farmers in this area raising cassava have an income of
B500 to B700 a month. The farmers involved in the pig raising
project earn an average of B4,000 a month.
The social and developmental concomitants are unmistakable
to a visitor to the village. Individual farmers have acquired
big-ticket consumer goods, ranging from refrigerators to television sets for the home, and from motorcycles to pickup trucks for
increased mobility. More important, not only do all the children
in the village attend primary school, many go on to secondary
education, and a number of them are planning university careers.
A visit to the home of one farmer who had been a tenant
farmer, growing mainly rice before he was included in the project, revealed, in addition to a television set, a blackboard and
a literacy game with pink and blue plastic letters in his living
room, where three evenings a week he teaches his preschool children, his wife, and his mother to read and write.
The economics of this farmer's life clearly tell his tale.
As a tenant farmer he produced a rice crop worth about B30,000 a
year, of which he got to keep B4,500. It took four months to
produce the crop, and he spent the remaining eight months as a
casual laborer, earning an annual income of B10,000 to B15,000.
Now his pig raising alone brings him B3,000 a month, and in addition to growing his own vegetables for family consumption, he
produces most of the fodder for his pigs and is participating in
the mango scheme.
He does, however, report a social problem that troubles him.
His former neighbors, who are still tenant farmers and casual
workers, no longer regard him as one of their own. They see him,
with some suspicion and a great deal of envy, as a rich farmer
with whom they no longer feel comfortable. At the same time,
there are now many more farmers wishing to join the CP project
than the company can handle. This problem, in which a successful
rural development project focuses on a limited number of people
who then become an elite among their neighbors, is classical,
worldwide in its manifestation, resistant to easy solution, and
predictable from the outset of action.
CP recognizes the problem and is challenged by it; yet in
these early years of experimentation there is little it can do
but to create the models of village development, plan for additional projects, and hope that others will be encouraged by the
success of CP ventures with rural people to invest in the replication of the system over the full spectrum of agricultural opportunities that exist in Thailand. Meanwhile, CP must first
cope with the traditional habits and conservative attitudes of
small-scale Thai farmers who are reluctant to change production
techniques practiced for centuries, and even more reluctant to

switch from food crops such as rice and cassava to cash crops which normally relate to a highly volatile market. The company has addressed the general problem by giving farm families in the settlement project enough acreage to grow both food and commercial crops, as well as involve themselves with pig production. To further encourage change, CP assures the producers of a steady market at stable prices.

For the Company

Return on investment for the company has three dimensions. A financial ROI begins the very first year of operation. Tactically, the company considers the first five years of each project the developmental phase, after which the training and direct supervisory functions of the company are attenuated. The second dimension of the company's ROI comes into play at the stage when the company encourages the farmers to manage their own affairs via a board of directors made up of selected farmers, with the company assuming an advisory role, compensated by a management contract. The third dimension, which can be measured from the start-up of a village project, is the provision by CP of inputs such as feed and breeding stock, at a reasonable profit, and the provision of the processing and marketing, also at a reasonable profit. Long range, the company sees the college-educated children of these prosperous farmers managing their own family farms, with minimal outside services in either technology or management; at the same time, they will become increasingly larger customers for CP products and reliable suppliers of raw material to CP.

Payoff to CP in money terms was not quantified. It is indicative, however, that each village project has been profitable by the end of the first year of operation, and the corporation has invested B69 million in the four model villages to date. Financing has come largely from banks responding to feasibility studies prepared by CP.

Finally, return to CP has grown as the company has learned to manage the system with less application of executive time, including the time it takes to negotiate bank financing. It is expected that in the future, each village will require less managerial input, as farmers themselves become more and more competent in the administration of their own affairs. Encouraged by the early success of its satellite farming/procurement system, CP is planning to develop additional villages as sources of supply. Though an expansion in the number of villages means an expansion of CP management time devoted to the villages, it is hoped that efficiency, growth in raw material supply, and growth in the village market for CP products will more than compensate for increased costs of operation.

For the Consumer

The payoff of the CP program for the consumer is a better

product, that is more easily available at a better price.   CP's
pig raising enterprises illustrate this. The company developed a
hybrid pig for Thailand that grows faster, requires less feed,
and produces a higher percentage of meat than the traditional
Thai pig. The company began to work on this and on related technologies in the 1960s, and by the late 1970s was able to produce
a locally-bred and -raised pig that is up to world standards in
quality. With company encouragement, the technology spread.
When CP started its pig raising operations with the high-quality
hybrid, its market share was 100 percent. Today its market share
is 40 percent of an enormously enlarged base. At present, Thailand produces a hog population of 5 to 6 million head per year.

POLICY IMPLICATIONS

For Companies

The CP experience demonstrates that it is possible to meet
both profit and social criteria of performance at the village
level, as well as satisfy investment concerns for short-term returns as well as for long-term corporate growth.

For the Host Country

Until recently, the Thai government pursued what was essentially a welfare policy vis-à-vis the farmer.   It treated the
farmer as a backward child, poor and uneducated, and provided
handouts in the form of free seed, subsidized fertilizer, and
support prices. But it offered neither the full package of know-
how and services nor the motivation to make the farmer self-
supporting.
In addition, the government's attitude toward the private
sector in agriculture was that the private sector would exploit
the farmer, and was therefore not to be trusted. This attitude
is beginning to change as the government realizes that it cannot
create meaningful rural development alone. At this stage, the
government is thinking in terms of cooperation from the private
sector in rural development, and has long-term intentions of
encouraging private sector activity in agribusiness, with the
government gradually pulling out.   The kind of constructive cooperation that is possible is illustrated by CP's village projects and particularly by the farmer-recruiting process, which
involves the public sector in a very direct way, but leaves the
final decision to the private sector, where final responsibility
for success of the project lies.
A conceptual difference remains between the government and
the private sector over what rural development is and means. The
government is still inclined to think of rural development as
helping poor farmers in subsistence areas, while the private sec-

tor thinks of rural development as supporting motivated farmers
to cultivate products that meet market criteria, helping to create economically and socially self-sufficient, self-sustaining
communities.

It would be useful if the Thai Investment Board would provide the same tax and duty incentives for agriculture and agribusiness that it provides for industry. Furthermore, government
financial institutions that now exist for industry should have a
parallel network of financial institutions for commercial
agriculture. At present, government financial institutions in
agriculture are limited to servicing subsistence farmers and
farmer cooperatives.

Conceptually, what is needed on the government side is
greater recognition that any country must have a strong agricultural base in order to industrialize successfully, and that agribusinesses like CP can contribute to building, expanding, and
reinforcing this base by assisting farmers to attain new levels
of profitability and social awareness. Public policy should encourage agribusiness investment and help motivate management to
invest in the capability of Thai farmers to reach competitive
levels of production. This kind of interaction between the public and private sectors of all industrialized countries, and of
the more successful developing nations, has been basic to economic growth and social progress.

For the Donor Country

In the past, U.S. policy has channeled USAID funds only to
governments and to the military. The new emphasis on the private
sector, and direct contact with the private sector, with government encouragement and support, is likely to bring a positive
dynamic to the entire aid process. The allocation of USAID resources toward bringing together the private sector of the donor
country with the appropriate partner in the host country will
undoubtedly have more immediate and direct results than channeling funds to government organizations and institutions, where
demonstrable development results may or may not be achieved.

8
Productos del Monte: A Vegetable and Fruit Canning Operation in Mexico

Simon Williams

SUMMARY

Productos del Monte (PDM) is a wholly owned subsidiary of the Del Monte Corporation. PDM entered Mexico in the early 1950s, not as a manufacturer but as an exporter of canned goods, selling through a Mexican distributor. Between 1957 and 1960, the company investigated the feasibility of growing a wide range of fruits and vegetables in Central Mexico. In June 1962, PDM completed its first pack at its cannery in Irapuato, consisting of tomatoes, tomato products, and chilies. By 1982, sixty-nine items were offered for sale. With the exception of canned white asparagus exported to Europe, all products are for the Mexican market.

PDM, along with several other food processors in the area-- for example, Campbell Soup Company (Chapter 13, Section 3), Bird's Eye Foods, and most recently, Green Giant (Chapter 13, Section 3)--pioneered in the development of a "satellite farming" raw material supply system that became a powerful force in revo- lutionizing the agricultural economy of central Mexico. Companies like PDM played a decisive role in justifying public investment in supportive infrastructure, particularly in irrigation, trans- portation, and communication. By 1983, PDM was contracting 8,750 acres, held by 140 farmers, 130 of whom were private land owners, and 10 of whom were ejidatarios (members of a land tenure system unique to Mexico). Contract farmers supply 80 percent of cannery requirements; the rest is purchased on the open market, or, with regard to asparagus, is grown under company control on farms leased or owned by PDM. Historically, PDM and other food proces- sors in Mexico have tended to contract more with larger-scale commercial farmers than with small-scale farmers. This case study notes some serious problems that this emphasis has created and the new directions the company has taken and may take as a consequence.

A staff of nine agronomists is responsible for the satellite farming supply system. Each year, to ensure fair and affordable prices to both farmer and company, the staff calculates on-farm production costs and discusses these with farmers before setting the contract price.   PDM does not extend normal credit for crop practice.   Each farmer must negotiate credit needs with banks, using the PDM contract only as verification of ability to manage a loan.   On the other hand, a fundamental aspect of farmer loyalty and the relationship of confidence and trust between agronomist and farmer is the willingness of PDM to provide credit additions for such emergencies as a severe and unexpected pest infestation or a personal crisis.   PDM helps to minimize the investment of farmers in heavy equipment by maintaining an extensive pool of agricultural machinery that, with the approval of an agronomist, is rented out at a cost well below company cost of capital, operation, and maintenance. A key to the success of the procurement system is the constant contact between agronomists and farmers during a crop season.   PDM does not conduct crop research in the traditional sense, but the staff constantly seeks out improved practices elsewhere for adaptation locally.

COUNTRY BACKGROUND

The color and character of Mexico are difficult to capture and comprehend.   The nation is an active compound of diverse and ancient indigenous cultures that have left their stamp on the physical structure, art forms, craft designs, rural clothing, and village customs of the majority of Mexicans, especially the rural folk.   Inextricably mixed with this legacy is the powerful influence of three centuries of Spanish colonial rule and four centuries and more of the pervasive impact of the Catholic church. These imports provided a unifying language and a widespread codification of values.   At the same time, they introduced the hacienda system of land use and an extravagant social order that essentially disenfranchised practically all rural people, reducing them to a state of peonage that lasted 300 years, a yoke of underdevelopment still borne by all of Mexico.

The manner of Mexico is also deeply rooted in the success of the 1810 revolution of independence from Spain and in the fierce sense of pride and nonalignment that marks Mexico today in world affairs, particularly as it tries to adjust to its entanglement with the economy, mores, and politics of the United States. But the avid thrust of Mexico into the modern world really dates back to the 1910 agrarian revolution, which threw off the last vestiges of the hacienda system, returned the beloved land to the people as their rightful patrimony, and led to the 1917 constitution, which has guided the country ever since. And, although the constitution does not specifically provide for this, since 1917 Mexico has been led by one absolutely dominant political party, the Partido Institucional Revolucionario (PRI). The PRI attempts to house and harmonize the needs of all people, in all walks of life, raising the question: In what proportions is Mexico a blend of democracy and autocracy?

Understanding Mexico, being able to distill from history the essences essential to a working understanding of the rules of behavior and law governing relationships between private enterprise and the Government of Mexico (GOM), has always been important but never easy for foreign investors. The financial crisis of 1982 thoroughly confused the picture, making the task that much harder. There is no better measure of the doubts and uncertainties generated abroad by the crisis than the decline of capital inflows from over US$1 billion in 1982 to less than US$200 million in 1983.

Some observers reckon that how Mexico deals with the financial crisis will have as profound an effect as anything that has happened in the country since the revolution for independence. Certainly, the Mexican government has taken drastic steps in its attack on the problem. Among other actions, nationalization of the banking system; currency controls; sharp and continuing devaluations of the peso; major cuts in imports, particularly in the areas of capital goods, spare parts, and luxury consumer items; a significant decline in public works; and withdrawal of a wide variety of subsidies--all strongly influenced by the terms of an agreement with the International Monetary Fund--yielded encouraging results in 1983.

Inflation decreased from well over 100 percent in 1982 to 80 percent in 1983, with a goal of 40 percent in 1984. National accounts were in a stronger position in 1983, and management of the huge external debt seemed to be well accepted internationally. The government of President de la Madrid has strongly endorsed support for the further development of the In-Bond Assembly (Maquiladora) Industry, both along the U.S.-Mexican border and inland. In December 1983, GOM officially created a national commission to facilitate and promote foreign investment (Comisión Nacional de Inversiones Extranjeras), within the Ministry of Commerce and Industrial Development. Although few would venture a long-range forecast for the economy of Mexico and the durability of traditional support for a mixed economy, short-range indicators are modestly encouraging. After two years (1982 and 1983) of negative growth, in 1984 the economy held its own, setting up conditions for an economic recovery beginning in 1985.

Agriculture and agro-industry are deeply entwined in this context of change and uncertainty, and though the share of gross domestic product (GDP) contributed by agriculture has declined from 14 percent in 1965 to an estimated 8.7 percent in 1982, Mexico cannot hope to resolve its current and future economic and social problems without sweeping improvements in the performance of its agricultural sector. Roughly half the population is rural. Roughly half the labor force is employed in agriculture and related agro-industry. Basic foodstuffs are in short supply. Imports of wheat, corn, sorghum, vegetable oil, oilseeds, nonfat dry milk, rice, and breeding animal stock head a growing list of requirements. Rural poverty continues to be the driving force of migration to the cities and to the United States, and remains a major drag on the entire economy.

Constraints on improvements in agricultural performance are formidable. Of Mexico's total area of 197 million hectares (1 hectare = 2.5 acres), GOM considers 39 million as arable, 78 million as range land, and 44 million as suitable for forestry. Yet in 1983, President de la Madrid reported that the total harvested area in 1982 was estimated at 16 million hectares, of which 34 percent was irrigated. It is difficult to imagine how this farmed area can be greatly expanded. Money for infrastructure improvement is in very short supply. Water for irrigation is limited and though nearly 90 percent of public expenditures in the agricultural sector during the last thirty years went for capital and current costs in irrigated areas, further expansion is becoming more difficult and less cost effective. On the other hand, rainfall is poorly distributed seasonally and unless irrigation is available, most land is idle in the winter. Not only is rainfall seasonal, it is also highly variable and may exceed or fall short of "normal" by 30 to 50 percent in one out of three years.

Beyond the classic limitations on agriculture imposed by climate, soil, topography, and other physical factors, the peculiarities of land tenure, agrarian law, and the pervasive role of government are powerful forces affecting the future of farming and food processing in Mexico.

Land Tenure

Land tenure falls into two dominant patterns, the ejidal system and the system of small-scale, privately-owned farms known as the pequeño proprietarios.

The ejidal system. This system arose out of the 1910 agrarian revolution in an effort to help formerly landless peasants make a transition from centuries of serfdom to responsible participation in their new democracy. Ejidal land belongs to GOM and is considered part of the national patrimony. About one-half of all land and roughly one-half of all rural people fall within the system, which is administered by the Ministry of Agrarian Reform.

Groups of ejidatarios (farmers) form an ejido (a community) and each farmer has a homestead, generally centralized and off the farmland. Some ejidos operate their land collectively and share in crop proceeds. The majority allow members to operate individually and freely. Most ejidal farms are smaller than twenty hectares; the majority range from one to ten hectares.

Rights to land use can be passed on to a surviving wife or children, but the land can never be sold or mortgaged. Individuals, groups, and an ejido itself can enter into supply, purchase, or credit contracts, and may organize profit-making businesses. Recent changes in agrarian law allow for joint ventures with private-sector, off-farm partners, although in practice this law has been little tested. It is intriguing to note that the Bank of Mexico (the central bank), utilizing the financial and legal power vested in a group of trust funds for agricultural development, is actively searching for such joint venture opportunities. The lead agency of the bank in this regard is FIRA (Fideicomisos Instituidos en Relación con la Agricultura).

Pequeño proprietarios. This system covers roughly 45 percent of all land and includes perhaps 45 percent of the rural population. Farm size is well defined by law. It varies up to several hundred hectares, depending upon such variables as the crop grown, whether the land is irrigated, and whether it is used for crops or as rangeland. The majority of pequeño proprietarios are small- to very small-scale operators, their farms ranging downward from ten hectares. An increasing number, however, operate units that are larger than the law provides for and have become truly commercial, well-capitalized, and highly mechanized units. This is accomplished by owners who control adjacent farms registered in the names of others who collaborate in evading the intent of agrarian reform. Some existing food-processing corporations, both Mexican and international, have found it convenient to contract for raw materials from these larger farms, with dubious propriety.

Agrarian Law

Agrarian law, another major influence, has a dominant theme, vital to appreciate. The land is the greatest heritage of the people and the benefits that derive from it must in the end flow equitably to the people. True, Mexico has yet to achieve this equity. True, the law keeps changing. It is often confusing and contradictory. It is violated often, and too frequently without redress. Probably few people have ever read all the law or could act upon it with authority. However, agrarian law captures a large part of the spiritual character of Mexico and to grasp it, to incorporate it into the design of an agro-industrial venture, is to come a long way toward a good fit into the country. The law suggests why a nucleus estate, as a self-owned source of supply for a food processor, would be at odds with policy. The law in its essence supports a decision to work with small-scale farmers in a contracted supply system rather than with commercial farmers. In other words, as one scholar in agrarian law put it: "The spirit of the law may be a far better light to follow in considering a foreign investment in agro-industry in Mexico, than the pathways to alternative structures defined by the codified rules."

The Pervasive Role of Government

A third and pervasive force is government intervention at every point along the food chain from farmer to consumer, and from farmer to export market. The volume, nature, and cost of agricultural credit is essentially dictated. The price of basic crops such as corn, sorghum, wheat, rice, beans, and coffee, is controlled by price floors. The price of some foodstuffs, raw or processed, is also controlled. GOM manufactures or imports all fertilizer; manufactures farm equipment and trucks; operates the largest retail food chain in the country; and subsidizes consumer costs in the face of competition from privately held supermarket chains. The railroads and airlines are public. GOM, in other words, is to be dealt with at every turn.

It is also true that Mexico has always taken great pride in its mixed economy. A wide variety of agro-industries, many owned outright or controlled by foreign private investors, have prospered in Mexico. Even during the current financial crisis and the extension of increasing GOM controls over the productive sector, there are many assurances that a strong, competitive private sector must exist alongside dynamic public participation in manufacturing and marketing. The point for new investors in Mexico is, however, that no industry in the country has a more continuous or more sensitive interface with government than agro-industry.

ENTERPRISE BACKGROUND

Productos Del Monte is a wholly owned subsidiary of the Del Monte Corporation, since 1979 a subsidiary of R.J. Reynolds Industries, Inc. PDM cans and bottles vegetables and fruits, the latter only sold in the form of jam. With the exception of canned white asparagus, which is exported to Europe, the entire product line is marketed in Mexico. Since its inception, investment in PDM has totaled approximately US$40 million.

The cannery is located in Irapuato, in the state of Guanajuato, roughly 200 miles north-northwest of Mexico City. Procurement of raw material and all manufacturing is centered in Irapuato. Overall company management, fiscal control, sales, and government relations are located in Mexico City.

Raw material flows to the cannery from three different sources: contract or satellite farmers, the open market, and farms operated by PDM. Contract farmers are located within a 30-mile radius of the plant, and supply roughly 80 percent of requirements. In 1983, material was received from 140 farmers, 10 of whom were ejidatarios. The contracted area was 3,500 hectares. The open market may, depending upon need and time of year, be anywhere in Mexico. PDM farms are operated by a wholly owned subsidiary, Frutas y Verduras Selectas, S.A., which farms asparagus only on six ranches, four leased and two owned. The total area farmed is 250 hectares. These ranches produced 25 percent of the asparagus canned in 1983; eventually it is planned that PDM will grow at least 50 percent of its needs. In such an event, PDM will take a major step toward operating a nucleus estate and will be unique among foreign-owned agro-industries in Mexico.

The decision to create Frutas y Verduras, which is really a nucleus estate, is understandable and pragmatic in terms of protecting a vitally important product line. Nonetheless, it places PDM in a predicament vis-à-vis public land use policy and the intent of agrarian reform. It may be broadly instructive to outline the origin and nature of the dilemma faced by the company.

Ideally, cultivation of asparagus requires relatively large areas of contiguous land. In the case of PDM practice, eight hectares would be a minimum. Several hundred hectares would be preferable. Equally important, asparagus farmers must be able to finance the crop. In 1983, per hectare investment in starting production was about 400,000 pesos (conversion rate in 1983 averaged P160 = US$1) per hectare, and having made the investment, the farmer must wait four years after planting before a first harvest. The combined prerequisites effectively eliminate truly small-scale pequeño proprietarios and ejidatarios from participating in the benefits of cultivating asparagus.

The result has been that as PDM pioneered the crop and provided limited financial assistance, such as soft financing of planting stock, it contracted with the commercial farmers of the area who had the land and had access to the necessary credit. Yet experience demonstrated that working with such farmers does not necessarily secure sources of supply.

It is an intriguing comment on human behavior, of relevance all over the world, that though PDM and neighboring agribusinesses introduced most of the vegetables grown in their area, the most successful farmers have become the most difficult in their contract relationships. As they have become wealthy and expanded their farms (in violation of the spirit, if not the letter, of the law), they have become independent of market security, technical assistance, and credit offered by PDM. They now tend to dispute prices; at times they break their contracts if prices at harvest rise beyond expectation. They have introduced an intolerable uncertainty into the flow of raw material.

Faced with this emerging situation, PDM had two choices. The more difficult one, which PDM decided against (although there is ample evidence that it can be managed in Mexico), was to catalyze the organization of groups of small-scale farmers and then to aggregate adjacent lands into suitable asparagus farms. This was judged to be too slow, too risky, and likely beyond corporate competence. The choice PDM made was to both rent and acquire land, farm it, and exercise control over production in the mode of a nucleus estate, while continuing to contract with some farmers with whom steadfast relationships were being maintained.

It may well be that the solution chosen by PDM will demonstrate how to help resolve a general problem in Mexico, namely, how to increase agricultural productivity so that the goal of food self-sufficiency can be reached. However, by depending upon company-owned asparagus farms and upon commercial farmers who are at risk because of the manner of land accumulation, PDM may be exposed to criticism over an apparent return to a colonial view of rural people and land use.

From the beginning, PDM has maintained an extensive Agricultural Department that provides technical assistance to contract farmers; seeks out new contract farmers as needed; searches for supplies in the open market; and maintains and supervises the use of a pool of PDM agricultural machinery (like pea harvesters) available for certain farm practices. The staff also assists contract farmers who may solicit PDM for credit over and above that borrowed from banks and supports the manager of Frutas y Verduras Selectas, S.A., himself the manager of the Agricultural Department.

In terms of manufacturing costs and selling prices, PDM operates under continuously trying conditions. The raw materials purchased by the cannery are priced without GOM intervention. Each year, prior to contract negotiations, the Agricultural Department makes careful analyses, crop by crop, of on-farm production costs, which then serve to help establish a price that is fair and understandable to all farmers and absorbable by the cannery. It is a compliment to PDM staff that there is widespread acceptance of the integrity of the calculations and the honesty of cannery management in its efforts to ensure a reasonable profit to both farmer and company. Inevitably, the policy and procedures followed have meant steady increases in raw material costs.

Yet in 1983, over 50 percent of the PDM product line was price-controlled, at levels generally inconsistent with rising costs of raw materials, manufacturing, and marketing. This situation has considerably narrowed the margin between cost and income, which, when combined with inflation and peso devaluation, has had a serious and negative impact on profit. In 1983, for example, PDM made a modest profit in pesos but generated a dollar loss of roughly US$1 million. Communicating the stark realities of the interplay of all these forces to GOM, so that corrective measures will be introduced into public policy, while managing the variables at play to reduce costs, surely presents PDM with one of its most challenging tasks for the 1980s.

History

Del Monte entered Mexico in the early 1950s, not as a manufacturer but as an exporter from the United States working through a Mexican distributor. By mid-decade, product acceptance encouraged the corporation to select a site for a cannery in central Mexico, in a zone where public investment in infrastructure, with an emphasis on irrigation facilities, promised a flexible, diversified source of raw material. At the same time, between 1957 and 1960, PDM began investigations into suitable practices covering a wide range of fruits and vegetables.

By June 1962, PDM completed its first pack, consisting of tomatoes, tomato products, and chilies. By 1982, sixty-nine items were offered for sale. At the start of operations, PDM focused entirely on the domestic market. In part, this decision was based on the promise of a rapidly expanding market among the urban middle class. The decision was also influenced by the fact that PDM marketing strategy had to fit into the worldwide network of production and distribution of its parent corporation, a constraint on the growth and profitability of PDM that persists today. The one important break in this pattern came with the introduction of white asparagus into the line, which as already noted, is exported to Europe via the Del Monte marketing organization there.

Del Monte entered Mexico at a most favorable time. During the late 1960s and throughout the decade of the 1970s (even after 1976, when the first devaluation of the peso foreshadowed the crisis of 1982), the economy of Mexico boomed. Rising income and expectations characterized millions of Mexicans clustered in the cities near the cannery at Irapuato. Changing diets favored consumption of PDM products, so there was a ready market, easily reached. Mexico flourished during those halcyon years. Did PDM?

Del Monte Corporation felt it inappropriate to reveal the profit history of PDM. It was pointed out, with justifiable pride, that for PDM to have operated continuously for nearly a quarter-century is a clear signal that the investment was solidly based and was justified by events. However, a caveat was sounded, withal indirectly, that return on equity may not always have lived up to corporate expectations. This may have been tolerable in the past. The crisis of 1982 raised new questions: Are the factors threatening private, foreign-owned agro-industries, such as inflation, devaluation of the peso, price controls, and import controls, manageable? Does PDM have the opportunity to reduce costs, modernize its plant, expand its market, shift to more profitable lines, reduce dependency on price-controlled items?

For the immediate future, Del Monte Corporation and R.J.Reynolds Industries seem to have decided that PDM should stay; that the efforts of GOM to correct its financial course can be rationalized satisfactorily; and that there are a variety of challenging but feasible ways for PDM to improve upon its performance and prosper with Mexico as the country recovers the pace of its growth. Therefore, in 1983, a new management team at PDM set in motion a "crisis plan" based on six short- and long-term changes.

1. Reduce the number of price-controlled items in the product line.
2. Build an in-house capability to design and fabricate machinery and machine parts required to renovate the plant. This project was initiated in 1983, under the guidance and tutelege of experts sent to Mexico from other Del Monte locations. The effort was herculean; results were very gratifying. The work of training and implementation will continue as intensely as possible. In combination with some easing of import restrictions promised for 1984 by GOM, the hope is that full operating efficiency can be attained in the near future.
3. Up-date the marketing information base. A 1983 study revealed that the data base was inadequate and outdated, resulting in weak or nonexistent distribution in large areas of Mexico and, perhaps, in export markets that might be penetrated without conflict with other Del Monte operations outside of Mexico. Corrective measures are already being taken. New data are being collected. Thirty-five product lines are being eliminated as new ones are being contemplated.

4. Up-date and tighten quality control. Another study in 1983 noted that quality control measures had been neglected, with resultant operating losses, as well as damage to the consumer image of the Del Monte label. Both the facilities and techniques of quality control have already been greatly improved.
5. Initiate a search for new methods of packaging. Packaging has become the single largest item of cost in manufacturing. A can or a bottle may be more expensive than the ingredients. This may be one of the most intransigent of the problems being faced, even though Del Monte Corporation has been at the forefront of packaging innovations in the United States. Not only is new packaging machinery costly, it is difficult either to finance or to obtain import licenses. Many new forms of packaging depend on materials no more practical to buy in Mexico than tin or glass. Still, management is determined to attack the problem.
6. Intensify government relations, in a major effort to obtain concessions that would ease the squeeze on profits resulting from unrealistic price ceilings on certain canned vegetable products, especially those produced in large volume.

Outreach

PDM outreach is confined essentially to the procurement of crops from contract farmers, and is the responsibility of the PDM Agricultural Department (AD). Although AD no longer conducts crop-practice research in a formal sense, it may, on occasion, conduct tests of new practices already being applied successfully elsewhere. Because of their continuous contact with contract farmers, year in and year out, AD staff may, in an informal way, interact much as any good extension worker would to answer a broad range of technical and farm management questions. PDM as a company and AD as a technical resource have a fine reputation in the area of contracting, an asset that is carefully nurtured and guarded.

AD is staffed with a director and eight other agronomists, augmented from time to time with new graduates of agricultural universities who serve as apprentices. Apprenticeship may or may not lead to a permanent AD job, but the graduate receives valuable hands-on experience while AD is given time to evaluate performance, should a staff vacancy occur. PDM has learned that AD must function as a close-knit team, and to do so, a basic requirement is good transportation and communication equipment. All full-time AD staff have, therefore, a late model pickup truck, with two-way radio-telephone systems linking the central office at the plant and all vehicles as they circulate in the contract area. Each vehicle is also in communication with any and all others. The 1984 AD budget is P28.4 million (about $168,000). As previously noted, the AD director also serves as manager of

Frutas y Verduras, S.A. and is supported by the AD staff as
needed.

Each agronomist is a crop specialist. It is his responsibility to contract the necessary supply and to provide technical
assistance for each step in the crop cycle. At such times as agronomists are between crop cycles, they assist others who may be
at the peak of their work. In this way, every farmer is visited
at least twice a week during his agricultural year. Specifically, AD services are as follows:

Technical on-farm assistance. This activity is the highest
priority, as it can make or break a procurement program. If it
is effective, it breeds responsible performance, respect between
AD and its suppliers, and loyalty over time as the ups and downs
of farming encourage or discourage participation.

Technical assistance starts with an evaluation of the land
being offered for a given crop and of the farmer himself. The
area is surveyed, to be sure it is adequate and to facilitate
calculations of costs of production, prices to be set in contracts, and income to be expected by the farm family. Soil suitability and availability of water are determined. If the practice calls for the use of machinery from PDM equipment pools, is
there access to the fields? If larger units of land are required
than the farmer can offer, is it feasible to aggregate holdings
with neighbors? As best he can, the AD agronomist assesses the
character, farming skill, and reputation of the farmer, as well
as the ability of the farmer to finance his credit. This is an
important consideration because PDM policy is to keep to an absolute minimum the money tied up in providing credit. As will be
seen, PDM does exercise flexibility and compassion in the provision of credit under emergency conditions, but insists that in
the first instance, farmers work directly with banks.

During a crop cycle, the AD agronomist offers constant guidance to ensure that each step in the recommended practice is
taken on time and with care. The object of this supervision is to
stimulate farmers to participate in each decision and to facilitate this role by educating the farmer about the reasons behind
the practice. If an emergency arises requiring additional credit
a farmer may solicit an agronomist, who makes a determination of
the validity of the request and what may be needed. The agronomist immediately makes his recommendation to the manager of AD,
who passes it on to the production manager of the cannery. The
production manager is empowered to grant the credit, usually in
kind. PDM maintains a stock of agricultural chemicals and other
inputs, which it purchases as cheaply as possible and dispenses
at cost.

AD staff provide a myriad of other on-farm services. If a
farmer needs transportation help, the staff may locate and intervene in negotiations with private firms, required at harvest. If
machinery is required from the PDM equipment pools, the agronomist may expedite the order. If the design of a small-scale irrigation system to serve a group of neighboring farmers is de-
sired, AD can help.

Technical off-farm assistance. This, of course, pays off
only when transferred to the farm. Such assistance is important
but less structured in the work program of AD staff.   There is a
never-ending search for techniques to extend the productive season and increase productivity. The first goal is to increase the
number of months during which the cannery can operate; the second
is to bring the daily throughput at the cannery into optimum balance with capacity. Associated lines of inquiry are: how to
bring contract production of all requirements ever closer to the
cannery to reduce the subsidy on transportation costs; and how to
educate farmers to their real costs, so that price negotiations
can be facilitated when contracts are up for renewal.

Facilitation of credit. As already observed, PDM contract
farmers are expected to arrange financing directly with banks. In
no case will PDM guarantee a bank loan.   It will advise a bank,
if asked, as to the existence and nature of a contract and will
record PDM experience with a farmer-applicant.   Over the years,
area banks have come to value both personal commendations from
PDM and the fact that a farmer has a PDM contract.   In general,
this policy has served its purposes well and PDM management feels
that farmers have truly benefited by their direct interaction
with credit institutions.   In any event, PDM has never faced a
problem when seeking contracts with producers, although turnover
does both complicate and add cost to the system, year after year.

Despite a basic policy that deflects most credit needs of
contract farmers to the attention of banks, PDM does tie up a
considerable amount of money in various forms of credit and subsidies, which over the years have been built into different crop
production practices. In 1983, for example, roughly P400 million
(about US$2.5 million) were in circulation as cash, value of
seed, subsidies to transport costs, and subsidies of the cost of
using PDM agricultural machinery. It may be useful to illustrate
how subsidies, intrinsically part of a credit system, and used in
part as an incentive for farmers both to contract the sale of
crops to an agro-industry and to adhere to recommended practices,
quickly becomes large, complex, and almost impossible to abandon
or transfer to an external source like a bank.   In the case of
PDM, these subsidies may include free seed, partial payment for
transport of crops to the cannery after harvest, partial payment
for the rent of agricultural machinery, total cost of aerial
spraying, and the total cost of technical assistance.

Most contracted crops require the use of imported seed. PDM
buys the seed and, except in the case of asparagus, supplies it
free to farmers.   In 1983, exclusive of asparagus, PDM invested
roughly P53 million (about $332,000) in imported seed. The case
of asparagus is especially illustrative.

Farmers buy asparagus planting stock from PDM, which imports
the seed and grows it to transplant size in a company-controlled
nursery.   This quality control is vital and permits PDM to guarantee performance if all other steps in the production practice
are followed.   Although PDM sells the planting stock at cost,
nonetheless the farmer must invest about P160,000 ($1,000) per
hectare at planting time or almost half his total investment in

starting a new asparagus crop. (By way of comparison, the total credit needs for pea production in 1983 added up to about P48,000, or $300, recoverable the same year at a profit.) The farmer must then wait four years for his first harvest. As an incentive, when PDM first introduced asparagus in the early 1960s, the company agreed to sell the planting stock on credit. For the first three years, the farmer paid no principal and no interest. Beginning with his first harvest, interest, at the same cost of money to PDM, is applied, and the loan becomes payable in four to five years.

When farmers are required to arrange and pay for transporting harvested crops to the cannery, PDM pays 50 percent of this cost as a direct subsidy, and has done so from the beginning of operations. Farmers who use PDM machinery pay only 50 percent of the real cost to PDM of owning, maintaining, fueling, and operating this equipment. Further, the availability of the machinery adds another burden of vigilance to the task of each agronomist, who must see to it that farmers do not order out PDM machinery when they own equipment capable of doing the job, just to save money.

Finally, when aerial spraying of pesticides is necessary, as with sweet corn, PDM provides this service free; when other specialized chemical treatments, like the inoculation of pea seed are required, this service is provided free; and farmers pay nothing for the technical assistance services provided by AD.

The technical assistance and credit program of PDM does work. Raw material of satisfactory quality and quantity generally arrive on schedule to the cannery. The beneficial contributions of PDM to the agricultural economy of the area are impressive and unquestioned. Still, as the company pushes ahead to implement its "crisis plan," several questions relating to the cost of the raw material procurement program persistently puzzle management. Is the methodology too costly relative to profit margins achievable in the product line? If so, how can outstanding cash balances be reduced, along with subsidies and the cost of AD itself? Has the chosen methodology led PDM into too paternalistic a mode vis-a-vis contract farmers? If so, how can the company achieve to a new, high level of a shared responsibility and risk taking with producers? Is PDM at risk because it depends so much on farmers who operate at the margins of agrarian law because their farms are so large? Can PDM afford to take a neutral position on this matter simply because it is customary practice and beyond any control by PDM? Is there additional risk of conflict with public policy due to the creation of Frutas y Verduras Selectas, S.A.? Would answers to these questions provide insights into methods PDM might use to relate procurement more closely to the development of small-scale farmers whose productivity, income, and advancement are of elemental importance to Mexico?

It was significant that these same kinds of questions were threaded through my conversations about PDM and other agro-industries of foreign origin with Mexican experts in banking, economic analysis, agrarian law, and government policy. Throughout, it was agreed that companies like PDM are vitally important to the food economy of the nation. It was also suggested that the industry could and should take more initiative in tapping the latent capability of small-scale farms to become a vigorous part of the commercial sector of agriculture. The significance of such initiative was emphasized many times by references to the belief of many in government that GOM should take a stronger, not a weaker, position in control over the productive sector.

PAYOFF

For the Farmer

A view of payoff depends as much on the values and perspectives of the observer as it does on the facts interpreted. There are two fundamentally different, though not necessarily conflictive ways of analyzing the case.

One view perceives a variety of benefits resulting from the presence of PDM that are unequivocal and unarguably benign. Several thousand people, never before so employed, receive regular income; in family terms, this means that some 15,000 to 20,000 people share this good fortune. New skills have been transferred to contract farmers, as well as new concepts of farm management and new visions of personal capability. A one-channel, assured marketing system has been provided. Payments from sales are prompt and the bases of contract prices shared in understanding with all concerned. Competent, continuous technical assistance has been made available. Emerging credit needs have been met. Dependency on bureaucratic machinery has been minimized.

PDM has contributed to a sense of security among its steady farmer-suppliers. They have a sense of having a strong, knowledgeable representative in faraway centers of power. The farmers believe that their local connection with PDM will, in fairness to everyone's self-interest, keep things going, good times or bad. In both qualitative and quantitative terms, the perspective of these observations projects a clear image of beneficial impact and raises the question: What more should be expected of a private, profit-making agro-industry?

Without detracting from the flow of benefits outlined above, a second view of payoff looks at PDM in light of this question, or, put another way, in light of the development issues that the PDM experience brings into focus. This second view perceives that the raw material procurement system evolved at PDM, with its emphasis on the use of large farms and its current trend toward company farms, may well generate a negative impact on the majority of rural people. The system encourages the buy-out of small-scale pequeño proprietarios and forces up the price of land. It encourages commercial farmers to flout the intent of agrarian reform. The system tends to discourage efforts to organize, train, and lead small-scale farmers so that in the aggregation of their talents, intelligence, and physical resources they can partici- pate more dynamically and share in economic progress. The system may be retrogressive philosophically because it downgrades the potential of the Mexican campesino, (the country folk) and finds reasons to bypass them in the process of commercializing agricul- ture.

My discussions of the PDM payoff to the people of Mexico, from the standpoint of integrated rural development, were not confrontational, nor were they held in an atmosphere of anti- business, romanticism, or innocence. The Mexicans interviewed unanimously supported the existence of private agro-industry, ex- emplified by PDM. The realities of survival in the ambience of Mexico today were not minimized. The necessity of being competi- tive and earning a profit were well understood. Conversely, the realities facing Mexico impose certain unusual demands on the in- dustry. Mexico must decrease its dependency on food imports. It must increase the productivity of the small-scale farms that pre- dominate in the agricultural sector. It must alleviate the pov- erty and inequity that permeate rural life. It cannot continue to blink at violations of agrarian reform under pressure from a few and because of the questionable argument that large-scale, capital-intensive farming and ranching is the only route to ef- ficiency. Private agribusiness, these Mexicans insisted, has a unique opportunity and responsibility to help resolve these dif- ficult, seemingly intransigent national problems.

A review of these complex issues, with both the president of PDM and the production manager of the cannery, brought out no fundamental disagreements. However, two things were made clear. Because PDM relates to a relatively small number of suppliers, any long-range value to Mexico of a shift to truly small-scale farmers would have to derive from the replicability of methodol- ogy employed. Any plan of action would require such a concept. Further, at this moment in PDM and Mexican history, the cost of developing a prototype, as well as the time required, could not feasibly be borne by PDM alone, nor allocated from the workload of the company Agricultural Department.

Subsequently, I discussed the matter with the director gen- eral of FIRA (Fideicomisos Instituidos en Relación con la Agri- cultura), at the Bank of Mexico. FIRA had been reviewing pre- cisely the range of issues noted above and would be extremely in- terested in facilitating a shift by PDM (and any other similar enterprises in the private sector) to closer long-range relation- ships with larger numbers of small-scale farms. FIRA support might take the form of grants-in-aid, soft loans, policy approv- al, and possible staff assistance.

The roots of FIRA's interest are intriguing. In contradis- tinction to many people in GOM, some leaders of FIRA recognize very clearly the actual and potentially great importance of the food processors in the private sector as engines of change. There also exists an appreciation that FIRA itself, holding both public funds and public policy in its trust, has an obligation to create and test innovative forms of partnership between the public and private sectors. As mentioned earlier in this chapter, one way FIRA has already responded has been to lead the search for investors who would enter into joint ventures of a profit-making nature with ejidos. The idea of such ventures, entirely novel in Mexico, is now embodied in law.

Two tentative steps were taken toward implementing action. The idea of a venture with FIRA was discussed with the president of PDM, who expressed keen interest in the possibility. Second, contact was made with Coordinación Rural, A.C., a skilled and experienced organization in the field of integrated rural development in Mexico (see Chapter 13, Section 12, and note name change to the Instituto para el Desarrollo Rural Integral Autosuficiente, S.C.). This organization expressed keen interest in collaborating with PDM and FIRA. The entire matter was left pending but with a commitment on the part of Coordinación Rural to develop a program of action for further consideration.

For the Company

No data were given to quantify the payoff of PDM to the Del Monte Corporation over the years. Clearly, by whatever standards were used, the return on investment was sufficient to keep PDM in continuous operation for over twenty years and to justify the current determined effort to stay in Mexico in the face of great difficulty and uncertainty. Del Monte rightly takes considerable pride in the fact that it has never withdrawn an operation from a country once the investment was committed.

In this sense, the sustaining power of PDM and its inherent strength in dealing with Mexico in the 1980s seems to be a source of considerable satisfaction to the people of Del Monte. In the qualitative sense, it is remembered with a deep sense of gratification that Del Monte was a pioneer in agro-industry in Mexico. As it learned, it taught. New crops and new skills were introduced, inculcated, and acculturated throughout the area surrounding the cannery. PDM contributed directly and significantly to rising farm income. The company created jobs and earned a position of recognized integrity and fairness among the rural people.

For the Host Country

The data speak for themselves. PDM employs 237 salaried, nonunion people; 208 unionized permanent workers at the cannery; and as many as 1,300 seasonal workers in and around the cannery. In addition, Frutas y Verduras Selectas employs 35 salaried staff and up to 400 seasonal workers on its six asparagus farms. Direct payroll in 1983 amounted to P210 million (roughly $1.4 million). Also in 1983, farmers received P560 million (about $3.7 million) for produce received at the cannery; PDM also purchased P50 million ($330,000) in supplies and services from local businesses. No data were made available regarding tax payments and foreign exchange earnings, but over the years it might be expected that both have been significant. Although there are no known studies of the subject, the multiplier or eddy effect of these large cash flows into the area economy from the cannery, year after year, must be among the important reasons for the vigorous economic growth of the Irapuato region.

POLICY IMPLICATIONS

The financial crisis in Mexico, precipitated by the inability of the country to service its foreign debt in 1982, brought with it a bewildering array of policy changes and implementation plans, arising out of every public and private institution in the country. GOM, naturally, has concentrated on financial matters relevant to inflation, foreign exchange earnings and control, and a balance between austerity and social disorder. Private organizations like PDM have focused on changes required to maintain income and competitiveness. Conditions in the country are such that it is not reasonable to direct separate policy comments to the company and to the host government in the form used in other case descriptions in this book. The policy implications of the PDM case for the United States as a donor country are also not relevant. The United States has not been involved in providing Mexico with development assistance for many years, and the role it may play in the future is not clear.

Yet, acceleration of agricultural and rural development is critically important to the success of Mexico's efforts to bring its foreign debt under control and to bring its economy back to the stage of vigorous growth that characterized the 1960s and early 1970s. Despite a long history of agrarian reform and public sector action, the goals of reform remain beyond the dreams of the great majority of small-scale farmers, their families, and their villages. Until the anchor of rural poverty and low productivity is weighed, all other remedies applied to the social and economic problems of the nation will fall far short of their intentions.

To correct the deficiencies of rural Mexico clearly is a complex, long-term, and difficult task. It is not likely to be accomplished by taking a single approach. But as a beginning, Mexico desperately needs novel techniques of integrated rural development that depart from the bankrupt policies of the past, that reject old institutional and ideological constraints, and that can be applied nationwide. The case of PDM suggests one such innovative methodology, never before tried in Mexico, to be centered on private sector management in collaboration with GOM and USAID.

The idea takes its inspiration from a unique set of circumstances. In the area of raw material procurement by PDM, four U.S. multinational agro-industrial corporations are neighbors and, except for their product lines and marketing methods, operate in very similar ways and share many common concerns. They are

PDM itself, Green Giant (Pillsbury), Campbell Soup Company, and Bird's Eye Foods (General Foods). They all use contract farmers as primary sources, with an emphasis on larger, commercial units. They all carry a staff of agronomists, provide technical assistance, and are highly regarded in the rural community. Their combined payrolls, purchases of farm produce, and payments to local businesses send a large cash flow into the area. Alone or in concert, these companies form a natural base of operations aimed at capitalizing past achievements to ensure that the small-scale farmers, their families, and their communities share equitably in the benefits of investment in agro-industry and move on to new high levels of development.

In the same area as the companies, at least three national programs of rural development, sponsored and financed by the Mexican private sector, have long operating experience at the village level among small-scale farmers. They are all open to collaborating with industry, to put their skills and experience in joint venture with the human resources of the industry. These three are: Coordinación Rural, A.C., a subsidiary of Ingenieros Civiles Asociados, S.A.; the Mexican Development Foundation (Fundación Mexicana para el Desarrollo), financed by a broad cross-section of all Mexican business and industry; and the Banco Nacional de México (nationalized along with all private banks in 1981), which has a credit and technical assistance program at over 2,000 sites throughout the country. These organizations can greatly enrich the experience of industry and help answer the questions most likely to preoccupy management: How is the job done? What skills are needed? How long does it take? What will it cost? What is the payoff? Is it too political? Is it appropriate for privately held, profit-making enterprises to take responsibility for long-term, integrated rural development programs?

FIRA, a division of the Central Bank of Mexico and a powerful public force in rural development, has already expressed a desire to collaborate with agro-industry to accelerate rural development. FIRA approval itself would be prerequisite to action; FIRA could also be important in gaining policy approval at the highest levels of GOM. Though they are unlikely to be adequate, FIRA does have financial resources to help back an industry-sponsored program.

It is therefore recommended to GOM, PDM, and the U.S. government that every effort be made to bring agro-industry operating in the same area as PDM, rural development specialists serving programs sponsored by the private sector of Mexico, and FIRA together as quickly as possible. The objective of this interaction would be to facilitate and accelerate the organization of a novel, private sector rural development program, which if successful could serve as a prototype for adaptation to all parts of Mexico and for export abroad.

9

San Miguel Corporation: A High-yield Hybrid Corn Seed Venture in the Philippines

Ruth Karen

SUMMARY

The San Miguel Corporation (SMC) is a large agro-industry conglomerate in the Philippines, serving both domestic and export markets. This case study focuses primarily on a recently established hybrid corn seed operation in South Cotabato, on the island of Mindanao. By 1985, or soon thereafter, SMC projects that the seed company will supply roughly 50 percent of the domestic market.

The seed company is comprised of a core farm of 1,250 acres, intended to supply all the raw material for a processing plant that dries, husks, shells, sizes, treats, and packages certified seed. There are no contract farmers in this system. In its broadest purpose, SMC expects to aid the nation and all corn farmers by providing the means to increase productivity by 100 to 400 percent or more. More specifically, the seed venture is conceived as a key element in a complex of closely integrated corporate businesses. For example, SMC operates large animal feed mills; these feeds use corn as the grain base. Increasingly in the years ahead, SMC plans to draw its corn supplies from farmers using company hybrids, which will not only simplify the marketing problem of the farmers,but is expected to lower grain costs, even as farmer income rises. In turn, lower feed prices will decrease the cost of meat, both enhancing the diet of more people and making SMC feeds more competitive in both domestic and external markets. Furthermore, SMC is a major grower of poultry, which again provides an internal corporate market for corn-based feed, also produced by SMC.

Within this dynamic system of corporate growth, SMC recognizes that its relationships with the large numbers of small-scale corn farmers who buy their seed and sell their grain to the company is a key element. Therefore, the company's seed marketing program is geared to an expansive program: technical assistance, using a sales force of young men trained by SMC to double as agricultural agents; credit that may soon cover all inputs through harvest, at which time repayment will be made; and community development, which may go beyond the normal range of facilitating health, education, and recreation infrastructure to include intervention on behalf of a village with authorities the people have not yet learned to reach.

The SMC outreach to its customers/suppliers appears to be very successful in Mindanao, and the corporation is already planning to diversify its services, for example, helping farmers diversify their cropping patterns to include other cash and subsistence crops. The entire program of investment and development assistance is fully supported by public policy; in 1981, the government stated its intent to spur the socioeconomic development of the entire country by harnessing the private sector's entrepreneurial skills and initiative.

COUNTRY BACKGROUND

In a number of aspects, the economy of the Philippines differs from that of most other developing countries. The country has a substantial number of competent professionals, both technical and managerial. As a result, some of its industry and segments of its service sector are advanced by the standards of less-developed countries (LDCs). Nevertheless, 70 percent of the country's 53 million people still live in rural areas, many at subsistence levels. An indication of the potential that exists in the agribusiness sector is illustrated by the fact that at present all agribusiness output, defined in the most comprehensive terms (including agriculture, forestry, and fisheries), constitutes only 25 percent of the gross national product (GNP).

Government Policy

The Tenant Emancipation Decree. For several years, government policies have addressed this reality. The Filipino cabinet includes an agrarian reform minister, whose portfolio is to translate into action the concept, initially defined and articulated by President Ferdinand Marcos in the 1972 Tenant Emancipation Decree, that rural development requires an integrated approach under which farmers are given not only land and security of tenure, but are also provided with a package of services to help them upgrade their productivity and income.

In 1983, Agrarian Reform Minister Conrado F. Estrella, in a statement made at a convention of northern Luzon rural bankers, listed these services as

- Free legal assistance
- Education and training
- Infrastructure such as roads, bridges, electric power, and irrigation systems
- Formation of cooperatives
- Organization of farmer groups
- Supervised credit

The minister made a specific point of the importance of credit, noting that "Credit is of prime importance because much like the commercial and industrial sectors, the agricultural sector could thrive more speedily and meaningfully with the provision of adequate and liberally available credit." He added the barbed observation: "The attitude of considering the rural folk, especially the farmers, as non-bankable is no different from the judicial prejudice of pronouncing the accused as guilty before he is proven innocent" [18].

The Kilusang Kabuhayan at Kaunlaran (KKK). The Tenant Emancipation Decree, which laid the legal foundation for meaningful agrarian reform, was institutionalized on a mass basis in August 1981, with the establishment of the Kilusang Kabuhayan at Kaunlaran, designed "to spur the socioeconomic development of the entire country by harnessing the private sector's entrepreneurial skills and initiative" [19].

The sociopolitical thrust of the KKK is "to transform every barangay (the smallest political unit in the Philippines) into a productive and self-managing community by enabling residents to establish and run their own livelihood projects" [19]. The KKK established seven priority areas.

1. Agro-Crops. Primary production of root crops and vegetables.
2. Agro-Forestry. The primary production of energy; the cultivation of fruit trees, as part of integrated mountainside development, including water impounding schemes; and the promotion of ecological balance.
3. Agro-Livestock. Primary production of livestock.
4. Marine. Primary production of fish and other marine products.
5. Waste Utilization. The secondary processing of wastes from the primary production areas, converted into suitable products like wood chips, organic fertilizer, animal feeds, cottage crafts, and light-industry specialities.
6. Cottage and Light Industries. The secondary processing of raw materials for various small-scale manufacturing projects ranging from the traditional bamboo and rattan crafts to novelty items.
7. Shelter Components. Production of housing components such as standard concrete hollow blocks, clay-brick tiles, and woodworking products.

After establishing priorities, KKK proceeded to develop backward and forward linkages from the raw crop to processing centers, anchor projects, and trading centers.

The policy assumptions underlying the KKK strategy are that starting and managing a productive enterprise, however small, requires know-how in raw-material sourcing, production, financing, accounting, and marketing. As a KKK official elaborated during an interview: "Considering his educational level and lack of business experience, the KKK primary producer does not usually have the know-how and even the time to do all the major business activities. Practically on his own, the chances of success and prompt loan repayments are reduced."

To increase the odds of success throughout the KKK system, therefore, both anchor projects and processing centers are envisioned to involve the private sector most closely.. For example, in the case of anchor projects, KKK notes that private enterprise projects can include any or all of the following: marketing/ production, including contract growing/buyback arrangements, subcontracting, raw-material sourcing, processing, and countertrade; financial/equity participation; and technical arrangements such as transfer of technology and licensing arrangements.

Anchor firms in the private sector effectively link the primary producer both to the market, domestic and international, and to sources of production technology. Anchor projects are put together by a consultative body consisting of presidents of the banking, manufacturing, mining, and management associations, who work out macroeconomic policies with the KKK. Follow-through is provided by sectoral consultative groups that discuss and implement specific projects.

Sectoral consultative groups are deliberately limited in size to encourage action rather than debate. Membership ranges from ten to fifteen in each sector, and represents both big and medium companies, with all relevant functional facets of the industry: management, technology, and training.

COMPANY BACKGROUND

San Miguel Corporation (SMC) is a conglomerate engaged primarily in various aspects of agro-industry. The company has six major divisions: Beer; Magnolia, which includes ice cream, fruit drinks, and dairy products; Feeds and Livestock; Packaging Products--for example, glass, metal, paper, and plastic containers and closures; Agribusiness Projects, including hybrid corn seeds, shrimp fry, and green c offee beans; and Investments, covering a diverse mixture of products. In 1982, the company's total turnover was 5.61 billion pesos (end of 1982, P8.5 = US$1); the company had 21,522 stockholders; and employed 17,784 persons.

The Corporate Culture

The company's social philosophy is expressed primarily in its active participation in the organization, Philippine Business for Social Progress (PBSP), which undertakes self-help projects through proponent organizations in the areas of livelihood creation, technology transfer, human resources development, and expertise leasing. By the end of 1982, PBSP had funded a total of 590 projects, 93 of which were initiated in 1982.

The company has its own written corporate policy, subsumed under the concept of "profit with honor." The policy, made available by SMC's chairman for use in this case history, lists eight objectives, which are "indivisible and together represent the broad aims of the corporation."

• To be constantly aware of the aspirations of the people and of the nation, and to ensure that San Miguel continues to make a major contribution toward the achievement of these aspirations
• To manufacture, distribute, and sell throughout the Philippines food products, beverages, packaging products, and animal feeds, being ready at all times to add, modify, or discontinue products in accordance with changes in the market
• To diversify into fields that will ensure optimum utilization of management resources and a substantial contribution to corporate profits
• To seek and develop export markets for new products as well as for those already being produced by the corporation
• To generate a sufficient return on funds employed to ensure an adequate rate of growth for the corporation, and to provide satisfactory returns to stockholders
• To provide an environment that is conducive to the development of the individual and that encourages employees to realize their full capabilities
• To maintain the highest ethical standards in the conduct of our business
• To adopt a flexible and objective attitude towards change and to pursue an active policy of innovation [20]

The Approach to Agribusiness

San Miguel's corporate philosophy and strategy vis-à-vis agribusiness have been specifically defined [20]. The agribusiness ventures of San Miguel Corporation reflect a threefold commitment: to develop opportunities in the high growth agricultural sector; to increase food production; and to enhance the productivity of the nation's farmers.

In its agribusiness endeavors, San Miguel has forged a partnership with the Filipino farmer as the basic producer. Recognizing the farmers' intimate knowledge of their land and equipment, and their inherently low production costs, San Miguel adds its strengths in research and development, modern organizational skills, and resources in planning and marketing. The result of the partnership is enhanced efficiency in production and a productivity that increases the incomes and reduces the risks to farmers and hastens the development of the countryside.

The developmental thrust of San Miguel's agribusiness initiatives creates receptive new markets for its products, but there are other benefits as well. The agribusiness ventures are complementary to the main operations of the company and its affiliates. These ventures provide high-quality and adequate raw materials for the processing operations of San Miguel and its affiliates, for example, corn for poultry and livestock feeds formulation, and farm-fresh milk for Magnolia. Additional businesses create new demand and markets for the more established product lines. Thus, development of poultry and livestock and, more recently, of the shrimp business has spurred demand for feeds. Further, through its ventures in agribusiness San Miguel is contributing to increased production of crops and commodities with worldwide demand, thus generating foreign exchange earnings from exports--a national development strategy and priority.

Synergy thus ensues from the linkages of the various agribusiness projects with San Miguel's established products. In addition, San Miguel's ventures are congruent with national development goals. SMC's relationship with the farmer is a linkage that generates new opportunities and more progressive means of livelihood in the rural areas. In this context, a harvest of progress and prosperity is San Miguel's vision for its agribusiness ventures.

The company entered agribusiness in the 1950s, when it established a plant to utilize, as one of the ingredients in feeds, the by-products of its manufacturing operations. This paved the way for the development of the integrated poultry business, a modern industry that contributes significantly in meeting the country's requirements for food, particularly protein. Subsequently, the company expanded into hybrid corn seeds, green coffee beans, dairy products, shrimps and marine feeds, as well as soybeans, ramie, hogs, and cattle, through its subsidiaries. The following discussion focuses on the development of the hybrid corn seed enterprise in South Cotabato, on the island of Mindanao.

THE DEVELOPMENT OF HIGH-YIELD HYBRID CORN SEED

SMC first experimented with a corn project in the late 1950s, but was prevented by the government from continuing this experiment. At the time, activities in rice and corn were limited by law to enterprises owned 100 percent by Filipino citizens. About 30 percent of SMC's widely distributed shares are held by non-Filipinos, including citizens of the United States.

Responding to this law, the company turned over to the Agricultural University at Los Baños the research and feasibility studies it had done. In 1974, when these studies had produced no action, the law was amended, and the company began to look again at a hybrid corn seed project.

Corporate Motivation

The motivations of SMC to continue its hybrid corn seed undertaking range from the macroeconomic, to the sociopolitical, to the corporate-specific.

Macroeconomic reasoning starts with the fact that a corn farmer in the Philippines traditionally produces less than one metric ton (mt) of corn per hectare. With the hybrid seed developed by SMC, plus appropriate use of fertilizer and herbicides, the farmer can harvest between four and seven metric tons per hectare. Since 1.3 million farmers throughout the Philippines grow corn on plots ranging from one to five hectares (1 hectare = 2.5 acres), the potential on the production side is self-evident, as is the increase in farmer income with all its developmental implications. Further, in terms of balance-of-payment considerations, vital for the Philippines at this juncture, the country is currently in a position where it must import corn. Success of the company's seed corn venture and the resulting widespread use of the high-yielding seed corn could make the Philippines self-supporting in corn within two years.

The company perceives social as well as political concomitants to the macroeconomic considerations. On the social side, per capita protein consumption in the Philippines is low, creating nutritional deficiencies in both children and adults. Increased corn production would ameliorate this deficiency in two ways: more direct consumption of corn by farm families (20 percent of the Filipino population use corn, not rice, as their basic staple in the diet); and more consumption of chicken, pork, and beef, as more economic production of corn helps lower the price of animal feed, in turn bringing meat prices within the purchasing power of the general population.

In the political dimension, the company is convinced that helping farmers and their families earn a decent livelihood will make them less susceptible to communist propaganda and promises at one end of the political spectrum, and less vulnerable to the incitement of Islamic rebellion and banditry at the other.

Finally, there are three corporate-specific reasons to pursue the production of high-yield, hybrid corn seed.

1. Increased production of corn, based on the seed supplied by the company and backed up by company extension services, will assure SMC of a dependable quality supply of corn for its feed plants.
2. Production of quality corn on the scale envisioned will make possible the export of corn to countries that already have expressed interest (Taiwan, Japan, and Korea). Lowering the price of feed for hogs, chicken, and beef will help make these SMC animal products competitive in the international market. Forty percent of the feed bag for hogs, chicken, and beef consists of corn.
3. Because many of the company's products are designed for the lower end of the market, increasing the purchasing power of farmers by upping net farm income makes these

farm families potential customers for a number of SMC product lines such as milk, ice cream, soft drinks, beer, and other milk and coffee products.

This economic reasoning has yet another and different competitive aspect. Farmers are well aware of their value to SMC as buyers. In Mindanao, a farmer who heads a KKK association that uses its government-extended credit to buy seed corn and other inputs from SMC, told me that, if the company would help the farmers set up their own drying and warehousing facilities for corn, the farmers would reciprocate. When asked just what this reciprocity would consist of, the head of the association said that the farm families he represented would then buy the company's food and beverage products. And he knew what these were.

Project Strategy

Corporate strategy is based on a set of basic assumptions articulated by SMC's president during an interview:

> The farmer contributes the land and the labor. He has a deep involvement in both and, with this motivation, can do better as a producer than a corporation can. The corporation can contribute expertise in management, organization, and its capability to get technology, either through its own research and development facilities, or by buying it on the world market.
> It is not easy to convince farmers to take the risk involved in breaking with tried and true practices that have fed his family, however meagerly, for generations. This applies whether the opportunities are presented by growing a new product or by engaging in new techniques to grow a traditional product. When the new hybrid rice was developed, with all its evident advantages, it took about twelve years for farmers in the Philippines to accept the new hybrid and feel at home with it. I believe it will take considerably less time for corn. My estimate is that it will take about four years. The momentum is already there.

When SMC restarted its venture into corn in 1977, the strategic assumption was that the key to the undertaking would be the availability of a high-yield seed adapted to Filipino conditions. Initially, SMC sent people all over the world to look for a suitable seed, but found that none proved viable, mainly because of pest and disease problems that were country specific. The company then proceeded to cross high-yielding seeds imported from abroad with local varieties that had developed resistance to local pest and disease problems. It did this in its own research and development (R&D) facilities, spending five years and P50 million on the process. By 1982, it was judged time to go into commercial production, while maintaining the ongoing search for improved strains.

Commercial Production and Marketing

In 1982, SMC established a production center in South Cotabato, on the island of Mindanao. (Although corn is grown throughout the Philippines, the most concentrated production takes place on the southern island of Mindanao.) The production center consists of a nuclear farm encompassing 500 hectares and a modern processing plant with the capacity to dry, shell, husk, size, treat, and package seed. SMC initially sold this seed to farmers using SMC's established distribution network. In practice, this meant piggybacking the seed on the company's beer sales. It also meant that direct company distribution went only as far as the SMC network of warehouses, where seed dealers picked up the product and handled retail distribution to the farmers.

The company discovered very quickly that selling seed via its own beer warehouses and through wholesalers was not an effective distribution technique. A new marketing system was put into effect, based on four interrelated lines of action.

1. SMC organized classes for farmers, in cooperation with leaders of farmers' associations and, where possible, with technicians of the Ministry of Agriculture, on the characteristics of hybrid corn and the technology of growing it. It did this at the provincial level; the village level; and occasionally, in an impromptu, ad hoc fashion, responding to farmer interest in a particular locale.

2. SMC organized demonstration plots on a farmer's own land. The strategy was to give the farmer free seed for one hectare of land; teach him how to plant and take care of the crop; and invite neighboring farmers to observe the process during planting, fertilizer application, spraying, and perhaps most important, harvesting.

   At harvest time, when the results of the farmer's venture were most clearly evident, the company cooperated with its demonstration farmer in organizing a harvest festival for his neighbors. These festivals attract between 50 and 200 farmers and their families, and the company sees these occasions both as a marketing effort to generate sales of seeds and as a consciousness-raising exercise to make farmers aware of their own production potential.

3. The company moved from delivering seeds to wholesalers to dealing directly with farmers, primarily through KKK-supported farm associations. For this purpose, it hired a sales force of young men whom it trained to double as extension agents. The company plans to support this sales/extension agent network with senior technical representatives as soon as the scale of production and processing makes this an economically viable proposition.

4. The company is considering switching from its strategy of providing free seed for demonstration farmers and selling seed to other farmers to a strategy of advancing to all

farmers seeds, fertilizer, and chemical inputs at cost, and balancing the books at harvest time. In a discussion, the manager of the Mindanao operation explained the reason for this change in strategy: "Dealing directly with the farmers as we do here, we found out that small farmers simply do not have enough cash to pay for the seed, fertilizer, and chemicals they should be using. And farmers don't know how to deal with banks. So we may have to bridge that gap as another aspect of our outreach."

PAYOFF

For the Company

The company's expectations are fourfold: a stable quality supply for its feed operations and its downstream animal products; a stronger market for its other product lines, with resulting better profitability in both these aspects of corporate activity; an increased market share of corn seed (SMC's market share in 1983 was 24 percent, targets are 33 percent for 1984, 44 percent for 1985, and 50 percent-plus thereafter); and a return on investment of 20 percent on funds employed, which includes amortization of research and development activities.

The company originally calculated that it would achieve these targets at a production scale of 2,000 metric tons (mt), which it expected to reach in 1986 or 1987. Actually, when processing began in 1982 production reached 125 mt; by 1983 this had grown to 500 mt, with break-even income scheduled for 1984 at a production rate of 1,000 mt. However, economic conditions in the Philippines changed drastically at that time. Two devaluations of the peso in 1983 alone moved the break-even point to 1,500 mt. SMC remains optimistic about reaching its market share and return on investment targets, although the target time frame had to be extended.

During this time of both growth and economic uncertainty, SMC has continued its development programs. The initial cost of developing a satisfactory hybrid was P50 million. The company allocates P5 million annually for ongoing research, and P2 million annually for extension services. SMC also has a budget of P1 million per year for advertising, and is considering shifting some of that money from the media to community development, responding to the desires expressed by the farmers. Considering the competitive elements involved in marketing the company's wide range of products, and the farmers' awareness of their competitive clout as consumers, the company perceives this kind of outreach program as a component of advertising.

These early years of seed development and start-up of the corporate farm and seed processing plant paid their way less in cash than in operating experience, and the company is now reviewing the various changes that suggested themselves.

The first problem/opportunity the company is addressing is the need for postharvest services. Existing drying and storage facilities were sufficient for corn produced in the traditional way, but are already insufficient for the expanded yields that have resulted from the hybrid seed, and will clearly constitute a major bottleneck in the future. The KKK organization has formed a joint venture with a private company to produce shellers and dryers, and is looking for private sector partners to construct warehouses and silos, and to provide trucking and transportation facilities for the expanded corn harvest. SMC is looking at the possibility of participating in facets of this postharvest business; as a matter of corporate strategy, it would prefer to buy corn from farmers directly rather than from traders, as it does now.

A second change the company is considering involves expansion into new crops, in production, processing, or both. For example, SMC is looking at the possibility of using corn as a base to produce corn oil, and to use corn-based high fructose as an ingredient in some of its snack foods. The high fructose would replace sugar, both because corn-based fructose will deliver better nutrition, and because the company believes the sugar industry in the Philippines is no longer viable under present economic conditions.

SMC is also considering encouraging farmers who use its high-yield seed to diversify and further increase their income through intercropping and crop rotation. Crop rotation would primarily involve the production of peanuts. Company market research shows that there is a domestic market for peanuts as well as an export market in Japan, Australia, and Hong Kong.

The product the company is considering for intercropping is a special variety of coconut that could be used to create new food products. Intercropping corn and coconut is possible if the plot is laid out in a way that lets sunlight come through the coconut trees to reach the corn planted beneath.

Another product diversification possibility, in which the KKK organization is interested, is commercial production of mangoes for which SMC would set up a processing plant. The company already uses mango ingredients in a number of its products. At present, it buys mango puree from outside suppliers. Encouraging farmers to cultivate mangoes and setting up an SMC processing plant would serve a corporate purpose comparable to that of producing corn for its feed mills: It would assure a dependable, quality supply.

A third change the company has initiated revolves around the content and structure of its extension work and other outreach activities. For example, the company intends, regionally, to build on its local experience in institutionalizing an ongoing dialogue with local political and social bodies, including barangay captains, mayors, and parent-teacher associations, to ascertain what communities would like to see in the way of company involvement. This dialogue, as tried and tested, takes place at meetings scheduled on a bimonthly basis, usually held in the nearest school in the evening. The meetings are unstructured social events, d uring which informal exchanges are facilitated.

In Mindanao, this informal but ongoing dialogue has already had some interesting results. When, for example, during a typhoon in 1983 some cows strayed from the company's nuclear farm, a nearby community notorious for its banditry and particularly for its cattle rustling rounded up the cows and returned them to the company. The barangay captain of this community, at one of the bimonthly get-togethers, intimated that one of the reasons for this extraordinary behavior was the fact that SMC disseminates the offspring of its Holstein breeders to the community, gives bulls away to upgrade local cattle, and markets the hogs of local farmers.

Another result is the end of pilferage from the processing facility. Shortly after the processing facility began operations, some small motors were stolen from its workshop. The company complained about the theft at one of the get-togethers in the local school. Shortly thereafter, the stolen motors reappeared, deposited in a neat little pile in the schoolyard.

At the corporate level, the company is considering a systematic grant program to help establish a rural youth organization modeled after the 4-H clubs of the United States. SMC is also looking at expanded contributions to village health programs, adult education, nutrition programs for preschool children, and other activities that relate directly to the needs of the villagers. Included among these is hands-on assistance to farmers in "self-help settlements," where the government clears land and allocates it to landless farmers, who get title after five years if they demonstrate that they can make productive use of the land. SMC outreach programs in this area would consist primarily of supporting these farmers in developing new crops for which there is a domestic need, such as a high-protein winged bean, alkaloid plants for medicinal uses, macadamia nuts, and tropical alfalfa meal, as well as export crops, including sorghum, soy bean, peanut oil, and vegetable seeds.

For the Farmer

The payoff for the farmer, the family, and the community was delineated by the captain of the barangay in South Cotabato in which the company's seed processing plant is located. Barangay captains are elected every six years by men and women over eighteen years of age. The last election in this barangay, with a population of 4,000, took place in 1982. The barangay captain (who is a woman and a farmer) cultivates a medium-size spread of 50 hectares, representing an aggregate of family owners consisting of brothers, sisters, and parents. The farm traditionally grows corn, along with cotton, sorghum, peanuts, and pamelos (a giant grapefruit). The barangay captain began using SMC hybrid corn seeds in 1982, achieving a 300 percent increase in yield within one year.

Speaking about her community, the barangay captain observed that "people have improved their houses, bought cattle, bought bicycles, bought radios, and, most important, they eat better." She also noted that in her barangay, the SMC nucleus estate and processing plant provides off-farm jobs, an important contribution to the economic base of the community.

For the individual small-scale farmer, the economic bottom line is a production increase of 100 to 400 percent, the net income from which can certainly help, if not always totally resolve, the high cost of risk in any agricultural activity. A case in point is the experience of an association of Moslem farmers in Mindanao.

This association has 118 members, cultivating a total of 207 hectares in corn. All use SMC hybrid seed. The group obtained financing of P795,430 in 1983 from the local KKK organization. This financing, supplied largely on a chit basis, with the chits exchangeable for products, financed the purchase of the new hybrid seed, fertilizer, chemicals, spray knapsacks, and herbicides.

The farmers ran into two problems inherent in the feast-or-famine dimension of all agriculture. One was a worm infestation, the other was a flood. These problems were exacerbated by the farmers' lack of adequate drying facilities. Despite these problems, the production resulting from the hybrid seed made it possible for this farmers' association to pay back 70 percent of the loan the KKK had extended, and to negotiate for a rollover of the remainder and a new loan of roughly the same amount. With these results under their belt, the farmers plan to allocate a maximum amount of the new financing to corn production using the SMC hybrid seeds. The farmers figure that, with the hybrids, they will be out of debt in two years.

This association and its interaction with the SMC sales representative/extension worker demonstrates another element in the payoff of the hybrid seed venture. Although the company representative works with farmers in every aspect of corn production, he also doubles as a consultant on any problem a farmer or the farm group brings up. As one farmer put it, "he's our plant doctor." This intimate and easy relationship encourages farmers to ask SMC for help, whereas before they had nowhere to turn. While I was visiting the Moslem Farmers' Association, for example, the group indicated that it would like the company to provide corn-drying facilities and perhaps a shelter. Group members also felt free to say that they would like help with village authorities to improve educational, health, and athletic facilities. One extension project discussed was the construction of concrete-surfaced basketball courts for village elementary schools, which could also serve as drying areas for corn. What is significant is that SMC is giving serious consideration to these suggestions.

Another example of farmer benefits is the experience of an association of Christian farmers, also in Mindanao, and also with a first season of hybrid corn planting covering 215 hectares planted by 98 farmers. As the chairman of the association put it: "Despite our seasonal problems, it was an eye-opener to the old-timers. Under the old system, the farmers of this association got a yield of 1.5 tons of corn per hectare. This year, the average yield has been 4.5 tons per hectare, and our best farmer improved his yield to 7.9 tons."

This farmers' association had obtained a loan of P818,430 from the KKK organization, which it was able to pay off in full after the hybrid seed corn harvest. The association also achieved an underrun on estimated production costs. With this record, the association requested, and received, a rollover of its loan for the next season, plus an additional credit facility to buy two dryers and the materials to construct a drying platform. The cost underrun served as collateral for the additional credit. The government also agreed to subsidize for the association 50 percent of the cost of a solar dryer and a warehouse.

The farmers in this village asked the company to extend its outreach effort by organizing more classes for farmers, developing more demonstration farms, and offering more technical assistance. The chairman of the association said: "I need help to educate the farmers to the new ways. Government extension agents try, but there is a limit to what the Ministry can do. In any case, the more help we get in every aspect of extension work, the better off everybody will be. And no one is as competent as the company, especially in keeping us informed on new varieties and other new developments." He added that he would like to see more corporate involvement in other outreach services such as health, water, and education.

Reviewing his association's books, this farmer offered a set of figures representing average returns for the members of his association for 1982, when they did not have the hybrid seed, and 1983, when they did. The figures are interesting because they illustrate not only the difference in gross income for the farmer, but also the difference in net income, which takes into account the considerably higher investment made by the farmer for the inputs required in hybrid-seed production, in turn emphasizing the critical importance of the credit system of SMC.

In 1982, with nonhybrid seed and an investment of P800, net return was P1,000 per hectare. In 1983, using SMC hybrid seed and an investment in inputs of P1,800, net return per hectare was P2,500. Thus, by increasing investment by 2.25 times, net return increased by 2.50 times. The real significance of this result to the farmer was the absolute increase in net farm income from P1,000 to P2,500 per hectare; the real return to the nation was an increase in corn production equivalent to adding 2.5 hectares of productive land otherwise impossible to obtain. If this result could be replicated widely throughout the corn belt of the Philippines, as is projected by SMC, it could be of great importance nutritionally and for balance-of-trade accounts.

POLICY IMPLICATIONS

For the Company

For the company, one policy implication is that working directly with small-scale farmers represents a range of business opportunities that strengthens vertical integration of company products and provides a horizontal extension of product lines for the domestic market, as well as for export.

Another policy implication is that a carefully structured outreach program that involves technical support in a number of ways, and includes social activities and contributions to community concerns formulated on the basis of an ongoing dialogue with relevant community groups, has direct bottomline results. It helps to create markets for company products; it serves as an innovative aspect of advertising; it alleviates, or even eliminates, law-and-order problems for company activities; and it creates a relationship with producers that represents a potential for additional profitable activities.

For the Host Country

For the host country, the policy implications were spelled out by a senior official of the KKK organization: "Until we develop our farmer, we cannot really develop the country. There is no way the Philippines can take off economically without a strong and viable agricultural base. Historically, the farmers have been neglected by all administrations, before and after independence. Now we are in a race against time. KKK may well be our last chance."

Assessing KKK, a knowledgeable source in the private sector said that the organization has indeed been imaginative and sound in its design of programs, but weak in their implementation. Too much of the KKK's money still goes to feudal leaders in the countryside and their political allies, instead of being channeled to the disadvantaged farmers. If small farmers were supported more effectively, both their income and their community standing would increase, and the political leaders, now still very hierarchical in the rural areas, would have to listen more attentively to their constituents.

For the Donor Country

For the United States, the major policy implication of the SMC venture into high-yield hybrid corn seed, stated by a number of sources, is that a significant part of USAID funds allocated to the Philippines should be channeled to agribusiness. The unique capability of agribusiness to stimulate agricultural and rural development is underlined in Chapter 1; the policy and action recommendations in Chapters 14 and 15, respectively, directed to agribusiness, host governments, and donor countries, provide the details of how these aid funds can be effectively applied to serve everyone's interests. In this regard, SMC and USAID would seem to be ideal partners for a joint venture following the structure outlined in Chapter 15.

10

Agro Inversiones C. por A.: A Fresh Fruit and Vegetable Export Project in the Dominican Republic

Ruth Karen

SUMMARY

Agro Inversiones Compania por Acciones (AI) was established in 1982 as a subsidiary by the Caribbean Basin Investment Corporation (CBI), a Florida-based agribusiness. AI is a fruit and vegetable enterprise located in the Azua Valley of the Dominican Republic (DR). Production is based on a satellite system of procurement, with some 110 small-scale farmers currently under contract to produce melons for packing and export to the United States. The primary investment of AI is in a packing plant. Twenty to 25 percent of its recurrent operating cost is allocated to extension services. The plan of AI is to expand rapidly to include the export of a variety of vegetables. The production and marketing design is based on supplying the winter market in the United States, when domestic supplies are insufficient to meet demand.

CBI/AI have been able to take advantage of an unusual set of circumstances to move quickly into a highly profitable operation. First, the Azua Valley is a showcase of agrarian reform in the Dominican Republic. About US$1 billion has been invested in land preparation, irrigation facilities, and supporting infrastructure. Farm families have been relocated on ten- to sixteen-acre farms and given a form of land tenure that motivates responsible land use. Receptivity to AI was very good. Second, by actions of the governments of the United States and the Dominican Republic, the development of nontraditional exports and the acceptance of these into the United States have been encouraged through strong and varied financial incentives. Third, the growing conditions in the Azua Valley are favorable to a management system with peak production in the winter. And fourth, CBI started operations with extensive experience in Caribbean Basin agriculture and agribusiness, as well as a working relationship with an established system of wholesale marketing throughout the United States and into Canada.

The impact of AI on the contract farmers is already a classical example of the power of agribusiness to generate change. Adaptation to new technology has been rapid. Net farm income has risen significantly. Farmer/company relationships are excellent. People's hopes are high. This, of course, is a tribute to the rural people; it is also a compliment to the competence of a staff of five Dominican agronomists who manage the technical assistance program. The company supplies seed and all other inputs on credit, which is recovered at the time of fruit delivery to the packing plant. A carefully structured contract covers every detail of mutual responsibility, reducing misunderstanding and conflict to a minimum. In other words, as AI enters its early years of operation and expansion, it has quickly established a harmonious and beneficial relationship with its supplier constituency.

It is too soon to predict how these relationships and the company design of its outreach program will stand the test of time. Nonetheless, as is true of all the cases described in this book, the interdependency of the company and the farmer is constructed essentially on economic grounds. Interaction, in consequence, relates primarily to rising income. Yet worldwide experience suggests that rural people have, and will come to express, a far wider range of needs that can become pressing once the first flush of excitement over rising income passes. The case of the CBI/AI experience in the Azua Valley, therefore, expresses both the importance and the desirability of having the outreach program of AI go beyond its present limits to include the broader, long-range aspects of rural development, that is, to take advantage of the "opportunity," as defined in Chapter 1, which is the theme of this book.

COUNTRY BACKGROUND

From almost every point of view, the Dominican Republic ranks among the more advanced of the nations in the Caribbean and Central America. Its per capita income in 1982 was US$955 (in 1980 dollars). Literacy is 69.7 percent, despite the fact that 600,000 Haitian refugees, most of them illiterate, live in the Dominican Republic.

The country has a relatively well-developed network of light industry, mostly manufacturing import-substitution products that are not competitive in world markets. The country also has a network of domestic financial institutions that are competent and enterprising in the context of the region. Not counting government financial institutions, the Dominican Republic has seventeen commercial banks and nineteen development banks.

The rural/urban population ratio is low by the standards of the area. The latest census (1980) showed that only 57 percent of the 6.3 million population was still rural, and expectations are that the 1990 census will show a fifty-fifty split of rural and urban residents.

At present, agriculture contributes over 30 percent of the gross national product. This includes sugar, a crop in which the

Dominican Republic ranks among the major world producers. U.S. purchases of Dominican Republic sugar added US$140 million in income to the country in 1983, reflecting the spread between the low world price for sugar and the price paid by the United States to producers with access to the sugar-import quota.

Development strategy in the past two decades has been based, as in most developing economies, on the export of one or two basic commodities and on the encouragement of import-substitution industries. This is now changing. The new thrust calls for development via four new directions: tourism, mining, export zones, and agro-industry. The first two are considered long-term strategies; export zones and agro-industry have been identified as the sectors that can produce dynamic development in the shortterm.

The new thrust is buttressed by the financial policies of the Central Bank, whose development arm currently allocates as much as 85 percent of its funds to agricultural ventures, with almost half of the remaining 15 percent channeled into industries in the agribusiness sector. In addition, the Central Bank has itself developed a number of feasibility studies for agribusiness enterprises.

The most seductive incentives, however, for agribusiness ventures in the Dominican Republic are very recent, and come from two sources: the governments of the Dominican Republic and the United States. On the DR side, the incentive is the favorable peso conversion rate for agricultural exports. Whereas the official conversion rate of the Dominican peso (DP) in 1983 was still one to one (DP1 = US$1), agricultural exports were entitled to the parallel rate, which in early 1984 was in the vicinity of DP1.80 = US$1 and by mid-February had risen to DP2.50 = US$1. On the U.S. side, the Caribbean Basin Initiative, which offers duty-free access to the U.S. market for defined periods to a number of exports from the Caribbean, became effective January 1, 1984.

At the operational level, agribusiness activities in the Dominican Republic are based on the comprehensive agrarian reform that was launched by the administration of President Joaquin Balaguer in the 1960s. The reform had two important results. In the first instance, the government distributed land, in large part the enormous holdings acquired by General Rafael Leonidas Trujillo and his family, to formerly landless peasants, in parcels of 60 to 100 tareas (6 tareas = 1 acre). This created a sizable number of farm families, with farming experience going back over generations, who had for the first time a direct personal stake in their output. Under agrarian reform, these new farmers (parceleros) do not get title to their land. They do get a lifelong lease that is extended to the next generation if anyone in that generation remains on the farm and works the land. Interviews with parceleros showed that as a practical matter, the farmers consider the land their own, and are fully aware of their effective equity stake in any use to which they put their "parcel."

The other important result was that the government made major, and on the whole successful, investments in every aspect of the physical, financial, and social infrastructure for the implementation of meaningful agrarian reform. It built dams, irrigation systems, and a network of market access roads. It electrified most of the rural areas where land had been allocated under the agrarian reform. It built schools, health clinics, community halls, and, in some regions, housing. It created an agrarian bank that, despite its cumbersome procedures, does provide up to 100 percent of the financing parceleros need, at a substantially preferential interest rate.

The Azua Valley, where the Caribbean Basin Investment Agribusiness Group, Inc., venture is located, is a prime example of the positive impact of agrarian reform in the Dominican Republic. Before the government focused its efforts on the Azua Valley, it was a backward, poverty-stricken area that had once been forest land but had been turned into a semidesert when its timber resources were cut down indiscriminately to yield mahogany for furniture and charcoal for fuel.

In the period from 1978 to 1982, the DR government invested close to US$1 billion in rehabilitating the Azua Valley. Today, the Azua Valley is one of the most attractive areas in the Dominican Republic for agricultural production. In addition to a major domestic company, which uses it primarily for the growing of tomatoes, the valley has already attracted three foreign investors, from the United States, Mexico, and Israel, who are working with parceleros to grow agricultural products, largely for the export market. CBI Agribusiness Group, Inc., joined the ranks of foreign investors in the Azua Valley in 1983.

ENTERPRISE BACKGROUND

The Caribbean Basin Investment Corporation is a small, Florida-based company established in early 1982 by five private investors. Within its first year, CBI had launched agribusiness enterprises in Jamaica (cattle raising), Panama (a finance company for agribusiness and light manufacturing), the Dominican Republic (cattle, hogs, and poultry raising), and was conducting a feasibility study on the production of edible oils in Barbados. In 1983, CBI created a separate company, CBI Agribusiness Group, Inc., designed to function as a management and technical assistance enterprise in services to agribusiness in the Caribbean Basin. Three of the original investors in CBI, with considerable experience in agribusiness in the United States and the Caribbean area, are actively involved in the management of both companies at the top level.

The enterprise in the Dominican Republic, Agro Inversiones C. por A., is a joint venture between R.D. (Republica Dominicana) Vegetable Products Inc. (a holding company CBI created for all its ventures in the Dominican Republic), which has 70 percent of the equity, and private Dominican investors, who hold 30 percent. The Dominican investors take no active part in the management of the enterprise, and consider their equity participation a portfolio investment only.

Discussing the corporate philosophy that dictates their agribusiness activities in the Caribbean, the shareholder-managers of CBI argued that small- and medium-sized companies are, in many ways, better suited to agribusiness enterprises in the Caribbean than are large multinational companies. Small companies, they feel, reflect more accurately both the investment conditions and the managerial elements of the host countries in the Caribbean. Small companies can react more quickly to evolving conditions in the host country. Small companies can transfer agricultural technology more easily because they can get to the root of local problems more quickly and can respond more effectively to local social conditions.

"It is a natural relationship," says Francisco Hernandez, president of the CBI Agribusiness Group. "Personally, and as a corporation, we have experienced many of the same problems that we encounter in these ventures in the Caribbean." The CBI executive pointed out, however, that a certain size is necessary to undertake such ventures. The parent company, he maintains, must be substantial enough to have the financial and managerial resources to create and support the enterprise, and to be able to command the in-house expertise to provide the technology transfer that will make the enterprise profitable. It is important for that expertise to encompass both production and marketing. Also, the parent company must have some experience in operating internationally; and it is a considerable plus if the company has had direct commercial contact with the host country, either in terms of products sold or of services provided.

Employing a quantified yardstick, the parent company must be substantial enough to be able to afford up-front risk money of $50,000 to $100,000 to finance an undertaking in its development stage, and have in-house expertise of at least ten persons at the managerial level who can contribute to the creation and supervision of the enterprise. Using another quantified yardstick, the parent company should have minimum U.S. sales of $1 million a year before overseas activities are undertaken, if the United States is targeted as the sole or major market. All these criteria are met by CBI.

Investment Motivation

The corporate motivation for the CBI venture in the Dominican Republic is based on three classic factors. First, the soil, climate, labor, and proximity to market give fresh fruit and vegetable cultivation a competitive price advantage. Second, harvesting and packing can be maximized in the winter months, when U.S. demand far exceeds the ability of U.S. farmers to produce. For example, production of fresh fruits and vegetables in Arizona, Texas, Florida, and southern California meets less than 10 percent of U.S. and Canadian winter demand. Third, CBI has a well-functioning relationship with an established marketing system in the United States and expert knowledge of the grading, packaging, and export/import procedures required to move the output of the Azua Valley enterprise into the market with a minimum

of delay, spoilage, and rejection.   CBI exports all the quality
melons it produces in the Dominican Republic to Corky Foods Corporation, a Florida-based food brokerage organization.   Corky
Foods, in turn, sells to supermarket chains and food wholesale
firms throughout the United States and Canada, as far north as
Ontario and as far west as California.
     These bottom-line motivations were enhanced by U.S. legisla-
tion permitting, as of January 1, 1984, duty-free access of a
range of Dominican agribusiness products to the U.S. market and,
on the DR side, by investment incentives for enterprises engaged
in the production of nontraditional export crops.   These incentives include an 85 percent duty exemption for imports of machinery; 100 percent financing; peso conversion at the favorable parallel market rate rather than the official rate; and the export
of capital and profits to a full 100 percent.
     CBI management is convinced that making the best possible
use of this combination of economic factors requires substantial
equity participation by the parent company in the enterprise, and
a hands-on presence for the long term. It believes that in agribusiness the most effective transfer of technology takes place
when new production techniques are taught to small-scale farmers,
who then develop a personal stake in the successful application
of the new technology and become increasingly responsive to new
and better technologies as they evolve.
     Finally, the CBI president noted that a meshed, long-term
commitment by the company and the farmers results in a new range
of quality supply for the consumer. This applies to consumers in
the United States and Canada, as well as to Dominican consumers,
who as a result of increased purchasing power derived from a successful transfer of technology become customers for a wider range
of products, food as well as other consumer goods. As the president of CBI notes: "A successful transfer of technology to small
farmers is a pipeline for development."

Investment Strategy

     CBI's strategy for its agribusiness undertakings in the
Caribbean is three-pronged.

- To create a local company in which local investors have
  an equity share.
- To retain management control either through an appropriate equity split or via management contract.
- Not to own any land, or as little as possible, either directly or through the local company.   When necessary for
  a pilot project or a demonstration nucleus farm, CBI will
  lease land.   The company is convinced that for sociopolitical as well as production reasons, the land should
  belong to local people, and preferably to the farmers who
  work it.

It was the third ingredient of this corporate strategy that propelled CBI to locate its Dominican Republic enterprise in the Azua Valley. The site was ideal for agricultural production. The government had provided an effective irrigation system, electrification, farm-to-market roads, and above all, a large number of working farmers with a sense of security about tenure and management control over their farming enterprise and the economic return on their labor.

After only one full year of production experience, CBI is convinced that despite some unexpected technical problems it encountered in the valley, expansion into other products is desirable. The company has already run pilot projects on four other products: eggplant, cucumbers, bell peppers, and different varieties of squash. It has reason to believe these vegetables will prove as successful, in terms of production, marketing, and return on investment, as the melon project has already proven to be.

Management Strategy

The CBI managerial strategy provides top-level supervision of Agro Inversiones by the president and chief executive officer of the CBI Agribusiness Group, who has twenty-five years of agribusiness experience in Florida as well as in pre-Castro Cuba. The managing and administrative directors of the CBI Agribusiness Group double in both capacities for Agro Inversiones. The president of Agro Inversiones is a Dominican, a trained CPA who functions as chief financial officer at corporate headquarters in Santo Domingo. The field manager, who lives in the Azua Valley, is a U.S. agronomist from California with ten years of experience in tropical agriculture, gained mainly in Central America and the Caribbean. His staff includes five field agronomists, all of them university-trained Dominicans. CBI also supplies, from its headquarters in Florida, product managers and technical assistance consultants on a revolving basis. These experts provide on-site investigation and advice on fertilization, fumigation, and irrigation techniques, and on the operation of the packinghouse.

The packinghouse, located at the field station in the Azua Valley, has state-of-the-art cleaning, cooling, sizing, and storage facilities. It is run by a staff of five processors, plus twenty laborers. At its field station in the valley, Agro Inversiones also employs four permanent employees in its storage facilities and five in its mechanical shop.

The company negotiates individual contracts each year with 85 to 110 farmers. The contract is a highly specific legal document, running to five pages, which spells out in precise detail the mutual obligations of the parcelero and the company. The contract covers not only the purchasing commitments of the company and the production commitments of the farmer, but also systems of classification of the product, including arbitration procedure; details of transportation, payment, and financing;

conflict resolution and contract termination procedures; and of course, the price to be paid to the farmer for his product.

The contract's fourteen clauses commit the company to purchase the farmer's total production suitable for export on a stated acreage, even if problems arise on the corporate side either for mechanical or marketing reasons. A clause covering classification of the product stipulates that a representative of the government's agrarian bank must be present every day for the product classification procedure. Two symbiotic clauses require the company to provide seed and technological assistance, and require the producer to tend his field and harvest his product in accordance with company instructions. Another set of clauses calls for the farmer to provide free access to his field by appropriate company personnel, while the company provides free access for producing farmers to the packinghouse. Typically, the contract also calls for a commitment by the company to furnish all necessary inputs, the cost of which is deducted from payment to the farmer when he delivers his product.

The price to be paid for the product is negotiated each year between the company and farmer associations. These farmer associations were originally set up on a geographic basis by the government's Agrarian Reform Institute when it distributed the land. Since they are voluntary associations, the original memberships have shifted, essentially moving from a geographic base to one of congeniality, based on social and entrepreneurial factors. For example, one of the associations with which Agro Inversiones negotiates each year is called "La Brillante," because the fifteen farmers who belong to it consider themselves the most brilliant producers in the Azua Valley. Agro Inversiones negotiates with five farmer associations each year, with negotiations taking place thirty to sixty days before planting time. Melon-growing farmers have the option of selling to the Israeli and Mexican enterprises as well as to Agro Inversiones. As a result, price negotiations contain a genuine competitive element.

With the double incentive of strengthening its relationship with the farmer associations with whom it negotiates, while augmenting its own role as a good corporate citizen, Agro Inversiones reaches out to the community with some social services. These range from the operation of an emergency health clinic and providing bonuses at Christmastime, to such minor but creative aspects of community involvement as providing baseball uniforms and equipment for all members of the farmer associations.

PAYOFF

For the Farmer

Throughout the Azua Valley, employment between 1980 and 1983 rose 38 percent, and the per capita income of parceleros in the valley is three times the national average. With the technology transfer and the extension services extended by the four companies now active in the valley, yields for parceleros have doubled and in some cases tripled. Many parcelero families have acquired television sets and motorcycles; have improved their houses; and are sending their children to high school and university. An informed guess has 10 percent of the parcelero children in the Azua Valley going on to higher education.

The encouraging payoff for the parceleros is the result of crop rotation and crop change as well as the higher yields achieved through the corporate technology transfer. Traditionally, farmers in the Azua Valley planted about 20 percent of their land in plantains and 80 percent in sorghum and corn, most of which they sold. Whereas plantains are a year-round crop, sorghum and corn can be grown during a season running from April to September, making it possible for the farmer to devote his land and labor to a more profitable cash crop from October to April. Most Azua Valley parceleros now use the October to April season to raise either tomatoes or melons. The proven returns on these crops, especially melons, have led more enterprising parceleros into enlarging their melon acreage. For example, in 1983, net return to the parcelero in the Azua Valley from his tomato crop averaged DP50 per tarea, while the payoff for melons was DP80 to DP90 per tarea. In addition, a melon crop can be obtained in 65 days, while a tomato crop takes 120 days. During the 1983/1984 season, 16,000 tareas, out of a total of 40,000 tareas in the valley, were dedicated to the cultivation of melons and vegetables for export.

Pinpointing the payoff to the farmer in individual terms, one parcelero with eight children reports:

> I got my own land in 1971--60 tareas. I don't own it, but I have the right to work it for my lifetime, and my son has the same right when I die. It can be taken from me, or from him, only if I sell it, or if I let it lie idle. I don't intend to do either.
>
> In 1971, I started with plantains and tomatoes. I could only plant 10 tareas of each, because at that time, there was not enough water. In 1978, I had 30 tareas in plantains, 30 in tomatoes. I moved into melons during the 1980/1981 season, producing mainly for the Israeli company. Now I have 43 tareas in melons, 17 in plantains. This season all my melons go to Agro Inversiones.
>
> Here is my payoff: From 1971 to 1978, my income was DP10 per tarea. From 1978 to 1980, it was DP40 per tarea. In 1981, it was DP90 per tarea. Now, since I have moved mostly into melons, and grow two crops a year, my income is DP160 per tarea. I, my wife, and my two oldest sons do most of the work on the farm. For a few weeks during the harvest season, we hired about fifteen people to help.
>
> What do I do with the extra income? I spend it on my family, on clothes, on fixing up the house, and mainly

on education.   Two of my children are in high school,
and both intend to go on to university. I want both my
boys and my girls to have that opportunity.

Another source of income for the farmers, although small, is
appreciated.   After the packinghouse does its sorting, seconds
(melons whose size and appearance make them unsuited to the export market but whose quality and taste is the same), are returned to the farmer who has delivered them.   He, in turn, sells
them on the local market at one-tenth their export value.   Normally, three to five perfectly acceptable melons may be purchased
for one peso.   This means, in addition to representing income to
the producer, that lower-income Dominicans gain access to a nu-
tritious product that was out of their economic range in the
past.   The same procedure, and the same economics, will apply to
the vegetables planned for production--eggplant,   cucumbers,
squash, and bell peppers.

For the Company

The corporate payoff for Agro Inversiones has been above
expectations.   The CBI Agribusiness Group reports that, after the
first season, payoff has exceeded forecasts of return on investment (ROI). Agro Inversiones expected to complete the 1983/1984
season with gross sales of US$1.2 million, and figures on doubl-
ing these sales in the 1984/1985 season. This covers the production of melons only. For the medium term, including the production of vegetables, sales are expected to triple. The parent
company figures on an investment, for melons and vegetables, of
$1.5 million to $2 million, and expects to recover its capital in
full within two to three years. The operating cost-to-sales
ratio for the first season makes this an eminently probable forecast.

For the Marketer

The market organization involved in the enterprise, Corky
Foods, has increased its volume by 7 to 8 percent because of its
melon purchases from Agro Inversiones.   About 25 percent of the
corporate operating budget goes for agrochemicals, making it an
important new outlet for wholesalers of these products.   Put in
terms of operating cash flows, Agro Inversiones estimated costs
for the 1983/1984 season at roughly $400,000, on sales of $1.2
million.   Both sales and operating costs are projected to double
in the 1984/1985 season. It is significant that 20 to 25 percent
of operating expenses are allocated to extension services.

Corporate Changes

Its first year of successful operations has prompted Agro
Inversiones to consider making three substantive changes.

The most important concerns financing. During the first season, 100 percent of the financing for the inputs the company supplied to the farmers came from the government's agricultural bank, Banco Agricola. Although this is subsidized credit, offering an interest spread of three or four points lower than going commercial rates for loans of 90 to 120 days, the company has found that the executive time devoted to the elaborate documentation required by the bank, and the timing delays encountered in dealing with the bureaucracy, more than countervail the advantages of the interest spread. The company is therefore considering financing the farmers directly.

The second change concerns transportation. Melons are shipped from the Dominican Republic to Florida both by air and by sea. At present, the ratio is about fifty-fifty. This is expensive because the cost of air freight is roughly double the cost of shipment by sea. The price of air freight is also about twice the price the farmer gets for his product. The company wants to change the present ratio of transportation to making 70 percent of its shipments by sea, 30 percent by air. The difference in delivery time is only about six days which for melons is acceptable.

An alternative solution to the cost-of-transportation problem is for Agro Inversiones to operate its own chartered plane. If operated efficiently, especially when the vegetable product line is figured into the calculations, transporting its products through its own air freight operation would bring the cost down to somewhere near the present expense of shipping by sea.

A third change is another cost-cutting move along tactical rather than strategic lines. Agro Inversiones has discovered that there are some very talented mechanics in the Dominican Republic, including one at its own workshop in the Azua field station. It made this discovery when it wanted to buy a tool carrier for a tractor. The price quoted in the United States for the carrier was US$8,000. Instead of buying the carrier, the company bought drawings for a carrier. After two weeks of tinkering in the field station workshop, one of the company's mechanics had produced a workable version of the carrier at a total cost of $500. The company concluded that "we can save all kinds of money with in-house creative mechanics."

POLICY IMPLICATIONS

For the Company

Hands-on commitment and involvement at the managerial level, the technical level, and the field supervision level are essential for success. Given these three ingredients and the appropriate crop, a relatively modest scale of operations can produce a net profit on sales during the first year, and a respectable return on investment, including full recovery of capital, within two or three years. This applies even when there is on-site competition for the farmers' output.

For export-oriented products, it is vital to have a well-defined market plus a market organization, in the case of a bigger company; or a well-structured relationship with food brokers and wholesalers for a small company. Furthermore, because transportation is a major cost consideration in exporting, all available options have to be analyzed carefully and continuously. Financing, even if available locally at subsidized rates, may not be the most desirable form of credit. Given the snarls and obstacles of bureaucratic delays, it may be more cost-effective for a company to finance farmers directly.

From a sociopolitical point of view, in any operation designed for the long term, it is advisable for a company, particularly a foreign company, not to own land. If landholdings are needed for pilot projects or a nucleus estate, the land should be leased. From a sociopolitical perspective, as well as from a productive one, the most desirable arrangement is to work with producer farmers who own or have effective control of their own land and work it largely with their own family members.

For the Host Country

For the Dominican Republic, the primary policy implication of the CBI/Azua Valley experience relates to the payoff to the settled farmers and to the country that has occurred as a consequence of encouraging the participation of agribusiness. The relationship between the public and private sectors, in this case, has made it possible for the settlers to benefit economically and socially, while the company and the nation have profited as well. The policy question that arises has two parts: How can this partnership be extended throughout the country? What more can be done to ensure that the early impact of CBI and the other private agribusiness enterprises in the Azua Valley moves efficiently and in a planned manner into a long-range rural development program?

In terms of agricultural development throughout the DR, what has been done in the Azua Valley clearly demonstrates the required elements of public policy. Agrarian reform that efficiently prepares the basic infrastructure, including irrigation, electrification, farm-to-market roads, credit institutions, a network of health and educational facilities, and other elements vital to economic activity and social order lays the groundwork. The productive force is built by facilitating access to the infrastructure by farmers and their families and providing enough land to yield sufficient income for basic needs and enough more to motivate ambition. Tying the whole, in the early years of development, to an institution (agribusiness) capable of rapidly introducing superior technology, and to a processing and marketing organization that ensures those who produce raw material a fair return on their labor and their risk, puts the whole system into a dynamic profitable state for all.

In terms of attracting agribusiness into partnership with government, the Azua Valley/CBI relationship illustrates a variety of other measures that public policy should encourage. There needs to be a realistic exchange rate that applies to exports; conversely, there need to be duty concessions covering the importation of capital goods. Both of these financial incentives are vital to the maintenance of a competitive position in the marketplace. If agribusiness is foreign in origin, as is the case in the Azua Valley, government is well advised to allow reasonably untrammeled repatriation of profit and investment capital. From a development perspective, the cost/benefit relationships attendant on all these incentives should be made widely known so that the net gain to the people of a nation is understood and appreciated. Incentives to attract foreign investment into less-developed countries have been the target of misunderstanding and controversy for a long time, sometimes with justification. Agribusiness investment, relating as it does to food, poor rural people, and agrarian reform, is singularly vulnerable to criticism. Host government policy should promote careful calculation and adequate public education with respect to incentives offered to private investors.

Finally, to ensure the expansion and diffusion of the benefits of rural development when companies like CBI stimulate the process, the government of the Dominican Republic could initiate a policy that, perhaps in concert with donor countries, would encourage agribusiness to establish the development function within its management system. The joint-venture concept, and how it could be implemented to accelerate and extend rural development after agribusiness enters a rural area, is described in Chapter 15.

For the Donor Country

The CBI/Azua Valley project is in many ways a model exhibiting the benefits of sound investment and development policies. In this case, the agrarian reform program in the Azua Valley reflects a policy of aid from the donor country (the United States) to the Dominican Republic. Beyond the creation of a productive agricultural area, the Caribbean Basin Initiative taken by the United States, which established a policy of duty-free access of fruits and vegetables from the Dominican Republic, is an example of what a donor country can do to encourage agribusiness investment as an important component of agricultural and rural development. The implication of the immediate success of the CBI venture seems clear: Encourage more of the same. Taking a longer-range viewpoint, it would also seem desirable for U.S. development assistance in the Dominican Republic to work closely with agribusiness and the host government to facilitate follow-up, especially among the farmer beneficiaries of agrarian reform and company presence, along the lines of rural development.

11
Adams International: Tobacco Growing and Marketing in Northern Thailand

Ruth Karen

SUMMARY

Adams International (AI) is a joint venture tobacco company involving a Thai-Chinese family and W.A. Adams Company, Inc., of Durham, North Carolina. AI was organized in 1969, primarily to export leaf to Japan. In 1974, AI entered into a marketing agreement with Philip Morris, Inc., which provided for the sale of Thailand's oriental-type tobacco, if AI could meet price, quality, and quantity requirements. This agreement led to major new investments by AI and, for the first time, caused the company to establish its own satellite procurement system. By 1982, more than 40,000 small-scale farmers, for the most part in the underdeveloped northern and northeastern areas of the country, were cultivating oriental-type tobacco under contract.

After a difficult start, AI evolved an outreach organization that has proven most effective in transferring the technology for the cultivation of oriental-type tobacco. The heart of the program lies in the maxim laid down by the chairman of AI, which states that the farmers in the program must be thought of not just as producers but above all as human beings. The key to implementation is a staff of approximately 500 "village inspectors," who were selected from the more experienced farmers in the area, trained for their job, and who establish the close contact basic to confidence and loyalty. These village level inspectors report to and through a hierarchy of technical personnel, all of whom are visible to the rural people and have direct contact as needed with farmers, village leaders, and government personnel. The AI plan of growth and procurement has evolved smoothly and efficiently over the past eight years, to the mutual benefit of company, farmer, and nation.

As might be expected as a result of a corporate policy expressing deep concern for its rural constituency as human beings and not just as producers motivated by economic return, AI over the years has extended a variety of services to enhance the quality of farm family and community life. Yet, it has been cautious in the extent to which it feels it proper for a private company to take increasing social responsibility. Current events may be forcing management to examine its role in this regard.

There is a fundamental uncertainty in dealing with the highly competitive international market for leaf tobacco. AI is fully aware of this and for some years has been conducting research on alternative field crops and animal husbandry possibilities for introduction to the practices of its farmer associates. To date, encouraging productivity results have been attained, with crops like peanuts, sunflower seed, sorghum, corn, sesame seed, and tomatoes. Similarly, species suitable to the manufacture of fish meal have been cultured successfully. Clearly, the introduction of such new farming practices and crop marketing has great potential importance in diversifying and strengthening the economic base of both tobacco farmers and AI. Should this diversification take place in a way that maintains the satellite procurement system AI has created, the company inevitably will be drawn into a much deeper involvement, an ever-greater interdependency, with the rural people.

The speed with which diversification may proceed was brought into question when in the 1982/1983 season, the European Common Market (EEC) extended subsidies to Greece, quickly matched by the Turkish government in favor of its growers, permitting oriental-type leaf from these countries to compete successfully with Thai tobacco. The impact on Thailand and AI was serious, immediate, and negative. It is too soon to observe how AI will react to this competitive situation, or what impact will be felt among the small-scale farmers now engaged with AI.

COUNTRY BACKGROUND

Agricultural production is a mainstay of the Thai economy. Approximately 70 percent of the total population of around 50 million are engaged in agricultural pursuits. Yet agricultural output accounts for less than one-quarter of total GNP. Companies like Adams International, Inc., and Charoen Pokphand (Chapter 7), have successfully brought modern agricultural practices to traditional small-scale farmers, assisting them both technically and financially and providing a guaranteed market for their crops.

The three major problems in Thai agriculture (detailed in Chapter 7) are the scarcity of new land for farming; Thailand's dependence on exports, overwhelmingly agricultural, which makes the country vulnerable to fluctuating world economic conditions; and high population growth, especially in the underdeveloped rural areas.

COMPANY BACKGROUND

The W.A. Adams Company, AI's U.S. parent company, has an interest in Thailand that dates back to the late 1950s, when it became involved with the export of Thai tobacco, then totally controlled by the government's Thai Tobacco Monopoly (TTM). The joint venture was formed in 1969, and began operations by exporting Thai flue-cured tobacco to Japan. In the following years, the joint venture made substantial investments in a redrying factory and in a network of buying stations in the north of the country. The joint venture also helped the government monopoly in exporting its surplus tobacco to Japan, Korea, and the United States.

History

The big leap forward came in 1974 when Philip Morris, Inc., became interested in Thailand's oriental tobacco, a blend tobacco known as Thai Turkish, which at the time constituted only a small percentage of Thai tobacco production. The following descriptions covering the importance of the contact with Philip Morris, the plans developed by AI to take advantage of the market opportunity, and the company's current operations are taken directly from a letter written by the company chairman, Kosol Chongsuknirandr, to TTM in August 1976.

"Early in 1974, an official from Philip Morris Inc., one of the world's biggest cigarette manufacturers, visited us in Bangkok, and took an interest in the Thai Turkish sample we showed to him. A trial order of over 50 tons was shipped to Philip Morris that year, and this company was basically satisfied with the quality of our tobacco which we, with the cooperation of TTM, have improved over the years.
"Philip Morris advised us that being one of the biggest cigarette manufacturers in the world, they could buy all the Thai Turkish that Thailand can produce, provided the increases in quantity and price are regulated to avoid violent fluctuation. They insisted, therefore, that we should

● Invest in proper manipulation machineries to extract the sand out of the tobacco
● Maintain and improve its quality and grading standards
● Ensure availability of land and farmers so that production can be increased yearly
● Assure that we supply to Philip Morris on first priority basis
● Assure no big price fluctuation

"We wish to point out that up till then the only exports from Thailand carried out by us alone were less than 100 tons yearly, and that there have been no other buyers of substance in the international market. This commitment from Philip Morris was exactly what we needed to put Thailand on the map of Oriental tobacco producers, a supplier to a world-renowned company that buys over 50,000 tons of Oriental tobaccos annually."

In the two years following, the company responded to this new market opportunity with a seven-point action plan outlined below, again in the words of the chairman.

"In 1974 and 1975, we:

1. Bought and then expanded our tobacco manipulation plant in Ban Thai to ensure ample proper storage space for tobacco.
2. Imported from Greece one line of manipulation machines in 1974, and an additional line in 1975. Our facilities are now proclaimed to be the most modern outside of Greece.
3. Applied for and were granted a promotional certificate by the Board of Investments.
4. Applied for and were granted by the IFCT [a Thai industrial development bank] a loan of 5.6 million bahts [US$250,000] to expand our factory and storage facilities. [The conversion rate used throughout this case is B23 = US$1.]
5. Requested and received full cooperation from TTM to increase production of Thai Turkish from existing TTM farmers, and succeeded in increasing the production by more than 500 percent in two years. We bought for export 80 tons in 1974, 750 tons in 1975, and 1,700 tons in 1976, all through TTM.
6. Contacted and received full cooperation from the Public Welfare Department to introduce tobacco plantings in several big self-help settlements in different provinces in the northeast.
7. Introduced new Oriental tobacco varieties with seeds from Greece and Turkey."

In his letter to TTM, the Adams International chairman goes on to summarize the lessons learned in these first two years, and lays out plans and a strategy for the next five (Table 11.1).

"Our experience in expanding production shows that in areas where farmers have been planting tobacco for TTM and ourselves, the results are satisfactory; but in areas where farmers have little experience in producing Thai Turkish, the results are very poor. There is need, therefore, for our carrying out an integrated program to train and encourage more experienced farmers.
"We divide our territories into three main regions: TTM, Northern, and Southern.
"In the TTM region are those areas in Roi-Et, Mahasarakam, and Khon Aen, where farmers have been producing tobacco for years. In the Northern region are those areas north of our factory in Ban Thai; in the Southern region are the areas south of our factory. Each region is supervised by a fully qualified

agronomist under the overall direction of our agriculture manager. Under the agronomists are head village inspectors who supervise the work of a team of village inspectors. It is estimated that production per rai is averaged at 175 kilograms, and each village inspector can efficiently supervise 100 rais initially. Each village inspector is also provided a motorcycle by the company for easier contacts with farmers. We plan to increase our team of village inspectors (Table 11.1).

Table 11.1
Five-Year Development Plan
for Expansion of Oriental Tobacco Production

(Baht 23 = US$1)

The Five-Year Plan	1976/ 1977	1977/ 1978	1978/ 1979	1979/ 1980	1980/ 1981
Production targets (in metric tons)	4,000	5,500	7,000	9,000	12,000
Ban Thai/Roi-Et Staff	20	30	40	50	60
Seasonal Workers	800	1,200	1,600	2,000	2,200
Village Inspectors	250	325	425	525	650
Raiage (rai = 0.4 acres) under Cultivation	23,000	32,000	40,000	50,000	69,000
Farmers	15,000	20,000	23,000	26,000	28,000
Income to Farmers (baht in millions)	66	99	140	198	288
Company Investment (baht in millions)	4	10	20	10	4
Earnings in Foreign Exch. (baht in millions)	96	144	200	280	400

Source: letter from AI Chairman to the Thai Tobacco Monopoly.

"Each inspector is properly trained to advise farmers on all technical aspects of planting, curing, baling, and grading. He also has to motivate farmers to keep up with their work so that prior efforts and investments in agricultural materials will not be wasted due to negligence or laziness. Therefore, the village inspector is more than an advisor to the farmers.

"All agricultural materials necessary to produce a tobacco crop will be supplied by us to the farmers on a credit basis, cost of which is to be deducted from tobacco purchase proceeds. This is necessary to ensure the use of correct fertilizer and insecticides. At present, farmers in TTM areas pack their tobaccos in small bales of two kilos. This proves hard to handle as we have to repack every kilo in larger bales for proper storage.

Thus, new farmers under our direct supervision have been taught to grade tobacco properly and pack each grade in bales of 12 to 15 kilos. We hope that in due course old farmers can be converted into this type of packing.

Factory Operations

"One of the most important aspects of Oriental tobacco operations is to ensure sufficient storage space. Because of the delicate nature of the tobacco, each bale must be carefully stored to encourage proper air circulation through the tobacco. Also, there should not be too much pressure on the bales. Therefore bales should not be stacked more than four bales high.

"At present, we have space to store up to 2,000 mt of tobacco, or approximately 16,000 square meters, fully covered, in ventilated areas. A further 25 rais of land at the back of our present factory compound has been purchased for building more warehouses as our production increases each year. After the tobacco is bought, it is imperative to store it for at least two months before manipulation, to ensure that the first fermentation will take place. Our current manipulation capacity consists of two manipulation lines with three automatic packers. This means we can manipulate and pack 2,000 mt in five months, working two shifts for the last three months. Our plan is to increase to one more line of manipulation machines in 1977, and another in 1978, with corresponding increase in automatic packers each year. Concurrently we shall build a new factory in 1978 in Roi-Et, starting off with one line, then two lines, to take care of tobaccos produced in nearby provinces.

"Regarding manpower, we are currently employing a full-time staff of twenty to run the office and factory, supervising 800 seasonal workers. Full-time staff will be increased to 70 and seasonal workers will be increased to 2,200 by 1980/81, the last year of our five-year plan. Here, we think we are contributing much to the economy of the northeast by providing employment opportunities to local residents.

"The bulk of our present purchase has been handled through TTM. With the anticipated increase in volume, we will construct buying stations at strategically located points in each province to service the farmers. We have already opened an office in Roi-Et due to heavy volume of tobacco anticipated from this province. This office serves as a base for our team of village inspectors in the TTM region. Other offices will be established as the need arises.

Training Programs

"With our personnel requirements increasing year by year as our plan develops, it is clear that the training of people to staff various positions is the key to the success of the plan.

We have therefore established on a regular basis: an agricultural school for village inspectors and a class for tobacco grading.

"The first class for village inspectors started on July 19, 1976. The students were recruited by sending letters to universities and agriculture colleges in the northeast requesting recommendations of good students to participate in our school. Our representatives then went to these colleges and interviewed the students. The response from the colleges was very favorable, and we had no difficulty in recruiting our first sixty students. The students are paid a monthly stipend plus free board and food allowance on a daily basis to attend our school, at a total cost of about B2,300 (US$100) per student per month. The course itself runs for six weeks during which time the students will learn every aspect of tobacco planting and handling. Students will start their own seed beds and experimental plots as the course progresses to gain practical experience on the materials covered in the lectures. Field trips are also organized, paying particular attention to the many aspects of contacts with farmers. The school will run continually every year to train an increasing number of village inspectors. That number will reach 650 by 1980/81.

"Concurrently, grading classes are being conducted by our chief tobacco expert to teach our staff and workers the basic elements of tobacco grading. This course is being conducted on an informal basis; the class starts when the situation requires and normally lasts for two days.

Outreach Program

"Apart from the training of our staff to help the farmers, we are going to carry out consistent programs to recruit as many farmers as possible. In areas where the soil is not rich enough for other crops, farmers usually prefer to grow crops like tapioca and jute which need less intensive labor than Thai Turkish. But it has been found that while tapioca may yield the farmers B1,000 per rai, Thai Turkish may bring an income of B4,000 per rai for four months work. To encourage more farmers to grow Thai Turkish, we intend to stage competitions and award prizes to more productive farmers. Furthermore, we shall encourage social welfare activities in educational and religious functions in the villages in order to foster a community spirit in these areas.

"In carrying out the above programs, we think we are bringing in foreign investment and helping to improve the economic conditions of the country."

CURRENT OPERATIONS

Company Philosophy

The company's culture is shaped by the chairman, who is both a Chinese scholar and a businessman with half a century of international experience. His basic philosophy is "Listen, don't argue. Hear what others have to say, and be ready to change your own ideas and your own ways. If you know how to listen, what others say can only benefit you. In my long life, I have not met anyone who could not teach me something."

Current production by AI covers an area spread over regions that are together roughly the size of South Carolina, and contain some 16 million persons. In 1982, so far the best year in tobacco production in the company's history, more than 40,000 farm families were engaged in agricultural activity connected with the company. In Thailand, this is the equivalent of an impact on about 200,000 persons.

Managerial Strategy

The managerial pyramid of this enterprise starts with the board of directors, then the technical consultants who advise the board, then the line managers who report directly to this board. Next down the line are field managers, one for the North and one for the Northeast. Reporting to the field manager is a regional manager who is responsible for the network of buying stations. Reporting to the regional manager is a station manager who supervises the warehousing, cleaning, and packing facilities. Reporting to the station manager are head inspectors who are responsible for farmers in five to seven villages. The vital last link in the managerial chain is the village inspector, who deals with the farmers on a daily basis. Depending on the size of the village, a village inspector is responsible for one to three villages.

In 1982, the company had 600 village inspectors (50 less than projected for 1980/1981 in Table 11.1). When operations began in 1976, the company recruited all its village inspectors from agricultural colleges and, after some training, assigned them to the field. Within a year, half of the original group of 60 trainees had resigned. As one of the field managers, who had been with the company from the outset, put it: "They wanted to get away from the sun and the rice to a desk job in an office with regular pay and no demanding challenges." The remaining half were fired by the company because they proved unable to do the job.

The field manager explains:

They were too young to deal with the farmers. The farmers didn't respect them, and didn't listen to them.

Also, when they went to the village, their tendency was
to go to the headman's house and go to sleep rather
than visit with the farmers in their fields or their
homes and give them advice. Finally, and understandably, but it didn't help, their tendency was to look
for the prettiest girl in the village rather than the
best farmer.

With this experience, the company did a 180-degree turn in
its management practice. Instead of combing agricultural schools
for the most suitable students, it combed the villages for the
most suitable farmers. Often, but not always, these were the
village headmen. The company then trained these men in the
tobacco-growing specifics and, when necessary, in the minimum
literacy required. As a follow-through, the company set up a
system of continuing on-the-job training, which includes a road
show complete with slides, cutouts, and tests, as well as ongoing
seminars.

The company also supplies the village inspectors with such
hands-on teaching tools as a wall calendar in which each month is
illustrated with pictures that show exactly what the farmer needs
to do about his tobacco crop during that month. The pictures illustrate how to do it right and how to do it wrong, and how the
farmer can tell the difference. A comparable educational approach at this level has each seed packet the village inspector
hands his farmer wrapped in a cover printed with pictorial instructions on how to make a seed bed. In addition to instructing
farmers on the most useful agricultural techniques and keeping
them current on the latest agricultural developments, village inspectors conduct field demonstrations with farmers on the farmer's own land.

Recruiting village inspectors from among the farmers themselves has proven to be a highly successful management approach.
As a result, a comparable system is now applied up the line; that
is, head inspectors are recruited from among the best village inspectors and station managers are recruited from among the best
head inspectors.

At the regional level, managers are recruited either from
TTM or, in two cases, are former U.S. Peace Corps volunteers who
know and love Thailand, speak fluent Thai, and with company encouragement, have acquired the appropriate academic and business
experience.

Technical Strategy

The major technical change the company has introduced in its
strategy involves keeping track of its input/output cycle. The
company provides the farmer with all the inputs he needs, on
credit, with no interest. These inputs can consist of as many as
sixteen items, ranging from fertilizer, lime, insecticide, and
fungicide to spray pumps, water cans, plastic sheets, twine, nee-
dles, and burlap. The tobacco delivered by the farmers has a

dozen gradations, each with a different price. With 40,000 farmers receiving inputs and delivering product, record keeping is a serious accounting task. One of the company's field managers, a former Peace Corps volunteer with an interest in computers, decided to address that problem. With the help of one of the company's directors, who had friends at the Jet Propulsion Laboratories in California, a new company was formed, also in California, which after a couple of years came up with a small multiuse computer, appropriately called Discovery Multiprocessor. By 1983, that multiprocessor was not only keeping the company's 40,000 accounts in good order; it also handled all the company's other internal computing needs. In addition, Adams International organized a network of seventy dealers around the world who sell this same multiprocessor. They comprise a new affiliate of Adams International, called Action Computers (Thailand).

The company is also making technical changes in its product line. It is encouraging farmers who produce tobacco to engage in crop diversification. For example, the company has developed a peanut that is a Thai variety of what the company calls "the Carter peanut." Based on genetic stock from the United States, it has also adapted a sunflower seed variety for Thailand. Using Australian and U.S. stock, it has come up with a hybrid sorghum; and from Japanese stock, it has developed a corn hybrid. Stock from China, Hong Kong, and Taiwan, has been used in developing a sesame variety for Thailand. The company's newest thrust involves tomato seeds and the production of fish meal.

The product diversification program has three purposes. One is to provide a rotation crop designed for optimum production of tobacco that feeds back into the soil the nutrients that tobacco uses up. A second purpose is to increase the farmer's income and spread his risks of dependency on any single product market. The third, analogous to the second, is to spread the corporate risk should the decline in the tobacco market, which started in 1983, be irreversible. In the long run, AI might conceivably be led to market, and even process, crops other than tobacco, for domestic and regional consumption.

Outreach to the Rural People

As stated by the chairman of AI at the outset of the outgrower tobacco procurement program in 1976, the company realized that it could get neither the quantity nor the quality of product it required without a comprehensive outreach program. The key to success in this regard is the performance of the hundreds of village inspectors. These inspectors operate daily at the critical interface between farmer, farm family, village, and company. Their intimate relationship with the rural people builds the trust basic to loyalty and effective two-way communication. As is generally the case with agribusiness, the world over, AI has moved cautiously into the full range of rural development activities, but the company tries to make its relationship to growers a happy one. For example, a harvest festival is sponsored at the buying stations every year in August and September. A sizable cash prize is offered to the farmer with the best quality record in each of ten production areas. Another facet of community involvement is exemplified by the northeast regional manager. He teaches a course on the cultivation of oriental tobacco at the local agricultural college; supplies equipment and training to area vocational schools; and contributes sports equipment to primary and secondary schools.

The characteristics of a typical farm family, and their feelings about their relationship with AI, were illustrated clearly to me during a visit to Thailand. The family lives in a two-story house of brick and wood, with a good roof, a few domestic animals, and a vegetable garden. The household consists of husband, wife, three sons, and three daughters. Two of the daughters are married and there are three grandchildren, all of whom live in the family compound. The two younger sons, ages twenty-one and eighteen, attend a commercial school in the nearby provincial capital, and the father works as a teacher at the village elementary school. The farming is done by the mother and the oldest son, with the husband helping on weekends and everyone else pitching in as required. The family grows rice (the traditional crop of the region), chili, cotton, and tobacco. It has grown tobacco for ten years, starting with Virginia tobacco, then switching to the new oriental crop. Oriental tobacco, the family reports, requires more work and harder work, but also nets a higher income. Citing the economics of its activity, the family notes that rice brought in a gross income of B900 per rai, while tobacco produces a net income of B4,000 plus.

Discussing the relationship with the company, the family cited the fact that the company provides all required inputs on credit, interest free; guarantees the quality of the inputs; and buys their entire crop. In addition, the family referred to the frequent visits of the village inspector and his hands-on help with the tobacco crop, contrasting this with the extension agent for peanuts who is sent by the government. "The Adams agent comes once or twice a week the year round. The peanut agent comes twice a month and only during the season. With the Adams agent I can discuss all my problems and plans; the peanut agent is interested only in peanuts."

This farm family also notes a particular form of off-farm employment provided by the tobacco production process. Tobacco has to be strung, a task requiring primarily manual dexterity. Experience has shown that children can do this faster and better than adults. Payment for each string is 25 satang (satang 100 = B1), and schoolchildren of farm families are pleased with this opportunity to earn their own income, however miniscule. This practice appears to fulfill a function comparable to a newspaper route or babysitting for U.S. schoolchildren. This Thai farm family reported that the children spend their money on candy and books.

Outreach to the Government and Farmers' Organizations

The company maintains a close working relationship with the Thai Tobacco Monopoly and in effect acts as an export arm for TTM. In addition, company technicians meet with their opposite numbers at TTM to exchange technology and know-how. Unlike Adams International, which is actively and increasingly involved in crop diversification, TTM deals with tobacco only. In the tobacco sector, the two systems are essentially parallel, an arrangement that suits both TTM and the company.

Adams International maintains watchful diplomatic relations with the Thai government's Excise Department, which sets a minimum price for tobacco each year. That price is unrelated to the world market price and is set by the Excise Department in Bangkok on the basis of production costs for the farmer, which include inputs, land cost, labor, climate, and soil conditions, and allows for a profit of B3,000 per rai.

A special situation exists with regard to credit. Although the government maintains a credit bank for agricultural cooperatives that extends loans at a subsidized interest rate of 8 percent, there are no cooperatives among the tobacco growers in the AI system. Although the company would like to work with cooperatives to take advantage of both the availability and low cost of money, management does not feel that it can or should play a direct role in stimulating their creation. In turn, the growers under contract to AI have no incentive to form cooperatives because the company extends all the credit needed at no interest. This impasse is now a constant and it would require great skill and deliberate intervention by AI to change the program at this late date. Approaching its relationship to farmer organizations from a different perspective, AI cultivates connections with farmers' clubs that exist in large villages and small towns throughout Thailand. Basically, these clubs are social centers at which it is common for members to discuss their farming problems, such as new plant diseases. Depending upon the issue, it is traditional to seek solutions in the offices of the governor or mayor. In the areas in which AI is active, the farmers bring their tobacco-growing problems to the company. Obviously, this is an elegant method of communication that opens the way to deeper and broader explorations not only of farming problems but, should the farmers and the company wish to discuss them, of other concerns that bear on mutual welfare.

PAYOFF

For the Farmer

The payoff for the farmer has been sharply increased net income, without displacement of subsistence food production. Although in absolute terms cash income increases have not been great, in relative terms the growers of oriental tobacco for AI

evidence significant enhancement in the quality of life. Beyond
on-farm net return, AI outreach has provided a real measure of
simplicity and security to farm operations. All credit for tobacco cultivation is made available, on time and free of interest. Assured, single-channel marketing frees the family of worry
over price and market stability. Research and development on
other crops by AI, both to diversify farm income and as insurance
against a decline in the export market for tobacco, is a bright
light illuminating the future. Though much remains to be done
in the area of rural development, AI has faithfully served as a
vital agent of beneficial change. Table 11.2 summarizes the
economic impact on farmers since 1974.

Table 11.2
Payoff to Farmers in Baht

(Baht 23 = US$1, in 1983)

Year	Total Farmers	Total Raiage	Net Farm Income	Rai per Farm
1974	982	654	1,174	0.67
1975	6,000	4,400	1,799	0.73
1976	13,450	9,800	1,940	0.73
1977	24,550	17,700	2,068	0.72
1978	39,950	28,000	1,884	0.70
1979	32,550	36,500	1,217	1.12
1980	37,400	39,000	1,736	1.04
1981	39,700	42,400	2,372	1.07
1982	40,450	46,100	4,047	1.07
1983	27,263	32,379	3,292	1.19

Source: Adams International, internal report.

Because many of the people AI employs in its system of technical assistance, leaf collection, and leaf handling are rural in
background and come from the general area of tobacco farming,
payoff to the community of rural people may properly be viewed as
including the wages paid by AI to its employees. Table 11.3 summarizes these data.

For the Company

Oriental tobacco constitutes about 50 percent of company
sales and contributes roughly 50 percent to corporate benefits.
To achieve this condition, AI estimates its total investment for

Table 11.3
Payoff to Employees in Baht

(Baht 23 = US$1, in 1983)

Year	Total Employees	Average Salary	Total Wages	Total Income Farmers & Employees
1974	5	1,510	356,900	1,510,166
1975	21	1,740	1,609,020	12,404,570
1976	196	1,980	7,481,040	33,569,468
1977	238	2,210	10,808,940	61,590,048
1978	560	2,540	25,529,200	100,794,364
1979	423	2,780	20,552,220	60,169,539
1980	515	3,310	29,972,450	94,910,863
1981	631	3,800	41,665,400	135,839,918
1982	526	4,260	41,225,880	204,935,733
1983	495	4,600	40,941,000	157,962,362
			220,142,050	863,687,030

Source: Adams International, internal report.

the ten years, 1974 through 1983, at about $3 million. This investment includes fixed assets such as machinery, warehouses, and buying stations, and approximately 20 percent of the total cost has been allocated to extension services. Table 11.4 outlines the growth of the oriental tobacco business. Although not yet realized in a commercial sense, the expansion of AI resulting from its marketing agreement with Philip Morris has benefited the company by stimulating a program of research and development on alternative crops (or additional crops) to be cultivated by farmers. The implications of this investment may become more significant in the years ahead if the competitive position of Thai oriental tobacco on world markets deteriorates, owing in part to EEC subsidies to Greece, a major producer of this type of tobacco.

For the Importer

The payoff for importers of Thai oriental tobacco, primarily Philip Morris in the United States, has been a supply of tobacco for blending purposes at an initial price approximately 30 percent lower than that of traditional suppliers in Turkey and Greece. This picture changed in 1983 as a result of agricultural policies in the EEC. The EEC now offers subsidies to Greek tobacco producers, which make it possible for Greece to cut its price to roughly the Thai level and, for competitive reasons, Turkey has matched the Greek cuts. The expectation and the hope of Thailand is that as the world economy improves, demand will

Table 11.4
Payoff to the Company in Baht

(Baht 23 = US$1, in 1983)

Year	AI Cost Per Kg US$	Sales Obtained US$	Export Sales US$	Profit Baht	Profit US$
1974	$1.29	$1.35	94,429	88,134	4,197
1975	1.28	1.45	840,331	2,068,953	98,522
1976	1.45	1.63	2,134,256	4,949,380	235,685
1977	1.52	1.72	4,221,955	10,309,425	490,925
1978	1.72	1.69	5,904,153	-2,200,956	-104,807
1979	1.92	2.15	3,851,636	8,652,745	412,035
1980	1.98	2.21	5,878,728	12,848,079	611,813
1981	2.16	2.42	9,052,908	22,370,409	972,626
1982	2.18	2.33	13,512,821	20,008,254	869,924
1983	2.20	2.31	9,279,904	10,163,704	441,900
	$1.98*	$2.11*	54,771,121**	89,258,127**	4,032,820**

*   Average
**   Total
Source: Adams International, internal report.

pick up, providing adequate markets for Thailand as well as for Greece and Turkey. In the interim, the company is integrating the diversification program for farmers into its own operations.

POLICY IMPLICATIONS

For the Company

The company perceives two major policy implications in its operation. The first is a managerial approach formulated by the chairman in the maxim, "You have to deal with the farmer not only as a producer, but as a person." This policy is subject to constant review as the company expands and diversifies its operations, relates to more and more farmers, and gets drawn more and more deeply into technical transfers and increasingly complex processes of rural development. Cost of involvement will inevitably increase. New skills will be required of staff.

The second is that agricultural ventures in Thailand are conducted most effectively as joint ventures in the private sector. Indeed, the company is looking for joint venture partners in other product areas, for which the outside partner can contribute techniques or markets while the Thai company contributes its proven know-how in working with Thai farmers, Thai bankers, and the Thai government.

For the Host Country

The company feels that the Thai government should take a more active role in helping to market Thai agricultural products in other ASEAN (Associacion of Southeast Asian Nations) countries. Particularly, it could push for a reduction in the tariff on oriental tobacco. The current tariff for Thai tobacco in the other ASEAN countries is set at the same rate as tobacco coming from Greece and Turkey. In contrast, the EEC levies no import duty on Turkish and Greek tobaccos, but does have a duty for Thai tobacco. In the EEC, the company feels, the Thai government could argue for lowering the duties on Thai tobacco.

For the Donor Country

One recommendation emerging from this case study is that more be done by the donor country to develop and extend irrigation systems in the dry Northeast. Further, aid that stimulates and assists greater private sector participation in agribusiness and in the extension of improved farming practices to the major disadvantaged areas of the country would be most welcome. One example of such aid would be to facilitate access to information on the world experience of such corporations as AI concerning the response of private enterprise as time and events draw companies ever more deeply into the complex and subtle realm of rural development. Much has been learned about the difficulties and opportunities of relating directly and continuously to rural people whose lives become entwined with agribusiness. This book is indicative of the richness of knowledge waiting to be shared, but too often not shared.

12
Kenya Canners Limited: A Pineapple Plantation and Cannery in Kenya

Simon Williams

SUMMARY

Kenya Canners (KC) is a subsidiary of the Del Monte Corporation, which owns 95 percent of the equity. The enterprise is a classic example of collaboration by public and private institutions to promote agricultural exports and invigorate a rural area.

KC began operations in 1949, long before Del Monte came to Kenya. By 1965, the company was close to failure and contracted the services of Del Monte to manage operations. At that time, the Government of Kenya (GOK) also contracted with Del Monte to investigate the potential of Kenya for large-scale cultivation, processing, and export of pineapple. In 1968, the result was first, the purchase of KC by Del Monte; and second, the purchase of 8,800 hectares (1 hectare = 2.5 acres) by the government, which were then leased to KC for forty-eight years, renewable for the same term thereafter. This land was made up of four contiguous, unused, former sisal farms, so that no farmers were displaced. KC has since built a new cannery and operates a 4,000 hectare pineapple plantation. In addition, 400 hectares are in coffee cultivation; some cattle are being raised; and a major reforestation program is planned for erosion control and to supply charcoal and lumber to KC employees.

KC is not a satellite farming procurement system. All raw material comes from the central pineapple plantation. The rural development impact of the company derives from its employment and training of some 6,000 people. The enterprise has built several complete communities that house the majority of its employees and include a variety of health, educational, and recreational facilities. KC does reach out to the small-scale farmers in the area by providing technical assistance in the cultivation of pineapple for the local fresh-fruit market.

For the first time in its history as a Del Monte subsidiary, KC is currently actively exploring an outgrower system of procurement. The plantation has reached its maximum feasible area and productivity has leveled off. The problem being faced is that

pineapple cultivation to supply a large-scale cannery is not feasible if carried on in scattered, small-scale farms. Inter-
estingly, after independence in Kenya groups of small-scale farms
were established on large estates formerly owned by non-Kenyans.
In addition to establishing clusters of farms, large units of
land were held back for single management systems operated professionally but for the benefit of the farmer members of what can
be a cooperative or a corporation. KC is working with one such
cooperative to determine the feasibility of utilizing its large
estate for pineapple cultivation. The rural development implications of this experiment are considered below.

COUNTRY BACKGROUND*

Agriculture is the backbone of the economy and lies at the
heart of social and political life in Kenya. Currently, even in
the face of a recent decline explosive in relative importance,
the agricultural sector provides nearly 40 percent of the gross
domestic product (GDP), 34 percent of manufacturing inputs,
65 percent of nonpetroleum exports, and 65 percent of total employment. In a country having no natural resources aside from
land, people, and wildlife, and almost no mineral deposits other
than soda ash, gemstones, limestone, and fluorspar, the vital
importance of vigorous growth in agriculture and agribusiness to
the future prosperity and stability of the nation is clear and
pressing.

The agricultural sector is dominated by four characteristics
of particular importance to investors.

Private land tenure. Ninety-nine percent of the farms and
ranches are privately owned, even though tribal culture is strong
in rural Kenya. Approximately half this land is in about 3,000
so-called "large farms," ranging upward from 20 hectares to well
over 40,000 hectares (1 hectare = 2.5 acres). These farms yield
45 percent of marketed production. The other half is the property of approximately 800,000 smallholders, 70 to 75 percent of
whom farm less than 3 hectares. These farms have become increasingly important to the agricultural economy since independence
and now account for 55 percent of marketed production and 80 percent of all production.

An intriguing development has been the transfer of ownership
of some purchased large expatriate farms to groups of smallholders organized into either companies or cooperatives. In either
case, part of the land is divided into individually owned small
farms and part is farmed as an estate, with paid management.

Increasing productivity on smallholder land is of the highest priority in Kenyan planning. Land tenure realities and the

---

* This same statement is included in the case report covering the
Mumias Sugar Company (Chapter 3). It is repeated here for the
convenience of the reader.

pressing need for more food production exercise a pervasive influence on public policy, popular attitudes, and the design of public and private investments in agro-industry.

Explosive population growth. Kenya has one of the highest rates of population increase in the world. Officially designated at 3.8 percent a year, the figures of 4.0 to 4.2 percent are more widely held to be true. This steadily increases pressure on the land, as indicated by a World Bank estimate of a 0.88 hectare decline in the amount of good farmland per capita from 1970 to the year 2000. The decline in good farmland per capita has also forced agriculture and animal husbandry into marginal areas, with serious negative impact on soil erosion and water conservation in the same vicious cycle that plagues nations throughout the world. Although it is not the sole factor at work, population pressure on the land has surely contributed to the slowdown in farm production growth from an annual rate of 6 percent in the 1970s to a 1983 rate of 2.4 percent [9].

Improved agricultural practice constrained. Improved agricultural practice on smallholder farms is inhibited by the very high cost of all chemical and machinery inputs, weakly structured credit systems, traditional practices, and inadequate pricing and marketing policies. Further, despite high levels of unemployment and underemployment in rural areas, there are acute shortages of labor throughout the country at critical times in a crop rotation. Among the myriad reasons for labor shortages are more children spending more time in school, very low wage for hard work, traditional patterns of the distribution of labor, and migration to urban centers.

Powerful and pervasive force of GOK. Finally, and very importantly, GOK is a powerful and pervasive force affecting practically every aspect of commercial agriculture and agribusiness. It fixes prices and the cost of labor. Public corporations may compete with private enterprise. Marketing boards control much of the domestic and export market. GOK dictates the movement of foreign exchange, the Africanization of management, and the requirements of training, to name but a few of the interventions of the public sector. Yet despite first appearances, GOK exhibits considerable flexibility and pragmatism. Granted that negotiation is never easy and is always slow, it is, nevertheless, always possible. The structure of a few existing agro-industries best illustrates the point.

Some ventures are parastatal and managed by public corporations, for example, the Kenya Tea Development Authority (Chapter 13, Section 3); other parastatals are managed by foreign partners, such as the Mumias Sugar Company. CPC International (Chapter 13, Section 7) has been granted the first commercial exception to the rule that all grain must be purchased from GOK and can now negotiate for maize at the farm gate. East Africa Tannin Extract Company (Lonrho-UK, Chapter 13, Section 6) wholly owns and operates a 46,000-acre diversified farm-ranch, which helps support a central manufacturing complex. East Africa Industries (Unilever, Chapter 13, Section 4) is developing a source of vegetable oil-seed using land leased from absentee owners and managed under contract to private, profit-making companies.

Kenya Canners, Ltd. (Del Monte, Chapter 12) leases long-term its entire 22,000-acre estate (10,000 in pineapple) from GOK, but owns and operates a cannery and controls all export marketing of its canned product.

Two of these enterprises have been isolated for more detailed analysis, namely, the Mumias Sugar Company and Kenya Canners, Ltd. This report highlights the former.

ENTERPRISE BACKGROUND

Kenya Canners Limited (KC) is a subsidiary of the Del Monte Corporation, in turn a division of the Food and Beverage Group of R. J. Reynolds Industries, Inc. Del Monte owns 95 percent of the equity; the Development Corporation of Kenya owns 2 percent; and the remaining 3 percent is owned by twenty-four individuals (one Englishman and twenty-three Kenyans). Del Monte has invested US$36 million in the enterprise to date.

Kenya Canners is comprised of three distinct elements: the estate, the cannery, and the areas of housing. The estate is leased on a long-term basis (forty-eight years, renewable for an equal term) from the Kenyan government. Specifically, the land use pattern is as follows:

- 4,000 contiguous hectares are under pineapple cultivation, under the sole management of KC. It is judged that no further extension of the pineapple plantation will be feasible. Expansion of production, therefore, will depend upon the development of an outgrower program, now under consideration.
- 400 hectares are cultivated for coffee, a well-established crop in the region.
- About 2,000 head of cattle are grown out, fattened on cannery waste; a small breeding herd is maintained. However, KC does not consider itself permanently in the cattle business and plans to eliminate this activity in the years ahead. The breeding herd will be kept as a source of meat for employees.
- In areas not otherwise suitable, KC is developing a reforestation program to supply charcoal to employees, to serve as an erosion control system, and to provide lumber. In support of the program, KC operates a tree nursery. This type of land preservation, applying multiuse forestry practices, is of keen interest to GOK.

The cannery and its associated facilities (a training center, shops, and offices) is a modern plant with a throughput capacity of roughly 170,000 mt of raw pineapple a year. Management estimates that this input could increase as much as 15 to 18 percent with modest changes, and feels that the market for this increased production is available. This perceived marketing opportunity, combined with production limits of the plantation, have stimulated current interest in the development of an outgrower program.

The housing areas, distributed around the cannery within reasonable walking distance, incorporate some 3,300 houses owned by KC and provided free to workers in the factory and on the plantation. Historically, the distribution of housing has been based on a combination of factors such as position, length of service, and need. Those who must (or choose) to live elsewhere receive a housing allowance of 15 percent of base salary.

KC employs 6,000 people at the peak of the season; 5,500 on the average: 2,500 are regularly employed in production and engineering, training, research and development, and various other functions of administration; 3,000 to 3,500 are utilized on the plantation and in other areas of agricultural activity.

No exports go to the United States. All canned goods are sold to and through Del Monte International into European, Middle Eastern, and other foreign markets. KC also sells a small amount of fresh-fruit to the GOK Horticultural Crops Development Authority, for air-freighting into European markets. Although the authority fixes the price of fresh-fruit, this is nonetheless profitable for KC because the fresh product brings a higher net return than canned products. It is significant to note that despite the wide range of GOK marketing boards and the extensive involvement of GOK in price controls, KC markets its canned goods free of price control or any other government intervention. Presumably, this is in recognition of the fact that canned pineapple is now a major foreign exchange earner for Kenya, and that Del Monte is best able to maximize sales and protect the competitive position of KC products. KC management notes that it is currently earning over 300 million Kenyan shillings (US$22.2 million) a year in foreign exchange. The conversion rate used throughout this chapter is the 1983 rate of KS1 = US$0.074.)

History

Kenya Canners Limited was first organized in 1949 by Theodore West, a British businessman, and C.W.P. Harries, whose mother, O.M.A. Harries, was the pioneer in Kenya who developed pineapple for the fresh fruit market of the country (circa 1910) at Thika, about thirty miles east-northeast of Nairobi. The company struggled along until 1958, when it was taken over by the Tancot Group, an established East African company. Tancot launched an expansion program that increased the cannery potential to over 20,000 mt per year of pineapple and mixed vegetables. However, all raw material procurement was based on outgrowers in the Thika area. Apparently, the outgrowers were not properly organized, were not provided with the necessary technical assistance or financial support, and were not suitably located. In any event, the enterprise was in very poor condition by 1965.

At that time, KC entered into an agreement with Del Monte to manage the Thika cannery. At the same time, Del Monte was invited by GOK to investigate the potential for expanding pineapple cultivation and processing, both for export of canned goods and for marketing fresh fruit locally. By 1968, Del Monte decided to exercise its option to purchase the majority shareholding of KC. This decision was facilitated by GOK, which had acquired the defunct Anglo-French Sisal Estate at Thika for long-term lease to KC. The government then went on to purchase three more large estates, all more or less contiguous to the former sisal plantation, laying the foundation for a 1972 decision by Del Monte to implement a major expansion program, including the construction of a new cannery. It is important to note that unlike the situation at the Mumias Sugar Company (Chapter 3), where many farmers were bought out by the Government of Kenya, no smallholders were involved in making land available to KC.

Since the early 1970s, KC has become a successful and important part of agro-industry in Kenya. It has brought thousands of acres of land from abandonment to a high level of productivity. As noted, KC offers employment, housing, and other benefits to some 6,000 people. The company appears to have established good relationships with its two unions, the Kenya Plantation Workers and the Food and Allied Workers Union. Despite occasional gossip heard to the contrary, GOK seems to hold KC in high regard and makes no effort to participate financially or seek control of the company.

More than anything else putting pressure on KC in its effort to remain competitive in world markets is inflation, tied to import controls. Tin plate costs have gone up 400 percent over the past several years. Tires, fuel, spare parts, energy, and many other basic items have also increased dramatically in cost. KC has worked diligently to decrease plantation costs and increase efficiency at the cannery, but it remains a serious question for Del Monte as to whether or not GOK will take the necessary actions to reduce the risk to manageable proportions. (See Chapter 8, the case of Productos Del Monte from Mexico for an identical problem Del Monte faces there in canning vegetables.) Negotiations on the subject are constant. KC management could not reveal the substance of these talks except to indicate the generally held belief that the industry was too important to endanger.

One corrective measure offered to all exporting industries by GOK is the "export compensation scheme." Prior to 1982, this provided a 10 percent rebate on the FOB value of exports to a given level; plus an additional 15 percent if this first level was exceeded. In 1982, in an economy move, the government eliminated the rebate. There was such organized resistance to this decision by industry that the incentive was reinstated in 1983. The 10 percent rebate level was maintained as before and the entire package of rebates was made more attractive by increasing the second level rebates from 15 percent of FOB values to 25 percent.

Although this success in getting GOK to reinstate the export compensation scheme was encouraging to KC, management is concerned that Kenyan industry, foreign-controlled or not, has no truly effective voice with which to address GOK. The Kenya Association of Manufacturers is weak; the Kenya Chamber of Commerce is not highly regarded; and the Federation of Kenya Employers tries to confine itself to matters of employment and wages. Finally, there is the Investment Advisory Council, set up by GOK to facilitate entry of foreign capital and help in the search for local joint venture partners. Yet negotiations on critical issues, such as duties charged on imported tinplate for cans, depend on individual companies doing the job.

OUTREACH

Outgrowers

Until recently, KC had no outgrower program. All fresh pineapple was produced on its own plantation. Recently, two farms lying adjacent to the plantation, owned by absentee landlords, each about twelve to sixteen hectares, were contracted and are cultivated by KC as integral parts of its own estate. Actually, as the production limits of the estate have been reached, KC has been studying more intensively the opportunities for further development of an outgrower program.

The outgrower situation is a complex one. Farmers delivering fruit to the cannery must expect to receive 50 to 70 percent of the price they could receive in the local fresh-fruit market. On the other hand, the fresh-fruit outlet is limited and subject to considerable wastage. Alternatively, yields would increase under KC direction and there would be a guaranteed market, in all more than compensating for lower prices (although KC staff has not made actual calculations to prove the point). To obtain the highest net return, KC estimates that groups of outgrowers would need to aggregate twelve to twenty hectares. This is not a simple task. The topography of the area is hilly, cut with ravines, and not well served with secondary or tertiary roads. This could force very high transportation costs on the system. All of these factors have been discouraging.

The one current possibility for approaching outgrower production, which is being carefully nurtured, has its roots in a bit of Kenyan history. After independence at the end of 1963, GOK began purchasing large farms that had been owned and operated by expatriates for redistribution to the indigenous people of Kenya. Some of these were organized into companies, others into cooperatives. In some instances, those who purchased shares established small individual farms; other shareholders remained absentee and organized production around professional management. Many cases reflect a combination of methods in the practice of land use. Part of the owned area is divided into small farms with resident operators; the remainder is operated as a corporate farm, under paid management, with the profits (if any) divided among the shareholders.

One such enterprise, a cooperative, lies about 25 kilometers from the KC estate. The area owned is about 3,200 to 4,000 hectares. There are approximately 1,000 shareholders, some resident on farmsites or homesites, many more living elsewhere. The primary cash crop is coffee. The cooperative members have aggregated a large area for this purpose and it is operated professionally, under the terms of a contract with a coffee estate management company. In its search for acceptable outgrower sites, KC observed that roughly 800 hectares of land, owned by the cooperative in one block, was not being utilized and might be well suited for pineapple. With approval of the cooperative board, KC set up a 2-hectare test and demonstration plot, which did prove the area to be potentially suitable to pineapple and within the capability of the cooperative to bring into production, with technical assistance provided by KC. The transport distance to the cannery is reasonable; the road access acceptable.

As of early 1984, a two-man team from Kenyan Canners, comprised of the director of Research, Training and Agricultural Extension (an expatriate with many years of experience in Kenya with pineapple) and the manager of Personnel and Industrial Relations (a Kenyan with a master's degree in business administration, earned in the United States), have been working with the cooperative. Their task is to evolve a satisfactory contract for production and sale to KC. From the perspective of KC, it is felt that the agreement should cover a minimum of ten years. To assure proper practice, technical and other forms of assistance might also be required. A pool of machinery will be needed. For the cooperative to own the equipment, if it proves feasible, would be best for all; if not feasible, KC might find it necessary to own, operate, and maintain the machinery, as it does on its own plantation.

The cooperative board of directors has full responsibility to find the credit financing needed for the project. Based on its own operating costs, KC estimates that it will require an investment of roughly KS25,000 per hectare ($740 per acre) up to the first harvest, eighteen months after planting. To move ahead prudently and within the bounds of possibility, KC has suggested that the project be started with 100 hectares.

Education

KC has created a fine school system associated with a private enterprise in Kenya. Five schools have been built and are maintained by KC. Four of these are at the elementary grade only and are run by GOK, which pays the teachers and covers all other costs. The fifth school, which carries on through secondary level, is wholly owned and run by KC, which pays all teachers and finances any deficits at the end of the year. In recent years, this deficit financing has averaged KS250,000 a year (US$18,500). Enrollment in all five schools is about 1,250 to 1,300; in 1983, 93 percent of these were children of employees. The KC private school, in contrast, had 240 pupils in 1983, of which 25 percent were children of employees and 75 percent children of people from all over Kenya. This school charges tuition in an effort to attain self-sufficiency, and it emphasizes a curriculum permitting graduates to enter universities throughout the world. There are plans to structure the educational program so that graduates may plan their university careers in Kenya or overseas. This unusual and considerable investment in, and direct responsibility for, the education of children of employees and Kenyans generally is a matter of great pride and satisfaction at KC and is an outreach regarded with considerable favor by GOK.

In another area of education, KC has encouraged its director of Research, Training, and Agricultural Extension to work closely with nearby Kenyatta Agricultural School in the development of their curriculum, as an aid to generating a practical, problem-solving, and critical view of Kenya's rural problems. This is done purely as a public service.

Research

Also as an outreach of a public service nature to the rural community at large, going beyond any KC commercial interest, KC finances a series of demonstrations that provide small-scale growers of fresh pineapple who sell in the local markets with information on the costs and benefits of different kinds of practice: using or not using fertilizer with different proportions of ingredients; using herbicides or not; applying water or not, among other arrangements of variables. Field days are utilized to follow the course of growth and yield and to communicate the varying rates of return on investment of both time and money. The entire emphasis of this outreach program is on fresh fruit production and marketing. The project is not intended to build a reservoir of potential outgrowers for the KC cannery.

Housing, Medical Care, and Other Services

As noted earlier, KC provides 3,300 housing units to its employees. These units are distributed about the cannery and plantation area to form several communities. This housing is provided free. Each area is served by a medical dispensary, staffed with aides who have been trained to perform simple health-care functions. A corporation doctor makes the rounds of these dispensaries daily and takes care of more serious matters. Medical care is also free. Each housing area is served by a store, privately managed by the successful bidder for the opportunity. Once the management is settled, KC does not intervene in the business. It is estimated that over the last twelve years, KC has spent KS35 million (US$2.6 million) on its programs of education, housing, and medical care.

Training

KC participates in the National Apprentice Training Program. For this purpose, a training center has been in operation for the past fourteen years. The facilities and organization of the center must be approved by the Ministry of Education, and the cost of maintaining and carrying out the programs of the center is partially borne by a levy of KS4 per mt of agricultural product. GOK is authorized to pay back 60 percent of this levy, based on satisfactory performance, but the payback by GOK does not cover all costs. KC subsidizes the difference.

The center provides a three-year program for craft apprentices and a four-year program for technician apprentices. The latter program involves a higher level of skill and leads to a higher starting salary and increased job status. The net cost of a three-year program has been about KS17,000 per student (US$1,258). GOK controls the basic course context through the inputs of the Ministry of Labor and the Federal Directorate for Training. The company certifies the apprentices and directs the center and its staff.

Graduate apprentices are not obligated to go to work for KC. Out of 220 students trained over a period of fourteen years, 170 have gone elsewhere; 50 work for KC. Lately, this trend appears to have been reversed. For example, in 1983, it was expected that 23 of the 27 trainees would go to work for KC. Part of the reason so many now stay is that the program includes twenty weeks of hands-on experience in the cannery. Since pineapple-processing machinery and supporting maintenance is unique in Kenya at KC, students are attracted to jobs that have become familiar and cannot be replicated elsewhere.

There is an apprentice hostel provided at no cost to the student. A tool box is also given to each student. KC can claim half the cost from GOK; the apprentice buys the box at half price, paying for it over three years.

PAYOFF

For the KC Employees

The payoff to the people who work at KC has been considerable. Some 6,000 people have jobs and they and their families have security and improved quality of life. Housing, schooling, and medical services are better and are immediately available. Upward mobility on the job is fostered by the Apprentice Training Program and in other ways. KC pays out some KS60 million (US$4.4 million) directly in salaries each year, in addition to the millions of shillings spent by KC to subsidize housing and other social services. The workers, their families, and their unions are all treated with respect. However, as suggested below in the section on policy recommendations, the adequacy of those benefits might be challenged in terms of human development goals.

For the Company

No figures were given to quantify the payoff to KC or Del Monte, Yet the longevity and vigor of KC indicate that return on investment has been sufficient to sustain the enterprise.

For the Host Country

The payoff for Kenya has been positive and constructive from the beginning. Past failure in efforts to bring pineapple production and exports to commercial success had failed; KC made it work. The cost to GOK of acquiring the land leased to KC has been a good investment and the major financial risk in the enterprise was taken by Del Monte. Unproductive land is now fruitful. Steady employment has been created for 6,000 to 6,500 people, enhancing the quality of life for many thousands more who are members of workers' families. Foreign exchange earnings have ranged from US$22 to $30 million a year. KC has been meticulous in financial reporting and in its adherence to tax law. KC has contributed a model educational facility, well worth replication elsewhere in the country, and its training center meets every standard set by the Ministries of Education and Labor. In all honesty, it is difficult to see how GOK could be critical of the returns on its original invitation to Del Monte to help Kenya develop its pineapple potential.

POLICY IMPLICATIONS

For the Company

The major policy concern of KC is to maintain its products at a competitive price in the different markets it serves. Management is well aware of this fact. There is constant effort to interact with GOK. The efficiency of the plantation and the cannery has improved steadily. However, there are two additional matters of policy which might well receive closer attention in the search for lower costs and long-range stability. Both tie in closely to the expanded role KC might play in stimulating rural development.

KC management noted that with a relatively minor new investment, the cannery could put through more pineapple than the plantation is likely ever to produce, and that the market is there for the product. Logically, this implies development of an outgrower program, and KC is working on this. The evolution of the outgrower project under consideration and the nature of the land tenure system involved--a cooperative estate, partly occupied by resident small-scale farmers and partly set aside in a large block for development as a cooperative plantation--raise several policy considerations both for KC and for agribusiness ventures everywhere.

If it is important to the future income of KC to obtain the pineapple from cooperative land, and if the cooperative members cannot themselves afford to take the risk with their own capital but will take all the risk if they borrow the money, then is this an equitable arrangement when one compares Del Monte resources with those of the cooperative members? Granted that KC is leading the cooperative to an excellent new source of income and that by establishing a one-channel marketing system, with technical support, it reduces the risk. However, what KC has invested in a 2-hectare test is as nothing compared to the investment in 100 hectares by the cooperative.

On the question of what the cooperative can and cannot afford to risk, it would seem logical that KC ask the question and help find an answer. My impression was that the nature of the cooperative membership was not clearly identified. Who are they; what social and economic level do they represent; what responsibility might they be expected to accept? With such a data base, the reality and fairness of asking the cooperative to finance a 100-hectare, semi-commercial test of pineapple cultivation might be better evaluated.

KC is indeed helping to create an exciting opportunity to accelerate rural development, touching the lives of several thousand people, and building a model that might be widely applied, in Kenya and elsewhere. If, upon further investigation, it were to be shown that KC cannot take on the burden of financing the credit needed and that the cooperative either cannot or should not accept the risk, might not this be a perfect opportunity for the USAID mission in Kenya to enter into a joint venture with KC? AID could invest in the credit, using a deferred repayment schedule, with soft interest terms. KC could then accelerate and manage the system. The training and guidance given to the people could be intensified, hastening the transfer of full responsibility. The question here is: Who takes responsibility to bring these forces into play? KC would seem to be the logical and proper center of responsibility, first to be sure of the facts, to avoid any error in judgment as to who can do what; and second to negotiate with USAID, whose current emphasis in Kenya is to foster the role of private enterprise as a force for rural development. The concept of joint venture between private enterprise and USAID is discussed further in Chapter 15. The objectives of such a venture, which integrates commercial goals and the goals of rural development, were defined in Chapter 1.

A related long-range policy matter concerns the future envisioned for the 6,000 people who work on the plantation, in the cannery, and among the service departments that together form KC. The KC environment, while benign in so many ways, is nonetheless definitely limiting to upward mobility for the majority. It might be predicted, therefore, that if nothing is done beforehand, some agitation will eventually foment, with people demanding more pay; more benefits; a faster outreach. KC could be vulnerable, as are all foreign companies with large plantations and factories at their core. The landless may demand some land. All may demand a bigger share of the profit. Some may demand a share of ownership. There is no need to write a scenario of chaos or gloom. But human history is so replete with documented support for the possibilities of trouble that it would seem a sound recommendation to KC that it adopt policies that help anticipate the changes in attitude and behavior likely to occur over time in the political ambience of Kenya. This will allow management to respond creatively and promptly.

The example of the retail stores established in each of the residential communities built by KC is illustrative of past policy and what a relatively small change might accomplish. As was noted, these stores are run for profit by people who have bid for the privilege. Each store serves a large number of families. The question immediately comes to mind: Would it not be better for development purposes and for the sake of long-range harmony between workers and KC for the families in each area to own the store that serves them and share the benefits of profit?

There is so much to be gained. It would generate significant savings (or earnings) for each family; 1,000 families buying their essential foods, soap, candles, pots and pans, dishes, among dozens of other simple items, surely generates a very large cash flow in the course of a year. With such purchasing power and attendant possibilities for wholesale buying, moderating markup, and low overhead charges (housing for the store supplied free by KC), many forms of advantage are attainable by the people. In the long term, an even more significant developmental gain is possible if the people participate more in such economic and social projects as the store. The cumulative educational impact could greatly affect personal attitudes; a sense of participation and achievement; a sense of the meaning of capital, savings, and investment; and an appreciation of organization, mutual responsibility, and honesty. Without trying to exaggerate the human development impact of several stores, it is nonetheless true that development is a complex process that achieves its ends by integrating a multitude of gains, each arising from a modest activity. Giant steps forward are rare in development. A chance to take a small step should not be lost. It therefore seems reasonable to suggest to KC that as a first pass, the way the stores have been integrated into the life of the workers at KC be reappraised. What would it take to do it differently, at what cost, and at whose cost? What benefits might justify a change?

For the Government of Kenya

In general, the policies of GOK, as they affect KC, are reasonable in light of circumstances and are not constraining, with one exception: the rationality and speed with which new regulations are conceived and issued, bearing upon import duties and export duties.

Manufacturing costs, for all industries, have risen sharply in recent years. In the case of agro-industries like KC, which export their entire line in cans, a rise of 400 percent in the cost of imported tin plate, strongly affected by import duties, becomes a threat to survival. Indeed, the East Africa Tannin Extract Company, Ltd. (Lonrho-U.K.), in Eldoret, Kenya, has recently been squeezed out of world markets for canned mushrooms because of can price, even after setting in operation one of the most efficient, low-cost systems of mushroom production in the world. Tied inversely to tin plate costs is the question of export duties and whether or not additional rebates can be used more creatively to alleviate the impact of importing irreplaceable manufacturing inputs.

The policy recommended to GOK is basically directed to procedures rather than to substance. GOK and the managements of export industries are in constant negotiation on matters of mutual concern: reducing foreign exchange outflows; increasing GOK revenues; maintaining the competitive position of Kenyan exporters; protecting jobs; promoting new foreign investment; and keeping the transfer of technology and skills to Kenya a lively, enriching process. However, the analytical procedures used by GOK often lack rationality and seem to take too long. Regulations need to be issued quickly and frequently in order to sustain a balance between costs and competitiveness. Management claims that clear, current, and accurate data are being supplied to the appropriate ministries; what is needed is the force of a policy that minimizes delay and pinpoints decision-making on very specific issues affecting very specific industries. Global policies and industry-wide regulations are, it is said, simply not functional.

In terms of rural development, as was recommended in Chapter 3, GOK needs to exercise dynamic leadership if the full benefits of agro-industrial investments are to be realized. But GOK should recognize the likelihood that no investor or prudent manager is likely to risk scarce resources on an extended socioeconomic development program unless encouraged by public policy that makes the will of government unequivocal. GOK should also reckon with worldwide experience, which suggests that the will of government is ineffective unless backed by collaboration in financing and by the allocation of other resources necessary to facilitate the task.

For the Donor Country

The following points are taken, essentially verbatim, from the case report covering the Mumias Sugar Company, also in Kenya. Mumias and KC share many of the same achievements, problems, and opportunities. Insofar as U.S. policy can or might take advantage of the presence of these two enterprises in Kenya to accelerate rural development in the country, what can be suggested for Mumias is relevant to KC.

With reference to agro-industries already in existence in Kenya, U.S. aid might be extended programmatically to ensure that any opportunity created for vigorous integrated rural development is not lost. This policy would be independent of the source of capital in the venture. Rather, it would emphasize the importance of well-managed, profitable, rurally sited enterprise in catalyzing socioeconomic progress. For example, in the case of KC, U.S. aid might focus on the needs and potential of the cooperative farm being considered by KC as the site for its first outgrower program.

In point of fact, every one of the more than ten agro-industrial enterprises studied or contacted briefly in Kenya evidence exciting opportunities to build on commercial success to

achieve new heights of extended benefits in rural development.
Yet, not one company was prepared to take financial and operational responsibility without the full policy support of GOK and
without financial support arising outside of their business cash
flows. On the other hand, no one with whom the idea was discussed was disinterested in the possibility of a joint venture
with aid agencies that would not detract from the profit-making
function, even if it risked beyond traditional corporate limits
on activities in development.

Beyond capitalizing on development opportunities generated
by existing agribusiness, it would seem desirable for the aid
agency to relate as closely as possible to investors considering
new investments in agriculturally related, rurally located enterprises. This would help ensure that feasibility analyses included the costs of integrating the production function with the
function of development. In this way, the implications of success in economic terms could be examined for their impact on people and on the opportunities to be anticipated relative to area
socioeconomic dynamics. Such early collaboration between public
and private investors could help in the invention of the means to
blend corporate and developmental objectives into harmonious,
financially viable management systems. All this would require
strong policy backing on the part of the U.S. government, both to
influence acceptance of the approach by GOK and to ensure adequate financial resources for the country AID mission.

A policy that supports the training of Kenyan professionals
in a very wide spectrum of fields has always been basic to U.S.
aid. This policy might well be extended to include rural development as an adjunct to agro-industrial enterprise. It may be
timely to give recognition to worldwide experience that suggests
that agronomists or other technicians, economists or other social
scientists, or politicians, however skilled, do not necessarily
make good managers of integrated rural development. This even
more likely to be true when development goals are integrated with
those of a profit-making agro-industrial system. Therefore,
training for the field needs to emphasize its own unique professional character and provide special content suitable for the
task.

13
Interaction Between Agribusiness and the Small-Scale Farmer: An Inventory of Experience in Less-Developed Countries

Simon Williams

INTRODUCTION

It may be recollected from Chapter 1, which introduced the purpose of this book, that this inquiry was initiated as part of a search for the answers to two questions:

1. How can new investment in agribusiness be accelerated and widely extended throughout Africa, Asia, and Latin America, to help improve the performance of national food systems and the global network of supply that they comprise?
2. How can the resources of agribusiness, once in place--resources of money, management skill, technological knowhow, research capability, international operating and marketing experience, entrepreneurial energy, and good will--be applied in such a way as to speed up rural development to help relieve the compounded miseries of poverty, hunger, malnutrition, poor health, and social inequity, that plague the world?

In the persistent search for answers to these questions, it is significant that there has been so little investigation into the enormous spread and variety of existing agribusiness investment experience. Surely, as long as the development role of agribusiness is queried in terms of ideology and passion, with little or no information drawn from our heritage of knowledge about the impact of billions of dollars of investment along the food and fiber chains that bind all of humanity together, there can be no valid response to these two queries.

It was from an awareness that the future of agricultural and rural development, in terms both of policy and methodology, could be much more widely conceived if we could capture the past and current agribusiness experience that this inventory project was conceived. As presented, the inventory is but a beginning, a bit of evidence verifying the richness of the storehouse of lessons to be learned if the effort to gather the data is maintained. The hope is that more will be done, and continuously. A plan has been drawn to develop a computerized, rational method to store and retrieve information in both descriptive and analytical ways. The goal is to put in place a true state-of-the-art resource that can reveal the essential harmony between investment and rural development goals.

The sixty-four notations in the inventory, which for convenience include the eleven cases described in more detail in Chapters 2 through 12, are but a representative sample, although it is felt that they fairly illustrate the diversity, richness, and utility of the knowledge "out there" to be tapped. Actually, the projects included provide direct access to literally hundreds of additional cases. The doors are open to an examination of the more than 200 companies in which the Latin American Agribusiness Corporation has a financial stake; the same can be said of more than 100 agro-industrial ventures of the Commonwealth Development Corporation. There is an opportunity to integrate the data in this inventory with the files of the Fund for Multinational Management Education, Agribusiness Worldwide, Enterprise and Development, Olsen's Agribusiness Report, the Overseas Private Investment Corporation, and many other institutions that have been gathering relevant information. The multinational companies contacted operate much more widely than is revealed by the cases described in this report. Examples are Booker Agricultural International, British-American Tobacco, Unilever, Castle and Cooke, Del Monte, Nestlé, Ralston Purina, and Tate and Lyle Technical Services, which are all willing to share information should the investigation proceed.

1. NUCLEAR ESTATES

These are enterprises with a core processing plant; plus a farm or plantation operated by the plant to produce part of the raw material requirement; plus a system of obtaining additional raw material by means of contracting exclusively with small-scale farmers. The following cases are examples of nuclear estate enterprises. The area of operations is given in parentheses.

- Commonwealth Development Corporation (Worldwide)
- Gulf and Western Americas Corporation (Caribbean Basin)
- Higaturu Oil Palms/Higaturu Processing Pty., Ltd. (South Pacific Ocean)
- Kenya Seed Company (East Africa)
- Mumias Sugar Company Limited (East Africa)
- Tenneco Sahara Agricultural Venture (Northeast Africa)
- Texaco Agro-Industrial (Nigeria) Ltd. (West Africa)
- Vuvulane Irrigated Farms (Southern Africa)

COMMONWEALTH DEVELOPMENT CORPORATION (CDC)
London, England

The Commonwealth Development Corporation is generally considered to be one of the pioneers of the "nucleus estate" design
of agro-industry, and with investments in fifty nations, CDC is
undoubtedly the largest repository of experience relevant to
agro-industry involvement with small-scale farmers to be found in
the world. Four examples of CDC investments are cited in this
book: two as detailed case descriptions (the Mumias Sugar Company in Kenya, Chapter 3, and the Vuvulane Irrigated Farms in
Swaziland, Chapter 4); and two in this inventory--(the Kenya Tea
Development Authority and the Higaturu Oil Palm/Processing enterprise in Papua, New Guinea). There are over 100 more cases awaiting description and analysis.
A CDC publication provides this description:

CDC's constitution and powers are laid down by Acts
of Parliament, consolidated in the Commonwealth Development Corporation Act 1978, which charges the Corporation with the task of assisting overseas countries in
the development of their economies. It does so by investing its funds in development projects which not
only help to increase the wealth of those countries but
also yield a reasonable return on the money invested.
Its area of operations covers Commonwealth countries
which have achieved independence since 1948, the remaining territories dependent upon Britain, and, with
ministerial approval, any other developing country. To
date, the Minister has given CDC authority to operate
in Bangladesh, Cameroon, Costa Rica, Ecuador, Ethiopia,
Honduras, Indonesia, Ivory Coast, Liberia, Philippines,
Sudan, Thailand, Vanuato, and Zimbabwe; and in Rwanda,
Sri Lanka, Tunisia, and Zaire in which countries the
Corporation had not invested.
By virtue of the terms of reference set out in the
Act which require CDC to pay its way, CDC operates on
broadly commercial lines. It does not make grants but
offers investment in the development of resources. In
general, it chooses its projects with due regard to
their development value to the country concerned rather
than for their profitability. Close relations with
overseas governments are maintained through CDC's regional and country offices in order to ensure the economic development of the countries concerned [10].

CDC's 1982 Annual Report and Summary Accounts notes that
there are 250 or so CDC projects in fifty countries, with combined long-term capital resources amounting to an estimated
£2,500 million, of which CDC has provided 500 million. Table 13.1
illustrates the financial operations and structure of CDC.

Table 13.1
Commonwealth Development Corporation Five-Year Summary (in millions £)

	1982 £m	1981 £m	1980 £m	1979 £m	1978 £m
Group Balance Sheet					
Investments	467.2	403.6	346.8	319.7	281.9
Provisions	(56.5)	(44.1)	(42.6)	(36.3)	(32.2)
Net investments	410.7	359.5	304.2	283.4	249.7
Fixed assets	4.7	4.5	3.9	3.3	3.1
Other debtors less (creditor) items	(4.7)	(1.9)	0.7	(1.7)	9.4
Cash and deposits less overdrafts	20.9	16.4	23.9	25.0	21.0
	431.6	378.5	332.7	310.0	283.2
Financed by					
Loans from HMG	335.5	313.2	283.3	270.3	247.9
Reserves	82.4	49.8	32.2	21.5	16.3
Provision for interest equalization	13.1	14.9	16.7	17.3	18.0
Secured and other loans	0.5	0.5	0.4	0.8	0.9
Minority interests	0.1	0.1	0.1	0.1	0.1
	431.6	378.5	332.7	310.0	283.2
Group Revenue Account					
Operating surplus	31.1	35.2	31.6	30.8	28.2
Other items	8.9	(2.0)	3.2	(0.7)	1.3
Interest payable	(16.2)	(14.8)	(14.3)	(13.8)	(13.8)

Provisions	(6.0)	(4.2)	(6.2)	(1.7)	(12.4)
Taxation	(3.7)	(6.4)	(3.4)	(7.1)	(7.1)
Transfer to general reserve	6.6	5.7	10.9	9.6	4.3
Group Source and Application of Funds					
Source of Funds					
Cash and short-term deposits	15.1	21.0	25.0	23.9	16.4
Drawn from HMG	34.1	28.9	20.3	38.4	33.0
Self-generated funds	12.8	29.4	31.0	31.7	25.7
	62.0	79.3	76.3	94.0	75.1
Application of Funds					
New investments	33.1	53.1	47.7	72.8	52.1
Fixed assets	0.3	0.7	0.6	0.5	0.3
Working capital	7.6	0.5	4.1	4.3	1.8
	41.0	54.3	52.4	77.6	54.2
Closing cash and short-term deposits	21.0	25.0	23.9	16.4	20.9
Drawn from HMG, less principal and interest paid to HMG	4.1	15.2	(0.2)	16.1	5.1
New capital commitments to projects in the year	59.1	82.7	80.8	94.7	102.9
Total invested or committed at year end	374.7	445.7	512.3	590.1	703.8
Total undisbursed commitment at year end	104.3	136.2	165.4	186.5	236.6

Source: Commonwealth Development Corporation. 1982. Annual Report and Summary of Accounts [13].

According to this report, CDC is authorized to borrow £750 million on long and medium term, and up to £20 million on short term. Of the £750 million, up to £700 million may be borrowed from U.K. Exchequer funds. The Minister may, by order with the consent of the Treasury, increase borrowing up to £850 million, of which not more than £800 million may be borrowed from exchequer funds.

CDC Chairman Lord Kindersley, states in the report:

> Nearly one-and-a-half million acres in 30 countries are under commercial crops, forestry, or being grazed by cattle. A further one million acres are being farmed by some 400,000 smallholders growing cash and food crops. Very large tonnages of agricultural produce are shipped, earning considerable sums of foreign exchange and reducing the need for food imports. Industrial enterprises supported by CDC produce goods not only for home consumption, thus saving foreign exchange, but also for export. Savings in foreign exchange due to reduced imports of oil result on an ever increasing scale from greater use of alternative sources of energy such as water, geothermal steam, and local coal deposits. As a result of all these CDC-supported activities, hundreds of thousands are in paid employment or being helped to earn a livelihood, and many are receiving training in professional and technical skills. In addition to those direct benefits, food production on a sizeable scale and widespread secondary development is taking place through small enterprises which have sprung up around the CDC projects in order to meet the needs of the workforces [13].

GULF AND WESTERN AMERICAS CORPORATION (GW)
La Romana, Dominican Republic

In 1967, Gulf and Western acquired the South Puerto Rico Sugar Company (incorporated in New Jersey in 1900), which consisted of property and sugar mills in Florida, Puerto Rico, and the Dominican Republic (DR). In the DR, the purchase included 275,000 acres, of which 12,000 were used for sugar cane cultivation and 130,000 were used for livestock pasture. There was also a sugar mill, a furfural plant, a railroad system, and other related facilities. The purchase was made six years after the assassination of General Rafael Leonidas Trujillo, and during this time, as the country experienced eleven governments and total turmoil (including a civil war which broke out in 1965 and which was quelled by a mixed army from the United States and other members of the Organization of American States), the area under GW suffered from total neglect and seethed with social and political unrest.

Development Opportunity

GW decided first to completely modernize the sugar mill and the plantation, in order to bring the property into a competitive and profitable enterprise. It then removed expatriate staff and initiated a long range plan to diversify the agricultural base of the operation. It also was decided to develop tourism in La Romana, as a profitable and quick means of generating employment for local people and earning foreign exchange for the Dominican Republic.

There was much to be done to enliven and enrich the social and economic conditions of the essentially rural people in eastern DR. To diffuse an image of the corporation's intentions and policies and to help concentrate attention on these developmental issues, GW created the GW Dominican Foundation in 1973. This foundation has provided a channel for financial support of projects in health, education, recreation, community development, and cultural affairs. Over US$10 million has been granted to citizens' groups and nonprofit organizations since the foundation began its work. An agricultural school was established in El Seibo; a classroom building was built at the Central University of the East in San Pedro Macoris; over $2 million has been granted to public and private schools in La Romana, enabling the city to achieve the highest levels of education in the country.

In 1976, GW created the Agricultural Company of Central Romana Employees and Workers. They then donated 33,000 acres of arable land to this worker-owned and -managed enterprise which produces vegetables and sugar cane. In October 1984, Gulf and Western announced that it was selling its agribusiness enterprises in the Dominican Republic. Indications are that all operations will proceed as they were.

HIGATURU OIL PALMS PTY., LTD. (HOP)
AND HIGATURU PROCESSING PTY., LTD. (HP)
Papua, New Guinea

Higaturu Oil Palms Pty., Ltd., and Higaturu Processing Pty., Ltd., were incorporated in 1976 as a fifty-fifty joint venture of the Commonwealth Development Corporation and the government of Papua, New Guinea (total investment over US$17 million at exchange rates effective over the past years; the investment figure is thus approximate). In 1982, CDC subscribed approximately US$2.2 million in addition, as equity. Various loans have been made by CDC, the German Finance Company for Investments in Developing Countries, and the European Investment Bank. The oil palm estate, at the end of 1982, was 11,157 acres; smallholder (settlers) production was harvested from 11,353 acres. The oil mill has a capacity of 60 metric tons per hour. Some 1,800 persons are employed at the mill and on the estate; 1,400 smallholders are dependent on the project (about 10,000 people directly impacted) [4].

Development Opportunity

CDC's responsibility includes general management of HOP and HP. HOP manages the estate; provides administrative and accountancy services to HP; provides technical assistance to smallholders; and supplies seedlings at the cost of production. HP, in turn, purchases, processes, and markets all fruit; the government sets the price on fruit. HP also provides technical services to a government-owned transport company for the integrated enterprise. The government's responsibility to the outgrowers is met by the Smallholders Management Organization (SMO), which operates under the direction of the Department of Primary Industries. SMO has particular charge of land clearing, plot layout, and settler selection. It also provides infrastructure, technical assistance, credit, and bulk purchase and transport of all inputs. SMO organizes the harvest and sets quality standards. It is important to note that SMO, not CDC, has the responsibility of dealing with the day-to-day problems of the smallholders.

It is thought that cash income of the smallholders will stabilize at about US$1,750 per year (based on currency values of several years ago), roughly three times more than might be expected from the basic food crops cultivated in the area. The full developmental implications of this oil palm/settlement scheme are far from clear. Whether or not SMO has both the mandate and the capability of building on HP/HOP as a center of wealth production, to create socioeconomic development beyond anything to be expected of the impact of one enterprise, was not clear from the literature relating to Higaturu or from discussions held in London at CDC headquarters. However, as with all CDC projects, the investment has established an infrastructure for development. It is to be hoped that the investment in SMO will be sufficient to capitalize on the opportunity in the years ahead.

KENYA SEED COMPANY LIMITED (KSC)
Kitale, Kenya

Kenya Seed Company Limited was formed in 1956, as a private company, by a group of farmers, in response to demand for seed of improved grass and legume varieties developed by the Grasslands Research Station at Kitale (now the National Agricultural Research Station). Since then, as crop research has grown and diversified, KSC produces and markets the seed of sunflower, maize, wheat, barley, and most recently, horticultural seeds. The company receives new cultivars from government breeding programs, and organizes multiplication of certified seed with contract growers around Kitale. KSC operates its own seed-drying, -cleaning, -testing, and -packaging plant; it provides a management service to farmers under contract that provides machinery, inputs, and credit, enabling these farmers, usually with extensive land holdings, to produce large quantities of seed. A wholly owned subsidiary manufactures and markets seed driers.

Finally, KSC leases 3,500 acres from the Agricultural Development Corporation for research and production purposes. Current value of the company is about US$10 million. In 1981, gross turnover was about US$23 million. The company's development has for the most part been financed from profits. Equity holding has altered until the Kenyan government, through the Agricultural Development Corporation, has become the majority shareholder.

Development Opportunity

Without doubt, KSC has played the major role in the commercialization of crop research in Kenya. There is no practical way to measure the economic return to farmers of all scales, and to the nation. The main reason for its remarkable impact, other than the quality of its product, has been the nationwide marketing system worked out with the Kenya Farmers' Association Ltd. (KFA), a cooperative through which thousands of agricultural input distributors, cooperative unions, and individual storekeepers in even the most remote parts of the country can draw supplies from KFA depots. These depots, in turn, are located so that no supplier is beyond a source reasonably distant from the outlet. A countrywide price for seed was established. The marketing system placed ultimate responsibility on local people who knew the farmers and were known as people of confidence. Local stockers best understood the quantities needed and the timing of demand. The KSC marketing system and the history of its evolution are famous the world over. The problems faced, the difficulties overcome, and the lessons learned could be instructive to any enterprise, anywhere in the Third World, facing a widely scattered market with a very large number of small-quantity buyers. An excellent review of KSC may be found in "Kitale Maize: The Limits of Success" [21].

MUMIAS SUGAR COMPANY LIMITED (MSC)
Mumias, Kenya

This case is presented in detail in Chapter 3. In brief summary, Mumias Sugar Company Limited is a joint venture of the government of Kenya (70.76 percent share); the Commonwealth Development Corporation (17.18 percent); Booker Agricultural International, managing directors (4.42 percent); Kenya Commercial Finance Corporation (5.0 percent); and the East African Development Bank (2.64 percent). There are three components of the enterprise, namely a sugar mill; a plantation of 8,500 acres operated by MSC and providing roughly 12 percent of cane requirements; and an outgrower program involving 23,000 small-scale, freeholder farmers under contract, who supply MSC with 88 percent of cane requirements. The outgrowers are organized into the Mumias Outgrowers Company, which represents farmer interests

before the government of Kenya and MSC, as well as being the
administrator of a complex and extensive credit system. All sugar
produced by MSC is consumed in the Kenyan market; the mill supplies the internal market with roughly 50 percent of demand. The
government of Kenya sets the price on cane delivered by outgrowers and on sugar sold by MSC. The government also markets the
sugar to the public.

Development Opportunity

Sugar production at MSC began in 1973. In ten years, the
enterprise literally transformed the agricultural pattern of the
area and converted a large, poor, sub-subsistence region into a
productive system, with 5,000 people fully employed; 9,000 people
with seasonal employment; and 23,000 farm families the recipients
of a large cash flow. Clearly, the achievements of the project
took every bit of energy that could be focused on the job. However, the dynamic changes that have been wrought in the economic
and social conditions of the hundreds of thousands of rural people whose lives have been impacted by MSC clearly present both
problems and opportunities for the future. The question now is:
Who is responsible for guiding the next steps to be taken by the
rural people to ensure that the benefits inherent in the continued presence of MSC are captured, in such a way that it truly reflects a better quality of life, at home and in the communities
of which they are a part?

TENNECO SAHARA AGRICULTURAL VENTURE
Akkad Plain, Republic of the Sudan

According to a publication of Tenneco, Inc., "Farming the
Sands of Sudan" [22], in 1978 the corporation formed a joint venture with Sahara Engineering Company of Khartoum to establish a
"model farm of the future," essentially a core demonstration (yet
of commercial size) that, after becoming established and successful, would work with neighboring agricultural societies to help
modernize their practices and diffuse the benefits of the enterprise. By 1981, a modern 320-acre farm had indeed been established. The first wheat crop was harvested; a small grape vine-
yard was in place; peanuts and sorghum had replaced the poor
wheat, which had been grown at the wrong site. The farm operation includes buildings, fencing, water wells, and an overhead
linear irrigation system. This has stimulated local farmers, who
could not afford to buy pumps, to form agricultural cooperatives
to bring water from the Nile River through common irrigation canals. The cooperatives now plan to transform as much uncultivated
land as possible to commercial levels of productivity.

Development Opportunity

The original stimulus for this investment by Tenneco was a plan being explored at the time by Egypt and Sudan that if implemented would have greatly expanded trade between the two countries. The thought was that the project, advantageously located in northern Sudan in terms of transportation of exports to Egypt, might be able to take a favorable competitive position as a supplier of basic foodstuffs. By 1984, it seemed clear to Tenneco that negotiations intended to lead to the trade pact were likely, at best, to go on for a long time and a decision was made to sell the enterprise. As of early 1985 there was a good possibility that a Sudanese consortium, led by the Sudanese Agricultural Development Company and including several private investors, would buy the core farm. The consortium has indicated its intent to continue to implement the Tenneco plan. This would involve collaboration with the farmer cooperatives in the area to bring all the cultivatable land possible into commercial production.

TEXACO AGRO-INDUSTRIAL (NIGERIA) LTD. (TEXAGRI)
Lagos, Nigeria

Texagri was incorporated in October 1975, to convert cassava to gari, a basic staple in the West African diet. An estate of roughly 6,000 acres (somewhat less than 2,000 planned for cassava production and, eventually, some 600 to 1,300 acres planned for corn) was put together with the help of local chiefs and the collaboration of 141 small-scale farmers who leased their farms except for 4 acres kept for subsistence farming. Texaco, Inc., holds 60 percent interest in the company; 15 percent was given to the farmers; the balance is owned by other Nigerians. Plant capacity, at maximum, is 7 metric tons of gari per day. Texaco has invested nearly US$4 million, in the form of equity and medium-term loans; it expects that further significant loans will be necessary to complete the project and place it on a fully economic basis.

Development Opportunity

Texaco has developed Texagri as a commercial model for replication by others throughout West Africa [23]. Though it hopes to recover its capital in the long run, Texaco also perceives itself and other corporations operating in the area as having a responsibility in helping to solve the food problem. It has established the Texagri estate on a poor site and is demonstrating a problem-solving technique to the Nigerians. Texagri, from the outset, has also emphasized the need to involve farmers both in improved farming practice and in ownership of processing facilities. Finally, Texagri has worked closely with scientists at the

International Institute of Tropical Agriculture in Ibadan, and the University of Ife in developing systems of control for weeds and insects, in turn contributing to a speed up in the process of applying research findings on farms.

Since its inception, Texagri management has been willing to share its experience with other agro-industry venture capital organizations. In both 1981 and 1982, the Texagri venture was reviewed at the Agri-Energy Roundtable in Geneva. These presentations may be obtained from the Roundtable headquarters, 2550 M Street, N.W., Washington, D.C. 20037 [24, 25].

VUVULANE IRRIGATED FARMS (VIF)
Mbabane, Swaziland

This case is presented in detail in Chapter 4. In brief summary, the Swaziland Irrigation Scheme (SIS), Mhlume Sugar Company (MSC), and the Vuvulane Irrigated Farms (VIF) form an inter-related agro-industrial complex created by CDC (United Kingdom) with an equity investment of roughly US$40 million. SIS is a large estate, 76,000 acres, producing sugar cane, citrus, and beef cattle for both domestic and foreign markets. SIS also manages an irrigation scheme that serves the entire complex. MSC is a large sugar mill, supplied in part by SIS, in part by its own plantation of 12,000 acres, and in part from VIF. VIF is an out-grower project that operates as a separate entity controlled, as of 1984, by the Swazi Nation. MSC is jointly owned by CDC and the Swazi Nation, and as of 1984, SIS will be converted to a joint venture of a similar nature.

Development Opportunity

The entire operation goes back to 1950, when CDC acquired all the land occupied by the three ventures. In agricultural and rural development terms, CDC converted a wasteland into a fruitful agricultural area, now employing between 4,000 and 5,000 people (depending upon the season), and, with the creation of the VIF in 1962, integrated small-scale farmers into the complex. By 1984, VIF included 263 families resettled from other parts of the country, with access to about 4,000 acres of the best land in the overall enterprise.

The critical issues of the future relate more to questions of rural rather than agricultural development. This is the result of the gradual conversion of more and more of the ownership and control from CDC to the Swazi Nation. As noted, in 1984 VIF reverted entirely to Swazi ownership and even though CDC retains a management role, it is far from clear as to what the impact on the settlers will be after two decades of essential freedom from traditional tribal control. It may be assumed that if Swazi participation in the ownership of SIS allows for the same effective management as is evidenced at MSC by CDC personnel, there is little reason to worry about the venture as an efficient, competitive, for-profit enterprise.

2. MODIFIED NUCLEAR ESTATES

These enterprises are essentially nuclear estates with the difference that contract farms are a mixture of both small-scale and larger, more commercial operations. Two cases are described.

- Leche y Derivados, S.A.(Central America)
- Productos Del Monte, S.A. de C.V. (Middle America)

LECHE Y DERIVADOS, S.A. (LEYDE)
La Ceiba, Honduras

According to a report in Agribusiness Worldwide (July-August 1983) [26], "Leyde is an example of how small dairy operations can succeed in spite of government controls and an uncertain supply system. . . . Leyde currently supplies a major share of Honduras' milk production and is serving as a development model for other Central American countries." Since 1976, Leyde has received strong financial support from the Latin American Agribusiness Corporation (see under "Financial Institutions" below).

Development Inventory

Leyde was organized in 1972 by two Honduran dairy farmers, in the face of two national government-owned dairies and price controls on pasteurized milk. (In Honduras there is no requirement to sell only pasteurized milk at retail.) Leyde produces about 10 percent of its raw milk needs on its own farms. The remainder is procured from some 350 farmers: about 46 percent are small-scale operators (10-25 cows, with up to 50 acres of land); 31 percent milk 25 to 50 cows and farm up to 100 acres; 21 percent milk 50 to 100 cows and farm up to 200 acres; and 2 percent are larger and more commercial in all aspects. All milking is by hand, and because of capital and technical capability limitations, milking by hand is expected to be the common mode for a few more years.

Leyde sales increased fivefold during its first two years of operation and continue to grow as more modern systems of milk handling and production are introduced and as the product line expands into pasteurized natural and skim milk, butter, flavored milk, sour milk, and cheese. The next big developmental step for Leyde is to establish a technical assistance program that will take advantage of the new high levels of income flowing to the farms by upgrading the genetic quality of stock, improving animal protection and health, and encouraging better animal nutrition. Though this was not mentioned in the Agribusiness Worldwide report, Leyde is also considering a wider diffusion of ownership among the dairy farmers upon whom the company depends.

PRODUCTOS DEL MONTE, S.A. DE C.V. (PDM)
Irapuato, Mexico

This case is presented in detail in Chapter 8. In brief summary, Productos Del Monte, S.A. de C.V., is a wholly owned subsidiary of the Del Monte Corporation, in turn a division of the Food and Beverage Group of R.J. Reynolds Industries, Inc. PDM cans and bottles vegetables and fruits, the latter in the form of jams only. With the exception of canned white asparagus, which is exported to Europe, the entire product line is marketed in Mexico. Since its inception in the early 1950s, investment in PDM has totaled approximately US$40 million. PDM employs 237 salaried workers and up to 1,700 seasonal laborers.

Development Opportunity

Roughly 80 percent of raw material requirements is supplied by contract farmers within a thirty-mile radius of the cannery. In 1983, fifteen to forty farmers were under contract, ranging in farm size from several acres to several hundred. In addition to purchases made in the open market, PDM also receives asparagus from a wholly owned subsidiary, Frutas y Verduras Selectos, S.A., which has six farms, four of them leased, two of them owned. In a special sense, Frutas y Verduras operates as a nucleus estate, which now yields 25 percent of asparagus requirements; plans are to supply the cannery with 50 percent of requirements in the years ahead.

PDM maintains an Agricultural Department, currently with nine agronomists who develop contracted sources of supply and offer a variety of technical assistance services that ensure follow-through on recommended practices. Though PDM encourages farmers to use private and public banks for crop-practice financing, the company does extend credit in kind under special conditions of need, if recommended by the Agricultural Department staff.

Over the years, PDM has pioneered the introduction of new crops and improved practices, which, taken together with the impact of its payroll and local purchases, has markedly improved the economic conditions of the area. However, because of a tendency both to contract with larger commercial farms and to farm directly, the potential benefits of the investment may not have reached as many small-scale farmers as might be thought possible. The implications of this issue are discussed at length in the enlarged case report presented in Chapter 8.

3. NEARBY PROCESSING AND CONTRACT FARMING

This category includes enterprises that obtain 100 percent of their raw material through a system of contract farming, using small-scale operations primarily, but possibly including larger-scale, commercial farms as well. The following cases give an overview of this type of enterprise.

- Alimentos Congelados, S.A. (Central America)
- Cadbury (Nigeria) Ltd. (West Africa)
- Campbell's de Mexico, S.A. de C.V. (Middle America)
- Cigarette Company of Jamaica Ltd. (Caribbean Basin)
- CoopeMontecillos, r.l. (Central America)
- Gigante Verde, S.A. (Middle America)
- Hindustan Lever, Ltd. (Southern Asia)
- Jamaica Broilers (Caribbean Basin)
- Kenya Tea Development Authority (East Africa)
- Nestlé (Middle America)
- Pinar (Middle East)
- Southland Frozen Foods, Inc. (Caribbean Basin)

ALIMENTOS CONGELADOS, S.A. (ALCOSA)
Guatemala

Alimentos Congelados S.A. is a bulk freezing plant, processing okra, broccoli, cauliflower, and brussel sprouts, primarily for export and repackaging in the United States. There are plans to expand into the export of fresh vegetable products. ALCOSA is a wholly-owned subsidiary of Hanover Brands, Inc., of Hanover, Pennsylvania. Hanover purchased ALCOSA in 1975, with some financing from the Latin American Agribusiness Development Corporation (U.S.); processing capacity was expanded in 1981, with financing from the Overseas Private Investment Corporation (U.S.). ALCOSA employs up to 400 people, depending upon the season; roughly half of them have steady employment at the factory.

Development Opportunity

ALCOSA contracts production with about 2,400 small-scale farmers in central Guatemala, and despite some historical problems in company/farmer relationships, management estimates that many thousands of additional farmers are willing and able to contract if ALCOSA could handle the produce. Of great interest to potential investors in agro-industry is the experience of ALCOSA in sourcing its supply of raw farm product. At first, the company farmed on its own and decided after several years that this was both costly and inappropriate. In a second stage that also only lasted for several years, contracts were made with commercial-sized farms, many with absentee owners. Neither the owners nor their hired labor had prior experience with vegetable growing. It became apparent that the small-scale highland farmers, the majority of whom had intensive farming experience, would be the most effective and efficient source of supply. As of 1984, highland smallholders produce all raw material frozen by ALCOSA except for okra, which is grown in a different climatic zone.

ALCOSA has had a sweeping impact on the highland villages it deals with. The ups and down of socioeconomic relationships between the company, its professional staff that deals directly with the farmers, and the farmers have been the subject of several detailed studies well worth examination [27, 28, 29]. It should be noted that during a visit to the headquarters of Hanover Brands, some concern was expressed that in practically all of the writing about ALCOSA, the writers had not discussed their questions, criticisms, or analysis with top management at Hanover. Hanover consequently feels that some of the information presented is not precise and that some of the interpretation of management behavior is neither fair nor accurate.

CADBURY (NIGERIA) LTD.
Zaria, Nigeria

Cadbury Ltd. was drawn into an investment in tomato-paste production, located in Zaria, in the North Central State of Nigeria, in late 1971. For some years prior, Cadbury had been importing paste from Spain, packaging it in several mixes, and marketing to the retail trade and to the military. In 1969, the government levied a 100 percent import tax to encourage the development of a domestic enterprise, to be located in the North Central State and based on a tomato supply to be expanded among the small-scale farmers of the area. Cadbury was invited to enter into a joint venture with the state government and, with some reluctance, accepted. The Food and Agriculture Organization (FAO) of the United Nations, at Cadbury insistence, agreed to participate by providing a technical expert in tomato cultivation. [30]

Development Opportunity

The project area is normally dry and barren, so the tomato-growing area had to be in the river basin. This was surveyed by FAO and the State Ministry of Agriculture and when suitable sites were identified, village chiefs were then approached, the project explained, and each was requested to organize groups of twenty-four farmers to cultivate eight acres of tomatoes in separate but contiguous plots. Three groups were formed the first year; forty in the following years. It has not proven possible, under the conditions of project administration, to attain a production level adequate to the needs of the Cadbury factory. There are plans under consideration to create one large commercial farm to serve as a core plantation and, in combination with the small-scale farmers who stay in the scheme, to meet factory raw material requirements.

Earlier documentation suggests that the project sponsors and Cadbury did not deal effectively with tribal culture [30]. Farmers did not live up to their commitments to sell the crop to Cadbury. The chiefs were given responsibility to market the tomatoes to Cadbury and to disburse payments. They took advantage of the scheme to benefit their kin and skim off some of the cash returns to others. The price set by Cadbury was less than half that paid in the fresh vegetable markets of the surrounding villages. Despite these difficulties, the project has continued in an effort to resolve the problems affecting on-farm production and factory efficiency.

CAMPBELL'S DE MEXICO, S.A. DE C.V. (CAMPBELLS)
Celaya, Mexico

Campbell's de México, S.A. de C.V., started production in Celaya, in central Mexico about 180 miles north-northeast of Mexico City, in 1962. Production was focused on a line of canned soups and vegetable juices for the domestic market. Most of the vegetables required had to be introduced for the first time to local farmers so before plant start-up, Campbells spent three years experimenting with seed selection and practices best suited to the area. It is interesting to note that the experimental work was not only prudent from the standpoint of ensuring low-cost, high-quality, dependable supplies, but was required to meet the terms of agreement between Campbells and the government of Mexico to "Mexicanize" vegetable growing and eliminate imports of any kind in a reasonable time. The Celaya operation flourished, although the sale of canned goods is reportedly dropping due to the financial crisis that has plagued Mexico since 1982. Several years ago, Campbells invested in a modern new tomato-paste factory in Los Mochis, Sinaloa, in northwest Mexico, for bulk export to Campbells' U.S. operations.

Development Opportunity

In the case of the Celaya operation, practically all raw material is supplied by a relatively small number of contract farmers, a mixture of small farm owners (pequeño proprietarios) and farmers who do not own the land (ejidatarios) but operate almost as free agents under the ejidal land tenure system (described fully in Chapter 8). Farmers do not receive credit, but are creditworthy in the eyes of the banks if they have a Campbells contract. Practices are specified and supervised by Campbells staff. Quality standards and amounts to be bought under guaranteed prices are clearly specified. If there are surpluses of fresh produce, Campbells agronomists try to help with marketing. When this enterprise began, it shared a common experience worldwide. At first, production was contracted with larger, more commercial, farms. This very quickly proved troublesome (again, see Chapter 8 for more on this subject) and gradually the switch was made to smaller-scale units where the kind of intensive farming practice demanded was acceptable.

When Campbells developed its paste plant at Los Mochis, it avoided privately owned farms entirely and now obtains its entire tomato requirement from a group of nearby ejidos, where the relationship is welcomed and the results most satisfactory.

CIGARETTE COMPANY OF JAMAICA, LTD.
Kingston, Jamaica

The Cigarette Company of Jamaica Ltd., is an affiliate of Carreras Group Limited, which is in turn affiliated with Carreras Rothman Limited of England. The cigarette company is the contractor for almost all Virginia-type tobacco grown in Jamaica; the company is also the sole cigarette manufacturer in the country.

Development Opportunity

All of the tobacco processed by the company is grown under contract to farmers who own land or to tenants or subtenants on eight large tracts, either owned or leased by the manufacturer. The average-sized plot devoted to tobacco, per farmer, is two acres. Every contract farmer is trained to grow the crop and receives supervision from the company technical staff. The contractor selects and provides seed; advances funds needed during production, harvesting, and curing; provides all production inputs; and at harvest, deducts the cost of services and supplies from the value of the crop delivered.

During the off-season for tobacco, growers are restricted from planting certain designated crops that might transmit or incubate insect or disease infestations damaging to tobacco, but other crops may be raised for home or market consumption. A small charge is made by the company for the off-season use of its land.

The company encourages the formation of growers' committees elected at each farming site, and works with them in training programs, administration, and consultations on technical and operating problems. Both management and growers seem to agree that the committees are a positive and constructive feature of the system. For further details see "Contract Growing of Flue-cured Tobacco in Jamaica" [31].

COOPEMONTECILLOS, R.L. (CM)
Alajuela, Costa Rica

CM (La Cooperativa Matadero Nacional de Montecillos), is one of the largest organizations of its kind in Central America. CM operates six wholly owned enterprises (abattoir, meat packing, meat processing, tanning, export sales, and retail sales) and also holds equity positions in several other businesses, including a gelatin plant, a printing company, and an export shipping line. Although CM offers no services to its cattle ranchers of a technical nature and is not organized to contribute directly to rural development, its history, organization of ownership, and incentives to members to work hard and loyally to ensure success are valuable sources of guidance to potential investors in agro-industry in Costa Rica and elsewhere.

Development Opportunity

Organized in 1964, CM was on the verge of bankruptcy in 1977. In a joint effort to save the organization, 500 members of CM and 283 employees (out of a force of 800) entered into an agreement with a consortium of banks to borrow the money needed. Cattle ranchers pledged their land and cattle; workers pledged 5 percent of their salaries for seven years. In exchange for worker support, the ranchers agreed that all present and future employees could voluntarily become co-op members and share in profits. Through negotiation, all agreed that yearly profits would be divided, 78 percent to the ranchers, each share based on cattle delivered; and 22 percent to workers, each share based on salary levels. As of 1983, membership was comprised of 1,042 ranchers and 780 employees, the latter holding 20 percent of total shares.

CM has no union. The membership is divided into groups of ten; each group elects representatives to the General Assembly. Each enterprise in CM has a labor arbitration committee of workers and managers; and each enterprise has an elected board, also made up of workers and managers, that deals with overall planning and policy. Many benefits flow to members of CM, including free medical and dental services, nutritional guidance to all families, health insurance, recreational facilities, and interest-

free loans to workers who desire further schooling. Obviously,
to bear these costs and still remain competitive, everyone must
remain highly productive and the production system must operate
at maximum efficiency. The current success of CM speaks well for
its management, its internal cohesion, and its philosophical
focus, the latter stemming from the Costa Rica Solidarity Union
movement. The union holds that owners, managers, and workers
must assist one another in the efficient operation of any business and, more important, should also jointly share in the risks
and benefits of the venture.

GIGANTE VERDE, S.A.
Irapuato, Mexico

Gigante Verde, S.A., is a wholly owned subsidiary of Green
Giant, which in turn is a subsidiary of the Pillsbury Company.
The Gigante plant is a new (brought into operation in 1983),
state-of-the-art facility, freezing selected vegetables for bulk
shipping to the United States for repackaging and marketing by
the parent company. All raw material requirements are procured
through contract farming. In 1983/1984, roughly 1,000 acres and
30 farmers were involved, with plans for a steady expansion during the next several years, with a target of 140 to 150 farmers.

Development Opportunity

Green Giant has entered an area that has long experience
with contract farming, and the company started its procurement
program in the basic form of other multinationals in central
Mexico, for example, Del Monte (Chapter 8), Campbell (see above),
and Birdseye. Farmers under contract receive technical assistance, financial assistance in the form of credit for seed, and a
boost with banks by virtue of their marketing agreements with the
company.
Yet, it is instructive to note that despite the general experience in the area that suggests the larger, more commercial
farms turn out to be troublesome, unreliable sources of supply
within a very few years, Green Giant initiated its procurement
program with just such farms. The justification is that despite
the risk, it greatly simplifies getting started and ensuring adequate supplies. It is far too early in the history of this enterprise to judge its rural or agricultural development impact. In
discussing the evolution of the Gigante Verde investment, there
was a sense of regret that very early in the planning stage no
consideration was given to alternative ways to contract out produce requirements in order to maximize development impact without
sacrificing factory performance.

HINDUSTAN LEVER LTD. (HLL)
Etah, Uttar Pradesh, India

This case is presented in detail in Chapter 2. In brief summary, Hindustan Lever Ltd. is part of the Unilever group of companies. Unilever equity in HLL is 51 percent. The remaining equity is owned by some 90,000 shareholders, among them all of HLL's 10,000 employees, whose stock purchases were financed by the company. Early in the 1970s, HLL decided to place a milk processing facility in Uttar Pradesh. It had immediate supply problems, with the plant operating at less than 50 percent of capacity. In 1973, the company was ready to close the plant. However, both its own employees and the governor of the state mounted a campaign to have HLL change its mind. The company agreed to stay and for the next two years streamlined factory operations and concentrated on increasing milk supplies. This experience led to the organization in 1976 of an integrated rural development program (IRDP), in recognition of the fact that the supply of milk could only be assured in the context of overall socioeconomic development in the milkshed.

Development Opportunity

IRDP began with the assignment of six supervisors from the factory to a careful, basic study of the area. They were asked to collect information on population, landholdings, irrigation infrastructure and use, cropping patterns, cattle numbers, farmer attitudes and felt needs, and in general, ideas as to how HLL might best work with farmers and their communities to improve agricultural output and the quality of life, without the company having to subsidize the IRDP in all its aspects. In response to the results of the inquiry, HLL structured a four-part program, emphasizing improved agricultural practices, animal husbandry, community development, and other special projects. Throughout, a carefully structured plan of participation between HLL staff, villagers, and public officials was put into effect. Starting with six villages in 1976, the IRDP covered fifty villages in 1983, impacting roughly 100,000 people. Farm income doubled over a cultivated area of 125,000 acres. The program continues to grow and diversify.

JAMAICA BROILERS (JB)
Jamaica

Jamaica Broilers was founded in 1958 by three men involved in the import of iced broilers. It is now the largest local pro-ducer of broilers in the country; it produces its own chicks; it controls grow-out through a system of contract production; it runs the largest feed mill in Central America and the Caribbean

Basin; it operates processing plants and a fleet of refrigerated trucks for distribution; and is starting to produce some of its own feed ingredients. Unique in Jamaica, the company introduced a stock ownership plan (ESOP) under which the employees own 25 percent of the shares, and all contractors hold 30 percent. The entire stock is held in an employees' trust until the stock is paid for out of dividends.

Development Opportunity

Management considers the contract farming system and the ESOP as two vital elements of success, along with continuing to reinvest much of the profit into diversification and vertical integration of the entire system from chick to market. In mid-1981, JB had 260 contract growers, each with an average of 14,000 birds. At the time the system was introduced, it was felt by authorities in Jamaica that the project would not succeed with Jamaican small-scale farmers; but despite conventional wisdom, it has succeeded. Contract growers must build to the specifications of JB and thereafter provide labor, utilities, and management. In turn, they receive free chicks, feed, veterinary services, nutritional guidance, and continuing technical assistance from an eight-person field team. In addition to these 260 farmers, JB employs 36 truckers and 450 workers. The entire staff, as well as the owners, are Jamaican. The enterprise appears to have been both profitable and beneficial in a broader sense to all involved.

For the future, JB management has expressd the belief that poultry consumption in Jamaica cannot be expected to continue growing at the high rate of the past decade. Nor can the country export competitively so long as it must import feed ingredients. Therefore, the center of corporate growth and the further development opportunity for the people of Jamaica lies in developing agricultural raw material for the feed mill, even while expanding the mill to balance crop yields with production capacity; in building export markets; and in extending animal production to include freshwater shrimp, fish, and dairy cattle.

This abstract is taken from an article in the October-November 1981 issue of Agribusiness Worldwide [32].

KENYA TEA DEVELOPMENT AUTHORITY (KTDA)
Nairobi, Kenya

The Kenya Tea Development Authority, a public monopoly, is included in this inventory because it is generally considered to be one of the largest and most successful smallholder agricultural development projects in the world. A public corporation, it is nevertheless intended to generate a profit, and its structure is as free of bureaucratic interference as could possibly be expected. Careful study of the history, organization, and operating results of KTDA may be of great value to any enterprise in the Third World that becomes deeply involved with large numbers of small-scale farmers as a source of supply.

Development Opportunity

As of late 1983, KTDA related to 137,832 smallholders, who produce tea on one acre (average) of their landholdings. The remainder of farmland, it was hoped, would be devoted to subsistence agriculture and possibly other cash crops. Farmers have the opportunity to own shares in thirty-four tea factories (five more are planned), each of which is a joint venture with KTDA and is run as a separate profit center. At one time, a number of the tea factories were joint ventures with CDC or British tea growers who had pioneered tea production in Kenya; all such shareholding has been or is being phased out and replaced by farmer participation. Equity investment at mid-1982 exceeded 13.5 million Kenyan pounds (K£1 = US$1.48, 1983 rate). The government of Kenya has supplied 20 percent of all financing apart from retained earnings. The remainder has derived from loans from the Commonwealth Development Corporation, the World Bank, the European Investment Bank, OPEC, and the West German government.

The structure of relationships between KTDA and the farmers and the various benefits that have accrued to the rural people and to Kenya are impossible to summarize in one paragraph. To do full justice to this important enterprise, the reader is referred to "Control, Accountability and Incentives in a Successful Development Institution" [33]; and the KTDA's Annual Report and Statement of Accounts, obtainable from KTDA, Rahimtulla Trust Tower, Moi Avenue, Post Office Box 30213, Nairobi, Kenya [34].

NESTLE
Mexico City, Mexico

The three cases of milkshed development with Nestlé as a joint venture partner with the government of Mexico, which are cited below, are presented in full detail under the titles, "The Chontalpa Plan," "Chiapa de Corzo," and "Guichivere," in material prepared for the Mohonk Conference of April 1981 [35]. These studies are available from the Fund for Multinational Education, 684 Park Avenue, New York, New York 10021. They are representative of Nestlé's worldwide experience in developing milksheds, that in their earliest stages, are located in remote rural areas, and hold the promise of being able to justify an investment in a milk processing plant.

Development Opportunity

The conference material notes that "Nestlé's principal business is as a processor of fresh milk into a line of powdered and condensed milk products. To assure a supply of raw material which is vital to the commercial interests of the company, Nestlé has developed support systems to local farmers by providing trained technicians on demonstration farms who teach methods for the general care of stock. The company provides financial assistance and sometimes imports purebred stock at its own expense and gives it to promising local producers. Occasionally Nestlé operates a feed mill and also sells medicines, fencing wire, seed, and other materials, all at cost or below. Apart from land upon which the milk processing factory and the demonstration farm stand, Nestlé owns no land or stock from which it could develop its own supply of fresh milk. Therefore, farmers have a guaranteed market and realize the company is dependent upon them for its supply of raw milk.

In Nestlé's corporate philosophy, milkshed development is in both the company's long-term commercial interest, as well as part of its social obligation and the company has been willing to collaborate in government schemes even when the company itself does not benefit directly from the increased supply of milk [35].

The projects in Mexico were not wholly successful, although technical transfers were made in every case. The reasons for what happened are carefully revealed in the case studies mentioned; it is most interesting that the greatest success was judged to have taken place at Guichivere, where more time was allowed, a lower Nestlé profile was maintained, and the first changes introduced were much simpler and initiated with a more realistic set of expectations.

PINAR
Izmir, Turkey

This case is presented in detail in Chapter 5. In brief summary, Pinar is a member company of Yasar Holding, which began as an industrial organization, mainly in chemicals, and moved into agro-industries early in the 1970s. Pinar itself, a milk processing and marketing enterprise, was launched in 1974 as the first private sector venture of its kind in Turkey. As of 1983, there were thirty-six government-owned and -operated milk plants, with a total capacity of 270 million liters a year, utilizing about 30 percent of the capacity, and generally operating at a loss, which is subsidized. In 1983, Pinar had a capacity of 70 million liters per year, operated at close to 100 percent of capacity, and made a good profit. Pinar has 900 shareholders: 40 percent is owned by Yasar Holding; 20 percent is in the hands of a bank and another holding company; and 40 percent is spread among both small- and large-scale farmers who supply milk to Pinar (a "small-scale" farm in Turkey averages 2.5 to 25 acres; "large-scale" farms range from 200 to 500 acres).

Development Opportunity

At start-up in 1975, Pinar operations involved 9,000 families in 150 villages, 7 cooperatives, and 50 big farms. In 1983, the company was working with 21,000 farmers, in 296 villages, with 68 percent of the milk supply from small-scale operators, 18 percent from cooperatives, and the remainder from 155 large farms. Pinar works with farmers through a three-tiered administration. First, and in daily contact with producers, are collectors, who are private, local businessmen who use their own vehicles to collect milk, deliver it to a refrigerated collection center, receive payment, and disburse proceeds to farmers. Second, also in direct contact with farmers, but with less frequency, are field representatives who supervise the collectors, resolve conflicts, and provide key extension services. Third are the inspectors, who fan out from headquarters and do whatever is necessary to see that the system works smoothly. The methodology of selection, training, and actual interaction at the farm level is obviously critical to the success of Pinar. Pinar works to upgrade animal quality, ensure health care of the animals, and increase yield; the company also encourages diversification of farm practices. To date, after ten years of experience, the Pinar operations have been beneficial in many ways, as perceived by farmers interviewed. Net farm income has increased. Herd size and performance is up. Field representatives have taken on an important, very personal extension role. Marketing milk to Pinar has not only provided a sense of security to the farmers, but has facilitated the flow of credit from banks as well.

SOUTHLAND FROZEN FOODS, INC. (SOUTHLAND)
Dominican Republic

Southland Frozen Foods, Inc., produces frozen okra in the Dominican Republic that is exported to the United States for marketing by the parent company. Raw material is obtained under agreements with some 2,500 individual farmers, on over 7,200 acres, in all the country's major growing areas. Until 1970, Southland got all its okra from Georgia and Alabama. However, by 1970 there was virtually no one to pick okra, and one of the company's best sellers was threatened. By 1973, Southland was obtaining okra from a few offshore sources in a haphazard and unprofitable manner. It then heard of a small freezing plant in Santo Domingo and contracted 500,000 pounds of frozen product; one-half the order was received and the Dominican company went bankrupt. Southland bought the local company with an investment of US$200,000. Over ten years, $1.5 million has been added, with plans for further investment. The Latin American Agribusiness Development Corporation (Section 11) has provided the bulk of the financing required.

Development Opportunity

When Southland began operations in the Dominican Republic in 1973, okra was not widely known, so it was necessary to transfer the full agricultural technology. For the first few years, the procurement problem was severe, and Southland indicates that it lost money continuously until 1982, when for the first time the full requirement of the plant was packed. Southland management emphasized that "the corporate commitment to a long term development project was essential to our success." Equally essential were the incentives received from the government: Class A Free Zone Status, allowing for the import of machinery duty free; a tax holiday for twenty years; and exemption from the requirement to return dollars earned from exports to the Central Bank. Southland employs about 65 full-time people and 500 hourly workers at the plant and in the management of its procurement system [36].

4. DISTANT PROCESSING AND CONTRACT FARMING

This category is made up of enterprises that obtain 100 percent of their raw material supply through a system of contract farming that uses small-scale farmers primarily but may include larger-scale commercial farms as well. Farming takes place some distance from the processing plants, distinguishing these enterprises from those described in Section 3.

- British-American Tobacco (Kenya) Ltd. (East Africa)
- Ceylon Tobacco Company, Ltd. (Southern Asia)
- Charoen Pokphand Group (Southeast Asia)
- East Africa Industries, Ltd. (East Africa)
- The Haggar Group (Northeast Africa)

BRITISH-AMERICAN TOBACCO (KENYA) LTD. (BAT)
Nairobi, Kenya

British-American Tobacco (Kenya) Ltd. was started in 1965, after the voluntary liquidation of the East African Tobacco Company, an operating company of the BAT group. The government of Kenya has a 20 percent share in BAT (Kenya); the Kenyan public (no details provided) owns 20 percent; and 60 percent is owned by the BAT group. Before 1975, the bulk of tobacco leaf processed in Kenya came from Uganda and Tanzania. In 1975, BAT (Kenya), building on ten prior years of research, embarked on an accelerated program to expand Kenyan production. By 1982, annual production had increased from 334 metric tons in 1975 to 5,211 metric tons.

Development Opportunity

BAT policy worldwide is to promote tobacco growing using small-scale farmers. Presently, 10,000 Kenyan farmers are registered suppliers. On the average, each farmer has 1.25 acres of land under tobacco. In 1982, 11,500 acres were planted, scattered throughout the country. In 1983, farmers earned US$3.4 million, net of the cost of inputs.

BAT has established a network of centers in its development program, each of which provide the infrastructure for provision of inputs, extension services, and for purchasing cured leaf. Two hundred extension workers are employed. In 1982, roughly $2 million had been invested in these centers. In order for farmers to be accepted into the program, they must have free land upon which to construct a curing barn (BAT will provide a loan for this); the land must be located near water; and the farmer must agree to plant trees to meet the fuel requirements for cured leaf. BAT has set up eleven tree nurseries to provide seedlings at nominal cost. (The seedlings were once provided free, but farmers sold them or refused to look after them.) Food crops are grown on a rotational basis with tobacco, effectively increasing food production.

CEYLON TOBACCO COMPANY, LTD. (CT)
Colombo, Sri Lanka

Ceylon Tobacco Company, Ltd., is a subsidiary of the British American Tobacco Company. During a visit to the company in Sri Lanka in 1983, Orville Freeman, Chairman of Business International, Inc., learned that CT operated a successful program of tobacco procurement among a large number of small-scale farmers under contract. This program began in 1950 and, with the exception of the chairman of the board, all personnel are Sri Lankans. Direct contact with the farmers is maintained by a staff of extension agents recruited from agricultural training institutions and trained for the job. A key factor in the satisfaction of both farmers and CT with the tobacco enterprise has been the policy of the Sri Lanka Tobacco Monopoly that permits rapid adjustments upward of both prices paid to growers and the price of cigarettes sold in local markets.

At the time of the visit to Sri Lanka, CT was going forward with an orchid project involving several thousand contract growers. They were being provided planning assistance, planting stock, other inputs, and marketing services. This enterprise is projected to sell in world markets.

The reader may note that this chapter describes several projects that have tobacco as the basic crop. In point of fact, practically all major tobacco companies follow similar, if not identical, practices in the less-developed countries, and there is no way of telling, without much more investigation, how many places in the world the British-American Tobacco Company, Philip Morris, R.J. Reynolds, and others have applied contract farming systems to large numbers of small-scale farmers. A comprehensive analysis of the overall impact of spreading tobacco cultivation might be of great value to the governments of less-developed countries and to development agencies.

CHAROEN POKPHAND GROUP OF COMPANIES (CP)
Bangkok, Thailand

This case is presented in detail in Chapter 7. In brief summary, the Charoen Pokphand Group is the largest agro-industrial firm in Southeast Asia. Started in 1921 to sell vegetables, the group has proliferated into a wide range of agribusinesses including fertilizer, agricultural chemicals, pesticides, machinery, animal feed, animal husbandry, and crop production. The company employs 10,000 worldwide; 6,000 in Thailand. CP is still privately held, with majority equity in the hands of the founding family and key executives. However, the company expects to go public within the decade.

Development Opportunity

After World War II, Thailand invested heavily in rural infrastructure. This did succeed in integrating rural people more than ever before into the total economy and did increase their standard of living, yet it soon became apparent that the aspirations of rural people could not be sustained by traditional production methods. Recognizing both a need and an opportunity, in 1977 CP launched a plan of agricultural and rural development to introduce a modernized version of pig production, mixed with improvements in and diversification of crop cultivation. Between 1977 and 1981, four experimental villages were established, all based on one system of animal husbandry, but each different in location and in certain aspects of crop production and land tenure.

These core elements characterize the four projects: farmers are settled on ten acres, two devoted to pig-raising and eight to be farmed freely; farm families receive a house, training, physical facilities for the pigs, and enough cash to live on until pig sales begin; if a family lives up to its responsibilities for seven years, title to the land and facilities are turned over to the family; and CP provides a project manager (a management trainee on a career track) who lives in the village for two to four years. Each village enterprise is intended to be profitable to both farmers and CP. To date, although results have varied, all four projects have met their return on investment demand. CP has invested US$3 million in the program since 1977.

An abstract is simply inadequate to do justice to this complex, subtle and yet comprehensive development plan. The reader is advised to study the detailed case report presented in Chapter 7.

EAST AFRICA INDUSTRIES, LTD. (UNILEVER)
Nairobi, Kenya

East Africa Industries, Ltd., is a major food processor and distributor in Kenya. For many years, the company had imported all of its vegetable oil requirements. Several years ago, it began a program to stimulate local production primarily of sunflower seed, and to a much lesser extent rapeseed, by means of contract farming. Corporate policy dictated that East Africa Industries would neither farm itself nor enter the crushing business. Oil, therefore, would be obtained by having seed produced under contract, bought by the company, and crushed on commission by existing millers.

Development Opportunity

The first phase of the program involved rather large farms of 125 to 250 acres, largely owned by absentee landlords. Operation of these farms, based on Unilever systems, was contracted to private farm management companies. In 1981, under the direction of the extension staff of East Africa Industries, an outreach to small-scale farmers was begun, which by 1983 had involved 1,500 to 2,000 farms, each contracting 1 to 2 acres for sunflower cultivation. (Rapeseed remains strictly the province of quite large-scale, mechanized units.) Inputs are provided on credit, and East Africa Industries guarantees to buy the crop. The farm families do the work, following directions from a technical staff. During the season, each farm is visited at least once each week. Unilever research calls for rape to be rotated with barley, and sunflower to be rotated with corn. In addition to disease and other forms of pest control of benefit to the oilseed crops, the grains flourish as the result of a synergistic effect not wholly understood.

Without questioning the benefit to Kenya of reducing vegetable oil imports, the management of East Africa Industries had some question about the cost/benefit relationships to the company. They were finding the capital cost of contract farming very

high, what with staff costs, financing credit-in-kind, financing
infrastructure maintenance and machinery services, among other
items. It was apparently too early in the program for any decision to be reached as to the future of the outreach program.

THE HAGGAR GROUP
Juba/Khartoum, Republic of the Sudan

This case is presented in detail in Chapter 6. In brief summary, The Haggar Group is a conglomerate of eleven companies with
a combined annual turnover of roughly US$81 million. Two of the
companies are agro-industries: the Sudan Tea & Coffee Plantation
Company Ltd. (STCP); and the Haggar Cigarette & Tobacco Factory
Ltd. One hundred percent of STCP is held by the Haggar families,
but there are plans to offer 49 percent to the public, preferably
to the farmers associated with the company. The cigarette company
was formerly owned completely by the Haggar family, but by 1983,
16 percent of equity had passed to employees.

Development Opportunity

The cigarette enterprise works with a network of 2,343
small-scale farmers who have been taught to grow tobacco in addition to their food crops. Haggar maintains a staff of sixty extension agents for the cultivation of tobacco, including forty
crop supervisors who live in the villages. The company provides
all inputs at cost plus transportation; finances the wages of the
farmers' work force; and cleans, processes, packs, and transports
the leaf at cost. For coffee and tea, the company supplies all
inputs at cost, and in addition, finances at subsidized rates of
interest the unusual costs of labor during the years from planting to first harvest. At the end of 1983, 102 family farms were
associated with STCP, mainly growing coffee. The domestic market
for coffee and tea, which is served essentially by imports, is
sufficiently large that there is a great expansion potential for
farmers and company alike over the next decade.
The outreach of the agribusiness activities of the Haggar
Group is considerable but quite traditional in most ways. Transfer of technology and financial support for crop practices, as
noted, and the system of relationships between company and farmers has succeeded in creating substantial goodwill and a willingness on the part of the farmers to try new things when suggested
by Haggar personnel. There are also some social benefits extended, such as the operation of non-profit stores and canteens, the
building of village schools, contributions to dispensaries, and
the extension of personal loans within carefully circumscribed
limits. The fact that the Haggar enterprises are located in
southern Sudan and that part of the country is historically
neglected and classically disadvantaged means that impact is

relatively very important, as is clearly revealed in the complete case report presented in Chapter 6.

5. DISTANT PROCESSING--DIFFUSION OF TECHNOLOGY

This category is unusual and is made up of enterprises with a commercial plantation intended to supply a distant company processing plant and to diffuse production and a farming-system technology among small-scale farmers. The goal is to build up industry-wide secure suppliers of raw material even while stimulating rural development. One example illustrates this type of enterprise in a singular way.

● Hummingbird Hershey Limited (Central America)

HUMMINGBIRD HERSHEY, LTD.
Belmopan, Belize

Hummingbird Hershey, Ltd., created in 1977, is a wholly owned subsidiary of the Hershey Foods Corporation, located in central Belize and created largely to demonstrate, under commercial conditions, that cocoa growing could be sharply improved by using existing technology and good farm practices. The intent of Hershey is to encourage small-scale producers, the dominant source of supply throughout the world, to stay in, or to enter into, cocoa cultivation by presenting both a practice and hard data on profitability. The concern of the corporation is that unless the trend toward decreased production can be reversed, all manufacturers of chocolate products will face a serious raw material shortage in the future. Though it is intended that the Hummingbird Hershey venture be profitable, the major thrust of the enterprise is to share knowledge and help in all ways to stimulate cocoa production wherever it is applicable and beneficial to small-scale farmers.

Development Opportunity

The estate in Belize is 1,800 acres, with roughly 600 acres in or nearing cocoa production. The plan is to have 1,200 acres in cocoa and 200 acres in citrus when development is complete. Project cost by mid-1983 was US$5 million. Eighty-five people are employed. Citrus, when ready, is expected to be sold to a nearby juicing plant. Additionally, the company is developing an animal feeding system utilizing cocoa pods in the ration. In every way possible, the goal is to illustrate the value of cocoa cultivation as a useful cash crop in a diversified small-scale farming system.

Hershey is already providing technical and marketing support in several other countries in the region, for example, in the Dominican Republic, with both government and private sector leadership; and in Haiti, in collaboration with the Mennonite Economic Development Associates, which receives assistance from USAID. Technical help is cordially extended to all who may inquire. The Hummingbird Hershey venture is a classic example of enlightened self-interest and represents an important kind of outreach for the consideration of agro-industrial organizations everywhere.

6. SELF-SUPPLIED PROCESSING PLANTS

These are enterprises that obtain 100 percent of their raw material supply from a farm or plantation controlled and operated by the enterprise itself. No contract farmers are involved.

- Brooke Bond Group,plc. (India, Kenya, Malawi, Tanzania)

- Dole Philippines, Inc. (Southeast Asia)

- East Africa Tannin Extract Company (East Africa)

- Egyptian-American Agricultural Company, S.A.E. (North Africa)

- Kenya Canners Limited (East Africa)

- La Perla y Anexos, S.A. (Central America)

- San Miguel Corporation (Southeast Asia)

BROOKE BOND GROUP, PLC. (BB)
Croyden, England

The Brooke Bond Group has strong interests in agriculture and agro-industry in India, Kenya, Malawi, and Tanzania. There is no indication that BB, in its plantation activities (tea and coffee primarily; in Kenya, also carnations, sisal, and cinchona) utilizes any form of outgrower supply system. Its rural impact is more directed toward employment, purchase of local services, provision of social services on the estates, and infrastructure development.

Development Opportunity

Clearly, the impact of many millions of pounds sterling invested in a diverse system of plantation production, raw material processing, and other industries in these four countries has had a marked effect on both rural and national development. Brooke Bond in India (where Brooke Bond India started seventy years ago as a marketing company) now has a sales team of 2,000 and is 60 percent locally owned. The BB literature notes that the capital realized from the share of stock, plus retained profits, has been used to maintain the efficiency of its roughly 15,000-acre tea estates and tea processing facilities, and to invest in other industries. For example, in a designated "backward area" east of Bombay, BB created a corned-beef plant, entirely for export, which draws on India's vast buffalo herds. A finished-leather plant has been built alongside the corned-beef plant to make full use of the buffalo hides. BB also has a paper mill at Bilaspur, another "backward area," and has three instant coffee plants with a large export commitment. It is to be noted that the BB plantation companies are 26 percent owned by Indian investors; in Kenya, 12 percent equity is held by local people.

This brief outline of the range of BB investments in India and East Africa is meant to be indicative; it is not complete. During a telephone interview, BB reported that it had been subject to some challenge relative to the level of wages paid to workers in these countries and had not wholly succeeded in explaining the reality of either wage controls or the potential distortions in an economy of violating the local norms.

DOLE PHILIPPINES, INC. (DOLEFIL)
Mindanao, the Philippines, South Cotabato Province

Dolefil is a wholly owned subsidiary of Castle and Cooke, Inc. (Honolulu), which set up operations on the island of Mindanao in 1963, and in the ensuing twenty-one years is said to have become one of the largest pineapple plantation/cannery/ export operations in the world. Adjacent to the cannery, Dolefil operates a modern manufacturing plant to produce cans from imported tinplate. Fresh fruit is exported to Japan; canned fruit goes to U.S., European, and other markets. Shipping is done from its own dock at Calumpang Wharf, jointly used by another Castle and Cooke subsidiary, Stanfilco, which produces bananas nearby. The Castle and Cooke operations in this area of Mindanao are clearly the dominant force for economic growth, and lie at the core of social progress and social controversy.

Development Opportunity

The developmental impact of Dolefil derives from employment of roughly 9,000 people; the training they have received; the eddy effect of payroll and purchases of local services and supplies; and expenditures on community services, welfare, and other development projects, such as improving potable water sources (an outlay over the years of about US$1 million). Dolefil does not have an outgrower program. It leases 20,000 acres from the

National Development Corporation, for a twenty-five-year period
subject to renegotiation. In addition it has farm management
contracts covering another 5,000 acres. By paying a set annual
rent and an annual premium based on the amount of pineapple harvested, Dolefil does the farming for these individual landowners.
Both of these land-use mechanisms have been subject to considerable controversy, both as to legality and as to the benefits ac-
cruing to the people under the acts of land reform. There can be
no question of the enormous economic impact of Castle and Cooke
investments in South Cotabato Province. There are, however, a
great many questions concerning the cost/benefit relationships
between Dolefil and rural development in the areas of housing,
health, land erosion, flooding, and chemical pollution, among
others. As these issues have arisen over the years of Dolefil
growth and the large increase in population through immigration
that it engendered, the range of conflict and the methods used
for their resolution provide a most instructive case history for
potential investors in agribusiness sited in rural areas. It is
fortunate that Dolefil has been the subject of a detailed study,
Multinational Managers and Poverty in the Third World, which
offers a variety of provocative comments on the role of private
enterprise in Third World development [37].

EAST AFRICA TANNIN EXTRACT COMPANY (EATEC) LTD.
Eldoret, Kenya

The East Africa Tannin Extract Company is a wholly owned
subsidiary of Lonrho plc., (United Kingdom). Lonrho and its subsidiaries are the largest food producers in Africa, ranching and
farming over 1.5 million acres, divided into large estates, with
and without involvement with outgrowers. These operations are to
be found in Kenya, Malawi, Nigeria, Swaziland, and Zimbabwe.
Clearly, the total experience of Lonrho in agricultural and rural
development deserves detailed investigation.

Development Opportunity

EATEC operates a 46,000-acre diversified farming and manufacturing facility, employing about 2,500 people. Twenty thousand acres are devoted to wattle, a species of acacia whose bark
is a source of tannin. Three thousand acres are in corn; 2,000
acres are in wheat. There are 5,000 head of beef cattle and the
company is starting a dairy. In addition, a plantation of eucalyptus trees is being developed to supply poles to the government
of Kenya for telephone and electricity distribution systems.
EATEC, utilizing a variety of its agricultural wastes, also produces mushrooms for both domestic and export markets, mostly
canned.
Wattle has always been basic to the EATEC operation, since
Lonrho purchased the farm in 1968. Originally, it had been hoped

that outgrowers would provide 40 to 60 percent of factory requirements. The company offered free, pretreated (for accelerated germination) seed; instruction in silvicultural practice and bark removal; instruction in converting the wood into charcoal for home use and sale; and free transport of bark from tree lot to factory. The program did not succeed. The market for tannin declined. Labor was said to be scarce and costly. Very little bark arrives at the factory from outgrowers, none of whom are under contract. Yet, management feels keenly that a tree lot is a highly desirable addition to the farms of the region and would likely cooperate with any agency from the outside that would take on the cost and responsibility of organizing a reliable and adequate outgrower system. This is particularly intriguing because EATEC is undertaking the development of its own diversified agricultural research program and intends to focus not only on higher-yielding monocultures, but also on profitable systems of multiculture that might be highly adaptable to small-scale agriculture in which tree and crop culture could be integrated.

EGYPTIAN-AMERICAN AGRICULTURAL COMPANY, S.A.E.
Ibrahimia, Alexandria, Egypt

The Egyptian-American Agricultural Company is a creation of EMCON International (Darien, Connecticut) located on roughly 2,000 acres of irrigated land adjacent to the Desert Road, between Cairo and Alexandria. It is a joint venture with the Nile Agricultural Development Company, a private organization, which holds a 40 percent share in return for contributing their lease of the land and water rights; 60 percent is held by a group of some sixty individual investors through a limited partnership. Simultaneously with the formation of the company in Egypt late in 1980, a marketing company, Four Seasons, was organized and headquartered in Switzerland. The entire project was planned for capitalization at roughly US$16 million. The enterprise is totally private in ownership and control.

Development Opportunity

At present, the company produces tomatoes, 80 percent of which are exported to Europe. Lettuce plantings have begun and plans are to include melons, broccoli, asparagus, and other crops as they are tested and adapted to the site. The farm, packinghouse, and associated activities employ up to 2,000 regular and seasonal workers. No outgrower program is either in operation or currently in the planning stage. All labor is recruited in the area, some from villages within the boundaries of the Nile Delta, as far as thirty-five to fifty miles away. As is the custom in Egypt, labor is supplied through a system of contractors and subcontractors. This method does deliver labor; it also raises serious questions about corporate responsibility for labor conditions, especially as the majority of field workers are girls and boys in their minority years.

The estate has the potential of being expanded to almost three times its present size, leading at least to the vision of a resettlement/rural development scheme, if financial and administrative assistance were forthcoming from development agencies. Management was intrigued by this long-range possibility but felt it would not be feasible for some years to come for the company to undertake such a project and support it from its own limited resources.

KENYA CANNERS LIMITED (KC)
Thika, Kenya

This case is presented in detail in Chapter 12. In brief summary, Kenya Canners Limited is a subsidiary of the Del Monte Corporation, which is now a division of the Food and Beverage Group of R.J. Reynolds Industries, Inc. Del Monte owns 95 percent of KC; the Development Corporation of Kenya owns 2 percent; 3 percent is owned by one Englishman and twenty-three Kenyans. Del Monte has invested US$36 million in the enterprise. KC processes pineapple grown on its own plantation; all canned goods are exported to and through Del Monte International into European, Middle Eastern, and other foreign markets. Nothing is sold to the United States. A very small quantity of fresh fruit is sold to the Government Horticultural Corps Authority, for airfreighting into European markets. KC employs 6,000 people in the cannery and on the estate during peak season; 5,500 are regularly at work.

Development Opportunity

The KC estate is an area of 22,000 acres, leased long term from the government of Kenya. Essentially, the land was aggregated by the government's purchase of four estates created before independence. In taking the land for KC use, no people were displaced. In effect, nonproductive land was reconverted to intensive agriculture. As of 1984, 10,000 acres were under pineapple cultivation; 1,000 acres grew coffee; 2,000 head of cattle were fed out and a small breeding herd was maintained; and on land not suitable for cropping, KC was developing a reforestation program, to supply charcoal and lumber for employees and to control erosion.

There is but one outgrower in the pineapple growing area. Yet KC is now giving serious consideration to expanding its supply beyond the plantation capacity, in the face of many difficulties caused by the topography of the area and a scarcity of land suitable for efficient pineapple production. This search for an opportunity to develop an outgrower system of contract farming

provides KC with a basis for planning the development both as a
sourcing device and as a stimulant to long-range rural development.   Chapter 12 describes at some length how KC might extend
the benefits of its presence in the Thika area, even while building a profitable expansion of its commercial enterprise.

LA PERLA Y ANEXOS, S.A. (LA PERLA)
Guatemala City, Guatemala

La Perla y Anexos, S.A., is a coffee estate of 8,645 acres
in northwestern Guatemala, a remote mountainous area near the
Mexican border. Ownership since 1942 has been in the hands of one
Guatemalan family.   The site is in the zone of El Quiché, one of
the places where insurgents have long campaigned to gain the support of the indigenous people, with dubious success.

Recognizing that the thrust of agrarian reform and the
search for social order had to be joined by the large landowners,
the family decided in the late 1970s on a bold experiment that
has yet to be fully implemented.

Development Opportunity

A multimillion-dollar loan has been essentially approved but
not yet actually funded by the Interamerican Development Bank,
for two purposes: to finance the purchase of 40 percent of the
common voting stock in the name of all the rural workers at
La Perla, to be placed in a trust until paid for from dividends
(a modified version of the Employee Stock Ownership Plan now
widely adopted in the U.S.); and to improve the infrastructure,
including road access, of La Perla and to diversify the agriculture to include other high value export crops such as cardamom
and macadamia nuts.

Eleven hundred acres have been set aside in an irrevocable
trust, for use by employees and their families for homes, community development to include all basic services, and subsistence
farming.   In 1983, two employee associations, representing all
350 employees, were legally created.   Their representatives are
working with management in the evolution of the entire scheme.
Further, in 1983 an Employee Civil Defense Force was established
to protect the estate.

The bottleneck to further comprehensive action at La Perla
is the funding capability of the Interamerican Development Bank
and the complex process of final evaluation of the loan application, which though approved in principle, has yet to be acted
upon after at least three years of negotiation.   The project has
caught the attention of the Republic of China (Taiwan), which
early in 1982 offered a technical assistance program to La Perla,
directed to teaching the workers how to plant vegetables and
other crops, raise poultry and pigs, and engage in fish-pond culture. This possibility is being explored.

SAN MIGUEL CORPORATION (SMC)
Manila, the Philippines

This case is presented in detail in Chapter 9. In brief summary, San Miguel Corporation is a conglomerate engaged primarily in various aspects of agro-industry serving both domestic and export markets. Among its many operations, SMC is a major producer of broiler chicks, broiler breeders, and dressed chicken. By the end of 1984, SMC will be the largest single source of improved hybrid corn seed, in a system where the company is also a major buyer of corn for the manufacture of animal feeds, some of which are consumed internally by corporate chicken enterprises. SMC employs just under 18,000 people; in 1982, sales were 5.61 billion pesos (US$660 million, at the exchange rate of P8.5 = US$1).

Development Opportunity

In 1977, after an earlier attempt to enter the field of hybrid corn seed production and marketing (1950), SMC started a breeding program to create corn hybrids suitable to the Philippines. After five years and an expenditure of roughly US$6 million, the company was ready to commercialize its experimental results. A production center was established in South Cotabato, on the island of Mindanao, consisting of an estate of 1,250 acres, with a modern processing plant to dry, shell, husk, size, treat, and package seed. Depending upon the stability of the peso, SMC expects to be at a break-even point by 1985 and to attain a return on investment of 20 percent, which includes amortization of research and development activities.

SMC uses a four-pronged technique. It organizes classes for farmers, in cooperation with leaders of farmers' associations; sets up practical demonstrations on farms and invites neighbors to observe the entire practice through the weighing of the harvest; organizes harvest festivals in cooperation with farmers who have demonstration areas; and uses a sales force of young men trained to double as extension workers.

Results of the first two years have been impressive. Yields have increased three- to fivefold and more; net return from corn has doubled and tripled. The hope is that on a countrywide basis, corn yield will increase dramatically, with a beneficial impact on family diet, directly from corn and indirectly by decreasing the cost of meat. Involved farmer associations are starting to invest in such capital goods as corn driers, and there have been marked improvements in life style: better homes, better sanitation, and better clothing, among other indicators.

7. PROCESSING PLANTS AND FREE-MARKET SUPPLY

Included in this category are enterprises with an investment in processing facilities supplied by competitive purchasing in the free market. Each has the possibility of changing the raw material system to a contract farming base.

- CPC Industrial Products (Kenya) Ltd. (East Africa)
- Livestock Feeds Limited (West Africa)

CPC INDUSTRIAL PRODUCTS (KENYA) LTD.
Eldoret, Kenya

CPC Industrial Products (Kenya) Ltd. is a corn wet milling plant whose primary products are starch and dextrose. It has a throughput of 7,000 to 10,000 metric tons of corn per year. Start-up was in late 1976. The plant equipment is a combination of used machinery brought to Kenya from CPC plants in other parts of the world. CPC owns 51 percent of equity; there is no estate nor are there outgrower programs. The plant employs about 150 people, three of whom are expatriates.

Development Opportunity

CPC started operations based on an eight-year purchasing agreement with the Kenya Cereals Board, setting a fixed price on delivered grain. After several years, the Cereals Board broke the contract and raised the price by 107 percent. During difficult negotiations relating to the source and cost of corn, CPC subsidized operating losses in an effort to keep the factory in Kenya. Finally, the Cereals Board granted the plant the right to buy corn directly from farmers--the first and only such exception ever made. CPC then entered into supply contracts with large-scale producers, including one commercial operation run by a public sector company. Management would like to facilitate an outgrower program (CPC does not wish to farm itself) but cannot, nor necessarily believes it should, undertake to develop such a program with its own resources.

LIVESTOCK FEEDS LIMITED (LF)
Ikeja, Nigeria

Livestock Feeds Limited was established in 1963, with an 80 percent shareholding by Pfizer, Inc. Following the Indigenisation Decree of 1977, Pfizer reduced its equity to 60 percent; the remaining 40 percent is held by 1,910 Nigerian stockholders.

LF is the largest animal feed miller in the country, with a 50 percent share of the market. There are about sixty feed millers in Nigeria [38, 39].

Development Opportunity

When Pfizer first entered Nigeria, its only relationship with the animal industry was through the sale of animal health products. Because the market was small, the company did everything it could to encourage an increase in poultry production. Along with other efforts, strongly supported at that time by USAID, the net effect was indeed a marked growth, soon introducing a shortage of feed that became a bottleneck to further progress. It was at this moment that Pfizer organized Lifestock Feeds. During the intervening years LF has become the largest Pfizer subsidiary in Nigeria. It operates four mills and has licensing agreements with thirty-four other millers who buy LF concentrates, mix according to LF formulations, and sell under the LF label. These franchise millers are scattered widely over the country in fourteen states.

In every way, LF has had a clear and significant impact on the successful and dynamic growth of the poultry industry. Recently, serious problems relative to imports of critical raw materials have begun to emerge and are not fully resolved. All millers depend upon the import of two key ingredients--corn and fish meal. When imports were cut off in 1982, the government promised to release enough grain from internal supplies to meet the needs of the industry; unfortunately, there were no such supplies. As of October 1983, when this problem was discussed at the Africa/Middle East Management Centre of Pfizer in Nairobi, Kenya, LF had but a three-month supply of corn left. Naturally, LF was trying to find sources, but as was said, "Pfizer has no intention of investing in direct corn farming or in an outgrower/contract farming program." Contracts, it is believed, would not be worth the paper written on. Because the poultry industry is now so large and vital in Nigeria, Pfizer feels that it should depend upon the outcome of industry negotiations with government to free up the necessary foreign exchange and import permits to eliminate the shortage.

8. CONTRACT FARMING AND MARKETING COMPANIES

These enterprises have no investment in a processing plant. They market raw material obtained through a system of contract farming, using small-scale farmers primarily, but in some cases include larger-scale commercial farms.

- Adams International (Southeast Asia)
- Agro-Inversiones C. por A. (Caribbean Basin)

- McIlhenny Company (Central America, Honduras)
- Press (Holdings) Limited (East Africa)
- Standard Fruit/Guanchis (Central America)
- Sudanese Gezira Board (Northeast Africa)
- United Brands Company (Central America)

ADAMS INTERNATIONAL (AI)
Bangkok, Thailand

This case is presented in detail in Chapter 11.   In brief summary, Adams International is a joint venture of a Thai-Chinese family company and the W.A. Adams Company, Inc., of Durham, North Carolina, formed in 1969.   In 1974, AI entered into a marketing agreement with Philip Morris, Inc., for the sale of Thailand's oriental-type tobacco, provided that AI could meet price, quantity, and quality requirements. This agreement has led to a major growth of the company, involving an outreach program to more than 40,000 farmers in three different parts of the country by the end of 1982. AI began in 1969 with 4 employees and now has 700, with plans for further expansion. Since the entry of Philip Morris into the scene, AI has invested about US$3 million in new facilities; 20 percent of this investment is directly related to the growth of the extension program.

Development Opportunity

The company's production area is spread over three regions, in total area about the size of North Carolina. Administratively, the AI agricultural manager is in charge of tobacco procurement. Under him are two field managers, each supported by a regional manager responsible for a network of buying stations, as well as for the work of a station manager who supervises warehousing, cleaning, and packing facilities.   Reporting to the station manager are head inspectors, who are responsible for relations with the farmers in five to seven villages. The vital last link in the managerial chain is the village inspector, who deals with farmers on a daily basis.   Depending on the size of the villages, an inspector is charged with one to three communities.   Village inspectors are selected from among the farmers and trained for the job.   In 1983, there were 600 village inspectors.

All agricultural materials necessary to produce tobacco are supplied on credit, free of interest, and repaid at harvest time. AI has also carried on the necessary research and extension work to introduce rotational crops, for example, peanuts and sunflower, vital to the maintenance of soil quality.   The accounts of all 40,000 participating farmers are handled by a computer system invented by one of the field managers who is a U.S. citizen and former Peace Corps volunteer. The computer itself has become a sales item in the AI line and is sold all over the world by an affiliate.

AGRO-INVERSIONES C. POR A. (AI)
Ciudad Azua, Dominican Republic

This case is presented in detail in Chapter 10. In brief summary, Agro-Inversiones C. por A., organized in 1982, is a joint venture between R. D. (Republica Dominicana) Vegetable Products, Inc., which holds 70 percent of the equity, and private Dominican investors, who hold 30 percent. R. D. Vegetable Products is a holding company created by the Caribbean Basin Investment Corporation (CBI) of Florida for all CBI ventures in the Dominican Republic. CBI also created the CBI Agribusiness Group, Inc., designed to function as a management and technical assistance company for agribusiness enterprises in the Caribbean area. Investment in AI is estimated at US$1.5 to 2 million. At the end of 1983, the entire emphasis of production was on melons to be exported to the United States, where CBI sells 100 percent of the melons to Corky Foods Corporation. Corky, in turn, sells to supermarket chains and food wholesalers throughout the United States and Canada.

Development Opportunity

The Azua Valley, where AI production and packinghouse activities are centered, is considered by some as a showcase of the beneficial results of agrarian reform in the Dominican Republic. Between 1978 and 1982, close to $1 billion was invested in rehabilitating the valley, once a forested land and later a semi-desert due to excessive cutting. Under agrarian reform, settlers (parceleros) do not get title to land, but do get a lifelong lease that can be extended to the next generation. AI contracts melon production with 85 to 110 parceleros. Seed is provided at cost; technical assistance is offered free; and the company provides all inputs on credit, which is paid for when the fruit is delivered to the packing plant. Meanwhile, AI is experimenting with other crops as part of a diversification program: eggplant, cucumbers, bell peppers, and squash, which it hopes to introduce into the Azua Valley soon. The field manager of AI is an agronomist from the United States with long experience in tropical agriculture; he has a field staff of five agronomists, all Dominicans.

A rehabilitated area, ready for the commercialization of its agriculture and settling in of new farmers, is always exciting in the vista it presents of opportunities for both agricultural and rural development. AI has taken an important first step by demonstrating the profit potential of the Azua Valley and the ability of the parceleros to adapt quickly to new and improved agricultural practices.

MCILHENNY COMPANY
Avery Island, Louisiana

For almost 120 years, McIlhenny Company has used a special variety of pepper for processing its internationally marketed Tabasco-brand pepper sauce. The fruit requires hand picking, and in recent years, as labor costs have increased and farm labor supplies have decreased, the company has gradually moved to Latin America for its raw material. In Mexico and Venezuela, Tabasco is produced by a licensed manufacturer. Peppers are grown by contract farmers in both countries. In Mexico, the manufacturer cultivates peppers on its own farm as well. These two countries, however, supply only a modest amount of pepper to the main plant in Louisiana.

Development Opportunity

Honduras has become the most important source of raw material for the U.S. operation, with roughly 50 percent of requirements met in 1983. McIlhenny has only two employees in Honduras, but they contract almost exclusively with some 300 small-scale farmers whose plantings range from two acres to three acres (with a few producing on twenty to thirty acres). The principal growing area is on the north coast, stretching from Santa Rosa de Copan to La Ceiba. It is interesting to note that in 1976, McIlhenny contracted directly with a Jesuit institution called La Fragua, which successfully subcontracted production. About three years ago, La Fragua phased out of pepper production, but many farmers stayed in the program.

The company provides growers with seed and as much technical assistance as they can "feasibly supply." There is a guarantee to buy a minimum amount (established by contract in pounds of red pepper), but traditionally McIlhenny has bought all the pepper harvested. The company rents land on which to build storage sheds, and for installing small hammer-mills for grinding. Empty white-oak barrels are sent from the United States, and once they are filled with the mash, can be stored indefinitely while awaiting export. The sheds, hammer-mills, and other small items constitute the only investment made by the company in Honduras. As the agricultural manager of McIlhenny says, "We have, however, invested immeasurable time and effort educating and training farmers, and many times over the years have shared expenses where producers have had crop failures due to diseases or other natural disasters" [40].

PRESS (HOLDINGS) LIMITED (PRESS)
Blantyre, Malawi

The origins of Press (Holdings) Limited extend back to 1960 when President H. Kamuzu Banda of Malawi formed the Malawi Press, a private company, for the primary purpose of publishing the Malawi News, the main publicity arm of the Malawi Congress Party. During the next two and a half decades, Press developed into the largest commercial, industrial, and agricultural organization in the country, with a total of seventeen subsidiaries, eleven wholly owned.

Development Opportunity

In agribusiness, the first company formed was the General Farming Company Limited, which by 1978 was growing tobacco on approximately 9,200 acres and accounting for 25 percent of national production. At that time, plans were being activated to establish two estates to be used for training tenant farmers and for research; to establish a Land Planning and Forestry Department to concentrate on the production of fuel wood; and a crop diversification program to expand corn and other cash crop cultivation both to feed the labor force and to market. In 1978, roughly 1,500 people constituted the work force.

Also in 1969, Press (Farming) Ltd. was organized, which now produces 33 percent of national tobacco production on 7,000 to 8,000 acres. In this scheme, there are 4,700 to 5,000 tenant farmers. Tenants are provided with communal holding barns and grading sheds. In 1976, Press (Ranching) Ltd., a wholly owned subsidiary of General Farming, was established on 64,000 acres secured in the Liwonde District. High-quality breeding stock was imported to help upgrade the local Malawi Zebu types. As a cash crop, Burley Tobacco is being introduced. Finally, this enterprise includes the only commercial production of pasture seed.

Obviously, the fact that President-for-Life Banda is the founder and chairman of Press (Holdings) has made life much simpler for this enterprise. Nonetheless, the form of the company is indicative of a private enterprise way of thinking, which might encourage foreign investors to look very closely at Malawi. During recent travels in East Africa, I heard constant references to the promise Malawi is holding out to agro-industrial investment. Finally, the report by Press from which this abstract is drawn makes no comment about the rural development impact of the farming companies, in terms of either policy and plans or direct outreach projects [41].

STANDARD FRUIT COMPANY (STANDARD)
AND THE GUANCHIS AGRICULTURAL AND
LIVESTOCK COOPERATIVE (GUANCHIS)
Santa Rita/San Pedro Sula, Honduras

This case is a classic example of how the coincidence of a grassroots, self-development project and the presence of a multinational agro-industrial corporation became mutually supportive, with significant mutual impact. It is also a case that raises a fundamental question for those concerned with maximizing the self-help aspect of rural development. Put another way, which factors limit the success of rural development when local leadership enter into successive stages of the process of change over the years? For a much more complete description of this complex, subtle, and instructive case, see the "Case of Guanchis," on file at the Fund for Multinational Management Education [42]; and the USAID Special Evaluation Study, Guanchis Limitada [43].

Development Opportunity

Guanchis is a cooperative that arose out of the closing of the United Fruit Company (now United Brands, Inc.) banana plantations in Honduras, in the San Pedro Sula area. Workers were out of jobs, and the land they hoped to farm was taken over by cattle ranchers and others by force, leaving these people in a desperate condition. Under the leadership of two determined men, a small group entered a decade of dramatic struggle against violence, bureaucratic obstacles, hunger, and poverty, clearly depicted in the "Case of Guanchis." Over the years from 1961 to 1968, Guanchis gradually prospered. It was legally recognized; it began to have access to the public credit system; it acquired a substantial amount of land for banana production.

While Guanchis was passing through its tormented early struggles, the Standard Fruit Company (a subsidiary of Castle and Cooke, Inc.) was slowly arriving at a conclusion that the times dictated a shift from production on its own plantations to sourcing bananas from independent producers. In 1968, Standard and Guanchis entered into a buy/sell contract that was so successful that it fundamentally influenced Standard to accelerate the application of this practice in all Latin American countries in which it had banana operations. Included in this system is the extension of technical assistance to producers. Thereafter, Guanchis developed a housing/community development scheme; it expanded into cattle, hogs, and poultry. There has been trouble in all these enterprises, raising serious questions as to the limits of management capability.

THE SUDANESE GEZIRA BOARD (GB)
Barakat, Republic of the Sudan

The Gezira Scheme is probably the largest unified irrigated farming enterprise in the world, spread out over more than 2 million acres lying between the Blue Nile and the White Nile, south of Khartoum. The Gezira Board is a government corporation that controls the farming activities of roughly 100,000 tenant farmers, whose land ranges in size from less than 15 to 40 acres. Between 1925 and 1950, the Gezira Scheme was a private enterprise jointly directed by two British companies, the Sudan Plantations Syndicate and the Kassala Cotton Company. It was conceived by the British Cotton Growing Association in the years before World War I.

Development Opportunity

The scheme constitutes 12 percent of the total area cultivated in the Sudan, although new areas to the south are being developed for agriculture by several large-scale projects. It remains true, however, that the farmers at Gezira produce most of Sudan's long staple cotton, constituting 30 to 50 percent of world production; and the scheme probably accounts for 50 to 60 percent of the commercial farm output of the country. Although cotton is the dominant crop, in recent years durra (a sorghum, the staple food of the people), wheat, peanuts, lubia (for fodder), vegetables, and Phillipsera (for fodder) have become significant in the six- or seven-year crop rotation now normal to local practice. The Gezira Board employs 50,000 to 60,000 people and has lost much of its plantation character. Although control over the cropping pattern is retained, supervisory powers over cotton production have been lessened and the board exercises virtually no control over other crops. Tenants now have a considerable say in the management of the scheme, through intermediary organizations with considerable political power. However, the board provides farm inputs on credit, arranges contract spraying, provides interest-free credit for needs beyond inputs, and offers technical extension services.

The value of this reference to the Gezira Board, even though it is now a public rather than a private enterprise, lies in an appreciation of the sheer magnitude of the organization and the system of administration, which has evolved in order to make the enterprise work at a profit. The case is also of interest because, as some critics suggest, the Gezira Scheme has put the people into a stagnant position after a first flush of rising incomes and expectations. The most comprehensive study of these matters is to be found in a book published in England by Tony Barnett, of the School of Development Studies at the University of East Anglia, The Gezira Scheme: An Illusion of Development [44].

UNITED BRANDS COMPANY
New York, New York

United Brands Company, which took over United Fruit Company several years ago, is one of the largest diversified agro-industrial enterprises in Central America. While the company has created subsidiaries quite independent of the assets purchased from United Fruit, operations in bananas, cacao, coffee, oil palm, and other crops have histories extending back to the turn of the century. United Fruit entered these areas and initiated an agricultural revolution which has had profound impact on the social and economic structure of every country in Central America. Because the role played by United Fruit in the development of this region was so central, so vital during three-quarters of the twentieth century, and so controversial, no comment about United Brands would be either fair or adequate without a careful analysis of the imprint of United Fruit on what it does in Central America, how it does it, and how it is received. Such an analysis is beyond the scope of this inventory. An important reference to the impact of United Fruit Company on the economic development of Central America is an unpublished report, prepared in 1967 by Projects International, Inc. [45].
Typical of the efforts of United Brands to develop its own favorable image in Central America are its operations in Costa Rica. Large tracts of land have been returned to the ownership of "associate producers," independent small-scale farmers. These farmers not only have gained landownership and have assured markets, but also receive technical assistance and other benefits from their association with the company. Indeed, United has established a separate company in Costa Rica, Compania Bananera Atlantico, exclusively to furnish technical and marketing assistance to independent banana farmers. United employs roughly 7,500 people in its six Costa Rican subsidiaries, four relate to bananas, oil palm, or vegetable oil products (the latter largely for domestic consumption).

9. SELF-SUPPLIED MARKETING COMPANIES

Self-supplied marketing companies are enterprises that have no investment in a processing plant but market produce from an enterprise-owned and -operated large-scale farm or plantation.

- MISR/American Agricultural Systems Company (North Africa)

MISR/AMERICAN AGRICULTURAL SYSTEMS COMPANY (MAASCO)
Cairo, Egypt

The primary purpose of MAASCO is the initial development and
subsequent management of farming and animal science projects and
agro-industrial enterprises, primarily but not exclusively in
Egypt. The three partners in MAASCO are the Management Services
Division of the Ball Corporation (U.S.); the MISR Iran Development Bank; and Sabbour Associates, the latter two centered in
Cairo. MAASCO does not itself invest. An early project of MAASCO,
in service to a group of Sudanese businessmen headed by Wadia S.
Girgis, is the development of newly opened land of some 5,000 to
6,000 acres, ultimately to produce potatoes, onions, and possibly
other vegetables. The production of peanuts for animal feed and
vegetable oil is also under consideration. Financing is in the
order of US$11 to 15 million.

Development Opportunity

The project site is actually leased by the Ministry of Agriculture. The first year will be used for a green fodder/cattle
feeding operation, to begin preparing the land for a cropping
pattern. A second crop (the first will likely be Sudan grass or
a grass/sorghum hybrid) of Berseen clover will follow, and thereafter peanuts, potatoes, and onions will be introduced.

It is hoped that by year six or seven, the estate will be
mature. Labor will be drawn from the region, to be obtained
through the traditional labor contractor. There are no plans for
a smallholder resettlement scheme at the moment.

10. SALES AND TECHNICAL SERVICES

The following four companies are enterprises focused on a
national or regional market that have extensive interaction with
farmers as part of their sales efforts, including technical
assistance, training, and often some type of credit.

- Ciba-Geigy Limited (Worldwide)

- Monsanto Central Africa, Inc. (East Africa)

- Purina, S.A. de C.V. (Middle America)

- Shell International Chemical Company Ltd. (West Africa)

CIBA-GEIGY LIMITED
Basel, Switzerland

Ciba-Geigy Limited has no direct investment in agro-industry, except in the sense of manufacturing and marketing insecticides, herbicides, and fungicides, and to a lesser extent, products for animal health. Correspondence with Ciba-Geigy indicates that it is often necessary to take what is called a "comprehensive project approach." This means that in building sales in an area where farmers may need both technical and financial help to apply superior practices (including company products), both credit and technical supervision are offered. Customers are advised as to the best seed stock, the appropriate pesticides, and methods of application. At first, Ciba-Geigy personnel may actually teach by applying the chemicals themselves. The company has found this to be a very successful way of demonstrating the net profit on the cost of chemical pest control, even while assuring the repayment of expenses and material costs that were advanced. Clearly, the work of this company would have to be examined in great detail to appreciate its developmental impact and to extract any methodology that might be generally applicable.

Development Opportunity

As with so many leads to the activities of individual agricultural chemical companies (see also Monsanto, below, and Livestock Feeds, Section 6), it is clear that practically every major company is multinational, and all carry out sales programs with a technical service mode that can be very helpful. More should be known about variations in methodology, success and failure, conflict resolution regarding health hazards, cost/benefit relationships, and other aspects of agricultural chemical manufacturing and marketing.

MONSANTO CENTRAL AFRICA, INC.
Nairobi, Kenya

Monsanto, in this case, is a distributor of agricultural chemicals. It neither farms nor processes agricultural raw materials. For the past several years, Monsanto Central Africa, Inc., operating out of Kenya, has spent roughly US$100,000 per year on the extension of what it calls the "Minimum Tillage Program." This program emphasizes the economic importance to small-scale farmers of using a biodegradable chemical weed control system (based on Roundup, a Monsanto product). The belief behind this program is that the future of African agriculture lies in bettering the performance of smallholders and, in so doing, laying the economic foundation for a growing market for agricultural chemicals. In 1983, the total Kenyan market for all chemicals was running at $25 million; 75 percent went to the largest farms and most of this goes to went to 300 large-scale units.

Development Opportunity

The base of the Minimum Tillage Program is the extensive distribution network Monsanto has built in African countries. In Kenya, for example, there are some 560 villages in which a private, small-scale, retail outlet exists, serviced by sales personnel (Kenyan) who work for distributors (not Monsanto-owned). Sales people are trained to demonstrate the tillage program. A local farmer-customer of the shopkeeper is first brought into the program. Then, field days are used to encourage replication. What works is the clear proof that weed control, a very difficult task, can be exercised in several hours of backpack spraying, saving literally hundreds of hours of scarce labor, thus overcoming labor shortages, erosion, evaporative loss of water, competition from weeds, and decreased productivity. In Kenya alone, in the first six months of 1983 some 8,000 farmers tried the chemical and changed their practices, with very impressive results. The program has been utilized for corn and vegetable farms, tea plantation start-up, canal clean-out in the Republic of the Sudan, among other applications, and is claimed to be a promising addition to techniques employed to increase productivity among small-scale, traditional, low-yield farmers.

PURINA, S.A. DE C.V.
Mexico City, Mexico

Purina, S.A. de C.V., has operated in Mexico for many years. It is the largest agro-industry in the country. The company employs 4,000 people, the majority of whom, by company policy, spend considerable time in the field. It is a matter of pride that between company staff and a network of 900 dealers and their employees (all independent enterprises), the system represents the single largest extension service in Mexico. Purina has a large investment in Mexico (no data given) but applying a policy that it considers basic to success, the company does not enter into production at the farm level, by means of contracts, nucleus estates, or any other way; all raw material is purchased in the free market or from government sources. Seventy-five percent of what Purina buys derives from crop allocations by the government. Prices are fixed at levels sometimes higher than the price at which Purina products can bear in the marketplace and sales drop significantly. This is causing a serious problem for the company, especially in these years of high inflation and constant devaluation of the peso.

Development Opportunity

The outreach program of Purina, which over the past several decades has had a profound impact on the growth of the animal industry, emphasizes instruction and certain kinds of financial assistance to the chicken farmer, piggery operators, dairy farmers, cattle ranchers, and dealers. This constant, nationwide program, led by a large staff of Ralston technicians and technical sales people, facilitates getting started in the business and operating at increased efficiency. In Mexico, Ralston has long believed that it is vital to itself and the country to give full attention to the start-up of large numbers of small-scale producers. To this end, the company has developed a wide variety of "family packages" that, with credit help, can put in place a profitable venture with a built-in capability to grow. For example, a dealer may offer a family twelve to fourteen cages, one to three hens ready to lay, and sufficient feed to proceed to first sales. Generally, the package is provided as a loan to be repaid after sales begin. At times, the package may be provided free if Ralston believes that a particular farm has special value as a demonstration unit. The package is almost ready at the time of assembly to yield a profit. The dealer and his staff remain as the local source of technical assistance. This kind of a package also exists for goats, milch cows, and pigs.

Ralston also operates a scholarship program (forty per year) for graduates of agricultural technical schools, which pays a salary for an eight week practical experience on a farm, leading to a job opportunity. Finally, the company maintains the country's most extensive, intensive, and accurate daily data-gathering system covering animal sales, prices of raw materials, availability of grain, and other critical information. These data, as well as all research data relevant to the industry, are made available to the government (which uses them without acknowledgment).

SHELL INTERNATIONAL CHEMICAL COMPANY LIMITED
Uboma, Nigeria

For many years, different Shell companies around the world have engaged in a variety of rural technical assistance programs. One of the most renowned projects involved the rehabilitation of the Borgo a Mozzana commune in Tuscany, Italy, dating back to 1956. Another example of more recent origin is a program called "Train the Trainers." In regional seminars, officials who themselves are engaged in agricultural extension training, receive roughly two weeks of intensive instruction in farm management and the safe use of agricultural chemicals. Perhaps the most extensive long-range rural development program of all has been going on in Nigeria since the early 1960s. The basic structure of the projects in Nigeria arose out of the Borgo experience, and the model being used for replication is located in Uboma, about fifty miles north of Port Harcourt, in what is called the "Oil Palm Belt" of southeastern Nigeria. As in all Shell projects, the objectives of the Uboma project are: to improve yields of major food crops; to improve diet with an emphasis on protein intake; to increase earnings; and to improve the quality of social services and infrastructure in the area [46].

Development Opportunity

The project was sponsored by Shell International and the Ministry of Agriculture. After an intensive socioeconomic study, project implementation began in 1964. One Shell agronomist (a Nigerian) and several assistants were the resident team. The land area of the project was twenty-five square miles, with six villages. In 1964, there were some 34,000 people, an increase of 14,000 in ten years. Per capita income was at least 15 percent below the national average. Farmers were busy six months and essentially idle six months. There was no off-farm employment. Infrastructure was very poor. Ten years later, even though hampered by the civil war of 1967-1970, Uboma was described by agricultural economists from the Universities of Ibadan and Nsukka as "a revitalized and rapidly developing rural community." Where rice had never grown, there were 1,600 acres in production, with one mobile and two stationary rice mills. Where only wild trees had been harvested, there were 864 acres of improved oil palms. Twenty-nine acres of fish ponds were productive; 70,000 pineapple stands planted; 88 acres of irrigated vegetables were under cultivation; 15 small poultry and 10 small piggery farms had been created. There were 17 farmer cooperatives, joined in the Uboma Farmers Cooperative Union, and most farmers were busy year-round. In 1978, the project was formally handed over to the local community and Shell concentrated on two other projects, one in Bondel State, started in 1971, and one in Rivers State, started in 1965 and reactivated in 1971. No data were available on the total cost of these programs, or on the combined impact of the program on the sale of Shell agricultural chemicals, or on the means whereby management was evaluating the payoff. In any event, the benefits to the people involved in the Uboma are impressive. Nigeria and other less-developed countries have been provided with a model form of agricultural rural development for widespread replication.

11. MANAGEMENT CONSULTANTS AND INVESTORS

These for-profit enterprises, often arising out of a corporate base of specialized skills and functioning as subsidiaries, are often called on to put together entire agro-industrial ventures and to manage them under contract. At times, the management contract is contingent on taking an equity position in the newly created company. The Commonwealth Development Corporation (Section 1 of this chapter) is occasionally in this position. To further illustrate this category of enterprise, two examples are given.

- Booker Agriculture International Limited (Worldwide)
- Tate and Lyle Technical Services Limited (Worldwide)

BOOKER AGRICULTURE INTERNATIONAL LIMITED (BA)
London, England

BA is a division of IBEC International (formerly the International Basic Economy Corporation) with a background of corporate experience in the sugar industry of the United Kingdom. In its evolution, BA is an example of a profitable consulting and management services enterprise growing out of an agro-industrial corporation and then gradually expanding the sale of services beyond the historical limits of the parent company's expertise. The role BA can play in the development of agribusiness in the Third World is typified in the case of the Mumias Sugar Company (Chapter 3).

At Mumias, BA has carried the full burden of technical and managerial responsibility. It conducted the agronomic research basic to a determination of the feasibility of commercial production of sugar cane. It established relationships with farmers and government officials prerequisite to effective collaboration both in the establishment of a sugar mill and in the evolution of a contract system of cane procurement. It designed and supervised the construction of the sugar mill. It designed and implemented training programs for mill labor and for the transfer of cane-growing technology to thousands of small-scale, traditional farmers. BA has managed the Mumias Sugar Company, under contract, from the outset of the enterprise. In a country and in a region lacking in the broad range of skills and experience necessary for the establishment of complex agribusinesses, BA was able to bring into play a competent team of professionals to do the job. BA does this worldwide; the ability to do so in a wide range of agro-industries is fundamentally what organizations like BA offer to the development process.

TATE AND LYLE TECHNICAL SERVICES (TL)
London, England

Tate and Lyle Technical Services is a peer of BA (see above), also with its origins in the sugar industry in the United Kingdom, and also providing a full range of technical and managerial services to investors in agro-industry, worldwide. Most

recently, TL has joined forces with two other development specialists in England: Masdar, with experience in smallholder agriculture, training, and management systems for integrated rural
development projects; and Mander, Raickes and Marshall, a well-
established expert in water resource development, infrastructure
design, and construction supervision. The three have formed a
consortium called Rural Development Indonesia, with expectations
of applying themselves worldwide.

An example of the services provided by TL is the role it
played in the establishment of the Royal Swaziland Sugar Corporation (Chapter 4). TL made the initial feasibility study. It then
established the sugar cane plantation, designed and built the
sugar mill, designed and supervised the creation of several communities for staff, mill workers, and plantation labor. In addition, TL was given the management contract and from its inception
the enterprise has had this form of administration. Finally, it
may be noted that TL holds roughly 9 percent of the ordinary
shares of the corporation.

Development Opportunity

While in no way reflecting a general policy of TL, it is
provocative to note a sharp contrast in the sugar procurement
system of the Royal Swaziland Sugar Corporation when compared to
the Mhlume Sugar Company of Swaziland, and to the Mumias Sugar
Company of Kenya (Chapter 3). Royal Swaziland depends entirely
on cane produced on the corporate plantation. Mhlume receives 12
to 15 percent of its raw material from 263 farmers resettled from
various parts of Swaziland on land provided by the Commonwealth
Development Corporation (Chapter 4). Mumias obtains 88 percent of
the cane requirements of the sugar mill from 23,000 small-scale
farmers who own their land. These three approaches to securing
cane supplies suggest that a comprehensive comparative study of
sugar mill operations throughout Africa might yield valuable
guidelines to optimizing the rural development impact of all
types of agribusiness which require extensive areas of land to
satisfy the demands of commercial processing operations.

12. FINANCIAL INSTITUTIONS

This section includes enterprises primarily concerned with
bringing about the establishment of agro-industrial ventures,
sometimes with loans, sometimes with investment, sometimes with
very soft credit lines, and even with grants, and in some cases
by participating in actual enterprise management. In all cases,
these enterprises have a strong corporate policy directing their
resources to ventures that contribute to agricultural and rural
development. In addition to the enterprises described below, the
Commonwealth Development Corporation, described under Section 1,
"Nuclear Estates," also functions as a financial institution.

- Adela Investment Company, S.A. (Latin America)
- Barclays Bank International Limited (Worldwide)
- Chase Manhattan Bank (Central America and Caribbean Basin)
- Latin American Agribusiness Development Corporation (Latin America, especially Central America and the Caribbean Basin)
- Private Investment Company for Asia (Asia)

ADELA INVESTMENT COMPANY, S.A. (ADELA)
New York, New York

Adela Investment Company, S.A., is a private investment company constituted in 1964 as a Luxembourg corporation, which for many years had its operating headquarters in Lima, Peru. As of the end of 1984, there were 290 shareholders from twenty-three countries. Over the years, Adela has invested, loaned, and leveraged more than US$2 billion, creating or assisting in the establishment of over 190 ventures, including several smaller-scale national development organizations with private sector sponsorship. Adela has usually invested as a minority partner, with the intent to divest its shares to local people as enterprises demonstrated their viability. For many years, Adela stood ready to provide management and technical services, and operated a well-recognized consulting arm known as Adelatec.

Development Opportunity

Adela has stated that its purpose is to foster socioeconomic progress in Latin America by stimulating private enterprise through providing development services, technology, and financing, including equity as a minority investor, to viable new projects and for the expansion of existing enterprises.

In many ways, Adela in its original form and statement was a private sector version of a development institution for Latin America in the image of the role of the Commonwealth Development Corporation (Section 1) in the countries of the former Commonwealth. In 1964 Adela was announced as a pioneering venture, with support from private enterprise all over the world, and during the next decade of growth, Adela roused an enormous amount of excitement and attention. Its influence and intervention became pervasive. Then, for reasons that are unclear, but surely partially due to the economic turbulence of the 1980s, Adela entered into a troubled time. Its portfolio is large. For the moment, it seems that Adela is in a holding rather than an active pattern. Adela is obviously a rich source of experience for those concerned with the role of the private sector in development.

BARCLAYS BANK INTERNATIONAL LIMITED
BARCLAYS INTERNATIONAL DEVELOPMENT FUND (BIDF)
London, England

Barclays International Development Fund was established in 1970, with the intention of filling a gap in the provision of assistance to projects that fall between the categories of pure aid and commercial finance. There are two main classes of projects that qualify for support: practical development projects and research studies. Some projects have a mix of development and research objectives. The fund has been built up over the years by an allocation from after-tax profits of the parent bank, and funds have been allocated in amounts varying between £50 and £50,000. A mixture of financial methods can be used to service a project: equity participation, which provides risk capital for entrepreneurs who may later buy out BIDF equity at a reasonable rate; interest-bearing loans, for varying lengths of time and varying interest; interest-free loans, for varying times; and grants.

Development Opportunity

Throughout the Third World, indeed even throughout the so-called "developed countries," there are innumerable situations where the incipient stages of commercialization of agriculture, industry, and commerce are constrained from further development by a lack of tangible security to facilitate borrowing or by a judgment that risk is too high. Yet, until the bottlenecks to risk capital are broken, the underpinning of the economy at specific sites cannot be strengthened and built upon, and cannot attract more and larger inputs of capital. Banks have always played a key role in investment financing, but rarely has a bank risked its own money, derived from the profit of the organization, to stimulate the early stages of growth in the productive sector of less-developed nations, as Barclays is doing. As a model, BIDF would seem to be an intriguing prototype for replication, not only by banks, but also by private sector industry and commerce.
It may be noted that BIDF tends to apply its funds in countries where Barclays is represented. As stated in private correspondence, "BIDF relies heavily on the 'good offices' of its local bank branches to keep in close touch with administration of a project's finances." In its literature, BIDF goes on to say that development projects are favored where the initial contribution generates a situation for continuing development, leading in due course to a healthy cash flow and normal finance arrangements. In addition, no conditions about an ongoing relationship with the Barclays Group are tied to BIDF support [47].

CHASE MANHATTAN BANK (CHASE)
Panama

Chase Manhattan Bank began its cattle credit program in Panama in 1950. At the time it was a pioneering venture for the bank and very quickly caused Chase to change its credit policy, with a return to what many might call "old-fashioned" methods of determining whether or not a loan was to be made, for example, loans based on the personal merits or apparent managerial ability of the borrower, the productive capacity of the operation, and the purpose of the loan. Further, the necessity to adapt traditional collateral demands to the realities of ranching in rural Panama forced Chase to employ a technical intermediary, a staff member who knew cattle, who could speak English and Spanish, and who was well trained in banking procedures and financial management. The early problems of Chase and a detailed description of how they were solved may be found in Agribusiness Worldwide, August-September, 1980 [48].

Development Opportunity

This is clearly a case where a decision by one enterprise, Chase, literally revolutionized the cattle industry and the rural areas where the bank has operated for over thirty-five years. During this time, Chase has loaned cattle ranchers roughly US$200 million and has only written off about $115,000. Panama switched in this time from being a net importer of beef and beef animals to becoming a major exporter. The number of animals held by Chase clients has increased by a factor of four. Chase itself has grown from its original branch in David to a total of six branches in the region; sixteen other banks have become involved. The regional economy in total displays a healthy vigor, even to the point where some claim that people who left the rural area years ago are beginning to return.

The Chase Panama experience is one of a number of instances around the world where a private bank was the first to perceive a long-range need, a way to meet it, and the pioneering role that a financial institution can play in creating a market for its own services within the context of basic rural development. Because the powerful force for change contained within the banking system of the world has not generally been focused on direct action in rural development, the Chase experience is of considerable importance as a contribution to methodology that might encourage greater involvement in the future.

LATIN AMERICAN AGRIBUSINESS DEVELOPMENT
CORPORATION (LAAD)
Coral Gables, Florida

The Latin American Agribusiness Development Corporation is a private investment and development enterprise, established early in 1970. Sixteen corporations, including five banks and the Adela Investment Company (see first case this section), share an equity of roughly US$5 million. The financial capability of LAAD is supported by a loan of $20 million from USAID, which in 1984 was expected to increase to about $24 million. Currently, LAAD has a role in over 200 enterprises, largely in Central America and the Caribbean Basin.

Development Opportunity

LAAD does not relate directly to the producers (farmers, fishermen, or others) or to rural development. However, in light of size and staff capability, LAAD feels that it can and does fulfill its development responsibility by working to expand and strengthen existing agribusinesses that do interact with rural people. Indeed, in recent years, LAAD includes in its project approval process an emphasis on enterprises that expand and make more secure the marketing of produce from small-scale farmers. Examples of such financing choices, which are briefly described in this chapter are: Alimentos Congelados in Guatemala (Section 3); Leche y Derivados, S.A. in Honduras (Section 2); and Southland Frozen Foods in the Dominican Republic (Section 3). Most of LAAD's participation is by means of loans. The actual and potential impact of LAAD on either national economies or rural development is a question impossible to answer in quantitative terms, without further detailed study.

PRIVATE INVESTMENT COMPANY FOR ASIA (PICA)
Singapore

PICA is a development finance and banking institution, that concentrates its attention primarily on Southeast Asia. Equity participation by a group of Japanese, European, and U.S. investors is in the magnitude of US$30 million. PICA provides financial assistance for the establishment of new enterprises and for the expansion and diversification of existing companies. Financing may include both equity and loan capital. PICA also provides advisory and consulting services. Unlike the Latin American Agribusiness Development Corporation, PICA intervention includes but is not restricted to agribusiness. PICA and LAAD are contemporaries; both have arisen out of a burst of interest and activity in the promotion of private sector investment in the Third World during the late 1960s.

13. BASIC DEVELOPMENT ENTERPRISES

These are enterprises that create the bases for establishing improved agricultural and rural development in the mode of self-sufficiency, sound business practice, and human development. They tend to emphasize participation by small-scale farmers and serve as models for agro-industrial enterprises that may choose to become deeply involved in rural development outreach programs.

- Alumina Partners of Jamaica Ltd. (Caribbean Basin)
- Consultores Del Campo, A.C. (Middle America)
- Fundacion Chile (South America)
- Instituto para el Desarrollo Rural Integral Autosuficiente, S.C. (Middle America)
- ITT/Institute of Cultural Affairs (Nigeria and Korea)
- LAMCO/Partnership for Productivity (West Africa)
- Massey-Ferguson Limited (Worldwide)
- Technoserve, Inc. (Worldwide, concentration in Africa and Latin America)

ALUMINA PARTNERS OF JAMAICA LTD. (ALPART)
Nain, Jamaica

Alumina Partners of Jamaica Ltd., is a joint venture of Anaconda Jamaica, Inc., Kaiser Jamaica Corporation, and Reynolds Jamaica Alumina Ltd., for the extraction of alumina from bauxite. Alpart Farms is a subsidiary that carries out six projects.

1. Land rehabilitation, in which mined-out land is brought back to its former or to a higher level of agricultural productivity.
2. Land resettlement, wherein residents who sell their land to Alpart for mining are moved to what is usually better quality land, several times larger than they formerly owned, and which is provided with a house of approximately the same size and of superior construction to the one left behind. These farmers are provided with technical assistance by Alpart Farms staff.
3. Cattle feedlot at Nain.
4. Cattle feedlot at Friendship.
5. Dairy farm at Pepper.
6. Research particularly as it relates to the use of local agricultural by-products for livestock feeds.

Development Opportunity

The Alpart venture was put together in 1966; start-up of
operations began in 1969. As with the LAMCO case (see below,
same section), Alpart and other mining and hydroelectric projects, and often an industrial complex associated with one or the
other, create unique and rich opportunities for agricultural and
rural development to take place around the peripheries of the
enterprises. Because many such ventures are sited in remote
areas, often with no preexisting infrastructure and little population concentration, the core wealth-producing activity becomes
the center of developmental responsibility, whether or not this
responsibility is expressed functionally in the corporate structure. As a general observation, large-scale mining and power generation projects, except for the creation of infrastructure and a
community for employees, have not demonstrated either leadership
or creativity in extending the benefits of their presence around
their sites; nor have governments capitalized fully on these investments. Considering the large number of such ventures scattered throughout the world, a great challenge and a marvelous
opportunity are "out there" to be faced [49].

CONSULTORES DEL CAMPO, A.C. (CONSULTORES)
Pátzcuaro, Mexico

Consultores Del Campo, A.C., is a nonprofit subsidiary of
Farm Centers International, Inc., a nonprofit rural development
enterprise based in San Francisco. This project is included despite its nonprofit status because it can so vividly illustrate
the profit inherent in financing simple, practical, on-farm improvements among traditional farmers, using low-cost, face-to-
face methods, and thus laying the groundwork for more rapid development in a free-enterprise, self-sufficient mode.

Development Opportunity

Consultores began activities in 1977, as an outgrowth of
lessons learned by Farm Centers International during another
rural development program in an area not far from Pátzcuaro,
which ran from 1964 to 1976. The first program was successful but
depended "too much on outsiders." Consultores works directly with
the farmers, using as a base other farmers who have been trained
to be technicians and local extensionists. The staff of Consultores are the trainers; the local technicians are the heart of
the day-to-day operations. Activities are directed at existing,
known problems of direct concern to income results. For example,
in the course of a single year, technicians work on field mouse
control (the dominant source of crop loss in the area), grafting
of fruit trees, pest control in the corn fields, disinfecting at-
tics, rat control before corn storage, requeening of bee hives,

fertilization of corn, and canning of fruit, among a host of
other interrelated activities. From the results of rodent and insect control alone, between 1977 and 1981 the value added to crop
production was over US$3 million. Investment in this project was
only US$136,000, and over 4,000 farmers benefited. To this may be
added the data reflecting an average increase in net return of
US$2,420 from ten acres of corn, when new practices (including
pest control) are followed.

Consultores is in many ways typical of thousands of inspira-
tional grass-roots projects around the world. But neither the
private sector nor the public sector (including international aid
institutions) have capitalized on these efforts to build upon
their results and to multiply their impact.

FUNDACION CHILE
Santiago, Chile

The Fundación Chile is a unique joint venture between International Telephone and Telegraph Corporation (ITT) and the government of Chile. The investment made by ITT resulted from an
agreement reached in 1974 between the corporation and the government regarding settlement of property expropriated by a previous
regime. Fundación Chile is a nonprofit organization providing
technical assistance to private industries and government agencies in the food sector.

Development Opportunity

It is to be hoped that the circumstances under which ITT
decided to help create Fundación Chile will not often be repeated. Nonetheless, what took place satisfied a need rarely met in
the structure and management of industrial development institutions around the world, namely, the need to bring private enterprise and the public sector together in promoting profit-making
agro-industries that are soundly conceived and that meet both investor and national objectives. The work of Fundación Chile needs
to be evaluated very carefully. If the payoff is as great as
might be anticipated, then the Fundación might well serve as a
model for private investors everywhere, and as a stimulant to
seek means of attracting joint-venture capital acceptable to both
partners.

The Fundación leans heavily on a variety of advisory boards
comprised of local business people, their customers, and members
of government agencies who meet with Fundación staff. In terms
of its mandate to concentrate on the food sector of the economy,
the technology departments of the Fundación are organized by conventional sectors of the industry (fruits and vegetables, grains,
dairy products, and marine resources). All departments bring

their expertise together with private sector participation in engineering, manufacturing, marketing, and business development.

INSTITUTO PARA EL DESARROLLO RURAL
INTEGRAL AUTOSUFICIENTE, S.C. (DRIA)
Queretero, Mexico

DRIA is an independent, nonprofit organization, formerly a subsidiary of Ingenieros Civiles Asociados, S.A. (ICA), a diversified, wholly Mexican-owned civil engineering and manufacturing corporation. DRIA, legally established in January 1985, is a direct outgrowth of Coordinacion Rural, A.C. (CRAC), a nonprofit subsidiary of ICA created in 1969 to initiate a national integrated rural development program. Between 1969 and the end of 1984, ICA invested over US$6 million in the evolution of CRAC methodology. After fifteen years of support, the board of directors of ICA made the judgment that the success of CRAC made it timely for the staff of the latter to move forward into the future as an independent institution and DRIA was established for the purpose.

Development Opportunity

DRIA methodology is based on four interconnected and vital processes: organization, training, and participation of local people; increasing net income from agricultural practices; investment in new local businesses and broadening the base of local ownership in this productive capital; and focusing newly created economic gain on the enhancement of personal, family, and community life. These processes flow together to generate economic self-sufficiency, even as they encourage change to occur in harmony with local needs and values. Based on principles of broad capital ownership, the methodology has proven to be flexible and adaptable to a wide variety of environments.

DRIA operates under conditions of national policy and land tenure that do not encourage a direct adaptation of the nucleus estate methodology widely used in Africa and Asia, but that do permit the physical and human resources of small-scale farmers to be aggregated under management into competitive, diversified, profit-making productive systems. A detailed description of the rural development methodology can be found in the publication, TECHNOS [50].

ITT/INSTITUTE OF CULTURAL AFFAIRS
Ijede, Nigeria

In 1978, International Telephone and Telegraph Corporation
(ITT) provided a three-year, $600,000 grant to the Institute of
Cultural Affairs (ICA), based in Chicago but with a network of
rural development projects all over the Third World, to help fund
two rural human development projects, one in Nigeria, the other
in Korea. When the grant was announced, ITT noted: "ITT believes
a new form of corporate responsibility is called for to improve
the quality and meaning of peoples' lives around the world. The
adoption of the villages will provide assistance for their own
self-development effort" [51].
Implementation of projects was assigned to ICA because of
its extensive and unique experience in stimulating the first
stages of change among traditional people and then building participation by the people to the end of self-sufficiency. ICA is
one of the largest private voluntary organizations in the world,
operating in the United States and internationally with a core of
several hundred full-time members of the staff (who receive a
stipend of the same order of magnitude as the Peace Corps) and
volunteers from all over the world who may number into the thousands at any moment in time. As part of the overall plan of work
designed by both ITT and ICA, ITT personnel volunteered in assisting villagers in the economic and social development programs
undertaken.

Development Opportunity

This case of corporate involvement in rural development is
included in this preliminary inventory of private sector action
because it demonstrates the vital importance of building a societal structure of thought, values, and activities that will support the growth of a system of free, private enterprise. As reported in Enterprise and Development, in Nigeria the results may
be summarized as follows.

Four industries have been created in Ijede: a sew-
ing factory, a motorized fishing fleet, a poultry industry, and a community farm. New construction included 17 community buildings and 123 private residences;
533 people have been involved in 26 training programs.
Five preschools have 112 three- to five-year olds en-
rolled. Nineteen healthcare workers have been trained
to combat dehydration, diarrhea, malaria, and malnutrition, as well as to immunize for measles, tetanus, po-
lio, and smallpox [51].

LIBERIAN AMERICAN MINERALS COMPANY (LAMCO)/
 PARTNERSHIP FOR PRODUCTIVITY (PfP)
Yekepa, Liberia

LAMCO is a joint venture of several Swedish industrial enterprises, Bethlehem Steel Corporation, and the Liberian government. It was created in 1955 after the discovery of iron ore;
open-pit mining began in 1963. When operations began, the community nearest the mine consisted of five thatched huts. LAMCO
created "Yeke's Town" or Yekepa, named after one of the original
inhabitants. The natives were subsistence farmers. There was no
cash economy. Over the next decade, LAMCO invested millions of
dollars in the mine and the infrastructure to support it, including a 167-mile railroad to Buchanan, where it also built a new
deep-water harbor, and a pelletizing plant. During this time,
Yekepa grew into the third largest city in Liberia, with a population of 18,000, and had also become a classical "company town,"
with total dependency on LAMCO.

Development Opportunity

In 1970, LAMCO decided that it must transfer responsibility
for the social and economic affairs of Yekepa to the people, and
at the same time initiate a program to ensure that Yekepa would
continue as a viable community after the iron ore is depleted
early in the twenty-first century. The company tried for three
years, by providing capital, loans, and technical assistance, to
transfer ownership and management control of a group of service
industries. This did not work. LAMCO then reached out for a development organization with the necessary skills to take on the
task of integrated development and chose Partnership for Productivity, a Washington-based nonprofit enterprise.
During the ten years of its association with LAMCO and
Yekepa, PfP has demonstrated remarkable success. During this
time, PfP has created 55 new enterprises and 750 nonmining jobs,
including a local transportation system, a woodworking company, a
forestry and sawmilling enterprise, a hotel and restaurant, a
poultry farm, a tailoring shop, among many others that are gradually fitting into a dynamic, interactive socioeconomic growth
pattern. PfP has created an appropriate technology development
center, and most importantly, it has set up a demonstration and
training farm seeking to diversify and expand the sources of primary wealth of critical importance to the future. Forty-five percent of PfP's total effort in Yekepa is now devoted to accelerating the growth of the agricultural sector of the area economy.

MASSEY-FERGUSON LIMITED
Toronto, Canada

Massey-Ferguson Limited supports the Developing Countries Farm Radio Network to help solve the world food problem. The program provides to communicators throughout the Third World packages of farm broadcast materials, such as scripts, cassettes, and reel-to-reel tapes, aimed at helping grass-roots farmers increase food supplies and achieve self-sufficiency. This activity links about 300 farm broadcast programs in over eighty countries, reaching an audience of an estimated 100 million people. The notice of this program in the March 1982 issue of <u>Enterprise and Development</u>, did not indicate either the Massey investment or the means by which the company has measured and evaluated the development impact traceable to the broadcast package [52]. The methodology is provocative in its implications for a universal question in development: How can information be brought inexpensively and continuously to large numbers of rural people?

TECHNOSERVE, INC.
Norwalk, Connecticut

Technoserve, Inc., was established in 1968 as a nonprofit development enterprise, and is included because of its purpose and the manner of its work. To quote from a corporate report,

It is the purpose of Technoserve to promote in the developing areas of the world, the establishment of viable commercial and industrial enterprises which will most directly meet the needs of low income groups for economic well-being and an improved standard of living; to encourage and respond to local initiative; to provide technical and managerial training; and to function as a catalyst in bringing together the necessary financial support essential to the development of small enterprises, not excluding those of a high risk nature [53].

Development Opportunity

Technoserve refers to its methodology as "self-help enterprise." It reacts to requests by local entrepreneurs or local development agencies, public or private. No cash grants or gifts are accepted. Every business assisted is expected to reimburse the cost of help provided, out of future profits. Technoserve provides experienced managers during start-up and helps train their replacements. Rarely is Technoserve able to offer direct financial assistance, but it does help find capital. More than most enterprises in the category of "private voluntary organizations" (PVOs), Technoserve has led the way in demonstrating to governments the validity of private, profit-making, well-managed business (in corporate or cooperative structures) in accelerating development all along the food chain.

By the end of 1983 Technoserve had given assistance during the year to 150 projects, to the benefit of roughly 600,000 people. The corporation maintains offices in El Salvador, Ghana, Kenya, Panama, Peru, and Zaire (a recent decision closed the office in Nicaragua). Of the global staff of 110, most are nationals of the country in which they work. Funding for Technoserve derives from the following sources, as reported at the end of 1982: USAID, 59 percent; churches, 10 percent; host country institutions, 10 percent; project fees, 11 percent; corporations and individuals, 6 percent; foundations, 2 percent; and, 2 percent from a variety of other donors. A current drive to increase corporate support is meeting with some success [53].

14

Optimizing the Role of the Private Sector in the Agricultural and Rural Development of LDCs: Policy Recommendations

Ruth Karen

The successful agribusiness enterprises in developing countries investigated in this study have four major actors.

1. The small-scale farmer who wants to move from subsistence agriculture into an active role in the market economy, and is ready to transcend traditional constraints to create socioeconomic conditions that offer greater opportunities for him and his family.
2. The company--foreign, domestic, or joint venture--that envisions the opportunity, takes the risk, and transfers the required technology in all facets of the undertaking (referred to as "the parent company").
3. The government of the country in which the enterprise is located (referred to as "the host government"), which promulgates the laws and regulations that directly affect the enterprise, provides and supports a range of institutions with which the enterprise necessarily interacts, and at times participates in the equity of an agribusiness enterprise.
4. The industrial country in which the parent company is based, which interacts both with the host government and with the operating enterprise in a number of ways. In this study that industrial country is described as "the donor country," and usually refers either to the United States or Great Britain.

These four actors are inextricably involved in a complex and subtle play. Though the farmers are essentially reactive rather than proactive, and at the threshold of a development program tend to be locked into their traditional style of life, they nonetheless have the key role. Whatever policies and projects are developed by companies, host governments, and donor countries, success in rural areas depends upon the understanding, acceptance, and response of the farmers, their families, and their communities.

Response is the key word. Rural people in the Third World do not make policy; they respond to it, and can make or break policy implementation. Policies concerned with transfers of

271

capital and technology, trade, the building of physical infrastructure, schooling, health, transportation and communication,
investment, law and order, prices, and the myriad of other elements interacting to make rural life more or less tolerable, more
or less free and dignified, more or less vivacious and hopeful,
almost always are designed in centers of power outside the rural
area.

Therefore, the policy recommendations are directed to companies, host governments, and donor countries. However, the recommendations are intended to go beyond the objective of facilitating the growth of investment in agribusiness to the more in-
clusive goal of utilizing the private sector presence in rural
areas to gain a constructive response from small-scale farmers;
to help these farmers and their families understand, value, and
inculcate the process of change as an instrument of progress; to
accelerate agricultural and rural development so that rural people can become better fed and housed, healthier, better educated,
and wealthier, as well as more self-sufficient and responsible
participants in the life and growth of their countries.

POLICY RECOMMENDATIONS

TO COMPANIES

The assumption here is that the paramount company goal consists of maximizing profit potential, minimizing risk, and
achieving a satisfactory return on investment. The research
shows that although some trade-offs come into play in all three
elements of the company goal, organizing small-scale farmers
around a corporate core achieves a satisfactory bottom line more
quickly than any alternative form of production organization.
Illustratively, the case history of an agribusiness enterprise in
Thailand (pig raising, Chapter 7) reports a return on investment
(ROI) with four dimensions.

1. The first dimension is a financial ROI that begins the
   very first year of operation. Tactically, the company
   considers the first five years of each project the developmental phase, after which the training and direct
   supervisory functions of the company are attenuated.
2. The second dimension of the company's ROI comes into play
   at that stage when the company encourages the farmers to
   manage their own affairs via a board of directors made up
   of selected farmers, with the company assuming an advisory role, compensated by a management contract.
3. The third dimension, operative throughout both processes,
   is the company providing inputs such as feed and breeding
   stock, at a reasonable profit, and doing the processing
   and marketing at a reasonable profit.

4. The fourth dimension is in the long term. The company sees the college-educated children of these prosperous farmers managing their own family farms, with minimal outside services in either technology or management, and at the same time becoming increasingly better customers for the company's products, and sources of supply for the company's processing and marketing activity.

A U.S.-based company operating in the Dominican Republic (Chapter 10), without the integrated structure of the Thai company cited above, also reported a satisfactory ROI the first year, and full recovery of invested capital within three years. It should be noted, however, that both cases involve crops with short production periods and, in the case of the Dominican Republic, the special advantage of duty-free access to the U.S. market. For tree crops and other crops with a longer cultivation and production cycle, the calculations for a satisfactory ROI would necessarily involve a different time frame.

For enterprises such as Agro Industrias C. por A., in the Dominican Republic (melons and vegetables for the U.S. winter market), the financial and operational policy implications are clear.

1. Hands-on commitment and involvement at the managerial level, the technical level, and the field supervision level are essential for success. Given these three ingredients, a relatively modest scale of operations can produce a net profit on sales during the first year, and a respectable return on investment, including full recovery of capital, within two to three years.
2. This applies even when there is on-site competition for the farmers' output.
3. For export-oriented products it is vital to have a well-defined market plus a market organization, in the case of a bigger company; or a well-structured relationship with food brokers and wholesalers for a smaller company.
4. Transportation is a major cost consideration, and available options have to be analyzed carefully.
5. Financing, even if available locally at subsidized rates, may not be the most desirable form of credit. Given the snarls and obstacles of bureaucratic delays, it may be more cost-effective for a company to finance farmers directly.
6. From a sociopolitical point of view, in any operation designed for the long term it is advisable for a company, particularly a foreign company, not to own land. If landholdings are needed for pilot projects or a nuclear estate, the land should be leased. From a sociopolitical perspective, as well as a productive one, the most desirable arrangement is to work with producer farmers who own their own land and work it largely with their own family members.

In the Philippines, the San Miguel Corporation (Chapter 9), a company with integrated operations in a wide range of food products, reports an ROI on its corn seed enterprise that spills over strategically into other aspects of company operations. Working directly with small-scale farmers represents a range of business opportunities that strengthen vertical integration of company products and provide a synergetic horizontal extension of product lines for the domestic market as well as for export.

A carefully structured outreach program that involves technical support in a number of ways, and includes social activities and contributions to community concerns, formulated on the basis of an ongoing dialogue with relevant community groups, has direct bottom-line results. It helps to create markets for company products; it serves as an innovative aspect of advertising; it alleviates, or even eliminates, law-and-order problems for company activities; and it creates a relationship with producers that represents a potential for additional profitable activities.

Whereas companies, in their feasibility studies for agribusiness ventures in developing countries, have corporate-specific strategies to determine the suitability of soil, climate, water, transportation, and appropriate financing mechanisms, useful policy implications generally emerge from the case histories in the areas of marketing relationships with farmer-producers, management, and macroeconomic aspects of the enterprise.

Marketing

Vertical integration works best. Thus, the San Miguel Corporation, with an internally integrated market for its corn seed enterprise, reports a four-pronged result: a stable quality supply for its feed operations and its downstream animal products; a stronger market for its other product lines, with resulting better profitability; an increased market share of corn seed; and a return on investment of 20 percent on funds employed, which includes amortization of research and development activities. The company's market share of corn seed was 24 percent in 1983; targets are 33 percent for 1984, 44 percent for 1985, and 50 percent-plus thereafter.

In Turkey, Pinar (Chapter 5), a milk-processing operation based in Izmir on the Aegean coast, developed a range of consumer products with which it successfully penetrated the domestic market nationwide, as well as developing an export market, primarily to the Middle East. In the Sudan, Haggar Ltd. (Chapter 6), notes that the payback for its tobacco operations is immediate, because it is vertically integrated in the production of blended cigarettes, which the company itself manufactures and sells. In contrast, the payback for the company's coffee and tea operations not only takes longer, because of the nature of the crop, but also requires volume or processing facilities for added value. The company points out that the highest payoff is obtained when coffee and tea operations are extended to include packaging and retailing.

Company Relationships With Farmer-producers

Farmer loyalty is vital. The secret of success in this relationship is stated succinctly by an executive of Adams International's operation in Thailand: "You have to deal with the farmer not only as a producer, but as a person." The multifaceted nature of this process is further spelled out by the manager of Pinar, who couches his recommendations in corporate-specific terms that nevertheless are applicable to all agribusiness undertakings in developing countries.

> Our company is aware of the fact that its own success depends not only on the increased population of milch cows it can induce and the higher yield and quality of milk it can help farmers produce. It knows that in Turkey, for small farmers, an economically viable and developmentally desirable farm requires an appropriate mix of livestock and crops, with a balance of food and cash crops. It knows, as well, that achieving this mix and this balance calls for sociopolitical and cultural skills as well as economic organization and technical expertise.
> Current plans call for a broad and diversified production base that would provide a market, and act as a technology transfer agent, for such integrated development.
> What should probably be added to the company's plans is a systematic effort to broaden its existing equity base to include among its shareholders as many farmer cooperatives and individual small farmers as is feasible, given economic realities.

As an operational matter, establishing a satisfactory ongoing relationship with its producers requires that the company offer not only a fair purchasing contract, but an appropriate mix of four additional contributions to the farmer's welfare.

First, competent, dependable, corporate extension services must be established that are responsible not only to the farmer's production needs but also to other needs that involve activities important to the farmer's economic base. This means that the extension agents give the farmers whatever help they can in the cultivation of crops or the raising of livestock even though such help does not represent a source of direct income for the company. It is vital, in this context, for the company to encourage a balanced use of land by the farmer. This means a division between food crops and cash crops that adequately meets the direct needs of both the company and of the farmer and his family. Typically, with small farmers in developing countries, this balance is tantamount to having no more than one-third to one-half of the farmer's land devoted to the market crop, with the remainder allocated to food crops for family consumption or for sale to the local market. An important fringe benefit of this arrangement is that the company/farmer relationship does not result in economic dependencies with explosive sociopolitical overtones.

Second, as far as corporate resources permit, the social environment of the farmer and his family should be improved and enhanced. This includes, but is not limited to, sports, health, education, and access to appropriate consumer goods.

Third, the company should act as a catalyst between the farmer and existing government institutions designed to serve the farmer. In most developing countries, competent bridge building is required between small-scale farmers and their needs and the bureaucracies intended to serve these needs.

Fourth, the company should assist farmers, in locally appropriate ways, to structure and strengthen their own organizations, and organizations involving their families and communities. Hindustan Lever Ltd. (a subsidiary of Unilever, Chapter 2), operating in the district of Etah, state of Uttar Pradesh, one of the least developed regions of India, has formulated "Ten Commandments for Rural Development," which, with relevant modifications and alterations, are applicable in any less-developed country (LDC). These "commandments" are noted in Chapter 2 but because of their general importance are repeated here both for emphasis and for the convenience of readers.

1. Establish credibility through honesty and integrity. These qualities have to be seen not only internally but externally as well. They are best conveyed by committed supervisors who are honest, apolitical, and corruption-proof, and can earn the respect both of elected officials from the village level up and of appointed civil servants from the district manager down.
2. Assure that plans are generated at the grass roots by the farmers themselves. There is an initial hesitation by the farmers to make such plans, but the resistance can be broken down by supervisors who know their business and their communities, and by management trainees who actually live in the villages. Both the supervisors and the management trainees have to establish the kind of relationship with the farmer in which they can say "no" as well as "yes" and still retain the respect and trust of the villagers.
3. Set up an effective organizational structure for follow-through. Frequently, government and voluntary agencies have marvelous ideas and brilliant concepts, but no one who is competent or interested enough to follow through.
4. Provide or organize financial support. The need is for on-site banking institutions that operate effectively at the village level.
5. Build a viable communications system, both physical and people-to-people. This includes roads that are accessible throughout the year, and every form of transportation.
6. Upgrade agricultural practices. This involves everything from water management to crop rotation; from seed improvement to livestock care.

7. Introduce animal husbandry, not as a replacement for existing cultivation of food or cash crops, but as a viable secondary occupation for the farm family.
8. Promote appropriate alternative energy resources, such as bio-gas fueled by cow dung.
9. Aid village industries, particularly those relevant to women.
10. Help to build health and educational infrastructure.

Management

At the top level of the enterprise, the company, wherever based, must reach for the best management--not the best it can spare, but the best it can muster. This applies to both executive and technical staffing. It is important to recognize that "the best," in this context, has to be defined in a way that exceeds narrow, or even broad-gauged, expertise. At the executive side, the top manager must not only know his product and his market, but must be sensitive to people in their social and cultural context. On the technical side, crop knowledge and people knowledge are pragmatically intertwined and equally important. The history of agribusiness companies in developing countries is replete with problems--and some outright failures--created by executives with unquestionable technical and managerial expertise who failed to relate effectively to the people in the undertaking's host country environment.

When the company is a foreign company, it is also advisable to work as assiduously as feasible toward the goal of replacing foreign management with local management. Systematic and thoughtful recruiting and training programs designed to achieve this goal are a major ingredient in the success of the enterprise over the long term.

For all companies, whether foreign or domestic, people contact works best when it is closest to the peer level. For example, one company discovered that for its hands-on extension services to farmer-producers, a team of local graduates from agricultural institutions did not work out. What did work was a system of recruiting extension agents from the farm families themselves and giving these best and brightest farmers the technical and administrative training they needed to become effective and respected extension agents.

At a more senior level of peer relationship, companies have found that local research and development is conducted most effectively when host-country technical and professional people, and indeed, more adventurous and experiment-minded farmers, are involved in the process as soon as feasible.

The Macroeconomic Area

In the macroeconomic area, successful agribusiness enterprises produce visible economic and social results. These penetrate the community both horizontally and vertically in measurable developmental terms. This enhances the image of the private sector in general and, where applicable, multinational corporations in particular, and validates their role as important engines of growth. In most developing countries, such image enhancement is important. In some, it is crucial.

Another macroeconomic consideration is the fact that successful agribusiness enterprises involving small-scale farmers in the developing countries substantially raise the purchasing power of those farm families. There are today approximately 1 billion small-scale farmers in the developing world. If, by way of the simplest of calculations, the income of all these farmers were raised by only US$100 per year, the stimulative effect on the global economy would be staggering, with multiplier effects not only for agricultural output, but for manufactured goods and services as well, both in the developing countries and in the industrialized world.

TO THE HOST COUNTRY

Almost without exception, political leaders in host countries today recognize the importance of agricultural development. Indeed, agriculture is, and always has been, the key to economic development. No country in human history, with the exception of a few merchant or military city-states, has ever prospered and built a sound economy without a solid agricultural base.

The problem is that while the importance of agriculture is clearly recognized, most host countries are at least baffled, and more often overwhelmed, by the magnitude, the complexity, and the political problems involved in carrying forward an effective, sustained program of agricultural development. There is no doubt that sound agricultural policies are difficult to develop and carry out. The time span required to put into place an appropriate land/people balance; to make credit and necessary inputs available to the grower; to construct storage, processing and marketing capacity; and especially to set in motion organized, self-sustaining rural development systems acceptable to rural people is far longer than the usual time span of a political officeholder. In addition, carrying out a sound, meaningful agricultural policy calls for changes that by their very nature shake up traditional social and management patterns, with the result that changes are fiercely resisted. This is true in industrialized as well as in developing countries, as even current EEC and U.S. policies demonstrate.

The problems host countries need to address most urgently fall into ten categories.

Food Policies That Have an Urban Bias

Food policies with a persistent urban bias may have short-term political payoff, but are clearly counterproductive in the long run. They slight agricultural producers, undercut production, and motivate mass population movements from country to city, creating in the process the socially explosive slums that bedevil almost every host country.

The clearest manifestation of this urban bias is price policy, with governments using a range of price-setting mechanisms to keep producer prices low, sometimes even below cost. An illustrative example, with counterparts in every host country, is the support price of cotton in Turkey. That price was set at TL70 (in 1983) when the market price was TL150.

Agricultural Taxation

In most host countries, the bias against farmer-producers manifest in pricing policies is equally prevalent in taxation policies. Agricultural output is taxed at too high a rate, a policy that extends even to such measures--clearly counterproductive from a macroeconomic viewpoint--as levying substantial taxes on agricultural exports and on imports required for optimum output in the agribusiness sector.

Exchange Rates and Exchange Rate Controls

In many host countries, exchange rates that overvalue the local currency are maintained, often for image concerns that have no realistic economic base. These currency value distortions are particularly harmful to farmers producing for export. A recent example of a reasonable policy in this area, leading to productive results, was a policy implemented by the Dominican Republic, which introduced a multitiered exchange rate, with the most realistic rate available to exporters of nontraditional products, specifically including agricultural products.

Restrictions on Internal Food Movement

Some host countries actually have laws or regulations that restrict domestic movement of food crops, mainly for political reasons. In many, indeed in most of the host countries, internal food movement is effectively restricted, and to a considerable extent prevented, by inadequate infrastructure and transportation as well as by inadequate and quite often non-existent storage facilities.

Credit Availability

Although most host countries make an effort to provide agricultural credit, with widely varying degrees of resource allocation and administrative competence, none of the host countries in the study has yet managed to get anywhere near enough credit to the small-scale farmers who constitute the backbone of the agricultural sector. Indeed, the case histories indicate that with rare exceptions, it is only when private sector companies, foreign or domestic, supply supervised credit themselves or act as catalysts and mediators between farmer-producers and host country financial institutions that small-scale farmers actually get the financial assistance that, in theory, has been designed for them.

Redistribution of Land

Evidence around the world has demonstrated that the family farm, with a landholding adequate to apply modern technology effectively, is the most productive size. The incentive that results when the producer benefits directly from his efforts cannot be duplicated by large holdings, whether they are privately held, communal, cooperative, or state-owned. Results from the factory-size organization of state farms and large collectives in the USSR are dramatic demonstrations of how not to organize agriculture. A system whereby the producer on the soil benefits directly from his efforts is the single most important element in increasing productivity. In most places in the world, this means producer ownership; and requires egalitarian land policies, adequately supported by the government. Adequate support, in this context, can be defined as a network of physical and social infrastructures that make possible economically rewarding farm production, and provide enough social services to induce farm families to resist the lure of the cities.

A demonstrative example of successful agrarian reform and its benefits is the effort made by the Dominican Republic in the Azua Valley. The reform that allocated land to family farmers was complemented by a web of infrastructure services, including irrigation, electrification, farm-to-market roads, effective credit institutions, health and education facilities, and help with housing. The result was a 300 percent rise in per capita income in less than a decade.

Expropriation or Nationalization of Food Industries

A number of host countries have pursued such policies with results that range from paralysis to financial disaster. This does not relate to enterprises in which the public sector holds an equity position, even the major share of ownership, as exemplified by the Mumias Sugar Company in Kenya (Chapter 3) and Mhlume Sugar Company in Swaziland (Chapter 4), so long as the business is professionally managed for profit and the government stays away from exercising any control over operations. However, where government owns and operates enterprises that compete with the private sector, as in the case of the milk industry in Turkey, indications are that it requires two to five times the resources that private companies employ; requires far longer to get into full production; and rarely becomes truly competitive in the marketplace. In many countries, public corporations tend to become protected, often to the detriment of quality and as a penalty to the consumer, who receives less at a higher cost.

Political Patronage and Bureaucratic Ineptness

Where government is involved in providing or supporting services to small-scale farmers, it is desirable to make farmer productivity, not political patronage, the yardstick. In the Philippines, for example, where the KKK (Kilusang Kabuhayan at Kaunlaran or National Livelihood Program, Chapter 9) is generally assessed as being both imaginative and sound in the design of its programs, the implementation of these programs is hampered by the fact that too much of the KKK's money still goes to feudal leaders in the countryside and their political allies, instead of being channeled to the producing farmer. If small-scale farmers were supported more effectively, desirable economic and political results could be achieved. Farmer income and community standing would increase, and the political leadership, now very hierarchical in the rural areas, would have to listen more attentively to its constituents.

An illustration of obstructive bureaucratic ineptness occurs in India, where the effectiveness of a comprehensive set of services the government offers its rural population is marred by bureaucratic corruption and by paperwork that is too incomprehensible and too cumbersome for villagers to understand and deal with. At present, the paperwork required for villagers to obtain any government service is daunting to a point where the overwhelming majority of the rural population simply has no way of obtaining the service to which it is entitled.

Private Sector Involvement

If host governments want to attract and support private sector activity in agriculture, domestic or foreign, the host country government will have to make clear its commitment to agriculture, its determination to implement policies it has proclaimed, and to honor promises it has made. This includes, but is not limited to, access to foreign currency; admittance of necessary expatriates; prompt approval of necessary imports; and as noted above, the development of needed infrastructure. Perhaps most importantly, it requires a commitment not only in the political and governmental institutions at the top, but in provinces and localities as well. Concurrently, the political leadership at all levels must lead the way in building public understanding and support of this commitment to the country's agricultural base.

Relations with Multinational Corporations.

Most governments' relations with multinational corporations in the agribusiness sector, whose technology organization, processing, and marketing expertise can make a major impact, have several special aspects of complexity. A blueprint for mutual understanding and successful collaboration is limned below.

Profitability and responsibility. Both multinational corporations (MNCs) and developing countries must recognize two fundamental facts: Private companies are (and by their structure must be) motivated to make a profit on their operations and investments, and host governments are (and naturally must be) concerned about the development of their countries. Each side should clearly recognize the legitimate interests of the other. The essential point is that governments must allow MNCs to make and remit a reasonable profit, while MNCs must acknowledge and fulfill the full range of their economic and social development responsibilities to the host countries. Further, it should be recognized by both sides that contributions to the progress of a developing country can be made in many forms, both economic and noneconomic (for example, training and educating people), and that all forms of contribution applicable to each investment should be given full recognition.

Information and reporting procedures. Access to certain kinds of information is often a key point of contention between MNCs and developing countries. On the one hand, governments often feel that MNCs are secretive and do not fully reveal their activities and practices. On the other hand, companies are sensitive about proprietary information getting into the wrong hands (for example, commercial competitors and social adversaries). If host governments wish agribusiness to reveal information to tax or other regulatory authorities, they must be able to guard against the misuse of that information.

Technology. Differences in the state-of-the-art of technology, including machine and instrument design; managerial, marketing, organizational, and other skills; as well as any other technical information that gives a company a competitive edge, lie at the heart of the gap separating developed from underdeveloped countries. There is no question that donor countries seeking to assist nations working hard to improve themselves should address the problem of how best to facilitate the transfer of technology. However, private companies cannot and should not be expected to give away skills and knowledge that may have taken years (if not decades) as well as great expense to develop. Nor is it reasonable that a country should expect to get something for nothing. Fair payments for technological contributions by MNCs to developing countries should be expected. If the technology is continuously updated by injections of fresh advances, these too should be compensated. However, payments should cease after a number of years during which no further advances are made.

    <u>Employment and labor</u>. Countries should clearly outline and communicate their manpower objectives and expectations to MNCs, and MNCs should do their best to fulfill those objectives. Where appropriate, free union activity should be permitted, but MNCs should not be picked out as targets for demands not made of local companies. MNCs should pay going wage rates as a minimum; on the other hand, if they offer more than the minimum, either in terms of direct pay or the provision of other benefits (for example, housing, schooling, lunch programs), the effect of such costs on the MNC's local operations should be taken into account by the host government.

    <u>Consumer protection</u>. Minimum international health and safety standards should be worked out, and a standardized international labeling system introduced. Any prohibitions or restrictions in process or product imposed by home countries should be revealed to host countries.

    <u>Competition and market structure</u>. Countries and MNCs should work out export and purchasing policies at the time investments are made, and they should clearly establish the length of time that such policies (and any restrictions on them) are to be in effect.

    <u>Transfer pricing</u>. Transfer pricing is a difficult and extremely complex area of international business. At the outset, two things should be honestly recognized: first, the host country must realize that the subject cannot be dealt with by simplistic slogans or formulas; and second, the MNC must acknowledge that there have in fact been cases of serious abuse of pricing policies.

    A reasonable transfer price for a product imported into a developing country for further use in an MNC operation in that country should cover the full costs (including R&D and engineering costs) involved in making and shipping that product, plus a fair profit <u>on the imported product</u>. The transfer price should <u>not</u> include any other "hidden" forms of return to the MNC, such as special services rendered by parent company specialists that are not reimbursed (or not permitted to be reimbursed) by the government, central bank, or host country subsidiary. Companies are sometimes tempted to take out returns for their investments via the transfer price when they are not permitted to charge what they consider reasonable royalties, service fees, trademark fees, and the like. It is the interrelationship of all these factors, affecting both local subsidiary and parent company profits, that makes transfer pricing such a complex area. The only reasonable way to approach this problem is through openness and honesty on both sides and through recognition that constructive economic activity is entitled to a profit for its efforts. At the same time, considerations of simple humanity and relative ability to pay must temper specific expectations of return.

    <u>Economic role of women</u>. Outreach programs need to address the role of women in the entire process of change, especially in rural areas where they are wholly responsible for the home and children, and do much of the work of crop production, processing, and marketing. It has been estimated that women do 78 percent of

the farm work in developing countries (yet all too often the farmer is referred to as "he). Though results and needs vary from country to country, the positive and negative effects of technology transfers on women tend to be constant. For example, women everywhere are interested in anything that lightens their workload and hence respond positively to domestic technology and to technology that provides easier access to water, heat, and light. At the same time, when large machinery, such as a tractor, is introduced and preoccupies men, women may be left with an even greater burden of manual tasks. In turn, some of these tasks may pass on to children, which may be detrimental to the child.

An Evolutionary Process

A classical description of host government thinking vis-à-vis agribusiness, as it might evolve anywhere in the Third World, is repeated with clear policy implications, from a discussion of policy recommendations to the host country in Chapter 7.

Initially, the Thai government pursued what was essentially a welfare policy vis-a-vis the farmer. It treated the farmer as a backward child, poor and uneducated, and provided him with handouts in the form of free seed, subsidized fertilizer, and support prices. But it offered neither the full package of know-how and services nor the motivation to make him self-supporting.

In addition, the government's attitude toward the private sector in agriculture was that the private sector would exploit the farmer and was therefore not to be trusted. This attitude is beginning to change as the government realizes that it cannot create meaningful rural development alone. At this stage, the government is thinking in terms of cooperation from the private sector in rural development, and has long-term intentions of encouraging private sector activity in agribusiness, with the government gradually pulling out.

A conceptual difference remains between the government and the private sector of what rural development is and means. The government is still inclined to think of rural development as helping poor farmers in subsistence areas, while the private sector thinks of rural development as creating and supporting motivated farmers to cultivate products that meet market criteria.

Conceptually, what is needed on the government side is the recognition that any country, in order to industrialize successfully, must have a strong agricultural base. Sound development is not possible by leapfrogging the agricultural component. A sound agricultural base raises farmer income which, in turn, increases demand for consumer industries; and that, in turn, creates the need and market for heavy industry. All industrialized countries, and all successful developing countries, have followed this pattern.

In this process, governments must remember that the private sector company is not a development agency, but it is an agent--a very dynamic agent--in the development process.

TO THE DONOR COUNTRY

Donor countries, if they are prepared to formulate the appropriate long-term policies, commit the indicated financial resources, and follow through with the required implementation at both the diplomatic and the administrative levels, can play a major positive role in development. They can exercise an important influence in guiding host countries toward formulating appropriate polices and implementing sound practices, thereby laying the foundation for sustainable economic and social development.

They can also furnish practical support and concrete incentives to private sector risk-takers, domestic and foreign, who are prepared to put on the line their expertise, their technology, and their shareholders' money to launch agricultural ventures that can make a meaningful contribution to the goals. of agricultural and rural development.

Policy and Implementation

At the policy level, donor countries must impress the governments of host countries with the imperative of making a clear commitment to the importance of the agricultural sector, and to its growth and expansion. This commitment must include specific undertakings to set product price levels that will stimulate the acceptance of new, and in many cases, untried technology and cultivation methods by small-scale growers.

As a political issue (clearly not an easy one to confront), this means that host governments must be persuaded to formulate and support an adequate agricultural policy rather than a cheap food policy. There is no doubt that this will require wisdom, insight, and political courage from host country leaders, who will need the staunchest possible support from donor nations.

This support must be expressed and delivered not only in donor country capitals but also, on an articulate and consistent basis, in the host countries. Donor country diplomatic personnel, starting at the ambassadorial level, need to understand that providing this support is a high-priority item on their overall diplomatic mandate.

At the implementation level, ambassadors and the directors of donor country aid programs should be directed to make contact at the highest level with the government of the host country in which they serve, beginning with the chief of state and including all appropriate ministers as well as other relevant government institutions. The thrust of this effort should not be to exercise pressure in the usual sense, but to convey unmistakably the support of the donor government for an active agricultural policy directed at the small-scale farmer and implemented by the private sector. For the United States specifically, it would be important to strengthen the staff of the AID director in the host country by assigning, at the highest possible level, a representative of the Bureau for Private Enterprise, with competence for and insight into private sector approaches and operations.

To host countries prepared to follow the policies described above, donor countries should offer the maximum assistance feasible in constructing the infrastructure networks, both physical and social, that will provide optimum conditions for agricultural growth through the instrument of small-scale farmer-producers acting in a private sector context.

Donor countries can provide a variety of practical services to the private sector that would help reduce risks inherent in agribusiness ventures in developing countries and would help companies function more broadly and efficiently in their outreach to rural people. Specifically, donor countries can increase the range and magnitude of programs that finance, or participate in the financing of, feasibility studies leading to investment. Normally, the identification and evaluation of investment opportunities is done by the companies themselves. However, quite often host government development agencies, local banks, and resident development assistance agencies such as AID missions will have identified but not thoroughly studied areas of investment important to a country and seemingly supported by available technology and market characteristics. Increasingly, host government promotional agencies and comparable institutions in donor countries meet to discuss the means of converting identified opportunity to actual investment, if a sound feasibility study can be provided. In these situations, policies of donor countries that allow for financial assistance in the conduct of feasibility studies can be most helpful. Potential investors may need to be convinced and may be reluctant to take all the risk; host governments may not have the money to finance the necessary studies. Since this kind of policy already exists in the United States, this recommendation is meant, first, to encourage a major expansion of effort, and second, to emphasize that it is in the field of agribusiness that less-developed countries have one of their greatest opportunities for both economic and human development.

The same kind of recommendations holds for appropriate insurance or reinsurance. Such coverage is available now through the U.S. Overseas Private Investment Corporation. Existing policy might be reexamined to ensure optimum support for agribusiness structured in satellite farming.

A third recommendation vis-à-vis private sector outreach to small-scale farmers relates to policies that affect the flow of agricultural supervised credit. Historically, large sums of money for credit have been granted and loaned by donor countries to host governments. This has encouraged the creation of public credit banks, few of which have succeeded in reaching the farmer. When bureaucratic constraints are in evidence, donor policy should permit funds to be channeled through agribusiness when an outgrower program exists. This would offer to the donor and the host government greater assurance of accountability and of the likelihood that more of the money would actually reach the farmer and be applied under careful supervision.

Finally, donor country policy that encourages the private sector to take on a more important role in agricultural and rural development should recognize that for many companies, going beyond the outreach programs illustrated in this book will be a new functional responsibility. In practical, operational terms, this suggests that the donor country should offer agribusiness management the services of development experts with a sound grasp of business realities and hands-on experience in working in rural areas, in developing countries. Such experts, under contract, could help train corporate staff. While fulfilling their training mission, these experts could also address the sensitive cultural, social, and political issues that inevitably arise when traditional practices on the farm and traditional patterns of family life and community organization are changed. (This relationship between agribusiness and donor countries is discussed in further detail in Chapter 15.)

On-Site Suggestions

Case histories in this study yielded a wide variety of policy recommendations from on-site sources that help reduce broad generalities to concrete terms. These specific recommendations have been noted throughout the previous chapters of this book as integrated summaries of interviews with many people and several are repeated below because of their singular applicability throughout the world.

In Thailand, it was observed that U.S. policy has channeled AID funds only to governments and to the military. The new emphasis on the private sector, and direct bilateral contact between the private sector of the United States and Thailand, with government encouragement and support, is likely to bring a positive dynamic to the entire aid process. The allocation of USAID resources to bringing together the private sector of the donor country with the appropriate partner in the recipient country will undoubtedly have more immediate and direct results than channeling funds to government organizations and institutions, where demonstrable development results may or may not be achieved.

In the Sudan, three positive action-points were put forward:

1. To find, or create, mechanisms that will channel funds as expeditiously and inexpensively as possible to "bush planters" for the production of cash crops to supplement their food crops and raise their living standard.
2. To devise ways in which a portion of counterpart funds (which will amount to the equivalent of $100 million in 1984) can be channeled to the private sector.
3. Using whatever policy-making leverage the U.S. government has to persuade the government of Sudan that encouraging private investment in agribusiness would be an effective method to make use of Sudan's comparative advantage of

arable land to raise the living standards of its people
and to contribute meaningfully to adjusting the presently
lopsided balance of payments.

In Turkey, it was suggested that the donor country can exercise its persuasive powers to move the Turkish government toward
a policy of letting the private sector do what it does efficiently and effectively while concentrating public sector attention on
infrastructure undertakings, economic and social, that are beyond
the private sector's competence or resources. It was also com-
mended that donor countries should provide scholarships for junior and middle management, not only in the public sector, but in
the private sector as well. Finally, in the technical area of
development assistance, it was urged that some USAID funds could
be allocated specifically for the importation of high-yield cattle and of frozen semen from the United States.

The people interviewed in the Philippines emphasized that
donor country funds should be channeled, at least in part,
through the private sector in the agribusiness area. Such funds
could be earmarked, for example, for appropriate research and development as well as a range of other private sector activities
in agribusiness designed to make small-scale farmers optimally
productive and increase their earning capabilities and purchasing
capacity. An example of how such donor country funds could be
used in innovative ways is the creation of a pilot project in
which the private sector would support a group of farmers organized as a cooperative or association by guaranteeing financing,
providing technology, and monitoring the farmers' activities for
a profit and loss orientation.

For the United States specifically, a final policy recommendation manifests an additional dimension relating to the vital
role of the United States as leader of the free world. That dimension was outlined in an editorial of Financier: The Journal
of Private Sector Policy.

> At a time when the world has grown bitter and skep-
> tical about U.S. leadership, agriculture could be the
> way for this country to reclaim the moral high ground
> it occupied not so many years ago, when it devoted its
> vast unharmed industrial power to rebuilding the world
> after World War II. In those helping, confident years,
> the United States exemplified leadership, in a moral as
> well as a material way.
> It has the stuff to do it again--to meet a great and
> growing material need, to feed the starving, to kindle
> hope, to regain confidence [54].

15
Optimizing the Role of the Private Sector in the Agricultural and Rural Development of LDCs: Action Recommendations

Simon Williams

INTRODUCTION

The policy recommendations covered in Chapter 14 have two basic objectives: to overcome the barriers to major increases in private sector investment in agribusiness in the Third World; and to ensure that existing and new investors take a position that allows local management to integrate commercial objectives and outreach to the needs of the rural people impacted, as a pragmatic as well as a philosophical matter.

Chapter 15 assumes that the barriers to investment are down and that investors are ready to reach out and take a share of the responsibility for rural development, as have the companies described in the cases included in this book. How is action taken at the interface between company and rural people? How is this action properly supported, by the company, by the host government, and by the donor country, in the short and long run? How, precisely, can the world capitalize on the presence of agribusiness in rural areas to help deepen, broaden, and hasten agricultural and rural development where the need is greatest?

Before going to specific recommendations, two points of reference need clarification. First, the isolation of agribusiness for specific attention in this book is not meant to exaggerate the power of the private sector to accelerate agricultural and rural development; nor is it meant to demean by contrast the important impact of literally hundreds of other kinds of organizations (for-profit and nonprofit) at work worldwide among rural people to enhance the quality of their lives. Rather, the intention is to emphasize that throughout Africa, Asia, and Latin America the need for development assistance far exceeds the resources of money and skilled labor being assembled for the purpose. Indeed, the need grows each year, and in a relative and absolute sense, support for aid activity declines. Therefore, the theme of this book underscores a singularly significant fact: Agribusiness investment all along the food and fiber chain from producer to consumer, within nations and linked into a world supply system, exists as a largely untapped source of energy for further development, enormous in scope, practical to utilize, irresponsible to ignore, and too exciting to contemplate idly. The most recently advanced evidence for this assertion is to be found within and between the lines of the cases included in this book.

Second, the action recommendations not only arise out of observations made in gathering the material for the cases and inventory covered in Chapters 2 through 13. They also reflect several decades of field experience, study, and analysis of the factors that govern the success or failure of agribusiness ventures in Third World settings, and the role the private sector has played and could play as a force for beneficial change among the hundreds of millions of disadvantaged rural people throughout the world. Because all this background bears directly on the choice and language of the action recommendations, it may be well to elaborate briefly the conclusions derived from past experience from which the recommendations take their logic, purpose, and validity.

BACKGROUND

With an unprecedented intensity of commitment, current U.S. policy directs that development assistance generally give priority to the role of private enterprise. The policy is a clear reflection of a widely held belief that the principles and methods of private enterprise, which organize knowledge, money, and people into productive and profitable businesses; which redistribute earnings through taxes, wages, purchases, dividends, and reinvestment; and which use competition in a free market to foster responsibility and service to the consumer, are ideal models to be replicated in the development process.

Focusing on agricultural and rural development raises a question: What is there about the international scene that gives this policy its sense of urgency? Looking back through the history of AID and agribusiness, both seem to offer cogent evidence of a dynamic partnership in generating world supplies of food and fiber, as well as contributing to the economic vitalization of agriculturally-based nations on all continents.

Agribusiness has invested literally billions of dollars in enterprises scattered into every corner of the earth. There has been a transfer of technology of all sorts. Hundreds of thousands of jobs have been created. Research centers, schools, communities, health delivery systems, and infrastructure in great variety have been financed. Tax receipts have grown; foreign exchange has been both earned and saved; and the litany could go on. AID, too, has long supported strengthening of the infrastructure basic to economic and social progress--schools, law, banking, research centers, transportation, and communications systems, among other critical elements. One need only scan the AID publication Horizons to be impressed by the wide range of activities directed toward minimizing the constraints to private enterprise [55].

Surely, the world would be a far worse place had not AID and
agribusiness done what they have over the past thirty years. The
fact is, however, that the world, particularly the Third World,
is a disordered place, and the heartland of discontent and disadvantage lies in the rural areas. Private enterprise is widely
suspect, and democratic, capitalistic values are under sharp attack throughout Africa, Asia, and Latin America. Economic and
political systems designed and forged in the past are under challenge everywhere. There is not a wholly stable government to be
found in the Third World. Hunger, malnutrition, and inequities
of all kinds touch and degrade the lives of more millions than
ever before in history. Tragic, forced migrations are legion.
Poverty is the hallmark of the majority. Conflict and confronta-
tion are spreading between and within nations in a manner that
confounds reason. Thus, the realities of the world situation do
generate a sense of urgency in response. The persistence of our
belief in a democratic free-enterprise society as the ideal
structure for the delivery of the good inherent in change does
entwine public policy with private enterprise.

This leads to a second question: What have been the critical weaknesses and limitations of past policy and implementation
in agricultural and rural development? The fundamental obstacles
to development I have observed worldwide and experienced over the
past quarter-century are described below.

There has been a puzzling reluctance to reckon with the reality that where hunger, malnutrition, poor health, poverty,
indignity, and inequity coexist with old, tenaciously held traditions that dominate thought, emotions, and life-style, response
to change is visceral. Neither a scientific nor a logical approach to change is entirely appropriate to such anguish. Yet
such an approach has been the spearhead of action in the development field since it was formally instituted in the mid-1940s. The
result has been that theory has built upon too many assumptions
proven false. Too many plans fail at the point of execution. Too
many bureaucrats and technical experts remain out of touch with
their rural constituencies. And too many businesses depend for
loyalty on isolated motivations such as job opportunity or increased net farm income, and then are surprised by apparent ir-
responsibility in the face of these benefits. Even where there
has been some appreciation of what makes people "tick," more
often than not rural development has been seriously inhibited by
the lack of time and money necessary to invest before the process
begins to payoff.

Relative to time, there has always been an unrealistic expectation of what is needed to bring traditional societies to the
point of intellectual and financial self-sufficiency; to the
point of dynamic balance between past and new values and patterns
of behavior. Hence, where program financing has been approved, it
is rarely maintained long enough. If anything of importance has
been learned about rural development during the past four decades
of development assistance, it is that for the process to be set
in steady operation, it takes at least five to ten years and
may still require the presence of skilled outside leadership for

an indefinite period thereafter. This is no different in its wisdom than the conclusion drawn by the majority of foreign investors in agro-industry in the Third World that, depending on the sophistication of the enterprise, it takes many years before it is prudent to turn over all managerial control to local staff.

Relative to money, in the case of aid agencies and host governments, the issue is less one of an absolute lack than it is one of attitude toward the investment. As noted above, unrealistic budgeting of time may simply cut off funding too soon. Tied to this attitude toward time, funding is frequently halted out of frustration over the apparent lack of results. Rural development cannot be neatly measured in terms of increased yields, or net farm income, or increases in irrigated acreage; only partial measures are possible relative to the incidence of disease, number of children in school, longevity, and other widely used indices of improvements in the quality of life. Least tangible in their early expression are the most meaningful achievements of rural development: a capacity to find solutions to personal, community, and technical problems; an ability to resolve conflict by other than violent means; an appreciation of the power of well-organized groups to multiply opportunities for further progress; a grasp of political activity within their system of government and an outreach to responsible participation; a vision of the future for men, women, and children; a grasp of the significance to daily life of such generalities as honesty, integrity of relationships, quality, sanitation, family planning, and nutrition. These achievements can be "seen" by anyone working continuously among rural people, but they have been most difficult to measure and communicate persuasively.

In the case of agro-industry, although many companies do finance a variety of programs in service to rural development, it is not likely now, nor has it been evidenced in the past, that many managers would recommend the allocation of sufficient money to support a full-scale and diversified program of extended and continuous rural development. This is not to say that, in general, the managers of plants in the Third World disagree with the need for such a program or even disavow responsibility. However, there continues to be widespread doubt as to the propriety of corporate involvement on so broad a scale. There is also an absolute shortage of money these days for the purpose. Inflation, currency devaluation, exchange control, high interest rates, depressed markets, and other factors have put a tight squeeze on profits.

Winning the hearts and minds of the great mass of rural people in order to accelerate the historic pace of change among traditional societies is a tough, enduring task. The job requires time, money, patience, and a fountainhead of knowledge ranging widely over many disciplines normally disassociated in technologically oriented enterprises. What is needed are the skills and personality of the highest levels of management, and these are in very short supply for application to rural development programs carried on in the ambiance of profit-making agro-industry.

The corollary is that nowhere in the world has adequate support been given to educating and training managers of change in rural situations.

Development has always been debilitated by fragmentation of effort and thought. Those working in agricultural development have long assumed that major advances in productivity and net farm income, for example, are a sufficiently powerful "engine of change" to set the whole rural development process in motion. Similarly, many managers of agro-industry feel that it is sufficient for business to create jobs, train their labor force, create a market for farm produce, transfer technology to farm and factory, pay taxes, and earn foreign exchange, leaving it to the public sector to capitalize on these effects by accelerating rural development in the area of enterprise influence. Traditionally, public international aid agencies, host country development agencies, and private enterprise have rarely joined forces to multiply and expand their resources for rural development promotion. Within Third World countries, it is uncommon for the variety of business enterprises and development agencies to have any idea of what is going on in each other's bailiwick. Across Third World national boundaries, interchange of experience, personnel, and resources is essentially nonexistent.

Closely tied to the fragmentation of effort and thought in limiting rural development, is a historical attitude that characterizes foreign investors and influences the range of commitment made by international, publicly supported aid agencies: Outsiders should not take responsibility for programs that intimately relate to social and personal development. This attitude is capsulized in the saying, "we cannot, we should not tell people what to do."

This position, often strongly identified in corporate and aid agency policy, both misses the point of rural development as a process and contradicts the logic of the situation created by an investor. The very essence of rural development methodology is that the change agent never tells anyone what to do. Rather, the secret of the process is its ability to awaken the mind to the nature and implications of alternatives; to free people from their bondage to poverty so that there is time to think and learn and deliberate; to choose for themselves, yet feel secure in asking for help and counsel. The road to sure failure in rural development anywhere in the world, no matter how autocratic the government, is to dictate change.

Equally significant, private and public investors in rurally sited agricultural or agro-industrial enterprises are generally the pioneers of change. The cases described in this report vividly illustrate the point. Every enterprise took a raw, backward area and with the cooperation of its people, and with admirable entrepreneurial energy, capital support, and effective management literally "made the desert flower." Large numbers of people were employed. Farm productivity increased sharply. Major cash flows poured into the area. In this sense, the company, not the government, made the decision to invest. Whatever public approval was necessary, the company, in a very deliberate way, was the driving force for change. Moreover, it is frequently the case that when agro-industry is located in a rural area, it stands alone, more or less removed from the center of government. If the company decides that "it cannot, it should not take responsibility for helping to guide people in their further development," and the government says, "we are unable," then are rural people, elevated to a new high plateau of opportunity, to be left high and dry, their futures foregone?

In times past, it may have been acceptable to say that having started the development process, private enterprise could, in good conscience, expect a host government to capitalize on the opportunity and take it from there. But this is not the case any more. No segment of society can be judged free of obligation if by its own choice it has generated the first significant movement of development machinery. An investment in agro-industry reflects such a choice. U.S. development assistance policy, which fosters investment, implies the choice. Host government approval of an investment proposal tacitly makes the choice. The price of future profits, to all, is the cost of total involvement in the never-ending process of rural development.

It may be remarked that these historic and current constraints on rural development assistance do not make specific reference to the backward condition of the people to be helped, nor to their diverse cultures and languages, nor to the manner and mode of their governments, all of which, it is said, place so many tough obstacles in the way of progress.

The reason for this needs a brief explanation. There are, of course, two distinct problems which a development program confronts: the reality of conditions in the country receiving aid which may resist modification; and how to design a delivery system whereby change occurs in ways which all agree are beneficial. Once a decision is made for aid to flow, then it would seem to be the responsibility of the agent of change, public or private in nature, to make it work. And, if it does not work satisfactorily, it would seem more appropriate to question the validity of the delivery system rather than blame the obstacles put in its way. Thus, in this book, emphasis in analysis, and in recommendations, are on correcting apparent weaknesses in the ways development assistance has been transferred.

From the foregoing a final question emerges: What specific, innovative action is needed to help overcome weaknesses in the past performance of rural development assistance, in a manner that adheres closely to the objective of integrating the action into the role played by agribusiness as a force for change?

ACTION RECOMMENDATIONS

The following series of action recommendations are directed simultaneously to agribusiness, host governments, and donor countries. All three are necessary to success in the long run; all three are beneficially affected by their interaction. All the

suggestions made focus on optimizing the interaction of agribusiness and rural people to ensure a harmony between their re-
spective needs, interests, and modes of behavior. In particular,
however, the recommendations are urged upon donor countries,
specifically the United States and its Agency for International
Development (AID), as the partner best able to provide the seed
capital required to finance a staff whose entire responsibility
would be to gain the approvals and tangible support prerequisite
to implementation.

RECOMMENDATION 1

Capitalizing on the presence of successful agro-
industrial enterprises in the rural areas of the Third
World to accelerate, extend, and sustain rural development in the zones of corporate influence.

This suggestion applies equally to present and future enterprises. Inherent in the scheme is the concept of "joint venture,"
with two flows of capital investment: from business investors
for the traditional purpose of establishing a useful, profitable
operation; and from public (development assistance) investors
taking the first risk on the payoff of rural development to the
company, to the host country, and to the rural people. Conceptually, the design of the system calls for the withdrawal of the
public partner once the rural development program demonstrates
its value to the company and as the rural people evidence a capability to operate in a self-sufficient, self-sustaining manner.
Public capital would flow to and through the agribusiness involved. In other words, the function of rural development might
be integrated into corporate management as a formal procedure,
with internal staff, or the function might be contracted out to a
competent intermediary responsible to management.
Recommendation 1 is rooted in several observations. A key
element in setting the process of rural development in motion
anywhere in the world is to create a source of new income, widely
enjoyed. There are various ways in which this is done: for
instance, by introducing improved agricultural practices that increase net farm income; by strengthening marketing methods to
ensure a higher rate of return to producers; or by setting up a
cottage industry. To this end, few techniques can claim to be as
effective as the establishment of an agro-industry. Regional
agriculture is frequently revolutionized. One-channel marketing
is introduced. New cash flows pour into the area. Jobs are
created. All this happens rather quickly, at little initial risk
to rural people or to their government. Without laboring the
point, agribusinesses of the world constitute myriad nuclei
around which development could crystallize. If the latent power
for rural development of this exciting and magnificent business
investment could be harnessed to a worldwide thrust toward development, the potential impact would be enormous. This resource
has never been systematically tapped.

Another observation, already noted, is that many top managers of agro-industry interviewed recognize the potential of their enterprises as instruments of sustained rural development. At the same time, most do not feel it is proper for business to exercise so direct an influence over social and personal change. Few felt comfortable with the idea of recommending the necessary allocation of money and personnel to support the full scope of an integrated rural development program; yet none rejected out-of-hand the suggestion of a joint venture with an aid agency, if the latter risked the capital and helped train a staff. In such a case, there would certainly be an openness to discuss the best way to integrate the function into the operation of their enterprises. It is taken for granted that host governments must give their approval to such an extension of company responsibility.

In a similar vein, host government officials were intrigued with the prospect of assigning some development financing and responsibility directly to agro-industry, without first passing through the bureaucracy where so much time, money, and energy is lost. True, as might be expected, suspicion is still universal as to the motives and integrity of foreign investors and foreign aid agencies regarding host country interests. But it is widely observed that a spreading and quiet pragmatism characterizes more and more government leaders in the Third World as they search desperately for solutions to rural problems. The thrust toward industrialization at all costs has weakened resource commitment to agricultural and rural development; and efforts to speed up the latter have too often been misguided and futile. Though politics in the Third World are unstable, it would seem that if agribusiness demonstrates its value to the achievement of national aspirations, getting approval for joint ventures in rural development between agro-industry and a foreign aid agency might not be as difficult as some might predict.

Finally, the recommendation is a perfect complement to major goals of U.S. development assistance. It helps tie together efforts to make private enterprise more attractive to foreign governments, in turn encouraging the flow of capital into rural areas. It acts as a stimulant to agricultural development. It helps diversify the base of rural economies. It brings economic growth into harmony with social progress. Implementation requires no major new requests for funds from the U.S. public. With strategic adjustments in the pattern of financial support now flowing from the United States for development activity, implementation could rapidly provide for a major test of validity.*

---

* As a matter of fact, a first exploration of a way to implement this recommendation will take place early in 1985. A major multinational agribusiness corporation from the United States has offered the site on a new venture in Central America for consideration. USAID will finance a prefeasibility analysis, in turn

RECOMMENDATION 2

Creating an international center for training managers of rural development, with special emphasis on two types of programs whose form and purpose converge over time: one starting from the base of an existing agro-industrial complex; and one starting at a primitive level of development and building toward attracting investment in the future.

The origin of Recommendation 2 lies in a worldwide shift in emphasis from agricultural to rural development, and the fact that a major cause of product weakness or outright failure is poor management. To appreciate the implications of the trend and the lack of professionally trained managers, two quotes are given below, taken from the context of international concerns. These texts define the scope of rural development and indicate indirectly the issue attendant to training.

To quote first from an informal memorandum on Human Resource Training for Rural Development in Latin American Countries, prepared for discussion within the Interamerican Development Bank.

In recent years, both Latin American governments and aid agencies have become increasingly interested in the multidimensional, integrated type of rural investment projects. Such projects, generally designated as "integral rural development" or simply rural development (RD) differ in a number of respects from the usual type of agricultural projects. The latter have typically focused on a single aspect (credit, irrigation, crop technology), while RD projects tend to be more complex or "systemic" and attempt to cover simultaneously a number of aspects. Furthermore, RD deals not only with farm production, but is concerned with upgrading the economic performance and social well-being of rural people. In this sense, RD projects tend to be spatially oriented, by concentrating on the incomes, employment, and welfare of a given population in specific rural areas. Virtually all the multilateral and bilateral assistance agencies have strong policy mandates related to a comprehensive attack on rural poverty, which favor this sort of an approach.

Initially, such projects focused on integrated agricultural promotion by providing several of the essential components on an interrelated set of farm developments (land development, credit, marketing, research, extension), but more recently the set of activities

leading to a proposal for a joint venture integrating both commercial and rural development goals, based on short-term and long-term considerations. This project will be part of a program of follow-up on the policy and action recommendations of this book.

which make up the RD package expanded beyond farm production to encompass other needs of the rural population, such as social services (health, education, nutrition, water supply); economic infrastructure (feeder
roads, electricity) and even linkages to the smaller
urban centers (rural industries, service centers, storage and supply facilities, etc.). If the area in question is a watershed or another type of ecosystem, RD
investments may also include conservation measures and
other ecological components.

The majority of such RD projects have also become
concerned with new institutional arrangements: the
strategy generally calls, on one hand, for strong peasant and village associations to insure grass-roots support and self-help, while on the other, for decentralized administrative mechanisms, in which the work of
the various governmental agencies can be suitably coor-
dinated at the action level and made more responsible
to local needs [56].

A more recent and formal statement was published by the
United Nations Development Programme in Evaluation Study No. 2--
Rural Development, a comprehensive and critical review of past
experience (June 1979).

The commonly held view which treats rural development as a sectoral category of programmes and projects
with special characteristics is too narrow. In this
report rural development is defined instead as a process of socio-economic change involving the transformation of agrarian society in order to reach a common set
of developmental goals based on the capacities and
needs of people. These goals include a nationally determined growth process that gives priority to the reduction of poverty, unemployment and inequality, and
the satisfaction of minimum human needs, and stresses
self-reliance and the participation of all the people.
National development strategies need to emphasize,
and not merely recognize, the agrarian core of most
Third World countries. Rural development must be considered both as an integral part and driving force of
the entire development process [emphasis added]. It
cannot be pigeon-holed into a sectoral "box" for it includes every sector of the economy. When the anti-
poverty, employment, distributive and participatory
goals of development are considered, rural development
takes an even wider significance, and demands far
greater attention than it has received in the past in
the majority of Third World countries [57].

These are grand and sweeping statements, and it is not necessary to accept every word at face value. What is important
however, is to recognize that such policy recommendations stem
from past failure in development efforts (hence, past weaknesses

in the design and management of development enterprises), and
that rural development is a long-term process, subsuming technology, marketing, finance, training, organization, human motivation, cultural form, political thrust, and other facets of
individual and societal behavior and structure. Recognition is
growing that the management of rural development enterprises requires specific professional training.

Where are these "ideal managers" to come from? The traditional and essentially correct answer is from a start made in
educational institutions devoted to the purpose. Unfortunately,
there is no such institution in the world today. True, bits and
pieces of such training are available. Schools of business, agriculture, and engineering, as well as departments of economics,
sociology, anthropology, and psychology all, to a greater or lesser degree, provide skill and sensitivity training that could be
basic elements in the equipment of a manager of an integrated
rural development enterprise. The Commonwealth Development
Corporation (England) offers some relevant training in its center
in Mananga, Swaziland. The United States Department of Agriculture includes some material in the courses offered by its Foreign
Development Division. The Project Planning Centre for Developing
Countries of the University of Bradford (England) does the same
in special short courses, as does the World Bank in Washington,
D.C. The Central America School of Business Administration in
Costa Rica; the Ph.D. program in rural development at the Davis
campus of the University of California; the bachelor's degree
program in the management of agribusiness at the Institute of
Technology in Monterrey, Mexico; and occasional courses set up by
the Organization for Research and Training (ORT) of Geneva,
Switzerland also touch upon the training required. The Israeli
Settlement Center in Rehovot; the Centro de Capacitación del
Desarrollo (CECADE) in Mexico; the Instituto Colombiano Agro-
pecuario (ICA) in Colombia; the Catholic University in Ecuador;
the College of Agriculture in La Molina, Peru; the University of
Costa Rica; the Universidad del Valle, Cali, Colombia; these and
no doubt other institutions in Latin America, Africa, and Asia
have all made course and program adjustments that approach the
training of administrators of integrated rural development enterprises.

However, nowhere is there a relevant academic content,
brought together solely with the objective of training the
managers-to-be or upgrading the performance of current managers
of integrated rural development. Such a curriculum, if it is even
thought reasonable to bring one together, has yet to be invented.
Recommendation 2 suggests that the necessary research and development be undertaken immediately. The lead time for a product to
be tested is likely to be two to three years; the creation of a
pool of talent would require at least an additional three to five
years. The entire field of rural development, whether integrated
with agro-industry or not, will be seriously constrained until
this particular personnel bottleneck is broken.

RECOMMENDATION 3

Organizing a carefully selected group of proven professionals in the field of agricultural and rural development, representing both the private and public sectors, to form the nucleus of a permanent research and development institution focused on the invention of practical methods of rural development that might best fit the management of agribusiness in its varied manifestations worldwide.

Recommendation 3 seems to reveal a contradiction. Chapter 1 emphasized the point that because agribusiness has dealt so effectively with the early stages of change in rural societies, and because the development assistance agencies like USAID have contributed so much to knowledge about the basic elements necessary to join into an efficient rural development process, joint venturing between both institutions is a feasible and forceful methodology through which to accelerate, extend, and diffuse progress to the goals of each. This argument remains intact. Nothing in this book contradicts the conclusion. It is time for the first joint venture prototypes to be set in place. However, because agribusiness and development agencies have been so separate, the totality of their valuable experience and creative energy has resulted in a vast, unfortunate dispersion of learning. This book barely touches on these riches; its assembly of cases is tantalizing in the benefits to mankind promised to those who can dig deeper and more widely, and in so doing, find novel ways to integrate the power for good inherent in agribusiness investment development assistance and host government collaboration. It is this clear vision of what yet remains to be learned, analyzed, and assembled into innovative approaches to rural development that has stimulated the recommendation for a permanent center of applied research and development, specifically focused on the interplay between agribusiness and the rural people impacted.

RECOMMENDATION 4

Establishing a major investment corporation in the United States patterned after the British Commonwealth Development Corporation (CDC) with a large capital base, which can provide equity and loan financing to agribusiness ventures that have a clearly defined policy of rural development and a longer-term payoff than alternative investment opportunities.

This recommendation takes its inspiration from the success and high level of development impact that characterize the Commonwealth Development Corporation (Chapter 13, Section 1). Despite public financing, CDC operates for profit. Because of its charter, which emphasizes the goal of benefiting the economic development thrust of host governments, CDC is able to take risks and exercise patience often beyond the traditional limits of private banks and corporations. The model of CDC is attractive because it has worked, and over a hundred agribusiness projects bear its stamp to prove the point. This is not to suggest that a sister institution created in the United States should be identical in every respect to CDC: for example, CDC often moves in the direction of financing governments into an equity position (see Chapter 3, Mumias Sugar Company, for an example of the method used). From the perspective of both tradition and development, the United States might prefer a system of equity transfer to farmers and workers in the image of Employee Stock Ownership Plans (ESOPs).

Recommendation 4 is not an alternative to the joint venture proposed in Recommendation 1. The CDC model implies an equity or loan position in the commercial aspects of agribusiness. The joint venture model implies direct financing to an existing agribusiness to cover the investment in rural development, as a function integrated into the management system. The two forms of financing could, of course, be considered as being complementary and could originate in one institution. This is a matter for further study. In concept and application, however, the two cash flows focus on different aspects of start-up.

The United States, of course, has taken a wide variety of approaches to facilitating the flow of investment and loan capital to the private sector, including agribusiness, including such devices as making loans to host country institutions created for the purpose; providing loans to private companies such as the Latin American Agribusiness Corporation; contributing a portion of the resources available to the World Bank family of financial institutions, the Interamerican Development Bank, and other regional banks. Recommendation 4 is not intended to demean the importance of these efforts. Rather, the basic thrust of the proposed action is simply that if agribusiness investment is badly needed in the Third World; if development assistance for agricultural and rural development is seen as best flowing through private enterprise (agribusiness); and, if rural development is seen as the critical mass in catalyzing the process of peace and security in the world, then the required action goes beyond dependency on institutions and arguments which have proven to be inadequate. More must be done. CDC illuminates one way to do more.

RECOMMENDATION 5

Intensifying the search for agro-industrial investment opportunities, particularly in modes which have clear-cut rural development components and which invigorate and diversify the search procedures.

This recommendation is rooted in three observations, which reflect quite different ways of seeking out investment opportunities.

In every country in which USAID has a mission, both AID and U.S. embassy staff give considerable attention to those factors in the environment that must be worked on to facilitate vigorous private sector activity, while focusing on projects and programs in the field of agricultural and rural development. Yet it is rare that these agencies have trained staff to actively and continuously search the country for agribusiness investment opportunities that might be both good for business and strong stimulants to rural development. It is even more unusual to find analytical procedures used to help define the development possibilities inherent in the nature of existing agribusiness. These oversights clearly reveal a lost opportunity. The presence of an AID mission is a major resource to draw on, and it would seem both prudent and imaginative to use the mission to search and promote without letup.

However, the search for investment prospects sponsored by AID through consultants or staff, when it has been instituted, has always been hampered by conflict-of-interest rules that keep the finder at arm's length to the investment. At the same time, investors are frequently discouraged from making a positive decision because of doubts that good management is available. It would seem that if the conflict-of-interest rules could be modified, the objectives of encouraging investment in agribusiness might be more easily reached. As an illustration of the point, some years ago a group of recent graduates of the Harvard Graduate School of Business, all ambitious, entrepreneurial, and undercapitalized, organized a business with this format: Any member of the organization would go anywhere in the world to seek out and determine the feasibility of investments for a client who would pay for transportation and subsistence, with one final proviso--if the client invested, the finder would stay on as project manager.

The writer has no record of the performance of this group--with the marvelous name "Interlink"--but the idea of linking good training, entrepreneurial energy, willingness to sacrifice for the reward, and investor interest seems to capture vital ingredients of the process of development in such a way that it is well worth further exploration. The United States is chock-full of this kind of creative intelligence and drive.

Another observation relates to the fact that sometimes investments can be first perceived through the "eyes" of a rural development need. A decade ago, while I was working in Mexico in the field of rural development, negotiations were initiated with a group of food importers in Scandinavia. The proposition was this: The importing countries were endlessly searching for and competing for foodstuffs, in fresh and processed form, which could not be produced in the northern tier of Europe. Meanwhile, there are many undeveloped parts of Mexico that have the inherent capability to produce at least some of the items needed. According to the deal negotiated (but never consummated because of a lack of money to finance continued contact), the importers in Scandinavia would finance a rural development program in return for a guaranteed percentage of the production (the remainder to serve local needs) at prices adjusted to the market but favorable to both farmers and buyers. There is nothing new about the basic idea of sourcing supplies under contract, but it is a relatively new and unexplored approach to financing rural development.

These three observations are not intended to exhaust the creative ways in which investment in agribusiness might be stimulated concurrently with rural development. They do, however, illustrate the point that investment promotion can and should be carried on in many innovative ways.

RECOMMENDATION 6

Intensifying the search for improved methodology to determine the cost-benefit relationships of programs of rural development.

For too long, programs related to rural development have been written off as either a donation from aid funds, or as a cost of doing business, analogous to buying insurance, deductible from before-tax income. This has been true largely because of the difficulty of measuring the value of education, improved housing, health care, and other components of a program. One result of this attitude toward financing rural development has been a resistance to incorporate the function of rural development in agro-industry simply based on its cost. Few tools of analysis are available to reveal, with clarity and in quantitative terms, whether the benefits outweigh the cost; whether investment in long-range rural development activities is a sound investment. If, then, responsibility for the management of rural development is ever going to fit comfortably into agro-industry, the image of cost needs to be converted to one of investment and the return quantified. This logic returns to Recommendation 3, since much more research than has been undertaken in the past is required. At present, the methods of analysis are in their very early stages of evolution. They need clarification and refinement. Fortunately, there are some economic analysts who are leading the way; they and others should be supported in an effort to accelerate the state of the art [58].

RECOMMENDATION 7

Creating a permanent Center of Information about the interaction between agro-industry and rural development worldwide.

This policy arises out of an astonishing fact. Except for a handful of well-documented cases, most of what agribusiness has done by way of investment and involvement with rural people has never been described in writing available to the public. The lessons learned, the results obtained, have essentially been lost in time, in private archives, or in reports to aid agencies that never see the light of day. In truth, this very important part of development history is denied to us all. The U.S. government declares development policy and moves implementation forward almost as though there were no past experience; yet relevant experience is legion. To the extent that it remains possible, this priceless heritage of knowledge should be recaptured for use by those entrusted with the future. As this overall report reveals, a mere scratching of the surface of this heritage illustrates its diversity, richness, and utility. What is "out there" should be identified, described, and analyzed. The data might best be made accessible by means of modern, computer-based systems of storage, rearrangement, and retrieval. What is in the bank could well become a decision-making tool for investors, managers, governments, aid agencies, and financial institutions. In descriptive terms, the case material could become a valuable educational resource.

To the degree that we are ignorant of past experience, we are all subject to higher than necessary risks of failure. Inevitably everyone is less creative, less innovative, and less effective. An investment in a data bank of the type suggested should pay off handsomely. Indeed, the rate of return should increase rapidly once the first deposits are made.

In Conclusion

The foregoing action recommendations and the policies they are intended to support arise out of a deeply held conviction not only of their importance, but also that they are timely, pragmatic, require no new allocation of money, and do not confront any major obstacles in the way of implementation. What is proposed is in total harmony with the purposes and needs of all concerned: rural people, their governments, agribusiness, and donor nations; what is recommended is supported by evidence taken from the cases reported and the analysis and discussion of the facts which thread the text and give this book its coherence.

However, it is fitting to conclude the book with one final reference to the farmer, the farm family, and all the other rural people whose labor and loyalty are vital to the success of agribusiness and any development program. The task of this book was to answer a basic question: Is there a role for agribusiness to play in accelerating and expanding agricultural and rural development in the areas of the Third World in which enterprises are located? It was natural, therefore, to emphasize throughout case descriptions and analyses not only what companies do, but also what companies might do in addition, with support from governments, to play the more important and expansive role in development. For some, this may appear to be an effort to organize development assistance by doing more "to" rural people, rather than by working "with" the people. To interpret this book as having a top-down orientation would be a grave error.

Long before work on this book began, the authors were committed to the belief that rural development could only take place and be sustained if the intended beneficiaries of a program come to understand, approve, acculturate, and participate in decision-making. Leadership, training and education, and internal resources may be required, but self-sufficiency and self-responsibility are the guiding principles of effective human

progress.   I have devoted thirty years to reducing these principles to practices which are effective among traditional rural
people, and it is through the lens of this experience that all
the evidence and all the recommendations in this book have been
examined and reexamined.   In its essence, the future envisioned
can be seen in the title of this book, "Agribusiness and the
Small-Scale Farmer: A Dynamic Partnership for Development."

Bibliography

SECTION 1

1. Freeman, Orville L., and Karen, Ruth. 1982. The Farmer and the Money Economy: The Role of the Private Sector in the Agricultural Development of LDCs. The Woodlands Conference on Sustainable Societies. Woodlands, Texas.

2. Karen, Ruth, and Haynes, Elliott. 1983. Toward an Unlimited Future: A Report of the Global One Hundred. Business International Corporation, New York.

3. Karen, Ruth; Fisher, William; and Sakoian, Carol K. 1979. Beyond Money: New Dimensions in International Corporate Giving. Business International Corporation, New York.

4. Williams, Simon. 1982. New Approaches to Agricultural and Rural Development: Nucleus Estates. Part I: The Mumias Sugar Company--Kenya; Part II: Higaturu Oil Palm Estates--New Guinea. Agribusiness Worldwide. June and October.

5. Williams, Simon. 1981. The Agribusiness Potential for Participation in Rural Development Worldwide. Mohonk International Conference on Multinationals, organized by the Aspen Institute for Humanistic Studies and the Fund for Multinational Management Education.

6. Williams, Simon. 1979. Agribusiness and Development. Wall Street Journal, December 7.

7. Etah Gramin Bank. 1981. Annual Report to the Board of Directors. Civil Lines, Etah, Uttar Pradesh.

8. Interviews and Internal Corporate Documents. 1983. Department of International Affairs. Unilever, London.

9. Kenya into the Second Decade. 1975. World Bank Country Economic Report. Washington, D.C.

10. Commonwealth Development Corporation. 1981. Partners in Development--Finance Plus Management. London.

11. Hazelden, E.J.R. 1980. Kenya Seed Company. Unpublished speech. Kitale, Kenya.

12. Commonwealth Development Corporation. 1974. CDC in the Swaziland Lowveld. London.

13. Commonwealth Development Corporation. 1982. Annual Report and Accounts. London.

14. Mhlume (Swaziland) Sugar Company Limited. 1979. Twenty-one Years of Progress--A History. Mhlume, Swaziland.

15. Tuckett, J.R. 1976. Vuvulane Irrigated Farms, Swaziland: A Report of the First Ten Years. Agricultural Administration, Volume 4, 1977.

16. Information Release. 1972. Vuvulane Smallholder Irrigation Scheme. Oxfam, Oxford.

17. Booker Agriculture International. London.

18. Bulletin Today. October 17, 1983. Manila (newspaper).

19. Kilusang Kabuhayan at Kaunlaran (KKK) Investment Folio. No date. Manila.

20. Annual Report. 1982. San Miguel Corporation. Manila.

21. U.S. Agency for International Development. 1980. Kitale Maize: The Limits of Success. USAID Project Impact Evaluation Report No. 2.

22. Tenneco, Inc. 1981. Farming the Sands of Sudan. Houston.

23. Texagri--Texaco's Unique Idea for Nigeria. 1979. The Texaco Star. Volume 66, No. 1.

24. Poupeau, Jean. 1981. Rural Energy Development: Oil Companies in the Agri-Energy Partnership. The Agri-Energy Roundtable, Geneva.

25. Poupeau, Jean; Morel, Robert; and Heys, Gilbert. 1982. Looking at Some Management Problems at Texagri. The Agri-Energy Roundtable, Geneva.

26. Freivalds, J. 1983. Leche y Derivados de Honduras. Agribusiness Worldwide, July-August.

27. U.S. Agency for International Development. 1981. The Social Impact of Agribusiness: A Case Study of ALCOSA in Guatemala. USAID Evaluation Study No. 4.

28. Harvard Business School. 1978. LAAD-Hanover-Finca Quetzal. Case Study 4-578-196. Cambridge, Mass.

29. Truitt, Nancy S. 1983. Chimachoy, Guatemala: ALCOSA, Subsidiary of Hanover Brands. Fund for Multinational Management Education, New York.

30. Morss, E.R.; Hatch, J.; Mickelwait, D.R.; and Sweet, C.F. 1976. Strategies for Small Farmer Development: Zaria Tomato Production Project. Volume II. Westview Special Studies in Social, Political, and Economic Development. Westview Press, Boulder, Colo.

31. Lewis, Robert G. 1983. Contract Growing of Flue-cured Tobacco in Jamaica. Agribusiness Worldwide, November-December.

32. Freivalds, John. 1981. The Growth and Integration of Jamaica Broilers. Agribusiness Worldwide, October-November.

33. World Bank. 1982. Control Accountability, and Incentives in a Successful Development Institution--The Kenya Tea Development Authority. Working Paper No. 550.

34. Kenya Tea Development Authority. 1980-1981. Annual Report and Statement of Accounts. Nairobi.

35. Froman, Jo. 1981. Nestle in Mexico: Chontalpa and Other Areas. Fund for Multinational Management Education, New York.

36. Staff Report. 1983. Frozen Okra Dominican Style: How and Why Southland Took Its Operation Abroad. Frozen Food Report. May-June.

37. Tavis, Lee A. 1982. Multinational Managers and Poverty in the Third World. University of Notre Dame Press, Notre Dame, Ind.

38. Livestock Feeds Limited. 1982. Annual Report and Accounts. Lagos, Nigeria.

39. Livestock Feeds Limited. 1983. Spanning the Years, 1963-1983. Lagos, Nigeria.

40. Truitt, G.A. and Edmunds, J. 1981. El Progreso, Honduras. Fund for Multinational Management Education. New York.

41. The Press Group. 1976-1977. Annual Report. Blantyre, Malawi.

42. Truitt, George A. 1981. Guanchis, Honduras--Castle and Cooke, Inc. Fund for Multinational Management Education, New York.

43. McCommon, C.M.; Rueschoff, N.G.; Tavis, Lee; and Wilkowski, J. 1984. Guanchis Limitada: A Case Study of an Agrarian Reform Cooperative and Its Long-Term Relationship with a Multinational Firm in Honduras. USAID Special Evaluation Study. Washington, D.C.

44. Barnett, Tony. 1977. The Gezira Scheme: An Illusion of Development. Frank Cass, London.

45. Bryce, Murray D. 1967. The Effects of United Fruit Operations on the Economies of the Banana Producing Countries. Projects International, Inc. (now Canadian Projects Limited, Vancouver, British Columbia).

46. Morss, E.R.; Hatch, J.; Mickelwait, D.R.; and Sweet, C.F. 1976. Strategies for Small Farmer Development: Ubomba Development Project. Volume II, Westview Special Studies in Social, Political, and Economic Development. Westview Press, Boulder, Colorado.

310

47. Barclays Development Fund. A Descriptive Pamphlet (no date). Barclays Bank International Limited. London, England.

48. Pitti, A. 1980. Protein for Panama: Financing Cattle Production. Agribusiness Worldwide, August-September.

49. The Alpart Story. A descriptive Pamphlet (no date). Alumina Partners of Jamaica. Jamaica, West Indies.

50. Williams, Simon. 1980. The Construction and Management of Integrated Rural Development: A Case History and Generalized Model. TECHNOS. January-February.

51. United States Council of the International Chamber of Commerce. 1981. Enterprise and Development. Volume 1, No. 4, October. New York, New York.

52. United States Council of the International Chamber of Commerce. 1982. Enterprise and Development. Volume 1, No. 9, March. New York, New York.

53. Technoserve, Inc. 1982. Annual Report. Norwalk, Connecticut.

54. Editorial. 1984. Financier: Journal of Private Sector Policy. Volume 8, No. 2, February.

55. Horizons. 1982-current. Volumes 1 through 4. U.S. Agency for International Development. Washington, D.C.

56. Carroll, T. mid-1970s. Human Resource Training in Latin American Countries. Unpublished Memorandum. Interamerican Development Bank. Washington, D.C.

57. Evaluation Study Number 2: Rural Development. 1979. United Nations Development Programme. New York.

58. Roemer, M. and Stern, J.J. 1977. The Appraisal of Development Projects: A Practical Guide to Project Analysis with Case Studies and Solutions. Praeger Publishers. New York.

SECTION 2--General References

Agency for International Development. 1984. Report of the Bureau of Private Enterprise. Washington, D.C.

Bell, Daniel. 1976. The Cultural Contradictions of Capitalism. Basic Books, Inc. New York.

Benne, Robert. 1981. The Ethic of Democratic Capitalism: A Moral Reassessment. Fortress Press. Philadelphia.

Bradshaw, T., and Vogel, D. 1981. Corporations and Their Critics. McGraw-Hill Book Company. New York.

Caribbean Group for Cooperation in Economic Development. 1980. Measures to Promote the Role of Private Investment in Caribbean Development. International Finance Corporation. Washington, D.C.

Charlton, Sue E. 1984. Women in Third World Development. Westview Press. Boulder, Colorado.

Christian Mission and Multinationals: Friends or Foes? 1982. Engage/Social Action. Washington, D.C.

Cleveland, H., and Wilson, T.W. 1978. Human Growth: An Essay on Growth, Values, and the Quality of Life. Aspen Institute for Humanistic Studies. New York.

Committee for Economic Development. 1981. Transnational Corporations and Developing Countries--New Policies for a Changing World Economy. New York.

Frank, Isaiah. 1980. Foreign Enterprise in Developing Countries. Johns Hopkins University Press. Baltimore.

Fund for Multinational Management Education. 1978. Public Policy and Technology Transfer--Viewpoints of U.S. Business. 4 Vols. New York.

Gaitskell, A. 1959. Gezira: A Story of Development in the Sudan. Faber and Faber. London.

Glynn, Leonard. 1983. Multinationals in the World of Nations. U.S. Council for International Business. New York.

Goulet, Denis. 1977. The Uncertain Promise: Value Conflicts in Technology Transfer. IDOC/North America, in Cooperation with the Overseas Development Council. Washington, D.C.

Hirschman, Albert O. 1967. Development Projects Observed. Brookings Institute. Washington, D.C.

Industry Council for Development. 1981. Development: Challenge, Opportunity, Responsibility for Industry? New York.

International Labour Organization. 1984. Technology Choice and Employment Generation by Multinational Enterprises in Developing Countries. Geneva.

Longstreth, B., and Rosenbloom, H. David. 1973. Corporate Social Responsibility and the Institutional Investor--A Report to the Ford Foundation. Praeger Publishers. New York.

Masden, Axel. 1980. Private Power: Multinational Corporations for the Survival of Our Planet. William Morrow and Company, Inc. New York.

McCormack, Arthur. 1980. Multinational Investment: Boon or Burden for the Developing Countries? W.R. Grace & Co. New York.

Novak, Michael. 1982. The Spirit of Democratic Socialism. Simon and Schuster. New York.

Ramesh, J., and Weiss, C. 1979. Mobilizing Technology for World Development. Praeger Publishers. New York.

Research and Policy Committee. 1981. Transnational Corporations and Developing Countries. Committee for Economic Development. New York.

Sherwin, Richard R. 1983. The Ethical Roots of the Business System. Harvard Business Review. November-December.

Vernon, R. 1977. Storm Over the Multinationals: The Real Issues. Harvard University Press. Cambridge.

Whyle, W.F., and Boynton, D. 1983. Higher Yield Human Systems for Agriculture. Cornell University Press. Ithaca, N.Y.

Williams, Oliver. 1984. Who Cast the First Stone--Church Groups and MNCs Need to Halt Their Battle. Harvard Business Review. September-October.

Wuthnow, Robert. 1982. The Moral Crisis in American Capitalism. Harvard Business Review. March-April.

Index